Empire of Influence

Indirect rule is widely considered as a defining feature of the nineteenth- and twentieth-century British empire, but its divisive earlier history remains largely unexplored. *Empire of Influence* traces the contentious process whereby the East India Company established a system of indirect rule in India in the first decades of the nineteenth century. In a series of thematic chapters covering intelligence gathering, violence, gift giving, and the co-optation of the scribal and courtly elite, Callie Wilkinson foregrounds the disagreement surrounding the tactics of the political representatives of the Company and recaptures the experimental nature of early attempts to secure Company control. She demonstrates how these endeavours were reshaped, exploited, and resisted by Indians as well as disputed within the Company itself. This important new account exposes the contested origins of these ambiguous relationships of 'protection' and coercion, while identifying the factors that enabled them to take hold and endure.

Callie Wilkinson is a Marie Skłodowska-Curie Postdoctoral Fellow at LMU Munich.

Empire of Influence

*The East India Company and the
Making of Indirect Rule*

Callie Wilkinson

Ludwig Maximilian University of Munich

CAMBRIDGE
UNIVERSITY PRESS

CAMBRIDGE
UNIVERSITY PRESS

Shaftesbury Road, Cambridge CB2 8EA, United Kingdom

One Liberty Plaza, 20th Floor, New York, NY 10006, USA

477 Williamstown Road, Port Melbourne, VIC 3207, Australia

314–321, 3rd Floor, Plot 3, Splendor Forum, Jasola District Centre,
New Delhi – 110025, India

103 Penang Road, #05–06/07, Visioncrest Commercial, Singapore 238467

Cambridge University Press is part of Cambridge University Press & Assessment,
a department of the University of Cambridge.

We share the University's mission to contribute to society through the pursuit of
education, learning and research at the highest international levels of excellence.

www.cambridge.org
Information on this title: www.cambridge.org/9781009311731

DOI: 10.1017/9781009311717

First published 2023

A catalogue record for this publication is available from the British Library.

Library of Congress Cataloging-in-Publication Data
Names: Wilkinson, Callie, 1990– author.
Title: Empire of influence : the East India Company and the making
of indirect rule / Callie Wilkinson, Ludwig-Maximilians-Universität München.
Other titles: East India Company and the making of indirect rule
Description: Cambridge, United Kingdom ; New York, NY :
Cambridge University Press, 2023. | Includes bibliographical references and index.
Identifiers: LCCN 2022043425 | ISBN 9781009311731 (hardback) |
ISBN 9781009311717 (ebook)
Subjects: LCSH: East India Company – History – 19th century. |
Great Britain – Colonies – Asia – Administration. | India – Politics and government –
19th century. | British – India – History – 19th century. |
India – Kings and rulers – History – 19th century.
Classification: LCC DS465 .W68 2023 | DDC 954.03/1–dc23/eng/20220926
LC record available at https://lccn.loc.gov/2022043425

ISBN 978-1-009-31173-1 Hardback

For my family

Contents

Figures

Maps

Acknowledgements

This book was written during a global pandemic, and from a position of professional precarity; it provided a much-needed refuge during a difficult time. Without institutional and personal support, I would never have had this creative outlet, and I am happy to be able to thank everyone who helped along the way. Funding from the Social Sciences and Humanities Research Council of Canada, the Cambridge and Commonwealth Trust, the Royal Historical Society, the Institute of Historical Research, and the Leverhulme Trust made research and writing possible. Chapter 5 originally appeared, in a modified form, as 'Weak Ties in a Tangled Web? Relationships between the Political Residents of the English East India Company and Their Munshis, 1798–1818', *Modern Asian Studies* 53, no. 5 (2019): 1574–1612, © Cambridge University Press 2019, and has been reprinted with permission. I would like to thank the editors and anonymous reviewers of *Modern Asian Studies* for helping to clarify my ideas at that early stage.

On a personal level, I am grateful to colleagues at Cambridge and Warwick who came to my aid time and again. Top billing must go to my PhD supervisor Renaud Morieux, who invariably asks the best questions and proposes the most exciting ideas; Renaud not only made the dissertation a pleasure to research and write but has remained a pillar of support ever since. I was very lucky to have Sujit Sivasundaram as my secondary advisor, not only because of his kindness and many insights (which certainly left their imprint on this book) but also because of the wonderful community he has created through the world history reading group at Cambridge; this book would not be what it is without Alix Chartrand, Steph Mawson, James Poskett, Tom Simpson, James Wilson, and Hatice Yildiz. As my external examiner and an expert in the field, Margot Finn has had a significant influence. She has supported me even at very difficult times. Also vital to my Cambridge experience was Larry Klein, who helped set me on this path as my MPhil supervisor, and Norbert Peabody, whose coffee and conversation meant a lot. At Warwick, Guido van Meersbergen was the very best office mate and helped in so many ways, not least by reading this book and making it better. Naomi Pullin was a great source of help and a role model when I needed it. A key moment in this book's development was the 'second viva' organized by Mark Philp, who has done so much to help me and other early career researchers at Warwick, and who deserves many thanks for all his efforts. Special thanks must also go to Mark Knights, who believed in this book when I had ceased to believe in it myself; his optimism and advice kept me going when I was beginning to falter. Josh Ehrlich read the full manuscript and was kind enough to give me the benefit of his insight and expertise. Laura Moncion has helped simply by being herself, a dear and much-loved friend, while Grace Ling and Zara Zalnieriunas have stuck by me through it all. Finally, Roland Wenzlhuemer and the directors of global dis:connect gave me an intellectual home when I needed it most, and I am so grateful to them for welcoming me into their community.

When it came to deciding on a dedication for this book, there were many possible candidates. My grandmother June Wilkinson passed away while it was being written, and I will always associate this book with memories of her. Meanwhile, my loving aunties showed their support in all kinds of ways throughout this process, reminding me that I had a support network when I needed it. Jamie Latham has done more than his fair share of cooking, cleaning, and sympathizing, and has made all kinds of sacrifices to make my research possible, including, but not limited to, moving to Germany. Before Jamie, though, there was Mom and Dad, who have believed in me the longest and who have made great sacrifices, too. In the end, I couldn't pick just one; this book is dedicated, with love, to every one of them.

Note on Translation and Transliteration

All foreign words not commonly used in English have been italicized. Where English terms are extant, they have been used and appear without italics. Accepted English spelling of foreign-language words has been determined using *Webster's Collegiate Dictionary*. Place names with accepted English spellings have been spelled in accordance with the UK's Permanent Committee on Geographical Names, with the exceptions of the historical Presidency capitals of Calcutta (now Kolkata), Bombay (now Mumbai), and Madras (now Chennai). Words from Persian and Marathi have been rendered using a simplified transliteration system without diacritical marks, using F. Steingass's *Comprehensive Persian English Dictionary* (1892) and J. T. Molesworth's *A Dictionary, Marathi and English* (1857).

Chronology

Residents

Courts	Residents	Years in Office
Delhi	David Ochterlony (1758–1825)	1803–1806
	Archibald Seton (1758–1818)	1806–1811
	Charles Theophilus Metcalfe (1785–1846)	1811–1819
Hyderabad	William Kirkpatrick (1754–1812)	1794–1797
	James Achilles Kirkpatrick (1764–1805)	1798–1805
	Thomas Sydenham (1780–1816)	1806–1810
	Henry Russell (1783–1852)	1810–1820
	Charles Theophilus Metcalfe (1785–1846)	1820–1825
Lucknow	Edward Otto Ives	1790–1799
	William Scott (d. 1804)	1799–1804
	John Ulric Collins (c. 1750–1807)	1804–1807
	John Baillie (1772–1833)	1807–1815
	Richard Strachey (1781–1847)	1817–1819
Pune	William Palmer (1740–1816)	1798–1801
	Barry Close (1756–1813)	1801–1810
	Mountstuart Elphinstone (1779–1859)	1804–1807
Nagpur	Henry Thomas Colebrooke (1765–1837)	1798–1801
	Mountstuart Elphinstone	1804–1807
	Richard Jenkins (1785–1853)	1807–1828
Gwalior	John Ulric Collins	1798–1804
	Josiah Webbe (1768–1804)	1804
	Richard Jenkins	1804–1805
	Graeme Mercer (1764–1841)	1807–1810
	Richard Strachey	1810–1816
	Robert Close	1817–1824
Travancore	Colin Macaulay (c. 1759–1836)	1800–1810
	John Munro (1778–1878)	1810–1820

Compiled using the *Oxford Dictionary of National Biography*, C. E. Buckland's *Dictionary of Indian Biography* (London, 1906), and V. C. P. Hodson's *List of the Officers of the Bengal Army 1758–1834* (London, 1927).

Rulers

Courts	Title	Rulers	Reign
Delhi	Mughal emperor (King of Delhi after 1803)	Shah Alam	1759–1806
		Akbar Shah II	1806–1837
Hyderabad	Nizam	Mir Nizam Ali Khan	1761–1803
		Sikander Jah	1803–1829
Lucknow	Nawab Vizier (King of Awadh after 1814)	Asaf ud-Daula	1775–1797
		Vizier Ali	1797–1798
		Saadat Ali Khan	1798–1814
		Ghazi ud-Din Haidar	1814–1827
Pune	Peshwa	Baji Rao II	1796–1818
Nagpur	Raja of Berar	Raghuji II Bhonsle	1788–1816
		Parsoji Bhonsle	1816–1817
		Mudhoji II Bhonsle (Appa Sahib)	1817–1818
Gwalior	Raja	Daulat Rao Shinde	1794–1827
Travancore	Raja	Avittom Thirunal Balarama Varma	1798–1810
		Gowri Lakshmi Bai (regent)	1810–1815
		Rana Varma II	1815–1846

Governors General

Years in Office	Governors General
1793–1798	Sir John Shore, first Baron Teignmouth
1798–1805	Richard Wellesley, Marquess Wellesley
1805	Charles Cornwallis, Marquess Cornwallis
1805–1807	Sir George Hilario Barlow
1807–1813	Gilbert Elliot Murray Kynynmound, first Earl Minto
1813–1823	Francis Rawdon Hastings, first Marquess of Hastings

Compiled using the *Oxford Dictionary of National Biography*.

Abbreviations

Add. MS	additional manuscripts
AHR	*American Historical Review*
APAC	Asia, Pacific & Africa Collections, British Library, London
BL	British Library, London
Bodl. Oxf.	Bodleian Library, Oxford
BRR	Benares Residency Records, Uttar Pradesh State Archives, Allahabad
For.Sec.	Foreign Secret Department, National Archives of India, New Delhi
FSC	Foreign Department Secret Branch Consultations, National Archives of India, New Delhi
FSP	Foreign Department Secret Branch Proceedings, National Archives of India, New Delhi
HJ	*The Historical Journal*
HRR	Hyderabad Residency Records, National Archives of India, New Delhi
IESHR	*Indian Social and Economic History Review*
JBS	*Journal of British Studies*
J. Earl. Mod. Hist.	*The Journal of Early Modern History*
J. Mod. Hist.	*The Journal of Modern History*
LIA	Letters issued by the Agent to the Governor General at Benares, Benares Residency Records, Uttar Pradesh State Archives, Allahabad
LRA	Letters received by the Agent to the Governor General at Benares, Benares Residency Records, Uttar Pradesh State Archives, Allahabad
MAS	*Modern Asian Studies*

MSA	Maharashtra State Archives, Mumbai
Mss. Eur.	European Manuscripts, Asia, Pacific and Africa Collections, British Library, London
NAI	National Archives of India, New Delhi
NAS	National Archives of Scotland, Edinburgh
NLS	National Library of Scotland, Edinburgh
NRAS	National Register of Archives, Scotland
NRR	H. N. Sinha, ed., *Selections from the Nagpur Residency Records*, 5 vols (Nagpur, 1950–1957).
ODNB	Oxford Dictionary of National Biography
P&P	*Past & Present*
PRC	G. S. Sardesai, ed., *English Records of Maratha History: Poona Residency Correspondence*, 15 vols (Bombay, 1936–1951).
PRCOP	Poona Residency Correspondence Outward Papers, Maharashtra State Archives, Mumbai
UPSAA	Uttar Pradesh State Archives, Allahabad
Wellesley Despatches	Robert Montgomery Martin, ed., *The Despatches, Minutes, and Correspondence of the Marquess Wellesley, K.G., during his Administration in India*, 5 vols (London, 1836; repr. Cambridge, 2012).

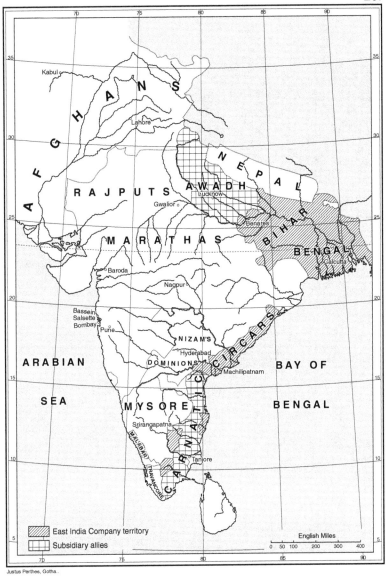

Justus Perthes, Gotha.

Map 1 'India in 1795', plate from Charles Joppen, *Historical Atlas of India* (London, 1907). © British Library Board. All Rights Reserved/ Bridgeman Images.

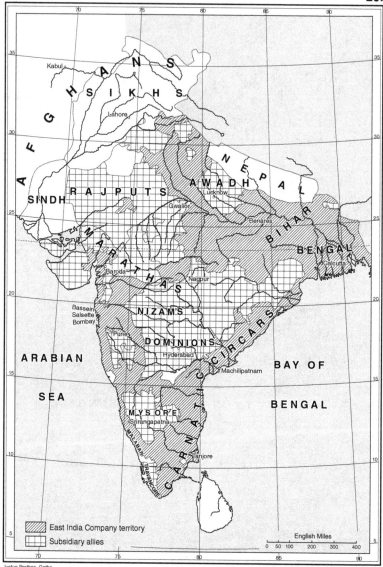

Map 2 'India in 1823', plate from Charles Joppen, *Historical Atlas of India* (London, 1907). © British Library Board. All Rights Reserved/ Bridgeman Images.

Introduction

In conventional accounts of Britain's empire overseas, the eighteenth-century 'revolution' in Bengal looms large. The story has been told and retold over the centuries, but the basic elements remain the same: the death of British captives confined in the much-mythologized 'Black Hole of Calcutta'; Robert Clive's 1757 victory over the nawab of Bengal at the Battle of Plassey; the definitive confrontation with the combined forces of Bengal, Awadh, and the Mughal emperor at Buxar in 1764; and the East India Company's assumption of the diwani in 1765.[1] The Mughal office of diwan conferred the right to collect taxes in what was formerly one of the richest provinces of the Mughal empire; this extensive revenue base is traditionally depicted as the launching pad for Britain's 'second empire' of conquest and exploitation.[2] The nawab retained nominal control over law and order within the province to begin with, and revenue collection was initially delegated to Indian deputies; in the end, however, this system of 'double government' proved short-lived.[3] By 1772, the Company had assumed formal control, claiming jurisdiction over a non-European, non-Christian population numbering into the millions.[4] As a result, generations of historians have looked to Bengal to detect the origins of the ideological and administrative mechanisms that would underpin the nineteenth-century empire on which the sun never set. According to one recent study, Bengal was the crucible wherein a 'new kind of imperialism' was forged, characterized by 'authoritarian government, territorial conquest, and extractive revenue polices', with

---

[1] On the language of revolution in Bengal, see Robert Travers, *Ideology and Empire in Eighteenth-Century India* (Cambridge, 2007), p. 31. The classic account is P. J. Marshall, *Bengal: The British Bridgehead – Eastern India 1740–1828* (Cambridge, 1988).
[2] Vincent T. Harlow, *The Founding of the Second British Empire 1763–1793*, 2 vols (London, 1952–1964), I, p. 3; C. A. Bayly, 'The Second British Empire', in *The Oxford History of the British Empire*, ed. Robin Winks, 5 vols (Oxford, 1999), V, pp. 60–62.
[3] Travers, *Ideology*, pp. 75–76.
[4] Tirthankar Roy, 'Economic Conditions in Early Modern Bengal: A Contribution to the Divergence Debate', *The Journal of Economic History* 70, no. 1 (2010): 184.

1

an 'emphasis on direct coercion and overt domination'.[5] Yet, fixating on Bengal obscures other, more pervasive and persistent forms of imperial power. The focus of this book is on the more nebulous, yet no less significant, history of British political influence beyond the borders of British India.

This history parallels, and indeed underpins, the more widely studied story of the Company's expanding territorial dominions. Just as the Company was working out how to defend and administer Bengal, a distinct yet complementary kind of empire was emerging in parallel. Nawab Vizier Shuja ud-Daula was also defeated at Buxar, but the consequences, for him, were very different. Rather than overturning Shuja's administration, the Company instead signed a treaty with him, one that guaranteed his independence but required him to pay subsidies in exchange for military protection. Over time, a network of similar agreements known as subsidiary alliances (for the payment of subsidies) began to take shape, founded on terms that were increasingly unequal, and overseen by Company representatives (called Residents) who intervened in the politics of nominally independent kingdoms with increasing audacity. The treaty concluded with the nizam of Hyderabad in 1800 marked a turning point in this process by placing key restrictions on the nizam's sovereign powers, requiring him to submit disputes with neighbouring polities to the arbitration of the Company and limiting his ability even to communicate with other courts except with the approval of the Resident.[6] These alliances were designed to obstruct the formation of hostile coalitions and finance the Company's armies at the expense of their allies' military establishments. They became the preferred mechanism for subordinating the Company's Indian rivals, and the basis for the Company's political and military dominance in the subcontinent. Despite a series of annexations in the mid-nineteenth century, the bulk of these alliances would persist until Indian independence. By this point, allied kingdoms, known as 'princely states', numbered into the hundreds and comprised almost a third of the Indian subcontinent and a quarter of its population.[7]

---

[5] James M. Vaughn, *The Politics of Empire at the Accession of George III* (New Haven, CN, 2019), pp. 35–36. See also David Armitage, *The Ideological Origins of the British Empire* (Cambridge, 2000), p. 3, where the second British empire is similarly distinguished as 'an empire founded on military conquest, racial subjection, economic exploitation and territorial expansion'.

[6] C. U. Aitchison, *A Collection of Treaties, Engagements and Sanads Relating to India and Neighbouring Countries*, 13 vols (Calcutta, 1909), IX, p. 72.

[7] Barbara Ramusack, *The Indian Princes and Their States* (Cambridge, 2004), pp. 52–53.

The subsidiary alliance system as it developed in India set an example that reverberated across Asia, Africa, and the Indian Ocean world. Whether rejected, modified, or imported wholesale, this model was an important point of reference as Britain's global entanglements increased and intensified across the nineteenth and twentieth centuries. Bengal has been described as 'the main laboratory for the development of new conceptions of empire' but this is only the case if we restrict our vision to a narrow definition of empire as direct rule.[8] As Ann Stoler has argued, by focusing on clearly bounded territories historians of empire have downplayed political and territorial ambiguity as defining features of modern imperial intervention. For Stoler, 'the legal and political fuzziness of dependencies, trusteeships, protectorates, and unincorporated territories were all part of the deep grammar of partially restricted rights in the nineteenth- and twentieth-century imperial world.'[9] From the vantage point of the northern Nigerian emirates, the Malay kingdoms, and the Gulf states, nominally independent but subject to Britain's overweening influence, the princes form a more meaningful precedent.

Despite having developed into a burgeoning field of study in their own right, the princely states rarely feature prominently in recent scholarship on the East India Company.[10] The reason has to do both with conventional narratives about the Company's development and assumptions about its essential characteristics. Percival Spear once summarized the Company's trajectory over the eighteenth century as 'from trade to empire, from embassies to administration', and, while Philip Stern has influentially refuted the first half of this formulation, the second continues to inform most scholarship on the eighteenth- and nineteenth-century Company.[11] Historians of the period have tended to study the Company's expanding bureaucracy. Robert Travers has attributed this trend to 'the strong historical association of European imperialism with modernity, and the concomitant sense of modernizing European ideologies confronting non-European "tradition"'.[12] The subsidiary alliance system has become something of a blind spot within this

---

[8] Travers, *Ideology*, pp. 4–5.

[9] Ann Laura Stoler, 'On Degrees of Imperial Sovereignty', *Public Culture* 18, no. 1 (2006), p. 137.

[10] For recent scholarship, see Chitralekha Zutshi, 'Re-visioning Princely States in South Asian Historiography: A Review', *IESHR* 46, no. 3 (2009): 303–313.

[11] T. G. P. Spear, *The Nabobs: A Study of the Social Life of the English in Eighteenth Century India* (Oxford, 1932), p. 130. See also Philip J. Stern, *The Company-State: Corporate Sovereignty and the Early Modern Foundations of the British Empire in India* (Oxford, 2011), p. 14.

[12] Travers, *Ideology*, pp. 16–17.

literature, failing in many ways to conform to the pattern of bureaucratization, standardization, and reform usually associated with the early nineteenth-century East India Company.[13]

When the Company's alliances are placed at centre stage, however, its empire in India starts to look very different. Existing scholarship usually depicts the early nineteenth century as an era of hardening racial hierarchies, wherein a reformed civil service valued abstract and institutionalized 'facts' over local, patrimonial knowledge.[14] At Indian royal courts, however, this ideal proved difficult, if not impossible, to translate into practice; after all, Residents were theoretically supposed to be working through existing structures rather than introducing new ones. Residents, then, had no choice but to accommodate themselves to the world of the court in ways that are more usually associated with the Company's early history as a supplicant to the Mughals than with this period of accelerated expansion.[15]

Because of the compromises that Residents were sometimes forced to make, Residencies are a revealing lens through which to examine the development of ideas and practices of empire as the Company emerged as paramount power. The Residency system might have survived and indeed been propagated across the Indian Ocean world, but its longevity belies the consistent problems to which it was subject, and the ideological conundrums that it posed. The disagreements that repeatedly flared up around it not only expose divisions within the Company that might otherwise have remained obscure but show how this period of experimentation and debate created opportunities for historical actors to try to bend these emergent systems to their will.[16]

To bring this process of experimentation into focus, this book centres on the changing relationships between the East India Company and allied Indian kingdoms during a period of intensive imperial expansion from 1798 to 1818, concentrating on the Company's most politically important contacts with Awadh, Hyderabad, Delhi, Travancore, and the Maratha polities of Nagpur, Pune, and Gwalior. This was a time

---

[13] Ranajit Guha, *A Rule of Property for Bengal: An Essay on the Idea of Permanent Settlement* (Paris, 1963); Uday Singh Mehta, *Liberalism and Empire: A Study in Nineteenth-Century British Liberal Thought* (Chicago, 1999); Jon E. Wilson, *The Domination of Strangers: Modern Governance in Eastern India, 1780–1835* (Basingstoke, 2008).

[14] The classic account is Bernard S. Cohn, *Colonialism and Its Forms of Knowledge: The British in India* (Princeton, NJ, 1998), pp. 3–4.

[15] Guido van Meersbergen, *Ethnography and Encounter: The Dutch and English in Seventeenth-Century South Asia* (Leiden, 2021); Sanjay Subrahmanyam, *Courtly Encounters: Translating Courtliness and Violence in Early Modern Eurasia* (Cambridge, MA, 2012).

[16] Cyril Lemieux, 'A quoi sert l'analyse des controverses', *Mil neuf cent* 25 (2007), pp. 91–92.

when many of the Company's most important alliances were concluded, but their long-term implications were only starting to become clear. In retrospect, relationships of 'protection' and coercion would become a distinctive attribute of the modern British empire, but at the turn of the century, the future role of indirect rule in cementing British global pre-dominance was not so evident.[17] The Indian alliance system is usually portrayed as an obvious measure designed to finance the Company's armies and create a defensive buffer around Bengal. This book, by con-trast, argues that the formation of the Company's empire of influence is a story of debate, resistance, and uncertainty, as colonial officials ques-tioned the feasibility of controlling purportedly independent kingdoms, and the appropriate methods to be employed for this purpose. These tactics were conditioned, enabled, and resisted by the activities of Indi-ans with varying interests and allegiances of their own. Far from being a simple political and military expedient, the subsidiary alliance system was a complex social, cultural, and intellectual enterprise, difficult to justify as well as to implement.

These problems are best appreciated through the eyes of the Residents, the men appointed to represent the Company at Indian royal courts. These were men who, in the words of their leading historian Michael Fisher, stood 'at the cutting edge of British expansion'.[18] They were the 'central yet slender thread that bound the Indian states to the British Government of India', individuals who powerfully shaped the devel-oping relationships between the East India Company and what would come to be called the princely states.[19] As such, the Residents found themselves at the centre of heated controversies about how the alliance system should operate, and what their own role and function at Indian courts should be. Focusing on the routine activities of Residency life, this book shows how the Residents navigated the conflicting pressures of court and Company, negotiating between political ideals and imperfect realities to build an empire of influence in India.

This empire of influence, though it overlapped with and underpinned the Company's territorial dominion in the subcontinent, also possessed distinct features. Whereas in British India, control was exercised through the Company's administrative and legislative apparatus, in allied states the mechanism of control was, primarily, advice. The goal was to cre-ate conditions in which this advice could not be ignored or gainsaid.

---

[17] On 'protection' in the nineteenth-century British empire, see Lauren Benton and Lisa Ford, *Rage for Order: The British Empire and the Origins of International Law* (Cambridge, MA, 2016), pp. 88–89.

[18] Fisher, *Indirect Rule*, p. 29.

[19] Ibid., p. 61.

In some cases, as in Awadh, the right to dispense advice was guaranteed by treaty (to be discussed in greater detail in Chapter 1). In practice, however, much depended on the Resident's ability to perform his authority convincingly. He had to act the part of someone with local as well as institutional support, someone with information, with resources, someone capable of following through on a threat if necessary. A lot depended, in short, on the Resident. In what follows, I will provide a brief account of who the Residents were and the conditions in which they lived and worked, before describing in greater detail their place within scholarly debates around the nature of empire and indirect rule.

I.1   Introducing the Residents

The potential problems of the Residency as an institution were anticipated by Company executives from the outset. Indian precedents existed, and in many ways formed the foundations upon which the Residency system was built; the role of early Residents as mediators and information gatherers paralleled that of vakils, the agents dispatched by Indian rulers to foreign courts.[20] Yet, the appointment of diplomatic representatives to act on the Company's behalf also raised all kinds of questions, including who would nominate and control them, and whether they might not create unnecessary expense and undesirable political entanglements.[21] The choice of designation for these officials reflects the minimal role that was originally envisaged for them. A 'resident' was a relatively humble and low-ranking officer within the European diplomatic hierarchy. The title reflected both the Company's status as a chartered corporation, and the determination of the directors (ultimately futile, as Chapter 4 will demonstrate) to sidestep questions of precedence and minimize the cost of ceremonial.[22]

The composition of this political line, as contemporaries termed it, fluctuated significantly over time. Military officers, being more numerous and cheaper to employ, initially dominated the service; many early Residents were soldiers who studied Indian languages while in the army.[23] With the foundation of staff training colleges at the turn of the nineteenth

---

[20] Ibid., p. 130. On vakils in regional politics, see for example Karen Leonard, 'The Hyderabad Political System and Its Participants', *Journal of Asian Studies* 30, no. 3 (1971): 569–582; Rosalind O'Hanlon, 'Entrepreneurs in Diplomacy: Maratha Expansion in the Age of the Vakil', *IESHR* 57, no. 4 (2020): 503–534.

[21] Fisher, *Indirect Rule*, pp. 133, 135.

[22] Caroline Keen, *Princely India and the British: Political Development and the Operation of Empire* (London, 2012), p. 6; Fisher, *Indirect Rule*, p. 49.

[23] Douglas Peers, 'Colonial Knowledge and the Military in India, 1780–1860', *The Journal of Imperial and Commonwealth History* 33, no. 2 (2005): 157.

century, the preference shifted towards college-educated civilians instructed in mathematics, natural philosophy, law, history, political economy, and the classics, as well as Indian languages, history, and culture.[24] Retrenchment in the 1820s cut this trend short; thereafter, Residents were once again more likely to be military officers. While C. A. Bayly and Douglas Peers have hypothesized that this military presence might have created a militaristic culture within the political line, it is worth noting that even though civilians predominated during the period under study, militarism prevailed, for reasons that will be explored in Chapter 3.[25] Regardless of their professional background, Residents usually belonged to the aristocracy or landed gentry, and were often connected to figures of influence within the Company. They leveraged these ties to secure appointments, usually starting out as secretaries or assistants and then working their way up the corporate ladder as vacancies emerged.[26]

Early Residents lived in houses furnished for them by the courts to which they were posted, but with time began to leave their imprint on the built environment of the cities in which they lived. At Delhi, Residents David Ochterlony (1803–1806), Archibald Seton (1806–1811), and Charles Theophilus Metcalfe (1811–1818) resided in a converted pavilion that had previously formed part of a palace belonging to the seventeenth-century Mughal prince Dara Shukoh.[27] This building was adapted and enlarged to suit British tastes, with the addition of a colonnaded portico and Ionic columns to costume the pre-existing Mughal structure in Classical garb.[28] At Lucknow and Hyderabad, grandiose Classical buildings were constructed to house the Resident and his guests, with room for hosting dinners, balls, and other entertainments for army officers, European travellers, and courtly elites (see Figures I.1 and I.2).[29] Not all Residencies were quite so ornate; at Pune, the Residency compound consisted of a scattering of bungalows far less impressive to the eye.[30] However large or small, the main Residency building was usually surrounded by smaller offices and houses

---

[24] Fisher, *Indirect Rule*, pp. 77–81.

[25] C. A. Bayly, *Imperial Meridian: The British Empire and the World 1780–1830* (London, 1989), p. 210; Douglas M. Peers, *Between Mars and Mammon: Colonial Armies and the Garrison State in Early Nineteenth-Century India* (London, 1995), p. 61.

[26] Fisher, *Indirect Rule*, pp. 88–89.

[27] Sylvia Shorto, *British Houses in Late Mughal Delhi* (Woodbridge, 2018), pp. 26–27.

[28] Ibid., p. 37.

[29] Dharmendra Prasad, *Social and Cultural Geography of Hyderabad City: A Historical Perspective* (New Delhi, 1986), pp. 49–51; Rosie Llewellyn-Jones, *A Fatal Friendship: The Nawabs, the British, and the City of Lucknow* (Delhi, 1985), pp. 88–115.

[30] James Welsh, *Military Reminiscences Extracted from a Journal of Nearly Forty Years' Active Service in the East Indies*, 2 vols (London, 1830), I, p. 208.

Figure I.1 Sita Ram, 'The Residency building in Lucknow' (1814), British Library, London, Add. Or. 4761, no. 4761. © British Library Board. All Rights Reserved/Bridgeman Images.

for the accommodation of its European staff, as well as gardens for their relaxation and enjoyment. Maria Sykes (whose husband was an officer in the subsidiary force stationed at Pune) observed in 1813 that the Residency compound was placed 'in most delightful pleasure grounds, where the apple and the pear, the peach and the orange, and almond and fig trees overshadow the strawberry beds and are hedged in by the rose, the myrtle, and the jasmine.'[31] Despite its humble architecture, the Pune Residency occupied a beautiful spot at the junction of two rivers, a setting much admired by European visitors who took advantage of the Residents' hospitality (Figure I.3).

As sites of sociability and consumption as well as statecraft, Residencies became important urban centres. At Hyderabad and Lucknow, bazaars (or marketplaces) sprung up to service them and the small population of non-official European residents (mostly traders and shopkeepers) flocked to the neighbourhood.[32] These spaces surrounding the Residency and associated military cantonments, and the people who inhabited them,

---

[31] BL, APAC, Maria Sykes Papers, MSS Eur C799, p. 55.
[32] Prasad, *Hyderabad City*, p. 16; Lewellyn-Jones, *Fatal Friendship*, pp. 95–97.

Figure I.2 Robert Melville Grindlay, 'The British Residency at Hyderabad, drawn in 1813' (1830), British Library, London, X400 (19), no. 19. © British Library Board. All Rights Reserved/Bridgeman Images.

fell under the jurisdiction of the Resident. As Michael Fisher has argued, by exempting Europeans and Indian dependents of the Residency from a ruler's judicial authority, extraterritoriality provided an important mechanism whereby the Resident established his own influence within the city, though, as an incident discussed in Chapter 3 will show, Company executives remained uncertain how far Residents should exercise these powers to punish offenders.[33]

The number of resident European officials varied from place to place. Most Residents were joined by two or three assistants, a postmaster, an officer heading the military escort, and a surgeon.[34] The number

[33] Fisher, *Indirect Rule*, p. 255.
[34] The members of the Residents' household are listed in published government registers and directories. See for example *A New Oriental Register, and East India Directory, for 1802* (London, 1802), p. 16.

Figure I.3 Henry Salt, 'Poonah' (1809), British Library, London, X123(13), no. 13 © British Library Board. All Rights Reserved/Bridgeman Images.

of assistants depended on the relative importance of the Residency in question; the Resident at Delhi, whose purview extended to Rajasthan, Punjab, and Afghanistan, had as many as eight assistants to fulfil a range of tasks, some more judicial and administrative than diplomatic.[35] Residents were permitted to recommend or consult on prospective candidates for these positions, meaning that the members of his household were often connected to him through ties of friendship, kinship, or patronage.[36] Sometimes these ties were close. At Hyderabad, William Kirkpatrick (Resident 1794–1797) was assisted by his younger brother James Achilles Kirkpatrick (himself Resident at Hyderabad 1798–1805); just over ten years later Henry Russell (Resident 1810–1820) was assisted by his younger brother Charles.

---

[35] House of Commons, *Return of Civil Offices and Establishments under Presidencies of Bengal, Madras and Bombay, 1817 and 1827* (London, 1830), p. 2.

[36] BL, APAC, Mss Eur F228/13, James Achilles Kirkpatrick to William Kirkpatrick, 23 August 1801, p. 133; Bodl. Oxf., Russell Papers, MS. Eng. lett. d. 163, Henry Russell to J. H. Casamaijor, 13 August 1811, p. 26.

This small circle of European men depended on a far larger number of Indian employees. By 1817, a typical office establishment included a head munshi (the focus of Chapter 5), up to three writers or copying clerks, sometimes a treasurer, and as many as forty further unspecified 'natives' fulfilling a range of tasks.[37] Added to this would have been the many table attendants, cooks, water carriers, tailors, washermen, grooms, gardeners, porters, watchmen and other staff without whom the Resident's elite lifestyle would have been impossible.[38]

Some of the Residents discussed in this book cohabited with Indian women, but, with the notable exception of James Achilles Kirkpatrick (whose marriage to Khair un-Nissa earned him Governor General Richard Wellesley's official disapprobation), these relationships rarely feature in their correspondence.[39] It is difficult to judge how they may have affected dynamics at court. The status and identities of these women remain, for the most part, obscure. Those whose personal histories are known did not have roots within the courts where the Residents were posted, though they may still have had networks of their own, and likely had useful knowledge to impart.[40] By forming a relationship with a well-connected woman of high status at Hyderabad, James Achilles Kirkpatrick once again appears to be the exception that proves the rule.

Very few Residents during this period had European wives while in office. Those who did are Henry Russell, who married a French Catholic resident of Hyderabad, Clotilde Mottet, in 1816, and Richard Jenkins, who married Elizabeth Helen Spottiswoode, the daughter of a Company man, in 1824.[41] Thomas Sydenham was briefly joined at Hyderabad by his sister, Mary Anne Orr (an officer's wife), from 1808; Elphinstone

---

[37] House of Commons, *Return of Civil Offices*, pp. 58–60.

[38] Thomas Williamson, *The East India Vade-Mecum; or, Complete Guide to Gentlemen Intended for the Civil, Military, or Naval Service of the Hon. East India Company*, 2 vols (London, 1810), I, pp. 186–187.

[39] On James Achilles Kirkpatrick and William Palmer's Indian wives, see Durba Ghosh, *Sex and the Family in Colonial India: The Making of Empire* (Cambridge, 2006), pp. 69–103. John Baillie appears to have had multiple partners and several illegitimate children; see NRAS, Fraser of Reelig Papers, B331, Edward Fraser to William Fraser, 3 February 1806, p. 5; B333, Edward Fraser to William Fraser, 21 December 1807, p. 6.

[40] William Palmer, who would become Resident at Poona, met his companion, Faiz Baksh, when he was Hastings's aide-de-camp at Lucknow; she was the daughter of a Delhi courtier (Ghosh, *Sex and the Family*, p. 83). Charles Metcalfe met his companion at the court of Ranjit Singh (Thompson, *The Life of Charles, Lord Metcalfe*, pp. 101–102).

[41] Bodl. Oxf., Russell Papers, MS. Eng. lett. c. 151, Henry Russell to his father, 3 October 1816, p. 175; 'Jenkins, Richard (1785–1853), of Bicton Hall, Salop and 7 Mansfield Street, Mdx', in *The History of Parliament: The House of Commons 1820–1832*, ed. D. R. Fisher (Cambridge, 2009).

reported that the two played Italian and Scotch airs on the flute and piano forte for five hours out of the day.[42] Apart from the occasional visitor and the officers' wives living in military cantonments, the Residencies were homosocial spaces. In their letters and journals, Residents report hunting, playing billiards, and reading aloud or studying with the male members of their household.[43]

Business hours were mostly spent reading and writing correspondence, interspersed with frequent consultations with ministers and occasional attendance at court levees (depending on the Resident's preferences). The Maratha courts usually appointed a minister to handle Residency business, while at Lucknow and Hyderabad the Resident interacted primarily with the chief minister. Consultations might occur within the palace precincts, at the Residency, or in the minister's own abode. In some cases, these relationships could become close; at Hyderabad, Henry Russell and his household frequently visited minister Chandu Lal's gardens, eating, drinking, and occasionally staying late into the night.[44]

Within the Company, the Residents' most important point of contact was the governor general or his secretaries, based in Calcutta. In the eighteenth century, the governments of Bombay, Bengal, and Madras had competed for control over the Residencies, but by the turn of the nineteenth century, Bengal had established its authority over key members of the political line.[45] It was to the governor general that the Residents studied here made their reports, and it was he or one of his secretaries who issued their instructions. It was the governor-general-in-council, in turn, who relayed the Residents' reports to the Company's Court of Directors and the parliamentary Board of Control in London. In addition to their official and demi-official exchanges with the governor general, Residents regularly corresponded with one another, partly out of necessity (they were responsible for keeping one another apprised of developments at their respective courts) but also because of feelings of personal and professional affinity, as Chapter 2 will show.

This official and unofficial correspondence, read alongside the Residents' personal letters and papers, reveals a world in flux. Focusing on an important but understudied period in the history of indirect rule, this book uses the papers and correspondence of the Residents to understand

[42] BL, APAC, Mss Eur F109, Mountstuart Elphinstone to John Adam, 15 January 1808.
[43] Bodl. Oxf., Russell Papers, MS. Eng. lett. c. 150, Thomas Sydenham to Charles Russell, 15 January 1806, p. 18; BL, APAC, Mss Eur F109/89, Mountstuart Elphinstone to John Adam, 5 July 1806.
[44] Hyderabad Central Records Office, *The Chronology of Modern Hyderabad 1720–1890* (Hyderabad, 1954), pp. 140, 143, 144, 147, 151.
[45] Fisher, *Indirect Rule,* p. 85.

how they tried to consolidate control despite resistance and unrest at court, and ideological division within the Company. In the process, characteristic narratives about the foundations of Britain's nineteenth-century empire, and the logic behind emergent strategies of indirect rule, begin to seem less certain.

I.2   Diving below the Waterline

Over half a century ago, two historians influentially pushed the boundaries of how the British 'empire' was defined. Criticizing their contemporaries for fixating on 'those colonies coloured red on the map', John Gallagher and Ronald Robinson memorably suggested that equating British overseas expansion with formal empire was 'rather like judging the size and character of icebergs solely from the parts above the waterline'.[46] This provocation generated decades of debate around the usefulness and validity of the concept of informal empire, particularly its application to Latin America.[47] Though contentious, these exchanges have been intellectually productive. Robinson and Gallagher encouraged British historians to look below the waterline (to borrow their famous metaphor) and see dominion as forming part of a wider repertoire of strategies for the pursuit of economic and political gain overseas. Key among these strategies was indirect rule.

Usually defined in opposition to direct administrative control, indirect rule encompasses various forms of imperial oversight. For the purposes of conceptual clarity, political scientists Adnan Naseemullah and Paul Staniland have identified three types: suzerain governance (whereby the princely or tribal state remains nominally independent and internally sovereign but recognizes the overarching authority of the imperial power); hybrid governance (whereby the imperial power and indigenous ruler share authority which they exercise in distinct but overlapping spheres); and de jure governance (where the imperial power has legal and administrative authority over the territory in question, but that control is enforced locally by intermediary political elites and strongmen).[48] These types, though implemented differently, are nevertheless founded

[46] John Gallagher and Ronald Robinson, 'The Imperialism of Free Trade', *Economic History Review* 6, no. 1 (1953): 1.
[47] For an overview of early debates, see William Roger Louis, ed., *Imperialism: The Robinson and Gallagher Controversy* (New York, NY, 1976); more recently, see Matthew Brown, ed., *Informal Empire in Latin America: Culture, Commerce and Capital* (Oxford, 2008).
[48] Adnan Naseemullah and Paul Staniland, 'Indirect Rule and Varieties of Governance', *Governance: An International Journal of Policy, Administration, and Institutions* 29, no. 1 (2016): 17.

on the same basic premise, namely, the desirability of working through existing institutions. All three are also calculated to fulfil the same essential purpose, that is, control. For Michael Fisher, this 'determinative and exclusive political control', recognized by both sides, is the defining feature of indirect rule.[49] The Residency system during this period largely conformed to what Naseemullah and Staniland describe as 'suzerain governance', with the Company controlling their allies' foreign policy while leaving their internal administration largely intact. Indirect rule was not a term used during the early nineteenth century, when colonial officials tended to speak in terms of 'influence', 'interference', 'connections', and, increasingly, 'ascendancy' or 'paramountcy'.[50] Still, as an analytical category indirect rule helps to remind us of broader patterns in the logic of colonial rule, encouraging us to address the big questions about why empires develop in the way that they do, and how they bend existing structures to their needs. In particular, studying indirect rule encourages us to think about power: what it is, how it is exercised, and the different forms it can take, some of which are less apparent than others.

This book is unusual in its chronological focus, since indirect rule is usually described as a late nineteenth- and early twentieth-century phenomenon. As a philosophy of rule, it is conventionally associated with Frederick Lugard and his book *The Dual Mandate in British Tropical Africa* (1922), widely considered the most influential statement of indirect rule's theoretical underpinnings and practical advantages.[51] Lugard's book marked the culmination of a late nineteenth-century process whereby indirect rule was implemented across the African continent as well as in Southeast Asia, Fiji, and the Persian Gulf. Two justifications have been advanced to explain its popularity. First, that it represented a means of bypassing the problem of resources at a time when the colonial state had limited funds and few staff, enabling what Sara Berry has described as 'hegemony on a shoestring'.[52] Second, that it was born out of the crises of the mid-nineteenth century, when experiences of the 1857 Indian Uprising convinced officials of the fundamental otherness of their colonial subjects, and the concomitant need to set empire

---

[49] Fisher, *Indirect Rule*, p. 6.

[50] See for example NAI, HRR, G. H. Barlow to Thomas Sydenham, 22 October 1806, pp. 380–385; BL, APAC, Cleveland Public Library Papers, wq091.92 Ea77p9, Archibald Seton to Marquess of Hastings, 6 June 1814, p. 113; BL, APAC, Mss Eur F88/405, Henry Russell to C. T. Metcalfe, 15 May 1819, pp. 61–62.

[51] Karuna Mantena, *Alibis of Empire: Henry Maine and the Ends of Liberal Imperialism* (Princeton, NJ, 2010), p. 173.

[52] Sara Berry, 'Hegemony on a Shoestring: Indirect Rule and Access to Agricultural Land', *Africa* 62, no. 3 (1992): 329.

on a firmer footing by grafting it onto pre-existing political and social structures.[53] Despite their different emphases, both explanations posit indirect rule as an alternative developed in response to the burdens and complications posed by direct rule.

The place of the early Residencies within this narrative is unclear. Given its establishment in the late eighteenth century, the context in which this system took shape was evidently different. Usually, the pragmatic justification is preferred as an explanation for its emergence. Scholarly convention holds that the Company's increased intervention into the politics of allied kingdoms was propelled by the need to ensure the smooth flow of subsidies to finance their armies. According to this argument, an aggressive form of indirect rule was foretold almost from the beginning.[54] The continued existence of these nominally independent kingdoms is viewed as a pragmatic measure on the part of the Company because of the almost self-evident benefits that indirect rule was seen to confer: that it was inexpensive; that it was practically effective; and that it was less likely to inspire Indian resistance.[55]

Because the development of the Residency system is usually portrayed as common-sensical and ad hoc, the cultural and ideological frameworks that informed its early evolution remain largely unexamined, the assumption being that there is little of interest to recover here. By contrast, the late nineteenth century has begun to attract historians interested in piecing together the theory of indirect rule and the status of the princely states within international law. These legal and intellectual historians have been enticed, no doubt, by the voluminous manuals and reports compiled by legal theorists and employees of the Foreign Office during this period. Based on this printed evidence, both Karuna Mantena and Lauren Benton locate the origins of a theory of indirect rule in India in the late nineteenth century, focusing on thick tomes authored by Henry Sumner Maine and Charles Lewis Tupper, respectively.[56] In so doing, the earlier history of these relationships is elided. The whole story is summarized in a sentence by Benton as a process whereby 'the princely states were quickly and clearly made subordinate to the British.'[57] There is little attention to the ideas and assumptions underpinning the early Residency

---

[53] Mahmood Mamdani, *Define and Rule: Native as Political Identity* (Cambridge, MA, 2012), p. 2; Mantena, *Alibis*, pp. 1–2.

[54] C. A. Bayly, *Indian Society and the Making of the British Empire* (Cambridge, 1988), pp. 89–90.

[55] Fisher, *Indirect Rule*, pp. 8–14.

[56] Mantena, *Alibis*, p. 2; Lauren Benton, *A Search for Sovereignty: Law and Geography in European Empires, 1400–1900* (Cambridge, 2009), p. 243.

[57] Benton, *Search for Sovereignty*, pp. 242–243

system, ideas that were largely implicit and constructed through experimentation and negotiation on the ground rather than elaborated in texts and treaties.

Disinterest in the early nineteenth century can also be explained in part by the almost magnetic effect of the 1857 Uprising. Traditional views of Indian rulers as pillars of imperial power during and after the rebellion have prompted historians to demonstrate the extent to which rulers continued to exercise political agency within their own domains, even at the height of the British Raj.[58] Recent examples that emphasize princely autonomy during this period include Manu Bhagavan's account of educational reforms in Baroda and Mysore and Eric Lewis Beverley's study of Hyderabad's connections with the Muslim world.[59] These analyses have revised our understanding of politics in the Indian princely states, incorporating them into wider debates in Indian and world history. Still, they are more concerned with recovering the agency of princes ruling under conditions of apparent thraldom than with understanding the process whereby the subsidiary alliance first took shape.

Historians who have addressed indirect rule's eighteenth-century origins have tended to adopt a regional focus.[60] As a leading power within the fragmenting Mughal empire and the first court to be connected with the Company through a subsidiary alliance, Awadh has generated the most interest.[61] Richard B. Barnett's *North India Between Empires: Awadh, the Mughals, and the British 1720–1801* (1980) is a classic of the genre. In adopting this lens, South Asianists have produced detailed case studies documenting the changing configurations of power at individual courts. Yet, this approach fails to capture the development of a Residency *system* defined by the movement of people and ideas between places.

---

[58] See for example Thomas Metcalf, *Aftermath of Revolt: India 1857–1970* (Princeton, NJ, repr. 2015), p. 222.

[59] Manu Bhagavan, *Sovereign Spheres: Princes, Education and Empire in Colonial India* (Oxford, 2003); Eric Lewis Beverley, *Hyderabad, British India, and the World: Muslim Networks and Minor Sovereignty, c. 1850–1950* (Cambridge, 2015).

[60] Karen Leonard's various studies of Hyderabad are particularly important here; see especially Karen Isaksen Leonard, *Social History of an Indian Caste: The Kayasths of Hyderabad* (Berkeley, CA, 1978). See also Zubaida Yazdani, *Hyderabad during the Residency of Henry Russell, 1811–1820: A Case Study of the Subsidiary Alliance System* (Oxford, 1976); K. N. Panikkar, *British Diplomacy in North India: A Study of the Delhi Residency, 1803–1857* (New Delhi, 1968).

[61] Rosie Lewellyn-Jones, *Engaging Scoundrels: True Tales of Old Lucknow* (Delhi, 2000); Muzaffar Alam, *The Crisis of Empire in Mughal North India* (Delhi, 1986); Michael H. Fisher, *A Clash of Cultures: Awadh, the British, and the Mughals* (New Delhi, 1987).

The synthetic studies by Michael Fisher and Barbara Ramusack most closely approximate the analysis undertaken here. Fisher's classic account provides a complete history of indirect rule within the Company, from 1764 to its abolition in 1858. Ramusack goes even further, tracing the history of the Residencies from their origins to independence in 1947. Both are impressive and widely cited works of scholarship that continue to dominate the field. Yet, both are also comprehensive overviews which, because of their broad coverage, necessarily do not furnish intimate details about what life at the Residency was like during any given period. These are political and administrative histories concerned with tracing institutional trends at the expense of details that do not fit. Whereas Fisher and Ramusack provide invaluable narratives chronicling change over the longue durée, this book casts a spotlight on a formative moment in the history of the Residency system, illuminating some of the messiness and uncertainty that might otherwise fade from view.

A key advantage of this roughly synchronic approach is that in narrowing the chronological scope, the emphasis shifts from big events to mundane realities. *Empire of Influence* is, above all, a cultural history concerned with the ideas and practices that constituted the day-to-day life of indirect rule during this experimental stage. By elucidating the conceptual frameworks within which the Residents interpreted events in the subcontinent, we can better understand the rules of political behaviour that they set for themselves. Delving into the details of day-to-day life permits us to see how and why these intentions did, or did not, translate into practice, and with what consequences. In turn, the routine problems of Residency life shaped Residents' ideas about how influence could, or should, be enacted going forwards. Only by reducing the scale of analysis can we tease out the relationship between ideas and practices and grasp how imperial influence operated on the ground.

Equally, narrowing the chronological scope enables this book to address a range of critical themes within the history of the Residencies, encompassing the broad spectrum of activities undertaken by the Resident at court. Histories of letter-writing, gift-giving, and flogging may not adhere to the same timeline, nor do they necessarily suggest a clear narrative arc; still, all are pertinent to how Residents understood and tried to express influence at court. Breaking with a traditional narrative structure permits us to bring topics that are conventionally treated separately within the same analytical frame.

Finally, by focusing on a small group of a dozen men, this book is better able to come to terms with the human dimension of the Company's history, counteracting a widespread tendency to treat the colonial administration as an 'agentless abstraction' to quote Frederick Cooper.[62] Such an approach, Cooper argues, obscures the ways in which people confronted the possibilities and constraints of particular colonial situations, and acted accordingly. This book is premised on the idea that imperial policies were mediated through human beings with complicated relationships both to the institutions they represented and to the societies in which they tried, to varying degrees, to immerse themselves. This is not a work of prosopography; the focus remains on ideas and practices rather than on individual biographies. Still, by incorporating examples of individual dilemmas, we are reminded that imperial influence was a fabric stitched together out of a series of interactions and can identify some of the factors that might have shaped how this process played out.

In so doing, I have tried to create space for acknowledging how feelings of loss, loneliness, jealousy, or contempt informed how Residents perceived India as well as how they behaved there. In this, I have been compelled by Ann Stoler's invitation to attend to 'how power shaped the production of sentiments and vice versa', to 'dwell in the disquiets, in the antipathies, estrangements, yearnings, and resentments that constrained colonial policies and people's actions'.[63] While in this instance Stoler was particularly concerned with the constitution and consolidation of racial boundaries through the regulation of interracial sex and procreation, her proposition seems equally relevant to the study of imperial governance more generally. Reading personal letters and journals alongside official reports restores some of the ambivalence and uncertainty that is elided in public records, exposing the fissures that emerged within the Company's administration. In the process, it also becomes possible to challenge certain assumptions about the Residents themselves.

I.3   Demystifying the White Mughals

Though the Residents of the early nineteenth century rarely figure prominently in the historiography on indirect rule, they have had a disproportionate impact on debates about cultural syncretism. As intermediaries living at the interstices of British and Indian societies, the Residents are alluring figures for historians interested in connectedness and cosmopolitanism. Indian royal courts, and their attendant Residencies, are classic

---

[62] Frederick Cooper, *Colonialism in Question: Theory, Knowledge, History* (Berkeley, CA, 2005), p. 25.
[63] Ann Laura Stoler, *Carnal Knowledge and Imperial Power: Race and the Intimate in Colonial Rule* (Berkeley, CA, 2002), p. 12.

'contact zones' where cultures mingled and overlapped.[64] A study of the Residencies intersects with wider interest in the 'middle ground', spaces where empires met, and lines of authority were blurred.[65] The Residents themselves, meanwhile, fit the rubric of cultural broker or go-between, agents who straddled cultural boundaries and made cross-cultural communication possible.[66] These were learned men, familiar with Indian languages, who immersed themselves to varying degrees in the swirling currents of courtly life. They partook of the symbolic exchanges that formed an essential part of Mughal ritual, chewed *paan* (a stimulating preparation of betel leaf and areca nut) and were christened with attar of roses. They smoked hookah and attended *nautch* dances; some took Indian wives. On the surface, at least, the Residencies seem like oases which, for a time, anyway, escaped what historian Sudipta Sen, among others, has characterized as the growing social and political distance separating Britons from Indians during this period.[67]

Unsurprisingly, some of the most well-known scholarship on the Residencies tends to romanticize them as sites of cultural fusion, as hybrid spaces on the margins of British India. In *White Mughals*, William Dalrymple depicts these courts as 'the borderlands of colonial India', as 'spaces where categories of identity, ideas of national loyalty and relations of power were often flexible, and where the possibilities for self-transformation were, at least potentially, limitless'.[68] This language is echoed in Maya Jasanoff's study of imperial collectors, where Lucknow is portrayed as a city that furnished its inhabitants with 'genuinely multicultural possibilities', offering 'the promise of reinvention in its cosmopolitan embrace'. According to Jasanoff, 'who you were, with whom you associated, and how you wanted to live were not either-or choices. You could bridge the boundaries'.[69] This strain of historiography resonates with a 'postmodern' intellectual tradition that uses the concept of border in a metaphorical sense to highlight the juxtaposition of cultures in

---

[64] Mary Louise Pratt, *Imperial Eyes: Travel Writing and Transculturation* (London, 2008), p. 8.

[65] Richard White, *The Middle Ground: Indians, Empires, and Republics in the Great Lakes Region, 1650–1815* (Cambridge, 1991), p. xxvi.

[66] See for example E. Natalie Rothman, *Brokering Empire: Trans-Imperial Subjects between Venice and Istanbul* (Ithaca, NY, 2012) and the essays collected in Simon Schaffer, Lissa Roberts, Kapil Raj, and James Delbourgo, eds., *The Brokered World: Go-Betweens and Global Intelligence, 1770–1820* (Sagamore Beach, MA, 2009).

[67] Sudipta Sen, *Distant Sovereignty: National Imperialism and the Origins of British India* (New York, NY, 2002), p. xxviii. See also Spear, *Nabobs*, p. 136.

[68] William Dalrymple, *White Mughals: Love and Betrayal in Eighteenth-Century India* (London, 2004), p. 16.

[69] Maya Jasanoff, *Edge of Empire: Lives, Culture, and Conquest in the East, 1750–1850* (New York, NY, 2006), pp. 58, 59.

particular places, tending to represent such spaces as 'zone[s] of cultural play and experimentation'.[70] Dalrymple and Jasanoff's findings have served to reinforce the historical commonplace that eighteenth-century understandings of human difference were more fluid and contextual than nineteenth- and twentieth-century conceptions of race.[71] The Residents, in this account, are used as evidence to suggest that Britons in India during this period acculturated and integrated into their new surroundings.

This emphasis on exchange and acculturation underplays the Residents' primary function as political agents. To be sure, Residencies were certainly seen to provide opportunities for staging cross-cultural encounters. Visitors to the subcontinent commonly toured Lucknow and Pune; both courts feature prominently in eighteenth- and nineteenth-century travelogues.[72] Here, European guests were treated to breakfast parties, hunting expeditions, elephant rides, and firework displays. Still, this veneer of polite sociability did not obscure the unequal dynamics at work in these places. For contemporaries, these were also sites of coercion and control, arenas wherein the Company asserted its right to dictate to its neighbours. Former Resident Richard Jenkins proclaimed to the 1831 parliamentary select committee that the subsidiary alliance system was 'the main source of our ascendancy, both military and political; it has grown with our growth; and strengthened with our strength. It is interwoven with our very existence'.[73] This statement might have been intended to burnish Jenkins's own reputation as a former Resident, but it was not an exaggeration. The objective of this book is thus to strip away some of the allure of the Residencies, to penetrate past the lavish exteriors of their palatial courts and the decorous, ceremonial forms and practices that Residents adopted to get at the heart of their work. This work involved espionage, patronage, war, and coercion as much as it did spectacle; the Residencies were as much spaces of empire as the courthouse or the counting room.

[70] Hastings Donnan and Thomas M. Wilson, *Borders: Frontiers of Identity, Nation and State* (Oxford, 1999), p. 39.
[71] See specifically Jasanoff, *Edge of Empire*, pp. 11–12. For fluidity of eighteenth-century conceptions of human difference, see Roxann Wheeler, *The Complexion of Race: Categories of Difference in Eighteenth-Century British Culture* (Philadelphia, PA, 2000), p. 15. For a critique of these conventions, see Shruti Kapila, 'Race Matters: Orientalism and Religion, India and Beyond c. 1770–1880', *MAS* 41, no. 3 (2007): 471–513.
[72] Examples include Maria Nugent, *A Journal from the Year 1811 to the Year 1815, Including a Voyage to and Residence in India* (London, 1839); Anne Deane, *A Tour through the Upper Provinces of Hindostan* (London, 1823); Godfrey Charles Mundy, *Pen and Pencil Sketches, Being the Journal of a Tour in India* (London, 1832); George, Viscount Valentia, *Voyages and Travels in India, Ceylon, the Red Sea, Abyssinia, and Egypt* (London, 1809).
[73] House of Commons *Report from the Select Committee on the Affairs of the East India Company*, 7 vols (London, 1832), VII, p. 24.

Incorporating the Residencies into this picture of the Company changes our views of British imperialism in India at the turn of the nineteenth century, an era that has been identified as particularly significant to its history. In *Imperial Meridian: The British Empire and the World 1780–1830* (1989), C. A. Bayly influentially depicted 1780 to 1830 as a vital phase of British imperial history characterized by territorial expansion, increased state intervention, and the development of new techniques of governance.[74] Building on this foundational history, the period figures prominently in recent studies dedicated to charting the hardening of racial boundaries and the emergence of modern governmentality in India, tracing how locally specific practices were reconfigured or displaced by abstract principles of rule in the realm of political ideology, land legislation, legal reform, and record-keeping and documentation.[75] The Residencies, however, do not neatly fit these overarching patterns. Here, Residents had no choice but to work within frameworks not of their choosing and were required to interact with Indians of various backgrounds whether they liked it or not.

How do we reconcile these two pictures of the Company's empire? Though *Imperial Meridian* is usually cited with reference to the centralizing, authoritarian impulses that it identified, the book also highlighted the patronage of indigenous landed elites as an important feature of the British empire during this period.[76] In so doing, Bayly had in mind not so much the merchants, bankers, and brokers who have long been recognized as indispensable to the Company, but rather the aristocracy of South Asia. In part, what the Residencies demonstrate are the points of commonality between British and Indian political elites that made empire possible. Although there were important differences between British and Indian political culture in the early nineteenth century (which this book will elucidate), there were also aspects of Indian courtly etiquette, patronage and service relationships, and gender and the family that aligned with British habits and assumptions. Contemporaries remarked more on contrasts and compromises than congruences, seemingly because many of the things that elite Britons and Indians had in common were also things that were taken for granted or assumed to be natural on both sides; yet these commonalities provided a foundation upon which understandings could be reached. Residents sometimes drew stark oppositions between British and Indian society, but their

---

[74] Bayly, *Imperial Meridian*, p. 8.
[75] Travers, *Ideology*, p. 25; Wilson, *Domination of Strangers*, pp. 2–3; Radhika Singha, *A Despotism of Law: Crime and Justice in Early Colonial India* (Delhi, 1998), p. viii; Bhavani Raman, *Document Raj: Writings and Scribes in Early Colonial South India* (Chicago, 2012), p. 2.
[76] Bayly, *Imperial Meridian*, p. 9.

assertions should be read critically. In so doing, these men were engaging in what legal historian Anthony Anghie has termed the 'dynamic of difference', the 'process of creating a gap between two cultures, demarcating one as universal and civilized, and the other as particular and uncivilized.'[77] Rather than taking the Resident at their word, we should make our own comparisons to better contextualize this dynamic process of interaction and exchange. The period was undoubtedly one of chauvinistic nationalism, but the example of the Residencies reminds us of the ongoing importance of strategies of negotiation and appeal, suggesting that patronage, gifts, and favours were as much instruments of imperial power as tax collection or the law. After all, it was by incorporating themselves into Mughal frameworks of submission and service that the Company had acquired its political and commercial foothold in India in the first place.[78] This book demonstrates the continuing importance of political interaction and exchange into the nineteenth century, even if the dynamics had shifted.

Though the Residents moderate our views on Britain's imperial meridian, it is also a case of the exception proving the rule; through the Residents, we see how determinedly the Company's executive tried to mould the Residencies to fit a bureaucratic pattern of their choosing, even in the face of determined resistance from Residents themselves. The Residencies were thus points of friction where some of the most intractable problems of empire played out. The Residents' close working relationships with Indian elites, for one, means that Residencies provide a useful site for thinking about the tension between domination and exchange upon which the Company's operations relied. The Residents were charged with conciliating Indian rulers and accommodating themselves to Indian political culture, all while maintaining the image of difference on which the imperial project in India was ideologically predicated. While Residents and their superiors believed, to varying degrees, that it was important to express political power in ways that were intelligible to the surrounding population and that resonated with local conceptions of political legitimacy, they were also wary of undermining the reputation for British moral probity and rule of law that they desired to cultivate. The Residents were thus put in a double bind. To establish themselves at Indian courts they had to engage, to some extent,

---

[77] Antony Anghie, *Imperialism, Sovereignty, and the Making of International Law* (Cambridge, 2004), p. 4.

[78] For a summary of early Company diplomacy, see Guido van Meersbergen, 'The Diplomatic Repertoires of the East India Companies in Mughal South Asia, 1608–1717', *The Historical Journal* 62, no. 4 (2019): 875–898.

with Indian political culture; in so doing, however, they threatened to subvert the carefully constructed differences, between 'civilized' Britons and 'barbarous' Indians, upon which the legitimacy of the Company's administration was believed to rest. Because of this paradox, Residents were in regular disagreement with their superiors about issues ranging from the purchase of gifts to corporal punishment.

As this suggests, the Residencies are also sites where the divisions within the Company most clearly come into view. Historians of the Company have long recognized the existence of an 'agency problem', whereby authorities in London struggled to control the activities of employees overseas.[79] Given their geographical distance from the Company's political centres, the Residents exemplify in perhaps its most acute form the distrust that distance could generate. As Duncan Bell has observed, from the perspective of nineteenth-century thinkers the problem of distance inhered, not simply in the practical, administrative difficulties posed by travel and communication, but also the attenuation of crucial bonds of loyalty and citizenship.[80] Suspicions about the corruptibility of the Residents' character were intensified by their relative isolation. The Residents, for their part, were liable to regard the Company's executive as a distant entity from which they could expect little support or recognition. As the man on the spot, Residents exercised significant discretionary power, but were easily scapegoated if problems emerged at court. Although the Residents and the governor general were in near constant correspondence, their relationship was fragile. Some Residents earned the governor generals' respect, even their deference, but good relations depended on the Resident's ability to anticipate and implement the will of government, a will that was not always clear or well informed where Indian allies were concerned.

Contrary to existing depictions of an 'agency problem', then, the reasons for the rampant distrust within the Company were more complex than the geographical distance separating Residents from London and Calcutta. Ideological divisions within the Company were compounded by wider transformations in British conceptualizations of public life and the duties of office. In Britain, the administration of William Pitt the Younger (1783–1801) took tentative steps towards abolishing sinecures, regulating the profits of office, and introducing salaries in place of fees.[81] These reforms reflected a greater demand for transparency and accountability, as official activity was increasingly dissociated from

---

[79] H. V. Bowen, *The Business of Empire: The East India Company and Imperial Britain, 1756–1833* (Cambridge, 2006), p. 151.
[80] Duncan Bell, 'Dissolving Distance: Technology, Space, and Empire in British Political Thought, 1770–1900', *J. Mod. Hist.* 77, no. 3 (2005): 531–532.
[81] Philip Harling, 'Rethinking "Old Corruption"', *P&P* 147 (1995): 151.

private life, and public assets were being more sharply distinguished from private wealth.[82] Similar attitudes operated within the Company; historians have described at length the anxieties about corruption within the Company in the eighteenth century, and subsequent attempts to reform it.[83] Efforts to refashion the Company's employees persisted into the nineteenth century, as evidenced, for example, by the foundation of the Company's college at Haileybury.[84] At the Residencies, the tensions generated by changing ideas of public office, and the shifting domains of private and public life, were at their most intense; by focusing on the Residents, it is possible to witness first-hand the divisiveness of an 'age of reform'.[85] For reasons that will become apparent in the course of this book, this emergent professional ethic proved particularly troublesome to inculcate or impose within the Residency system, long after the golden age of the nabob was supposedly over. In opposition to the wave of reformist enthusiasm coursing through the nineteenth-century Company, Residents like Mountstuart Elphinstone and Charles Metcalfe have been identified as 'Romantics', 'the true conservative element', who opposed 'the tendency that would transform British rule from a personal, paternal government, to an impersonal, mechanical administration', to quote Eric Stokes.[86] By situating these ideas within the courtly environments in which they took shape, this book exposes important practical and ideological divisions within the Company's operations.

Finally, as intermediaries working within and between British and Indian regimes, Residents were also well placed to reflect on issues of continuity and change. One of the driving questions of the historiography on 'British' India is the extent to which the Company's administration differed from existing Indian polities, and how far its expanding presence fundamentally transformed Indian politics and society.[87] Recent studies in the realm of tax collection, administration of justice, record-keeping, and the military have demonstrated how the Company drew on existing social and political structures and, in the process, reconfigured them in

[82] Peter Jupp, 'The Landed Elite and Political Authority in Britain, ca. 1760–1850', *JBS* 29, no. 1 (1990): 64.

[83] Bowen, *Business*, p. 182.

[84] Callie Wilkinson, 'The East India College Debate and the Fashioning of Imperial Officials, 1806–1858', *HJ* 60, no. 4 (2017): 943–969.

[85] For a full exploration of this period in British history, see Arthur Burns and Joanna Innes, eds., *Rethinking the Age of Reform: Britain 1780–1850* (Cambridge, 2007).

[86] Stokes, *English Utilitarians*, p. 14.

[87] For an outline of this debate, see the introduction to Seema Alavi, ed., *The Eighteenth Century in India* (Oxford, 2002), pp. 22–23.

profound and sometimes unexpected ways.[88] At Indian royal courts, the question of whether to adapt to existing political culture, or to remodel it according to British mores, had added stakes given the dangers of either undermining the existing regime, or inciting it to resist. Residents wanted to maintain the structural integrity of Indian administrations, while at the same time channelling their resources into the Company's coffers. Experiences at Indian courts forced Residents to reckon with the fact that their mere presence could provoke unexpected effects that worked against this political agenda, sending courtly politics spiralling in unanticipated directions. Some Residents even came to recognize the relative impossibility of maintaining the status quo given the intrinsically exploitative character of the Company's relationship with its supposed allies. The Residents therefore provide an ideal lens for examining contemporary perceptions of the nature and impact of imperial intervention during a period that C. A. Bayly identified as 'the first age of global imperialism'.[89]

I.4 Approach

Rather than constructing a broad chronological narrative, this book focuses on a brief, coherent, and historically significant unit of time when some of the most important subsidiary alliances were concluded. In 1798, the subsidiary alliance system was still in its infancy; its underlying principles and mode of operation were still in being worked out, and certain key Indian powers, notably the Marathas, remained outside its remit. By 1818, the subsidiary alliance system had brought most of central India under the Company's influence, but only after many years of debate within the Company, and resistance on the part of Indians of various backgrounds. It is this contested process, and the generation of Residents responsible for it, that lie at the heart of this book.

As a complement to existing works of regional expertise, the emphasis of this book is on detecting patterns across courts. This is not to suggest that the histories of these courts are interchangeable; to the contrary, their trajectories differed in important ways. Most obviously, they had different relations with the Company, resulting in varying levels of intervention by the Resident. At one extreme, the Resident at Delhi effectively ruled in

---

[88] Examples include Wilson, *Domination of Strangers*; Hayden Bellenoit, *The Formation of the Colonial State in India: Scribes, Paper, and Taxes, 1760–1860* (London, 2017); Raman, *Document Raj*; Singha, *Despotism of Law*; Seema Alavi, *Sepoys and the Company: Tradition and Transition in Northern India, 1770–1830* (Oxford, 1995).

[89] C. A. Bayly, 'The First Age of Global Imperialism, c. 1760–1830', *The Journal of Imperial and Commonwealth History* 26, no. 2 (1998): 28–47.

the Mughal emperor's stead following the Company's occupation of the city in 1803, and was accordingly charged with a range of responsibilities over neighbouring districts that other Residents did not have.[90] At the other end of the spectrum, the Residents attached to Shinde and the raja of Berar were essentially ambassadors with little influence over state administration, since neither Shinde nor the raja were then bound to the Company through subsidiary alliances. While these courts were all considered sufficiently significant for their Residents to fall under the direct purview of the governor general, they were important to the Company for different reasons. Nagpur's location at the centre of the subcontinent made it a coveted military and communications hub, while Travancore was considered as a likely staging post for a French invasion at the turn of the century as well as a valued source of timber and pepper. Awadh furnished money and military labour and occupied a strategic location as gateway to the North Indian plain.[91] Meanwhile, Company control over Delhi and Pune was seen to have symbolic significance because of their status as political capitals. Throughout the book, I have tried to bring some of these distinctions to the fore, indicating, as much as possible, where paths diverged as well as where they intersected.

Though the courts were unique in many respects, it is nevertheless worth considering them together because both British and Indian contemporaries explicitly made these connections and comparisons at the time, as Chapter 2 in particular will illustrate. The Indian political elite were attuned to developments at different political centres through the exchange of letters, ambassadors, and spies; this awareness informed their strategizing. The Company, for its part, was conscious of the scrutiny they were under and the ripple effect that could ensue because of shifts in practice or policy at a single court. The Company's aim during this period was precisely to divide political centres that had previously been in regular contact. By the same token, part of the strength of the Residency system was its networked character; Residents passed on information and experiences and learned from the examples set at other courts. The individual Residencies made up a system, a 'political line' (as contemporaries called it) characterized by the exchange of people and ideas; examining the Residents in isolation would obscure how this system operated. To demonstrate this point, throughout the book I have highlighted the ways in which exchanges between courts, and between their respective Residencies, shaped the development of ideas and practices of imperial influence.

---

[90] For British relations with Rajputana and the Cis-Sutlej States, see Panikkar, *British Diplomacy in North India*, pp. 42–99.
[91] Fisher, *Clash of Cultures*, pp. 1, 6, 18.

If the courts examined in this study differed significantly one from the other, so, too, did many of the Residents. Some fit the 'White Mughal' mould, either because they cohabited with Indian women, dressed in Indian garb, or delighted in Indian literature and history. Some, for example, were adepts in Indian languages; Thomas Sydenham was described in his obituary as 'master of the Arabic and Persian languages', and by a colleague in the political line as 'a most eminent Hindostannee in language & manners'.[92] Other Residents couldn't be bothered; as a young man, Charles Theophilus Metcalfe determined not to waste his time with Oriental scholarship, convinced 'that the Nations of Europe have so far surpassed any thing ever known in Asia that the world would not gain one atom of real information, from the disclosure of all, that is contained in Eastern languages.'[93] Some Residents were seemingly happy to remain in India forever, while others viewed their time in India as a liminal period to be endured before their real life could resume; in letters to friends, Mountstuart Elphinstone described his Company service as his 'period of transportation' (comparing himself to a convict) and despaired about the 'waste of years' separating him from his return to Britain.[94] Politically a few favoured conciliation, but growing numbers believed in the necessity of coercion, for reasons that will be explored in Chapter 3. Rather than trying to construct an ideal type or identify a paradigmatic example of how a Resident thought and behaved, then, this book instead recaptures the experimental nature of early attempts to consolidate the Company's political predominance. The Residents differed in their interpretations of what their influence should look like, and how it should be exercised. In drawing attention to this variety, the book illustrates the spectrum of possibilities available at this protean moment in the history of the Company's diplomatic line.

The examination of the routine practices of this small coterie of imperial officials might seem like a return to the study of 'great men', replicating the triumphal imperial accounts of the nineteenth century. To some extent, this focus on the Company's representatives runs counter to prevailing trends within global history, where there is a laudable preference for recovering the experiences of previously marginalized individuals at the expense of the subjects of nineteenth-century hagiography. In contrast to the convicts, captives, sailors, slaves, and indentured labourers studied by

---

[92] 'Memoir of Thomas Sydenham, Esq.', *Gentleman's Magazine* 86, no. 2 (1816): 374; BL, APAC, Mss Eur F109/89, Mountstuart Elphinstone to John Adam, 15 January 1808.

[93] BL, APAC, Mss Eur B233, Charles Theophilus Metcalfe to Joseph Goodall, 16 August 1803, p. 5.

[94] BL, APAC, Mss Eur F128/166, Mountstuart Elphinstone to Edward Strachey, 25 March 1813, p. 2.

historians like Clare Anderson, Residents like Mountstuart Elphinstone and Charles Metcalfe were recognized as leading figures in their own life-times.[95] They are, even now, sometimes described in terms bordering on veneration, as an 'extraordinary galaxy of distinctive stars in the political firmament'.[96] Of the four 'great men' of the 'golden age' identified by Philip Mason in his celebratory *The Men Who Ruled India* (1985), two were Residents; Metcalfe was described as 'the last and probably the great-est of the quartet'.[97] This lingering aura of adulation makes it even more important that we examine how these individuals self-consciously con-structed themselves to appear powerful and authoritative, usually at the expense of Indian elites who they worked systematically to disempower and discredit. In examining their professional trajectories, we see how their actions were shaped by the activities of Indians of various backgrounds, whether messengers, accountants, translators, or concubines. In their day-to-day work, the Residents were forced to respond to circumstances not of their making; they adapted in response to Indian resistance and relied on Indian aid. Throughout the book, but especially in Chapters 5 and 6, we see the significance of Indian actors to this history.

Although this book is concerned to bring the impact of Indian actors to the fore, it is in essence a history of British imperial ideas and prac-tices. As such, it relies on Company records and the Residents' personal papers. These sources, though voluminous and often rich in detail, are inherently problematic. To be sure, every archive is by its nature partial and incomplete; record-keeping is a selective process, and the decisions made about what to keep and what to destroy are both reflective and constitutive of an unequal world wherein some voices are amplified at the expense of others.[98] The importance of record-keeping to state-formation means that archives should be understood not as neutral repositories of information but as instruments whereby political power is exercised.[99] These traits are evident in imperial archives, too; nevertheless, imperial archives possess unique features that make them particularly suspect as windows onto the past. For the most part, imperial records represent an outsiders' point of view, with the testimony of indigenous popula-tions filtered through the prism of a colonial official's interpretation and

---

[95] Clare Anderson, *Subaltern Lives: Biographies of Colonialism in the Indian Ocean World, 1790–1920* (Cambridge, 2012).

[96] Ramusack, *Indian Princes*, p. 80.

[97] Philip Mason, *The Men Who Ruled India* (London, 1985), p. 116.

[98] Joan M. Schwartz and Terry Cook, 'Archives, Records, and Power: The Making of Modern Memory', *Archival Science* 2, no. 1–2 (2002), pp. 1–19.

[99] Peter Burke, *A Social History of Knowledge from Gutenberg to Diderot* (Cambridge, 2000), pp. 116–135.

recorded and preserved according to his priorities. The contents of imperial archives also served distinctive ideological purposes. These records
were used to construct and justify inequality along racial lines as well as
to give substance to the fantasy of an all-knowing colonial administration
which, historians argue, dramatically misrepresents officials' real grasp of
realities on the ground.[100] The Residency records are a product of their
imperial environment; their role was not simply to describe, but to reinforce political asymmetries. They must be read in terms of the functions
they were intended to serve, as well as the colonial common sense that
shaped them and was in turn shaped by them.

The Residents' personal papers can offer a valuable counterpoint to
official records; they contain evidence of uncertainty and dissent that
rarely features in letters destined for the eyes of their superiors. Yet, letters are not a transparent reflection of a person's inner life, either. Letters,
like records, are prone to damage, destruction, and redaction. Recent
scholarship on epistolarity emphasizes the extent to which letter-writing
was a performance, 'an "act" in the theatrical sense as well as a "speech-
act" in the linguistic.'[101] Letters were written with an audience in mind;
their language and contents were tailored for a purpose. An important
consideration for letter writers was the probability that their letter would
become public, given that it was common practice to forward letters of
interest to friends, kin, and colleagues, or to read them aloud in company.
Even when writing to family in Britain, then, Company men engaged
in understatement, misrepresentation, or embellishment; Sarah Pearsall, describing the correspondence of trans-Atlantic families in the late
eighteenth century, argues that many letter-writers used emotive and
sentimental language as a means of manufacturing intimacy with geographically distant friends and family, as well as out of a desire to conform
to literary and epistolary conventions that emphasized spontaneity and
sensibility.[102] Letters were therefore instruments through which Residents endeavoured to represent and thus in a sense produce identities
and relationships. The Residents' letters should be treated as part of the
repertoire of strategies that were used to cement their position at court.

---

[100] Tony Ballantyne, 'Archive, Discipline, State: Power and Knowledge in South Asian
Historiography', *New Zealand Journal of Asian Studies* 3, no. 1 (2001), pp. 89–90; Thomas
Richards, *The Imperial Archive: Knowledge and the Fantasy of Empire* (London, 1993), p. 6.

[101] Bruce Redford, *The Converse of the Pen: Acts of Intimacy in the Eighteenth-Century
Familiar Letter* (Chicago, IL, 1986), p. 2. Recent studies have emphasized the importance of the familiar letter was a way of producing and performing individual identities;
see the essays collected in Rebecca Earle, ed., *Epistolary Selves: Letters and Letter-writers,
1600–1945* (Aldershot, 1999).

[102] Sarah Pearsall, *Atlantic Families Lives and Letters in the Later Eighteenth Century* (Oxford,
2008), p. 15.

Whereas Residents' ties to friends and family can be gleaned from the many rambling letters that have survived, the interactions between Company Residents and courtly elites are some of the most compelling, yet often frustratingly opaque, aspects of the Residents' work. To understand these relationships, this book relies on the reams of letters and petitions authored by Indians of different backgrounds that fill the Residency records. These sources are crucial to our understanding of the Residents' place at court and his interactions with employees and royal family members, but they also raise problems of their own. Petitions are often highly formulaic, written in deferential language, with the aim of convincing. Though their language and format might vary, most letters submitted to the Resident were also written with some specific purpose in mind, and in accordance with epistolary conventions. These texts were instruments for making claims and cannot be read as objective representations of Anglo-Indian relationships. Still, they can be revealing. By identifying the demands that Indians made upon the Company, and the ways in which these demands were explained or justified, we can acquire some insight into how Indians at court viewed the Company, and what they hoped to gain from it.[103] As a result, we can reconstruct some of the transactions that prompted and sustained these cross-cultural relationships, making the Company's growing political influence at Indian royal courts possible.

I.5   Chapter Outline

Chapter 1 sets the stage by demonstrating the significance of the years 1798–1818, on which most of the analysis is centred. Specifically, it shows that while the developments of 1798–1818 can be situated within a longer history of political experimentation, this period nevertheless witnessed a crucial shift, in which a concept of British paramountcy was born out of a set of ideas and practices to be explored in the succeeding chapters. By comparing this period with the history that preceded it, and then briefly tracing its legacy over the following decades, Chapter 1 establishes this moment as one worthy of in-depth analysis.

The following three thematic chapters delineate the key strategies that Residents employed to establish positions of influence at court, and the

---

[103] Lex Heerma van Voss, *Petitions in Social History* (Cambridge, 2001), p. 6; Ravi de Costa, 'Identity, Authority, and the Moral Worlds of Indigenous Petitions', *Comparative Studies in Society and History* 48, no. 3 (2006), p. 670. On petitioning in India, see the special issue Rohit De and Robert Travers, 'Petitioning and Political Cultures in South Asia', *MAS* 53, no. 1 (2019).

obstacles that they confronted in so doing. At the heart of Chapter 2 are the tactics that the Residents developed for collecting and mobilizing political intelligence. Knowledge and knowledge-making occupy a central place in the historiography of colonial South Asia, but the Residents' crucial role in this process, as informants stationed at the courts of rival Indian powers, remains understudied. This chapter highlights the difficulties that the Residents encountered in trying to sew written, oral, personal, and institutional channels of information into a seamless whole. Chapter 3 considers the disputed role of violence as both an ideological justification for Company intervention and as a mode of imperial authority, contributing significantly to our understanding of eighteenth-century views on the use of force in imperial settings. Chapter 4 analyses the financial disputes that proliferated within the Residency system, highlighting the political and ideological dimensions of seemingly petty squabbles surrounding money spent on gift-giving and display. Together, these three chapters show how changing views of the Company's place in the subcontinent manifested themselves in the routine business of empire, exacerbating latent divisions within the Company created by distance, distrust, and conflicting interests.

The next two chapters focus in greater depth on the Resident's interactions with Indians at court, and the importance of these transactions to the evolution of the subsidiary alliance system. Chapter 5 examines the close yet controversial relationships that developed between Residents and their Indian secretaries, known as munshis. Although historians have long recognized the important roles that Indian experts played in the Company's operations, the focus has usually been on the mechanics of direct rule in 'British' India. Yet, the expertise of Indian cultural intermediaries was arguably even more important, as well as more contested, in the context of the Company's growing political influence over nominally independent Indian kingdoms. This chapter considers how relationships with Residency munshis were conceptualized and debated by British officials and reflects on the practical consequences of these relationships for the Residents and munshis involved. Chapter 6 emphasizes the importance of royal family members in shaping and resisting the Company's presence at court. Dynastic intrigue and revolt greatly complicated Residents' attempts to consolidate influence at Indian royal courts. This chapter shows not only how Residents sought to manage royal family members for their own purposes, but also how royal family members, particularly royal women, were themselves able to lay a claim on the Resident's services. Together, these two chapters bring to light the quotidian substance of the confrontation between British Residents and the Indian elite, showing how Indians of different backgrounds enabled, resisted, and profited from the Resident's presence at court. By its very nature, the subsidiary alliance system implied working with and through Indian elites, but, as these chapters show, this was far from simple or straightforward for colonial officials to do.

Taken together, these chapters illustrate the multifaceted nature of the Resident's work and the different, mutually reinforcing foundations of his influence at court. Yet, they also show that on all fronts the Resident's activities were questioned or undermined by colleagues within the Company as well as by Indians at court. Within the Company, contemporaries debated different styles of rule, and these practical and ideological divisions were exacerbated by mutual suspicions resulting from geographical distance and the blurring of personal and public interests in the diplomatic line. This process was further complicated by the need to work through Indian elites and administrators with interests of their own. Theoretically, the system of alliances was supposed to make things easier for the Company, allowing them to exercise political control over the subcontinent without shouldering the burden of internal administration. Practically, this influence proved difficult to enforce. Contrary to British hopes and expectations, Indian rulers often did not make for willing or accommodating instruments for achieving Company interests. This period would be remembered in nineteenth-century hagiography as one wherein the Company's supreme authority was established through the energetic activities of political and military masterminds, but the view from the ground, as we shall see, was far less triumphal.

1   A Time of Trouble

It was not easy being an annalist in an age of revolutions. The editor of the *Annual Register* for the year 1798 found it difficult to 'arrange, into any tolerable order or shape, so great a variety of counsels and actions, going on at the same time in so many different parts of the globe'.[1] Because Britain was at war with republican France in a conflict that stretched around the world, even a compiler of European history had to expand his field of vision to encompass 'the effects of European principles, passions, and projects, in Asia, Africa, and America'.[2] In the final weeks of May, Napoleon had launched a secret expedition to Egypt; by August, his ambitions were famously foiled at the Battle of the Nile. A few weeks later, a small French expeditionary force tried (and failed) to support the uprisings, collectively known as 'the Great Irish Rebellion of 1798', that had convulsed the island that summer. In the West Indies, meanwhile, Toussaint L'Ouverture blocked an attempted British invasion of the former French colony of St Domingue, cementing the gains made by the successful revolt of the island's enslaved population seven years earlier. Across the world, change was in the air.

Overall, the editor of the *Annual Register* did a fair job of summarizing this turbulent year, threading together disparate events into a single panoramic view. Despite his best efforts, however, one important incident escaped his notice. In May, Richard Wellesley, then Earl of Mornington, arrived in India to assume the role of governor general in Bengal. The omission is unsurprising, perhaps. From the vantage point of the *Annual Register's* many readers, Wellesley's disembarkation on Indian shores would probably have seemed trivial in comparison to the revolutionary events unfolding around the world. Yet, with hindsight, historians have recognized Wellesley's administration as a watershed in the history of the British empire in India. As C. A. Bayly observed, 'the political theory and practice of the Wellesley circle represented the first coherent

[1] *Annual Register* (London, 1800), p. iv.
[2] Ibid.

33

imperial policy in British Indian history.'[3] With time, Wellesley's contemporaries too would see him as a harbinger of change. Determined to make his name and fortune, Wellesley would transform the Company's relationships with neighbouring Indian states. Thus began a period in Maratha history known as the 'time of trouble'.[4]

This chapter sets the stage for the thematic chapters to follow by demonstrating the significance of the period 1798–1818 to the history of the Residency system. Though the Company first experimented with subsidiary alliances in the mid-eighteenth century, and the Residents began to emerge as political actors in the 1770s, this early history was one of fits and starts; it was from 1798 that a theory and practice of paramountcy was forged. British relationships with Indian kingdoms subsequently underwent profound changes, not least because of the abolition of the East India Company itself, but the vision of paramountcy that emerged at this moment continued to frame British attitudes to their empire in India. Events from 1798 to 1818 were explicitly cited as precedents for the sweeping powers claimed by the British Government of India as late as 1929. If the main tenets of the system persisted, however, so too did many of its problems, as Indian rulers continued to resist the unequal and ambiguous terms of the alliances promulgated by the British.

1.1   The Origins of the Residency System

The Residency system took shape within a dynamic Indian political landscape in which new regional powers were coming to the fore. Some were the creation of military entrepreneurs and can be roughly categorized as warrior states.[5] Prominent examples include the Marathas in the west and Mysore to the south. The Marathas were Hindu military elites who, having acquired land and status in the service of the Deccan Sultanates, wrested territory from the Mughal empire in the seventeenth century and were then integrated into the Mughal imperial framework through grants of land and titles. In the eighteenth century, Maratha territory expanded further, developing into a loose coalition of military estates divided among key dynasties: the Bhonsles in Nagpur; Shinde in Ujjain and then at Gwalior; Holkar in Malwa; the Gaekwads in Baroda; and the peshwa at Pune.[6]

---

[3] Bayly, *Indian Society*, p. 81.

[4] André Wink, *Land and Sovereignty in India: Agrarian Society and Politics under the Eighteenth-Century Maratha Svarajya* (Cambridge, 1986), p. 34.

[5] Bayly, *Indian Society*, pp. 21–22; Ramusack, *Indian Princes*, p. 12.

[6] Stewart Gordon, *The Marathas 1600–1818* (Cambridge, 1993), pp. 190–193; see also Stewart Gordon, *Marathas, Marauders, and State Formation in Eighteenth-Century India* (Delhi, 1994).

To the south, Mysore emerged as an important Muslim conquest state after it was seized and enlarged in the 1750s by one of the original Hindu dynasty's leading army commanders, Haidar Ali.[7] Finally, Travancore, as a fiscal-military state, might also be fitted into this category; Travancore became an important player in south India between 1734 and 1752, as Raja Martanda Varma carved out a new Hindu polity built on a large, European-style standing army.[8]

Alongside these warrior states were so-called successor kingdoms, former Mughal provinces that retained symbolic ties with Delhi but gradually broke free of imperial oversight. Of these, the most prominent were Bengal, Hyderabad, Awadh, and the Carnatic. In all these cases, nobles who had previously grappled for influence over the person of the emperor became increasingly dissatisfied with the gains to be made in the imperial court, and instead, from the 1720s, focused on consolidating their own fiscal and military bases in the Mughal hinterlands. The strict division of power between revenue manager and military commander that had formerly obtained in these places was abrogated, with power concentrated into a single, hereditary office. Revenues were diverted into provincial treasuries, reducing the tribute paid to the centre to ceremonial gifts and one-time contributions. War and diplomacy were conducted independently and in the name of the nominally subordinate, but practically independent, governor. More time was spent in provincial capitals rather than the imperial court and, concomitantly, more funds were dedicated to enhancing the architectural splendour of these spaces through the construction of mosques and palaces.[9] What emerged was a synthesis, a plural society wherein the old Mughal nobility, heavily concentrated within the capital, co-existed alongside Hindu warrior and administrative groups who controlled the countryside and played important roles within the central government.[10]

The East India Company had always engaged in local and provincial politics, but in the mid-eighteenth century, they developed a new,

---

[7]   Kaveh Yazdani, 'Haidar 'Ali and Tipu Sultan: Mysore's Eighteenth-Century Rulers in Transition', *Itinerario* 38, no. 2 (2014): 103–104.

[8]   Susan Bayly, 'Hindu Kingship and the Origin of Community: Religion, State and Society in Kerala, 1750–1850', *MAS* 18, no. 2 (1984): 186–187. See also A. P. Ibrahim Kunju, *Rise of Travancore: A Study in the Life and Times of Martanda Varma* (Trivandrum, 1976).

[9]   Barnett, *North India*, pp. 21–22.

[10]   Susan Bayly, *Caste, Society and Politics in India from the Eighteenth Century to the Modern Age* (Cambridge, 1999), p. 65; Karen Leonard, 'The Deccani Synthesis in Old Hyderabad: An Historiographic Essay', *Journal of the Pakistan Historical Society* 21, no. 4 (1973): 215–216. On the *samasthans*, see Benjamin B. Cohen, *Kingship and Colonialism in India's Deccan: 1850–1948* (Basingstoke, 2007).

more interventionist stance towards these regional powers. An important factor influencing this change in attitude was the growing French presence within the subcontinent. During this period, India became another theatre for staging imperial rivalries between France and Britain, with both the War of Austrian Succession (1740–1748) and the Seven Years' War (1756–1763) spilling over into conflicts fought between the French and English companies. These conflicts contributed to the militarization of these corporations, resulting not only in the expansion of the Company's forces (with the French setting the precedent for the recruitment of Indian sepoy battalions in 1748), but also the permanent presence of Crown troops from 1754. The French and English companies used their emergent military presence to support rival claimants to the thrones of the Carnatic and Hyderabad, transforming these disputes into a protracted proxy war that erupted in 1746 and rumbled on inconclusively throughout the 1750s.[11]

French military involvement was motivated by Governor General Joseph François Dupleix's desire to win territorial concessions from Indian allies, a strategy that formed part of his broader ambition to finance the French company's operations by securing an Indian tax base.[12] In Hyderabad, French officer Charles-Joseph de Bussy was able to install first Muzaffar Jang in 1750, and then Salabat Jang in 1751. In return for the provision of a force of 400 Europeans and 2,000 sepoys, Salabat Jang ceded control over Machilipatnam and adjoining districts. By the Treaty of Aurangabad, the French were awarded the Northern Circars for the maintenance of their troops. Bussy remained an important force within the politics of Hyderabad for almost ten years, until losses against the British in the Carnatic took their toll. Dupleix was then dismissed, and his expensive wars repudiated; in 1759 Bussy was recalled to Puducherry to support an assault on Madras, never to return.[13]

Dupleix and Bussy had left their mark within the subcontinent, however, by furnishing a model of how to make Indian alliances profitable. Although the first alliance concluded by the Company with Nizam Salabat Jang in 1759 was an ordinary alliance of mutual defence between equals, the English Company would conclude more financially motivated treaties

---

[11] For this paragraph, see T. A. Heathcote, *The Military in British India: The Development of British Land Forces in South Asia, 1600–1947* (Manchester, 1995; repr. Barnsley, 2013), pp. 22–23.

[12] S. P. Sen, *The French in India 1763–1816* (New Delhi, 1971), pp. 27–30.

[13] Sarojini Regani, *Nizam-British Relations 1724–1857* (New Delhi, 1963; repr. 1988), pp. 49–114.

with Hyderabad in future.[14] In a treaty of 1766, Nizam Ali Khan granted sanads (written orders or grants) for the Northern Circars in exchange for a guaranteed supply of Company troops when required. After the nizam allied with Haidar Ali against the Company in 1767, however, a new alliance was formed in 1768 that retracted this guarantee. Although the Company retained its hold over the Northern Circars, it promised only two battalions of sepoys and six pieces of artillery, to be paid for by the nizam while employed in his service, and to be furnished only if 'the situation of their [the Company's] affairs will allow of such a body of troops to march into the Deccan.'[15] Following the French example, the Company was determined to intervene only insofar as it profited them.

The fact that the French had effectively invented the subsidiary alliance system meant that in future the mere appearance of a French envoy at an Indian court would foment fears of a French-led, anti-British confederacy. This applied particularly to Hyderabad, where French influence remained strong. Writing more than half a century later, Henry Russell (then retired from his position as Resident there) noted how popular the French had been, and recalled that 'the common people at Hydrabad think that they do honour to an European by addressing him as "Monsieur Bussy," though it is upwards of 70 years since M. Bussy left the place.'[16] Though contemporary accounts of Bussy's time in Hyderabad suggest a more complicated story, British perceptions of the popularity of the French in India would continue to be used to justify the necessity of a Company presence at Indian royal courts.[17]

Despite the early importance of the Carnatic and Hyderabad, the Company's first subsidiary alliance was with the defeated Nawab Vizier Shuja ud-Daula in 1765. The alliance was formed in the aftermath of Buxar, a conflict which itself had been triggered by the Company's attempt to instate a puppet nawab in Bengal. The fact that Shuja marched into battle alongside the Mughal emperor Shah Alam II and the deposed Nawab of Bengal Mir Qasim indicates his significance within the Mughal empire as both nawab (or governor) of Awadh and vizier (imperial first minister), a title that Shah Alam II had made hereditary.[18] When Shuja finally surrendered to the Company, Governor Robert Clive determined to retain him as an ally. The treaty recently concluded with Shah Alam

---

[14] Ramusack, *Indian Princes*, p. 60.
[15] C. U. Aitchison, *A Collection of Treaties, Engagements and Sunnuds*, 13 vols (Calcutta, 1864), V, p. 25.
[16] House of Commons, *Report from the Select Committee on the Affairs of the East India Company*, 7 vols (London, 1832), VII, p. 172.
[17] On opposition to Bussy at Hyderabad, see Regani, *Nizam-British Relations*, p. 68.
[18] Fisher, *Indirect Rule*, p. 377.

at Allahabad had endowed the Company with tax collection rights in
Bengal, Bihar, and Orissa, and officials hoped that Awadh would act as
a buffer shielding their revenue-yielding territories from attack. As the
Court of Directors phrased it, 'we always esteemed the power of that
Soubah [meaning Shuja] the strongest barrier we could have against the
invasions of the northern powers' (referring to the Afghan incursions
that had periodically rocked northern India) and conceived that 'nothing could so effectually restore that country to its former state as putting
its natural prince in the full possession of his dominions.'[19] Awadh thus
formed a central plank in what historians term the 'ring fence policy',
whereby the Company endeavoured to secure its frontiers by using
Indian kingdoms as a line of defence against possible attack.[20]

The motives for retaining Shuja in power were pragmatic; the Company lacked the manpower, expertise, and above all the funds to administer his vast dominion.[21] Still, Shuja was saddled with paying sizeable
indemnities and helping to subsidize the Company's troops in exchange
for their services; he was also forced to permit duty-free trade within
his borders. Shuja's attempts to refashion his military in the Company's
image provoked stern injunctions that severely limited the size of his
army. Going forward, the Company was determined to render Shuja
dependent on their own forces, and to make him pay for the privilege.[22] Originally charged only with paying the extraordinary expenses
of Company troops serving in Awadh, Shuja was soon made to cover
these military charges in full.[23] As Governor General Warren Hastings
described it in 1774, 'every military operation which was before an accumulation of expense, and undertaken without an object of termination
in prospect, has become a source of economical advantages.'[24] Under
intense pressure from the Court of Directors to raise revenues and cut
expenses, Hastings's best option to make ends meet appeared to lie
beyond the borders of British India.[25]

Although Awadh became the first Indian state to conclude a subsidiary alliance, it took several years for the Residency system itself to crys-
tallize. At first, the nawab vizier's payments were overseen by military

[19] Court of Directors to Fort William, 17 May 1766, in C. S. Srinivasachari, ed., *Fort
William – India House Correspondence*, 21 vols (Delhi, 1962), IV, p. 183.
[20] Ramusack, *Indian Princes*, p. 65.
[21] Ibid.; Fisher, *Indirect Rule*, p. 378.
[22] Barnett, *North India*, p. 83.
[23] Cuthbert Collin Davies, *Warren Hastings and Oudh* (Oxford, 1939), p. 23.
[24] G. R. Gleig, *Memoirs of the Life of the Right Hon. Warren Hastings*, 3 vols (London, 1841),
I, p. 470.
[25] Travers, *Ideology*, pp. 101–102; Barnett, *North India*, pp. 90–95.

commanders stationed in the region. Only in the 1770s did Company executives begin to think seriously about establishing permanent channels of communication at Indian courts.

Warren Hastings was an important driver of this innovation, despite being initially averse to the idea. Hastings's concerns reflect the suspicions that Residents would be subject to throughout their history. As Hastings himself explained it,

> A cold implicit obedience to the orders of his superiors, which can accommodate itself to every change of opinions which a change of men may give occasion to, I do not expect from any man in that station capable of thinking for himself. Personal attachments or some favourite maxims will unavoidably get possession of his mind and influence his conduct, and these prepossessions will become more powerful in proportion to the length of time in which he has acted in such a capacity.[26]

Situated at a distance from Company headquarters, invested with discretionary power, and encouraged to take their place within courtly society, it seemed impossible to Hastings that a Resident could be trusted to unquestioningly enact the governor general's will. Sooner or later, a man like that, Hastings predicted, would go rogue. Still, the appearance of growing political influence on the part of military officers stationed near the court, particularly Captain Gabriel Harper (in command of Shuja's personal escort of Company sepoys), led Hastings to appoint his own proxy.[27] Factional divisions within Hastings's council meant that Nathaniel Middleton, Hastings's first choice, was replaced at intervals with John Bristow, the opposition's preferred candidate. Similar conflicts played out at Hyderabad and Pune, where Hastings competed with the governments of Madras and Bombay, respectively, for the power to nominate and oversee political agents at Indian royal courts. Despite these fluctuating appointments, the 1770s introduced the Residents as meaningful political actors, particularly at Lucknow, where Shuja's heir, Asaf ud-Daula, had made his capital.[28]

When nineteenth-century Residents described their political heroes, however, they were unlikely to name Nathaniel Middleton or John Bristow as exemplars. As it transpired, the Residency at Lucknow during this period would become more of a cautionary tale than a model for how a subsidiary alliance should work. Asaf ud-Daula always claimed to

---

[26] G. R. Gleig, *Memoirs of the Life of the Right Hon. Warren Hastings, First Governor-General of Bengal*, 3 vols (London, 1841), I, p. 327.
[27] Fisher, *Indirect Rule*, pp. 305–306.
[28] Ibid., pp. 128–129.

be a supporter of Warren Hastings but did what he could to evade the Company's burdensome financial demands. In frustration, the Residents meddled in an increasingly aggressive fashion in Awadh's affairs, ratcheting up their demands for cash and even assuming revenue collection duties in select areas to bypass the nawab's government. After Middleton was dismissed from his post and tried for insubordination for failing to liquidate Asaf's debts, Bristow followed Hastings's orders to their logical conclusion, pursuing extreme measures to collect what was owed. In the process, Bristow pushed the administration of Awadh to breaking point, inciting vicious mutinies within the army, unrest within the city, and chaos at court.[29]

By the 1780s, the Company was forced to introduce a new settlement that put a strict limit on the Resident's prerogatives in Awadh, clearly reflecting their sense of the political quagmire into which intervention could draw them. What they determined on was a clear division whereby the Company would provide troops in return for subsidies but would avoid intervening in the nawab's administration. Bristow was dismissed, and the Residents who succeeded him kept a conspicuously low profile.[30] In the late eighteenth century, the Lucknow Residency was thus seen to embody the dangers of a system of influence. In 1799, President of the Board of Control Henry Dundas, first Viscount Melville, cited Awadh as an instance of 'that species of mixed and double government, which has hitherto proved unpropitious to the happiness and prosperity of the governed, as it has to the safety, interests, and character, of the governors'.[31]

In the west, the Company was also forced to concede its inability to bend regional politics to its will. The islands of Salsette and Bassein were Maratha possessions that had long been coveted by the Bombay government; their acquisition promised guaranteed safe access to the port, revenues that would make Bombay less financially dependent on Bengal, and timber to support the budding ship-building industry. In 1772, the Bombay government dispatched Thomas Mostyn as first Resident to Pune in hopes of convincing the peshwa to cede the islands. Mostyn had participated in previous embassies to Pune in 1759 and 1767, so the Bombay government were confident in his linguistic and diplomatic abilities. Once in Pune, however, Mostyn found his negotiations blocked at every turn; his repeated requests to leave were finally accepted by the Bombay

---

[29] For this paragraph, see Barnett, *North India*, pp. 214, 221–222.
[30] Ibid., pp. 223, 228.
[31] Edward Ingram, ed., *Two Views of British India: The Private Correspondence of Mr Dundas and Lord Wellesley, 1798–1801* (Bath, 1970), p. 182.

government in December 1773.[32] By that time, hostilities loomed; Bombay had agreed to intervene in a succession dispute in support of Raghunath Rao, uncle to the infant peshwa. Bombay did manage to seize key Maratha possessions, but its plans were temporarily aborted by the newly ascendant government of Bengal, recently invested with supreme control over the Company's affairs through the Regulating Act of 1773. From the perspective of Bengal, Bombay's activities were a clear breach of instructions from the directors to preserve peace at all costs. Yet, although Bengal was determined to avoid a war, it was also unwilling to give up on the acquisition of Salsette and Bassein. The arrival of a French envoy at Pune raised further concerns. Mostyn made a brief reappearance as Resident, hoping to secure Salsette and Bassein and to counteract the Chevalier de Saint-Lubin's overtures. Once more, however, Mostyn's Residency was cut short by a renewal of conflict, as Bengal decided that supporting Raghunath Rao did in fact constitute their best chance of securing Salsette and Bassein. Almost ten years passed before a successor to Mostyn was appointed.[33]

War with the Marathas did not go well. Perhaps most embarrassing of all was defeat at Wadgaon, where Company troops were surrounded and forced to conclude a treaty on humiliating terms to secure their safe passage to Bombay. The pressures of an ongoing war in the Carnatic meant that the Company did not have the manpower to devote to war with the Marathas, either; to the contrary, the commander of the Company's forces in Madras desperately pleaded with the Bengal and Bombay governments to conclude a peace in western India at all costs after British defeats at Pollilur (1780) and Bidnur (1783) in the south. The overlapping First Maratha War and Second Mysore War demonstrated how dangerous Indian powers would be if they acted in sync.[34]

To negotiate a peace, the Company relied on the mediation of the Maratha Mahadji Shinde, further indicating their tenuous place amongst the country powers; Mahadji and his successors would continue to use the precedent set by the Treaty of Salbai to position themselves as the Marathas' political broker into the nineteenth century.[35] Mahadji's role reflected his pre-eminent place within the subcontinent, due in no small part to the successes of a large European-style army comprised of mobile artillery and professional infantry. By 1784, his reputation was such that he was invited to Delhi by Shah Alam II to secure the throne

[32] Sailendra Nath Sen, *Anglo-Maratha Relations during the Administration of Warren Hastings, 1772–1785* (London, 1995), pp. 2, 8–9.
[33] Ibid., pp. 86–102.
[34] Heathcote, *Military in British India*, pp. 35, 38–39.
[35] Gordon, *Marathas*, pp. 162–167.

and repress factional struggles, earning him the command of the Mughal army and the management of the provinces of Delhi and Agra.[36] When the Company finally determined to appoint another Resident at Pune in 1786, they consulted with Mahadji first.[37]

Meanwhile, the Company's alliance with Hyderabad remained uncomfortable. From the first, Nizam Ali Khan had been disappointed in the Company's very conservative interpretation of the alliance of 1768, according to which they refused to assist him in conflicts with the Marathas. Also at issue were claims over the Northern Circars. These coastal territories, whose revenues had previously supported the French force at Hyderabad, were occupied by the Company at the outbreak of the Seven Years' War in 1756. The Company's claims were confirmed by an imperial firman or charter in 1765, but in practice the Circars remained under the nizam's jurisdiction. He ceded them to the Company in 1766 in exchange for the payment of annual tribute, with the exception of Guntur, which he agreed could be assumed by the Company after the death of his brother, Basalat Jang, who held it in *jagir*. Tensions came to a head in 1779 when the Company made an agreement with Basalat Jang behind the nizam's back. Nizam Ali Khan responded by engaging the French soldiers formerly employed by his brother. To conciliate the nizam and secure remission of tribute, the Madras government appointed the first Resident at Hyderabad, John Holland, to negotiate. On arrival, however, Holland bypassed the Madras government and reported the nizam's grievances directly to Governor General Warren Hastings, who restored Guntur to Basalat Jang. The gesture of goodwill had little practical effect. The nizam refused to cede Guntur after Basalat Jang's death in 1782 as promised, and a succession of Residents resigned or were recalled after failing to reach a settlement. Finally, in 1788 Governor General Charles Cornwallis dispatched John Kennaway to demand the restitution of Guntur, all the while making military preparations to enforce his demands if requisite. The nizam did finally comply, but only under duress.[38]

Though clearly still willing to use force or the threat of force where necessary, the lesson learned from the overlapping First Maratha War and Second Mysore War seems to have been that the Company had narrowly

[36] Bayly, *Indian Society*, p. 8.

[37] In his memoirs, James Forbes describes 'the object of Sir Charles Malet's mission to Mhadajee Sindia' as being 'the conciliation of that chieftain to the establishment of his embassy at the court of Poonah.' James Forbes, *Oriental Memoirs: A Narrative of Seventeen Years Residence in India*, 2nd ed., 2 vols (London, 1834), II, p. 433.

[38] Regani, *Nizam-British Relations*, pp. 138–143.

avoided a crisis, and that it could not withstand a concerted attack. The India Act of 1784 bespoke the desire to place the government of India on a firmer footing. Rather than marking a sharp break, the Act was the culmination of a long-standing desire on the part of government ministers in Britain to extend their control over the Company's military and political operations, particularly given the increased presence of the British Army in the region. For them, it was essential that the Company be prevented from dragging Crown forces into troublesome and expensive overseas conflicts.[39] The 1784 Act institutionalized parliamentary oversight in the form of a ministerial Board of Control dedicated to overseeing the Company's civil and military affairs. The Act also firmly stated the British government's opposition to further warfare and territorial expansion, specifically prohibiting the Company from forming Indian alliances or concluding treaties unless attacked by a hostile power.

Despite these injunctions, it seemed clear that the Company needed Indian allies to survive. Pune and Hyderabad were both regarded as vital counterpoints to the rising power of Tipu Sultan of Mysore, who refused to accept a Resident at his court. In 1792, when the Company went to war against Mysore for a third time, both Pune and Hyderabad joined the struggle (nominally, at least). Residents Charles Warre Malet and John Kennaway were awarded baronetcies for their role in concluding defensive alliances with Pune and Hyderabad, respectively. Although the Company's Indian allies were not considered to have contributed materially to the campaign against Mysore, their neutrality was believed to have been a prerequisite to the Company's victory. When Tipu was finally defeated, the ceded territory (encompassing one half of his dominions) was distributed among the allies.[40]

Contemporaries in Britain were divided on the justice and policy of the Third Mysore War. A correspondent of Cornwallis, describing these debates in the House of Commons, was reminded a little of the American war; 'Tippoo has not such powerful and numerous supporters as *Jonathan* had [meaning Brother Jonathan, the personification of New England], but if the devil was to appear in the figure of an Asiatick Prince, and disturb the peace and quiet of the British Government, he would find some friends in this country'.[41] The Whigs expressed a decided suspicion of the tendency of Indian alliances to draw the Company into

---

[39] Bowen, *Business*, p. 72.
[40] Regani, *Nizam-British Relations*, pp. 151, 157–158.
[41] Lieutenant General Grant to Earl Cornwallis, 3 March 1791, in *Correspondence of Charles, First Marquis Cornwallis*, ed. Charles Ross, 3 vols (Cambridge, 2011), I, pp. 111–112.

undesirable wars.[42] They also questioned whether, by weakening Tipu Sultan, the Company were playing into the Marathas' hands.[43] On the government side, MPs voiced solid support for the war, but envisioned different desired outcomes; while prominent figures like Pitt and Dundas expressed an aversion to conquest, others argued that, as Colonel Macleod phrased it, '[a] war against such a tyrant ought to be carried to the greatest extremities'.[44] Ultimately, both the Commons and the House of Lords passed a vote of approbation, reflecting the belief that, whatever its initial justifications, the war's result was conducive to equilibrium in India. This was Cornwallis's own view; according to him, 'an arrangement of this kind, which effectually destroys the dangerous power of Tippoo, will be more beneficial to the public, than the capture of Seringapatam'. While Cornwallis conceded that '[t]hose whose passions are heated, and who are not responsible for consequences, will probably exclaim against leaving the tyrant an inch of territory, [...] it is my duty to consult the real interest of the Company and the nation.'[45] Defending the policy of his predecessor, Sir John Shore, first Baron Teignmouth (governor general 1793–1798), averred that to have deposed Tipu and divided his entire dominions among the allies 'would have thrown too decided a weight in the scale of the Mahrattas, already too powerful.'[46]

When Cornwallis and his contemporaries described their vision of how interstate relationships in India should operate, their perspectives were heavily informed by the same ideas of a 'balance of power' that operated in Europe. The goal was not peace so much as a low-level, tit-for-tat conflict of interest between equally balanced players, with the aim of preventing any single power (usually France or Spain) from establishing 'universal monarchy'.[47] In India, the belief was that by ensuring that different Indian powers enjoyed roughly equal military capacities, a kind of equilibrium could be maintained favourable to the Company's interests. As Shore phrased it, 'The spirit of Jealousy and Ambition which animates them all, is in one sense a collateral security to us; its operation [...] must necessarily tend

---

[42] Mr Hippisley, 28 February 1791, *Parliamentary Register 2*, vol. 28 (1790–1791), p. 315; Mr Fox, 28 February 1791, *Parliamentary Register 2*, vol. 28 (1790–1791), p. 315; Mr Francis, 28 February 1791, *Parliamentary Register 2*, vol. 28 (1790–1791), p. 311.

[43] Mr Francis, 28 February 1791, *Parliamentary Register 2*, vol. 28 (1790–1791), p. 311.

[44] Ibid., p. 318.

[45] Marquess Cornwallis to Sir Charles Oakeley, 20 February 1792, in *Correspondence of Charles, First Marquis Cornwallis*, II, p. 151.

[46] Holden Furber, ed., *Private Record of an Indian Governor-Generalship: The Correspondence of Sir John Shore, Governor-General with Henry Dundas, President of the Board of Control, 1793–1798* (Cambridge, MA, 1933), p. 145.

[47] Richard Whatmore, 'Vattel, Britain and Peace in Europe', *Grotiana* 31, no. 1 (2010): 90–91.

to invest the balance of power, in our Hands, where it should be steadily preserved without throwing a preponderance into either of the scales.'[48]

Prior to Wellesley's arrival, then, visions of the Company's role within the subcontinent remained limited. The intensification of Anglo-French rivalry mid-century had resulted in a growing militarization of the Company and a concomitant search for subsidies; partnerships with regional powers acquired additional significance owing to this combination of factors. Yet, it took time for the Residency system to take shape. Even once permanent Residents were appointed, their early interventions did not produce the desired outcomes, with the Awadh administration spiralling into chaos and the Company's armies experiencing humiliating defeats at the hands of the Marathas and Haidar Ali. The result of this period of existential crisis in the 1780s was a conviction of the importance, not of trying to control neighbouring polities, but of trying to pit them against each other. The overriding urge was to preserve the status quo. As Britain reached the apex of its imperial meridian, however, understandings of its role within the subcontinent shifted. Prominent figures within the Company began to insist on the necessity of 'tranquillity' in India, an imperative that they justified in increasingly moralizing terms as well as for reasons of security or financial solubility. These ideas formed the basis for a qualitatively different subsidiary alliance system that reached its culmination in 1818.

1.2   Primus inter Pares

On leaving England, Richard Wellesley had been enjoined to maintain the settlement of 1793. Yet, according to him conditions within the subcontinent had changed so considerably in the interim that a new, more aggressive approach was needed. The threat, as he described it, was threefold. First, Tipu Sultan of Mysore had been gaining strength since his defeat in 1793, building armies, cultivating ties with the French, and sending emissaries to insinuate themselves into the courtly politics of Indian powers. Second, the activities of Zaman Shah in the north raised the spectre of an Afghan invasion, which Awadh, in its disturbed condition, could ill withstand. Finally, in the context of a global war with revolutionary France, there was the possibility of a French invasion to consider, particularly in light of Napoleon's expedition to Egypt; it was conceivable, from a British perspective, that the French might exploit the disaffection of the Company's nominal allies to form an anti-British alliance.[49]

---

[48] Furber, ed., *Private Record*, p. 148.
[49] For this paragraph, see Richard Wellesley to Henry Dundas, 28 February 1798, in *Wellesley Despatches*, I, pp. 17; 24–26, 31.

To combat this triple threat, the Company needed effective supporters, but their Indian allies seemed to have grown weaker rather than stronger since the peace of 1793. In Hyderabad, Nizam Ali Khan had suffered doubly through a humiliating defeat by the Marathas at Kharda in 1795 and an insurrection led by his eldest son; his territories were disturbed, his revenues hard-hit, and his army, to Wellesley's dismay, dominated by French mercenaries.[50] To make matters worse, the nizam's declining health was made painfully evident by a bad stroke in 1796, causing a nascent succession crisis to develop as competing factions backed his two sons, Sikander Jah and Feridoon Jah.[51] In Pune, meanwhile, a succession crisis had placed the young peshwa, Baji Rao, under the thumb of Mahadji's successor, Daulat Rao Shinde. Daulat Rao was himself young, newly ascended to the throne, and facing the combined menace of unrest in his army, resistance in his territories to the north, and an armed insurrection led by the women of his predecessor's family.[52] All in all, Wellesley doubted the usefulness of these allies in the face of what he described as an impending crisis.

In this political climate, Wellesley advocated a new defensive system that would eradicate the French, eliminate conflict between the country powers, and establish the Company as the ultimate political arbiter.[53] Malcolm Yapp has argued that Wellesley did not seriously believe in the threat represented by Zaman Shah or the French, but instead saw it as a means of justifying his forward policy to resistant directors and Board members in London; to quote Yapp, the prohibitions enshrined in the India Act of 1784 'could be dissolved by the solvent of the external enemy.'[54] Whether or not this was Wellesley's intention, this was certainly what happened. In the name of 'security' and 'tranquillity', Wellesley set in train a pattern of aggressive intervention at Indian royal courts. In his own words, 'it is both our right and our duty to give vigour and effect to our subsisting alliance and treaties, by restoring to our Allies the power of fulfilling their defensive engagements with us.'[55] Rather than trusting

---

[50] Ibid., pp. 18–19.
[51] BL, APAC, IOR/F/4/8/705, Fort William to Court of Directors, 12 May 1796; William Palmer to Richard Wellesley, 26 December 1800, MSA, PRCOP, vol. 38 (1798–1801), p. 1079.
[52] Richard Wellesley to Henry Dundas, 28 February 1798, in *Wellesley Despatches*, I, pp. 21–23.
[53] Richard Wellesley to J. A. Kirkpatrick, 8 July 1798, in *Wellesley Despatches*, I, p. 104; Richard Wellesley to J. A. Kirkpatrick, 11 August 1798, in *Wellesley Despatches*, I, p. 159.
[54] M. E. Yapp, *Strategies of British India: Britain, Iran, and Afghanistan, 1798–1850* (Oxford, 1980), pp. 79, 159.
[55] Richard Wellesley to J. A. Kirkpatrick, 8 July 1798, in *Wellesley Despatches*, I, p. 104.

to a natural equilibrium between evenly equipped polities, the Company would impose balance from the top down, with force if necessary.

Wellesley's version of the subsidiary alliance system was pioneered at Hyderabad. Here, of primary concern was the prevailing influence of French mercenaries, particularly men like General Michel Joachim Raymond who, with his republican sympathies, were seen to form part of an anti-British conspiracy.[56] As Wellesley observed, 'can it be possible to provide a more ready channel for the intrigues of France, than would be offered by the existence of a body of 10,000 men, united by military discipline, and stationed in the dominions of one of our principal allies, and on the borders of our own?'[57] To expunge this republican menace, Wellesley relied on Resident James Achilles Kirkpatrick to negotiate a new treaty in 1798 that would require the nizam to disband the French regiments in his service and expel French residents from Hyderabad altogether. In 1800, Nizam Ali Khan agreed to a treaty of perpetual and general defensive alliance that established the subsidiary force on a permanent basis. According to this agreement, the Company took full control of his foreign affairs and contracted, in turn, not to interfere in his domestic concerns. This agreement provided the model for subsidiary alliances going forward.[58]

In Awadh, the justification for Wellesley's intervention was the ostensible threat of an Afghan invasion. To combat this peril, Wellesley pushed for a greater British military presence and, concomitantly, a greater fiscal contribution from the nawab. The subsidies due from Awadh had just been ratcheted up following the deposition of Vizier Ali and the accession of his uncle, Saadat Ali Khan, immediately prior to Wellesley's arrival. Already tense, relations between the Company and the nawab vizier now approached breaking point, as Saadat Ali first threatened to abdicate, then, according to William Scott's testimony (Resident 1799–1804), turned to drink to alleviate his despair.[59] Finally, a new treaty was agreed in 1801, whereby Saadat Ali made sizeable territorial cessions (encompassing Doab, Gorakhpur, and Rohilkhand) to purchase his freedom. By ceding these territories, the nawab paid off his debt to the Company, retaining his remaining territorial revenues in full. In theory, he had liberated himself from the Company's intervention.

---

[56] William Thorn, *Memoir of the War in India* (London, 1818), pp. 23–24.
[57] Earl of Mornington to the Right Hon. Henry Dundas, 23 February 1798, in *Wellesley Despatches*, I, p. 4.
[58] Regani, *Nizam-British Relations*, pp. 180–184.
[59] BL, APAC, IOR/H/235, William Scott to William Kirkpatrick, 12 January 1800, p. 497; William Scott to William Kirkpatrick, 13 March 1800, pp. 503–504.

48   A Time of Trouble

In practice, however, the terms of the treaty meant that the fates of the Company and Awadh would remain intertwined: first, because the nawab engaged to establish a government 'conducive to the prosperity of his subjects' (an article that would later be interpreted to mean that his sovereignty over this territory was conditional); second, because the treaty stipulated that he would 'always advise with, and act in conformity to the counsel of, the officers of the East India Company'; and finally, because the Company agreed to defend the nawab vizier against foreign and domestic enemies.[60] The Residents' letters from this period, which described Saadat Ali bursting into tears in public, would become grist for the mill of Wellesley's enemies within the Company and in parliament.[61]

Wellesley also appointed new Residents at courts that had heretofore remained largely outside the Company's purview. The Company had concluded a subsidiary alliance with Travancore in 1795 but the first Resident, Major Colin Macaulay (a Scotch evangelical and brother to the more famous Zachary Macaulay), was dispatched to Travancore in 1800 to liquidate its debts and oversee the payment of future subsidies. In 1805, Macaulay would negotiate another treaty that raised the subsidy and endowed the Company with the right to interfere politically to ensure its payment.[62] Meanwhile, in the Deccan, H. T. Colebrooke, a leading Sanskrit scholar and future founder of the Royal Asiatic Society, was dispatched to Nagpur in 1798 to negotiate an alliance.[63] In part, Wellesley hoped that by bringing Nagpur within the Company's sphere of influence, he could create a bridge across central India linking the Company's territories to the east and west; Hastings had nurtured similar aspirations, though the untimely death of his envoy, added to the larger problem of the ongoing First Maratha War, had forced him to abandon these hopes.[64] Just as importantly, however, Wellesley wanted to prevent Raghuji from allying with Shinde.[65] Wellesley's reasons for appointing a Resident to Nagpur were thus connected to his broader ambition to divide the Maratha powers, a strategy that would have profound implications for the future of the Deccan.

To understand Wellesley's Maratha policy, it is necessary to step back a few years. When Mahadji Shinde died of fever in 1794, his role as

[60] Aitchison, *Collection of Treaties*, II, p. 102.
[61] BL, APAC, IOR/H/235, William Scott to Neil Edmonstone, 2 February 1801, p. 511.
[62] Robin Jeffrey, 'The Politics of "Indirect Rule": Types of Relationship among Rulers, Ministers and Residents in a "Native State"', *Journal of Commonwealth & Comparative Politics* 13, no. 3 (1975), p. 263.
[63] Richard F. Gombrich, 'Colebrooke, Henry Thomas (1765–1837), administrator in India and scholar', ODNB.
[64] Sen, *Anglo-Maratha Relations*, p. 116.
[65] Richard Wellesley to Dundas, 6 July 1798, in *Wellesley Despatches*, I, p. 89.

Maratha power broker was taken up by his chosen heir, his nephew and adopted son Daulat Rao. Daulat Rao's political acumen was soon tested by the succession crisis that erupted in 1795, when Peshwa Madhav Rao fell (or jumped) from a balcony to his death. After weighing his options, Daulat Rao backed Madhav Rao's cousin, Baji Rao, son of Ragunath Rao, who had spent much of his life in exile. Daulat Rao's instrumental role in placing Baji Rao on the musnud, combined with his military might, put him in a position to dictate to the young peshwa. Hoping to incorporate Baji Rao into the subsidiary alliance system, the Company attempted to capitalize on this situation, arguing that an alliance with the Company would secure Baji Rao's independence from his supposed liege. Baji Rao remained impassive in the face of the Company's promises, however, until Daulat Rao's Maratha rival Yashwant Rao Holkar emerged to contest his place. When Yashwant Rao defeated Holkar and occupied Pune in late 1802, the peshwa fled to Company territory in Bassein, where he signed a treaty promising to bear the expense of a British force of not less than six thousand regular infantry to be stationed permanently in his dominions. Baji Rao submitted to British arbitration of his claims on the nizam and bound himself to consult with the Company on foreign policy decisions. In return, Baji Rao was reinstalled at Pune in the spring of 1803 under Company protection.[66]

The Company treated with Baji Rao as leader of a Maratha confederacy, investing him with sovereignty over the decentralized network of Maratha governments that he did not have; the interpolity dynamic was thus disrupted to an extent that other leading Marathas could not allow to pass uncontested. Within a few months, Daulat Rao Shinde and Raghuji had assembled their troops; the Second Maratha War had begun. The fighting in that year consisted of two distinct campaigns, as General Gerald Lake faced off against Pierre Cuillier Perron, commanding Shinde's troops in the north, while Arthur Wellesley confronted the combined armies of Raghuji and Shinde himself in the south. Arthur Wellesley made his name at the hard-fought Battle of Assaye, while Lake made Governor General Richard Wellesley's dreams come true by capturing Delhi. In December 1803, a settlement was reached.[67] The Company had established itself as the arbiter of the Maratha states, and the controlling power in Delhi. The Mughal emperor was reduced to a pensioner of the Company, his jurisdiction limited to the confines of his palace, where his activities were carefully scrutinized by

---

[66] Ramusack, *Indian Princes*, p. 71.
[67] Kaushik Roy, *War, Culture and Society in Early Modern South Asia, 1740–1849* (Florence, KY, 2011), pp. 117–122.

attentive Residents. Daulat Rao was stripped of his territories north of the Yamuna, and the Company signed a treaty with his former tributaries, the Rajput, Jat, Rohilla, and Bundela states. Finally, Daulat Rao became a party to the defensive alliance, according to which a subsidiary force of six thousand infantry was stationed within British territory, close to their shared border.[68]

In making these arrangements, the Company moved into territory that had been contested between Shinde and Yashwant Rao Holkar. Holkar, who had so far remained neutral, therefore entered the field in 1804. Despite early reverses, the Company were able to force Holkar to retreat into Punjab, and by 1805 had made a territorial settlement.[69] The Company's military reputation did, however, suffer minor damage because of the loss of men during the siege of Bharatpur in 1805. The Company's failure to breach the walls of this impenetrable fortress imbued it with legendary status in the eyes of Indian onlookers.[70] Holkar, too, derived military prestige from the conflict. Rumours of an intended confederacy, headed by Holkar, would continue to percolate throughout the subcontinent over the following years, as Chapter 2 will show.

Wellesley's treaties, annexations, and wars dramatically transformed the political landscape of India and provoked controversy at home. In addition to the measures already described, Wellesley led a full-scale war against Mysore resulting in the death of Tipu and the reinstatement of the old Wodeyar dynasty, and oversaw controversial annexations in Tanjore and the Carnatic. Wellesley's recall in 1805 constituted a renunciation of this process on the part of the Court of Directors and Board of Control in London. Their concerns were multiple; Wellesley's college in Fort William and his support for free trade threatened their traditional prerogatives (of appointment and commercial monopoly, respectively), while his wars were devastatingly expensive at a time when the Company was already in debt.[71] Yet, Wellesley's opponents also seem to have objected on principle to his acts of 'spoliation and extortion', at least judging by the impeachment proceedings to which he was subject.[72] On his return, Wellesley's enemies combined to attack him in parliament in a campaign spearheaded by James Paull, a former merchant who focused predominantly on Wellesley's conduct in

---

[68] Ramusack, *Indian Princes*, p. 71.
[69] Roy, *War, Culture and Society*, pp. 124–125.
[70] Peers, *Between Mars and Mammon*, pp. 166–167.
[71] C. A. Bayly, 'Wellesley [formerly Wesley], Richard, Marquess Wellesley (1760–1842), governor-general of Bengal', ODNB.
[72] HC Deb, 28 May 1806, vol. 7, col. 367.

Awadh, and the nepotistic appointment of his brother, Henry, as lead
negotiator of the alliance concluded there.[73] The motion to impeach
was defeated, but the debates surrounding it testified to the existence of
an uneasy alliance of Radicals and evangelicals opposed to 'the principle
of aggrandizement'.[74]

Wellesley's immediate successors in office repudiated his political
and military aspirations. Cornwallis returned to India as governor general in 1805 aiming to bring about a rapprochement with Yashwant
Rao Holkar and Daulat Rao Shinde. When Cornwallis died shortly
after his arrival in the subcontinent, the mantle was taken up by
George Hilario Barlow, who as acting governor general 1805–1807,
instituted Cornwallis's policies of retrenchment and conciliation.[75] As
Company diplomat John Malcom phrased it, 'hope seems still to have
been indulged, that peace might be preserved without our assuming
that paramount power which, the more it was within our grasp, the
more alarm it appeared to create in the minds of those who contem-
plated it at a distance.'[76] The Company's renunciation of their sphere
of influence north of the Yamuna, and their concession of Gohad and
Gwalior to Daulat Rao Shinde, were intended to symbolize this new,
more moderate stance.

Despite this disavowal, in hindsight Wellesley had created an insidi-
ous legacy. Arriving amid what he conceived to be an existential crisis
for the Company (or at least what he determined to frame as such),
Wellesley resorted to making far-reaching changes. Most importantly, he
insisted on positioning the Company as the ultimate political and military arbiter in the subcontinent. Hyderabad provided the model upon
which subsequent subsidiary alliances would be based as Wellesley tried
to assert full control over its engagement with the world outside its borders. War with the Marathas, meanwhile, provided an unprecedentedly
clear demonstration of the Company's military ascendancy, while territorial annexations, in Awadh and elsewhere, provided hard evidence
of its expansionary ambitions. Wellesley had many enemies within the
Company, not least for his warmongering, but his vision of a paramount
Company-state would have a long afterlife, thanks in no small part to the
generation of Residents that had grown up under his aegis.

[73] H. E. A. Cotton, 'The Story of James Paull', *Bengal Past & Present* 28, no. 55–56 (1924): 69–109.
[74] 7 Parl. Deb. (1st ser.) (1806) col. 367.
[75] Fisher, *Indirect Rule*, p. 57.
[76] John Malcolm, *The Political History of India, from 1784 to 1823*, 2 vols (London, 1826), I, 392.

1.3   Wellesley's Kindergarten

Like Warren Hastings before him, Wellesley was keen to stock the political line with men closely connected with him, men he felt he could trust to enact his views. This ambition formed part of his wider determination to transform the Company's civil service through his college at Fort William, which opened its doors in 1800.[77] Though founded on the anniversary of his victory at Srirangapatnam, Wellesley described the college as a symbol that the era of conquest was over: 'In the Civil Service we must now seek, not the instruments by which kingdoms are overthrown, revolutions governed, or wars conducted, but an inexhaustible supply of useful knowledge, cultivated talents, and well ordered and disciplined morals'.[78] Wellesley's college was intended to mould this new generation of statesmen; many key Residents were attached to the institution in some capacity, and were appointed to their posts through Wellesley's intervention.[79]

Perhaps unsurprisingly, many of the men trained up under this system resented what they viewed as the backsliding of the Barlow administration. Charles Metcalfe, the first student to enrol at Fort William and a firm favourite of Wellesley's, is a good example of this.[80] Writing to his father in 1806 from his post as assistant to the Resident at Delhi, Metcalfe expressed his dedication to Wellesley's plan 'to unite the tranquillity of all the powers of India with our own', contrasting it with Barlow's balance of power approach, which he described as 'barbarous, unwarrantable, and monstrous' owing to its reliance on divisions and disorder within Indian kingdoms for the future security of the Company. Detecting a 'loud cry that we are in danger from extended dominion', Metcalfe averred that '[f]or my part I can contemplate universal dominion in India without much fear.'[81] A year later, Richard Jenkins (who had distinguished himself as a student of Persian and Arabic at Fort William) described the concessions made by Barlow and Cornwallis as 'impolitic and dangerous', suggesting to Indian onlookers 'a want of confidence in our power and resources.'[82] Mountstuart Elphinstone, who also owed his early appointment as assistant at Pune to Wellesley's patronage, likewise

---

[77] Joshua Ehrlich, 'The East India Company and the Politics of Knowledge' (PhD diss., Harvard University, 2018), p. 136.

[78] Thomas Roebuck, ed., *The Annals of the College of Fort William* (Calcutta, 1819), p. xi.

[79] Ehrlich, 'East India Company and the Politics of Knowledge', pp. 145–146.

[80] Edward Thompson, *The Life of Charles, Lord Metcalfe* (London, 1937), p. 25.

[81] John William Kaye, ed., *Selections from the Papers of Lord Metcalfe* (London, 1855), pp. 7–8.

[82] David J. Howlett, 'Jenkins, Sir Richard (1785–1853), East India Company servant', ODNB; BL, APAC, Mss Eur E111, Richard Jenkins to Charles Russell, 22 February 1807, p. 11.

avowed in 1805 that 'I never could enter into the spirit of his [meaning Cornwallis's] late administration.' In Elphinstone's view,

> when our weak allies are to be delivered up to the rage of those whom they have exasperated by adhering to us [referring to the renunciation of influence north of the Yamuna] ... I confess I do not readily fall into the views of the government & feel no uncommon zeal for the success of its plans.[83]

In part, this emergent strain of hawkishness reflects the changing nature of the job itself. In the past, the Residencies were an attractive post for Company employees (usually soldiers) with a knack for Indian languages. While these were usually men of good reputation with personal connections to the governor general, they were not necessarily the Company's leading lights, because Residents' activities at this stage were limited largely to mediation, negotiation, and information gathering. These functions remained important, but under Wellesley the scope of the Residents' responsibilities expanded, as they were given greater leeway to intervene in courtly politics through the negotiation and management of subsidiary alliances. The Residencies therefore came to be seen as arenas where a man could make his political reputation. In 1806, Edward Fraser wrote confidently to his son William, then assistant to the Resident at Delhi, that the political line 'is really a great school, to train up young men in India to distinction & fortune there – and to fame and usefulness at home afterwards.'[84]

Many Residents did indeed have strong political ambitions. This is not to say that financial motives were unimportant; several were driven by the desire to pay off family debts, restore or purchase grand houses, or simply establish a competence.[85] Notably, though, both John Baillie (Resident at Lucknow 1807–1815) and Richard Jenkins (Resident at Nagpur 1807–1828) would become Company directors and MPs on their return to Britain, while Charles Metcalfe and Mountstuart Elphinstone's personal papers speak even more eloquently to their longing to leave their mark on the pages of history.[86] Writing to his former schoolmaster at Eton upon his arrival in India in 1803, Metcalfe described himself as 'a man

---

[83] BL, APAC, Mss Eur F109/89, Mountstuart Elphinstone to John Adam, 5 November 1805.

[84] NRAS, Fraser of Reelig Papers, B331, Edward Fraser to William Fraser, 30 April 1806.

[85] For Archibald Seton and Henry Russell, see Margot Finn and Kate Smith, ed., *The East India Company at Home 1757–1857* (London, 2018), pp. 153–175; 205–231.

[86] For John Baillie's and Richard Jenkins's parliamentary careers, see Martin Casey, 'Baillie, John (1772–1833), of Leys Castle, Inverness and Devonshire Place, Mdx' and Margaret Escott, 'Jenkins, Richard (1785–1853), of Bicton Hall, Salop and 7 Mansfield Street, Mdx.', both in *The History of Parliament: The House of Commons 1820–1832*, ed. D. R. Fisher (Cambridge, 2009).

ambitious of distinguishing himself', with an 'inclination for the diplomatique'; just over fifteen years later, in a letter to his sister, Metcalfe
explained his desire to remain in India by contrasting the opportunities
for government service available in Britain with the power he enjoyed as
Resident at Hyderabad, 'the Governor of a Territory 150 miles long &
the same broad, almost without control from the distance of the supreme
Government'.[87] Elphinstone's diaries, meanwhile, describe his yearning
for distinction and his inability 'to enter with spirit into affairs of moderate importance & to be satisfied with limited reputation.'[88] Men like
Elphinstone and Metcalfe shared Wellesley's desire to win glory on the
Indian stage. They were unlikely to be content with a restricted role at
Indian courts.

Putting aside the individual ambitions of the Residents themselves,
it is unclear how far a belief in non-intervention obtained even at the
higher levels of the Company. The persistent desire to meddle is particularly evident at Hyderabad. In 1804, under Wellesley, the Company had
nominated their own candidate for chief minister despite the opposition
of the newly crowned Nizam Sikander Jah, who reluctantly complied.
After Wellesley's departure, the Residents continued to support Mir
Alam in the face of Sikander Jah's clear preference for his own favourite,
Mahipat Ram, even requiring Sikander Jah to sign a memorandum in
1807 wherein he agreed to make the Resident's approval a prerequisite
for political appointments. In 1809, the Company again insisted on their
own candidate in defiance of the nizam's determined objections.[89] The
result was an uncomfortable compromise whereby the nizam's choice,
Munir ul-Mulk, was appointed diwan, while Chandu Lal, who enjoyed
Company support, was appointed to a rival ministerial position as *pesh-
kar,* responsible for the administration of the state and negotiations with
the Residency.[90] This awkward solution produced recurring problems
because it required the Resident to bypass Munir ul-Mulk and champion
Chandu Lal in the face of factional opposition. This close entanglement
with the minister rendered the Resident vulnerable at court because it
made him responsible for any misstep that Chandu Lal might make.
Chandu Lal, for his part, was forced to fight for his own survival.[91]

---

[87] BL, APAC, Mss Eur B233, Charles Theophilus Metcalfe to Joseph Goodall, 16 August
1803, pp. 3, 5; BL, APAC, Mss Eur F656/1, Charles Theophilus Metcalfe to Georgiana
Metcalfe, 24 June 1820, p. 3.
[88] BL, APAC, Mss Eur F88/370, Journal of Mountstuart Elphinstone, 4 February 1811,
p. 16; 27 June 1817, p. 32.
[89] Regani, *Nizam-British Relations,* pp. 191, 204.
[90] Ibid., p. 211.
[91] J. Sutherland, *Sketches of the Relations Subsisting between the British Government in India,
and the Different Native States* (Calcutta, 1833), p. 55.

Meanwhile, Sikander Jah seems to have become increasingly disillusioned with government. Despite early attempts to undermine the Company's influence, he gradually withdrew from political business, content to drag his feet and obstruct the Company's agenda where he could. Writing in 1812, Henry Russell wondered about the nizam's state of mind, observing that his abuse of the women of his household 'betrayed a ferocity of disposition which had never appeared in him before', and that his rambling conversation 'exhibit[ed] upon the whole a conduct strongly marked with all the characteristic features of insanity.'[92] Seven years later, Russell confirmed that Sikander Jah's 'dislike of his own Ministers' and 'his jealousy of our controul' (combined, Russell believed, with his preference for the life of the zenana or women's quarters) had 'gradually withdrawn him into a sullen, and total seclusion. He never quits his Palace, or holds a public Durbar [open court]: he is seldom seen even by his own Ministers, and he never takes any part in the business of his Government.'[93] The nizam was thoroughly alienated; the Company's behaviour could hardly be called conciliatory.

In 1809 and 1812, the Company were also forced (according to their view of things) to intervene to defend the territories of the raja of Berar from invasion. Raghuji had long resisted concluding a subsidiary alliance with the Company, observing, no doubt, that such an agreement was the mechanism whereby the Company insinuated itself into the politics of nominally independent kingdoms. Yet, Berar's place at the heart of the subcontinent, and its territorial contiguity with the Company and its allies, meant that a threat to Nagpur was a threat to the Company, regardless of its unaligned state. Again, the Company's intervention was conceived of in moral terms, as an inability to stand by and allow inter-state rivalries to play out unimpeded. As Governor General Gilbert Elliot Murray Kynynmound, first Earl of Minto, phrased it, it 'was for the Government of England to decide whether it was expedient to observe a strict neutrality amidst these scenes of disorder and outrage which were passing under our eyes in the north of Hindostan, or whether we should listen to the calls of suffering humanity'.[94] For Minto, the solution was clear. By the time he resigned his post in 1813, Minto, whose regime is

---

[92] BL, APAC, IOR/F/4/394/10019, Fort William to Court of Directors, 1 March 1812, pp. 1–2. See also Sutherland, *Sketches*, p. 54.

[93] BL, APAC, IOR/F/4/683/18885, Henry Russell to Thomas Hislop, Report on Hyderabad, p. 20.

[94] Emma Eleanor Elizabeth Elliot-Murray-Kynynmound, Countess of Minto, ed., *Lord Minto in India: Life and Letters of Gilbert Elliot, First Earl of Minto* (London, 1880), pp. 193–194.

usually remembered as an era of retreat from political intervention, was disillusioned with the moderate policy enjoined on him by the Company.

The administration of Francis Rawdon Hastings, first Marquess of Hastings, witnessed a return to the forward policies espoused by Wellesley, though this outcome was far from evident when Hastings first set foot on Indian shores. To the contrary, Hastings was convinced that the Company's straitened finances and uncomfortable circumstances were a direct result of the overbearing conduct of Residents at court.[95] With time, however, Hastings became convinced of the need for military intervention in the subcontinent. It became apparent to him, as well as to the Residents he superintended, that whatever the cause, Indian rulers were keen to escape the alliance system. Early British reverses during the Gurkha War (1814–1816) prompted a storm of intrigue, as Indian elites sought to exploit the Company's diverted attention for their own gain. Simultaneously, members of the political line were becoming sceptical about the extent to which their supposed allies were secretly fomenting banditry on the Company's frontiers.[96] Unable to pay their armies in the reduced circumstances brought on their heads by the defeats of the Second Maratha War, Maratha armies had little option but to concede to their former soldiers the right to make their living through pillage and plunder. Nagpur and Hyderabad were hit hard by these depredations, but so too was the Madras Presidency. Finally, Hastings was able to convince the directors that the aggressions of the Pindaris (as these mounted marauders were known) warranted a military response.

The Pindari War, or Third Maratha War (1817–1818), marked the end of large-scale, combined Maratha resistance to Company rule. At first, it seemed like some of the Maratha rulers, at least, might ally with the Company against the Pindaris. When Raghuji Bhonsle died in 1816, his nephew, Appa Sahib, proved willing to conclude the subsidiary alliance that Raghuji had so long refused. As it transpired, however, both Appa Sahib and the peshwa broke the terms of their respective treaties to mount a desperate challenge to the Company's authority. Despite initially profiting from the element of surprise, both were finally forced to flee their respective capitals. Appa Sahib was briefly reinstated by the Resident, then rebelled again before retreating into hiding. Baji Rao, meanwhile, was forced to surrender after a long and fruitless chase. Accompanied by an armed retinue, he proceeded to Bithur, a holy site

---

[95] Marchioness of Bute, ed., *The Private Journal of the Marquess of Hastings*, 2 vols (London, 1858), I, p. 44.

[96] BL, APAC, Mss Eur D585, John Adam Papers, Richard Strachey to John Adam, 12 June 1813, pp. 81–82.

near Kanpur where he lived out the remainder of his days on a Company pension, his activities closely supervised by a Company commissioner.[97] As one soldier and political agent phrased it, '[t]he grand and comprehensive system which the genius of Lord Wellesley planned has been successfully executed by Lord Hastings.'[98]

1.4 'Paramountcy Must Remain Paramount'

Although the Company had achieved relative paramountcy in central India by 1818, this was by no means the end of negotiation and resistance. The Third Maratha War certainly transformed the political landscape, but many of the states touched by it nevertheless lingered on. Appa Sahib may have died in exile, but unlike the peshwa he was succeeded by a nephew who retained varying degrees of control over Nagpur until the kingdom was annexed per the doctrine of lapse in 1854. Awadh would likewise remain independent until it was annexed for maladministration in 1856. Given his non-intervention in the conflict of 1817–1818, Daulat Rao Shinde retained relative independence for some time; Gwalior would once again fight to defend its independence in the war of 1843. Thereafter Gwalior, though militarily reduced, remained, like Hyderabad, ostensibly independent until 1947. The Company's so-called paramountcy was always uneven and ill-defined, leaving room for rulers and ministers to contest the terms of that relationship.

Looking towards the forests and mountain passes also suggests a different, longer timeline. In their struggle for control over the Marathas, the Company had concluded treaties with the Bhils and the Gonds, recognizing the independence of their 'little kings' as a means of controlling otherwise inaccessible territory by proxy. Yet, these groups soon proved resistant to the rules laid down for them by the British. Their continuing raids of lowland villages provoked Company attempts to pacify and settle them, which in turn incited open revolt. Though firmly ensconced in large capitals, the Company's grasp over the countryside, particularly 'zones of anomaly' which they perceived as 'wild', remained tenuous.[99] The intertwined processes of pacification, settlement, and deforestation intended to subdue unruly populations would continue into the twentieth century.[100]

---

[97] Roy, *War, Culture and Society*, pp. 126–128.
[98] Adam White, *Considerations on the State of British India* (Edinburgh, 1822), pp. 235–236.
[99] K. Sivaramakrishnan, *Modern Forests: Statemaking and Environmental Change in Colonial Eastern India* (Stanford, CA, 1999), pp. 34–35.
[100] Sumit Guha, *Environment and Ethnicity in India, 1200–1991* (Cambridge, 1999), p. 200.

Still, the period 1798–1818 witnessed a crucial shift. As one historian of the twentieth-century princely states has observed, 'the essential elements of British "paramountcy" – the system of "residents" at the princely courts, the regulation of successions, control over the states' foreign affairs – were all laid down in this period.'[101] Assumptions about the Company's right to intervene in and even control Indian politics gathered force during these years, with the disturbances of 1817 and 1818 acting (from a British perspective) as a powerful confirmation of what key members of the political line had long begun to suspect, namely, that neighbouring Indian kingdoms would never make trustworthy allies, and that the Company's influence would have to be imposed if their objectives in the subcontinent were to be achieved. This belief in the necessity, even inevitability, of intervention would continue to shape Company policy for the following hundred years or more.

To be sure, questions about the appropriate nature and extent of interference would never be conclusively settled. At different points, members of the 'interventionist' or 'non-interventionist' schools would emerge ascendant. Still, as Charles Metcalfe pointed out, the contrast was one of degrees. In his view, '[t]he difference between the interfering and non-interfering policy is not that of interfering on all occasions and not interfering on any, because, as the predominant power in India, interference is sometimes forced on us, however reluctant we may be to adopt it.'[102] The effect of the period 1798–1818 was to convince contemporaries of British responsibility for good governance and tranquillity in India and, in the process, to remove the option of complete non-intervention from the realm of possibility. Attitudes towards the appropriate degree of intervention or non-intervention might change over time, but belief in the right to intervene, even if only under certain circumstances, remained constant.

Wars and treaties from this period would be continuously referenced over the following decades as setting precedents for the Company's paramount responsibilities. For example, Governor General William Cavendish Bentinck felt that the Company's role in placing the infant Raghuji III on the throne in 1818 authorized them to reserve the right of 'rendering our advice effectual and of enforcing attention to it', even after Raghuji had reached his majority. In Bentinck's view, the Company 'may fairly demand from the prince who owes his existence to our support,

---

[101] Ian Copland, *The Princes of India in the Endgame of Empire, 1917–1947* (Cambridge, 1997), p. 15.
[102] Kaye, *Selections*, p. 237.

that the authority we have conferred and continue to uphold shall not be flagrantly abused.'[103] Nagpur's annexation in 1854 was justified in precisely these terms: 'Nagpore was a principality granted after conquest, by favour of the British Government, to the late Raja, on hereditary tenure; and we have no doubt of our right, on the failure of legal heirs, to resume the grant.'[104] The Third Maratha War was also invoked by Governor General Lord Ellenborough in 1843 to justify military intervention in Gwalior. Ellenborough argued that the Company had no choice but to assert its political control, or else face the resurgence of armed resistance as they had in 1817. The maintenance of tranquillity within the subcontinent was, he claimed, 'a duty, not to ourselves alone, but to humanity'.[105] The annexation of Awadh in 1856, on grounds of misgovernment, was directly informed by Wellesley's treaty of 1801, whereby the nawab vizier engaged to govern for the prosperity of his subjects. According to the interpretation of John Peter Grant, a member of the Supreme Council of India, Wellesley 'believed that he had a moral right to force upon that ruler [the nawab vizier] whatever in his judgment was then necessary for the general good'; Grant argued that 'the British Government should act now on the principle on which Lord Wellesley acted in 1801, and that, if it fails to do so, it will violate its paramount obligations to the people of Oude.'[106]

Assumptions from the period 1798–1818 endured even after the disruptions of 1857. Disorder and misgovernment continued to be invoked as the basis for circumscribing rulers' powers, as the government of India persisted in maintaining ministers in office against the sovereign's will, interfering in succession disputes, and even deposing rulers (as in Baroda in 1875).[107] When, in the late nineteenth century, government officials developed a legal theory based on usage that would justify these interventions and settle the uncomfortable question of the princes' status in international law, they were explicitly indebted to the principles of 1798–1818. Theorists like Charles Lewis Tupper identified the origins of their own system in the policy of Wellesley and Hastings; for Tupper, the first cardinal principle of the whole system – the maintenance of the supremacy of

[103] William Cavendish Bentinck, 'Minute on the Nagpur Treaty', 15 November 1829, in *Correspondence of Lord William Cavendish Bentinck*, I, p. 352.
[104] House of Commons, *Treaty between East India Company and Maha-Rajah Ragojee Bhonsla, 1826; Reports on Failure of Heirs of late Rajah of Berar, and Annexation of Berar Territory; Despatches and Correspondence with Lord Dalhousie* (London, 1854), p. 9.
[105] Algernon Law, ed., *India under Lord Ellenborough, March 1842–1844* (London, 1922), pp. 93–96.
[106] House of Commons, *Papers Relating to Oude* (London, 1856), pp. 207, 215.
[107] Keen, *Princely India*, p. 18.

the paramount power – dated back to this earlier period. The distinction that he drew was between 'the Indian political system and Indian political law'; whereas he viewed the latter as a contemporary phenomenon, in his mind 'the former was almost wholly constructed in the first twenty years of the present century.' As Tupper points out, these policies were not uncontested, and 'its consequences were left to be matters of conjecture or contradictory action'. Still, the assumption of paramountcy, the view of the Company as ultimate arbiter, remained constant.[108]

Perhaps the clearest illustration of the continuing legacy of 1798–1818 is the *Report of the Indian States Committee* (1928–1929). The committee was formed at the instigation of the princes themselves to inquire into the relationship between the 'Paramount Power' and the Indian states.[109] The committee toured fifteen states, predominantly Rajput kingdoms but also Baroda, Hyderabad, Mysore, Bhopal, Gwalior, and Kashmir, and then produced a report that was intended to lay the foundations for policy towards the princely states in future. In this report, the committee disputed the idea that the relationship between the British government and Indian states was a 'contractual' one, arguing instead that it was a 'living, growing relationship shaped by circumstances and policy'. To justify this belief, and to counteract what they perceived to be undue emphasis on treaty obligations, the committee tried to demonstrate that 'Usage has shaped and developed the relationship between the Paramount Power and the states from the earliest times, almost in some cases, as already stated, from the date of the treaties themselves.'[110] For example, they observed that despite article 15 of the 1800 treaty prohibiting the Company from concerning themselves with the nizam's subjects or relations, in 1804 the Company had nominated a of chief minister, and had, in 1815, come to blows with the nizam's two sons.[111] The committee thus laid out a sweeping vision of the prerogatives that paramountcy entailed, including complete control over external affairs and the right to intervene in internal affairs for the perceived good of the ruler, of the kingdom, or of India as a whole. Still, they refused to define paramountcy itself, largely because doing so would be to limit it. 'Paramountcy must remain paramount; it must fulfil its obligations, defining or adapting itself according to the shifting necessities of the time and the progressive development of the states.'[112] As the report attests,

---

[108] Charles Lewis Tupper, *Our Indian Protectorate* (London, 1898), p. 62.
[109] House of Commons, *Report of the Indian States Committee, 1928–1929*, 1929, Cmd. 3302, VI, p. 5.
[110] Ibid., p. 24.
[111] Ibid., p. 14.
[112] Ibid., p. 31.

1798–1818 did not provide an unchanging model to which subsequent generations of colonial officials adhered; to the contrary, the impact of 1798–1818 was to ensure that these relationships would change by convincing colonial officials that they could not and should not set contractual limits to their own right to intervene.

1.5   Conclusion

By tracing the history of the Company's relationships with Indian powers, this chapter has sought, not only to contextualize the analysis to come, but also to argue for the importance of 1798–1818 as a vital juncture in the story of these relationships. In 1798, the Company was still just one regional power among many (albeit a dominant one), its territories relatively limited, its Residents functioning like diplomatic representatives. The Court of Directors and Board of Control in London had expressed their aversion to schemes of conquest and their desire to avoid political entanglements, emphasizing above all the Company's commercial origins and function. To the extent that Residents engaged with Indian politics, therefore, it was largely to exclude European powers and military expertise from Indian courts, and to maintain the status quo in the subcontinent. Residents negotiated loans, subsidies, and war reparations as well as overseeing royal successions, but their intervention in Indian administrations was generally limited; in the Maratha states, Residents exercised very little control at all, and maintained only uneasy diplomatic relations interspersed with periods of war. By 1818, however, the scene had changed significantly. The Company had concluded key subsidiary treaties that brought previously recalcitrant kingdoms under their influence. In Awadh, the Company had annexed extensive tracts of territory and, despite the promises made in the treaty of 1801, continued to exercise significant influence over the nominally independent administration. Most dramatically, the Company took direct control over considerable portions of central India that had previously belonged to the peshwa. By the end of the period under study, British military and political pre-eminence in India was conclusively established, and the Company enjoyed direct or indirect control over most of the subcontinent.

In demonstrating the persistence of some of the ideas and practices that emerged during these transformative twenty years, the chapter has overturned old assumptions about the trajectory that these relationships took over the course of nineteenth century. Threads of continuity can be detected running through a period that has previously been presented as a series of vacillations leading up to a final rupture in 1857. There are reasons why this narrative has persisted, and the objective of this chapter is not to suggest that attitudes towards the Indian states were set in stone. Instead, the argument of this chapter is that the parameters for this debate were in many ways set by the period 1798–1818, and that many of the features that characterized the early system continued to inform it until the 1890s, the period at which an ideology of indirect rule for the princely states, a form of 'political law', is said to have emerged. By identifying themes and ideas that echoed through time, the objective of this chapter is to suggest that contrary to common assumption, 1798–1818 was not a time of unthinking action fuelled by existential crisis and pragmatic motives, but, instead, that it anticipated the problems that would continue to characterize the theory and practice of indirect rule for the following hundred years.

Having established this wider context, the question now becomes how some of the abstract problems posed by the subsidiary alliance system were manifested in the routine business of the Residencies, and how Residents, in turn, tried to resolve them in practice. The following chapters reflect the principal points of contention that shaped the developing Residency system, encompassing changing conceptualizations of imperial governance, international law, material culture, patronage, and dynastic power. We will start with perhaps the most fundamental aspect of the Resident's role at court: that of mediator and information gatherer.

2 Negotiating the Disinformation Order

When John Briggs recalled the tumultuous early days of the Third Maratha War (1817–1818), it was primarily to lament the loss of his library. Briggs was assistant to the Resident at Pune in 1817 and lost many of his earthly possessions when the Residency buildings were sacked and burned. He later alleged that the enemy specifically targeted Resident Mountstuart Elphinstone's books, 'which were believed to include many on alchemy and the occult arts, and to have given him almost magical powers'.[1] Whatever the motives of the men who consigned Elphinstone's papers to the fire, it was undoubtedly true that much of Elphinstone's strength, such as it was, resided in ink and paper: the credentials he carried with him on arrival at court; the archives he consulted; the reports he received from news writers and intelligencers; the letters he wrote. Part of what made the East India Company so effective was its ability to collect and collate information from across the subcontinent. According to historiographical convention, political control in India was made possible through a concomitant conquest of knowledge. Yet, an empire built on paper could be fragile. As the fate of the Residency library made plain, paper is easily reducible to ash. This chapter shows how the Residents collected and used political intelligence, while also emphasizing the practical obstacles and active resistance they encountered in so doing.

Interest in the production and circulation of information is an enduring feature of historiography on the Company. In their different ways, both Bernard Cohn and C. A. Bayly influentially drew attention to British desires to 'know the country'.[2] While Cohn emphasized the mutually reinforcing relationship between imperial state-building and officialising procedures, particularly the impulse to categorize and classify, Bayly proposed a different field of inquiry: 'the information order', a heuristic device encompassing the various, overlapping systems of

[1] Evans Bell, *Memoir of General John Briggs, of the Madras Army* (London, 1885), p. 52.
[2] C. A. Bayly, 'Knowing the Country: Empire and Information in India', *MAS* 27, no. 1 (1993): 3–43.

collecting and distributing political intelligence that crisscrossed the Indian subcontinent.[3] In *Empire and Information: Intelligence Gathering and Social Communication in India 1780–1870* (1996), a classic work populated by a rich cast of 'canny people' including astrologers, midwives, and religious mendicants, Bayly traced the changing nature of the Indian information order over the long nineteenth century and the Company's attempts to infiltrate and subordinate it. Most relevant for our purposes, Bayly highlighted the importance of Mughal institutions to the Company's dramatic imperial expansion, notably Persian newsletters, postal routes, and scribal communities with a tradition of state service.[4] By incorporating this pre-existing Indian information order, the Company, according to Bayly, was able to establish its influence across the former Mughal empire.

As vital nodes within this network, the Residents offer a useful entry point through which to reassess Bayly's classic narrative; if imperial control depended on the ability to 'listen in' on internal communications as Bayly suggested, it was the Residents who did most of the listening.[5] Bayly concluded that the accumulation of intelligence facilitated military victory and profitable governance, but the Residents' experiences indicate that the acquisition of knowledge, and the equation between knowledge and power, was not so straightforward. The uneven overlap of British and Indian information orders, identified by Bayly as the primary source of recurring 'information panics', was just one problem among many.[6] First, these information orders were also recognized vectors for the conscious or unconscious dissemination of forgeries, false information, and frauds as well as facts. Second, even the most authentic intelligence did not always prescribe a clear line of action. News could have unintended consequences; rumours that were demonstrably false could produce material ramifications. Residents did their best to anticipate these outcomes, but it was not always obvious how best to manage the flow of information within and between courts, nor were they always certain how much to report to their superiors in Calcutta. Residents devoted a significant proportion of their time and finances to gathering and processing intelligence but did not always deploy it in the ways we might expect. Whispers of hostile coalitions and planned assassinations sometimes accrued seemingly unheeded in Residency records, couched in phrases like 'it is said'.

---

[3] Cohn, *Colonialism and Its Forms of Knowledge*, p. 3; Bayly, *Empire and Information*, pp. 3–5.
[4] Bayly, *Empire and Information*, pp. 58–78.
[5] Ibid., p. 365.
[6] Ibid., p. 2.

What follows, then, is an analysis of the sometimes surprising ways in which Residents not only collected, authenticated, and analysed intelligence, but also ignored, suppressed, misrepresented, or diverted it. The first section introduces some of the basic features of the Residents' intelligence work, using the example of the Pune Residency to illustrate how intelligence was collected and recorded but unevenly pursued. The remainder of the chapter situates this case study in context through a broader discussion of the strengths and weaknesses of the procedures elaborated by the Residents in the years leading up to the Third Maratha War, first by examining the Residents' approach to letters and rumours, and then concluding with an analysis of divisions within the Company itself. What becomes clear is that distrust permeated the system at all levels, informing the Resident's relationship to his informants, to the court, and even to the Company.

2.1   Inside the Intelligence Department

Intelligence was vital to the functioning of the subsidiary alliance system; to enforce the terms of treaties, Residents needed to be able to identify when their conditions were being breached. Perhaps contrary to our image of courtly diplomacy, then, Residents spent much of their time ensconced in their offices. From their desks, they participated in a system of assembling and communicating political intelligence that spanned the subcontinent. Information travelled primarily via dak, a decentralized courier system with Mughal roots that, by the end of the eighteenth century, was increasingly monopolized by the Company.[7] Correspondence was then copied out and preserved in Residency archives to serve as a frame of reference for the Resident and his successors. On first arriving at the Residency, new appointees used these archives to ground themselves in local conventions and concerns.[8] There were no fixed guidelines for how a Resident should conduct himself, so Residents often based their decisions on the precedents elaborated in these papers.[9] The archives that historians now use to study the Residencies were therefore themselves mechanisms of Company power, repositories of social and technical knowledge that were deployed for political purposes.

As intelligencers, Residents had recourse to a variety of sources, not all of which they valued equally. The most reliable information, from

---

[7] Michael H. Fisher, 'The East India Company's Suppression of the Native Dak', *IESHR* 31, no. 3 (1994): 311–348.

[8] BL, APAC, Mss Eur F88/370, Journal of Mountstuart Elphinstone, 12 June 1811, p. 85.

[9] Fisher, *Indirect Rule*, p. 174.

the Residents' perspective, were the English letters, dispatches, and gazettes that reached the Residency by post.[10] In addition to their Company contacts, Residents also relied on methods devised by the Mughals to survey their own empire. An important source of intelligence were the *akhbarat* produced by news writers stationed at Indian courts across the subcontinent. *Akhbarat* are Persian-language newsletters reporting on events at different royal centres, modelled on the imperial court diaries describing the activities of the Mughal emperor and the events of his reign; their contents range from summaries of the ruler's eating habits and daily exercises to his political appointments and general assemblies. These newsletters, composed by professionals, were copied out and disseminated to subscribers across the subcontinent.[11] Like the Mughals before them, Residents occasionally tested the authenticity of *akhbarat* by dispatching confidential agents along each line of the network to relate conditions on the ground.[12] *Akhbarat* were also supplemented by more perfunctory communiqués from spies placed in military encampments recounting the mood and movements of Indian troops.[13] At court, Indian ministers and their employees reported on official business in exchange for salaries or a pension.[14] Information was also purchased from visiting merchants, religious mendicants, and the hircarrahs (or men of all work) who served as messengers. Mobile groups like these were particularly prized informants. Not only did they frequent the bazaars, pilgrimage sites, and army encampments around the country where people congregated and news was exchanged, but they were also able to draw on further networks of informants because of their commercial, institutional, and occupational affiliations.[15] There was an element of institutionalization to this process; reliable informants were

[10] When Mountstuart Elphinstone repeated the contents of a newsletter from Jaipur, he cautioned 'that the news was not to be considered authentic, as if it had been published in the Calcutta Gazette'. NAI, FSC, 25 April 1805, no. 81, Mountstuart Elphinstone to Marquess Wellesley, 19 March 1805, p. 1.

[11] For their transformation under the Company, see Michael H. Fisher, 'The Office of Akhbar Nawis: The Transition from Mughal to British Forms', *MAS* 27, no. 1 (1993): 48.

[12] Bell, *Memoirs*, p. 48.

[13] See for example BL, APAC, Mss Eur E111, Richard Jenkins to Charles Russell, 15 February 1807, p. 8.

[14] Fisher, *Indirect Rule*, p. 354.

[15] Chitra Joshi. 'Dak Roads, Dak Runners, and the Reordering of Communication Networks', *International Review of Social History* 57, no. 2 (2012): 169–189; Bernard S. Cohn, 'The Role of the Gosains in the Economy of Eighteenth- and Nineteenth-Century Upper India', *IESHR* 1, no. 4 (1964): 175–182; C. A. Bayly, *Rulers, Townsmen and Bazaars: North Indian Society in the Age of British Expansion, 1770–1870* (Delhi, 1993), p. 143.

accumulated over the years, passed from Resident to Resident, resulting in an increasingly sophisticated intelligence-gathering apparatus.[16]

What precisely the Residents were listening for, and where, changed over time. At first, Residents stationed in Awadh and Bengal were charged with tracking flows of revenue. Their primary responsibility was to ensure that reparations and subsidies were paid in full and on time, leading them to focus on the collection and distribution of resources within allied states. In the unsettled conditions of the eighteenth century, Lucknow, and later Delhi, also became important listening posts where Residents strained to detect signs of impending Afghan or Sikh invasions from the north. As Anglo-French rivalry intensified against the backdrop of the American War of Independence (1775–1783), increased emphasis was placed on monitoring the activities of French envoys and mercenaries at Indian courts, too. This period of Francophobia, though intense, was brief; Europeans were barred from allied Indian courts according to the terms of the subsidiary alliances concluded at the dawn of the nineteenth century, meaning that, apart from occasionally having to ferret out a few rogue deserters, once these treaties were concluded Residents no longer had to worry about shadowing European interlopers. Instead, Residents were primarily tasked with ensuring that their Indian allies were not corresponding with one another outside the Company's purview. According to the terms of these treaties, allied courts were not supposed to interact except through the mediation of the Company. Increasingly, the Resident's efforts were directed at enforcing this prohibition. Prior to his final defeat in 1799, the presence of Tipu Sultan's emissaries was the main source of uneasiness, but thereafter, the policy of subordinate isolation was mostly aimed at disentangling the connections between Maratha courts.[17]

As the symbolic centre of Maratha politics in the eighteenth century, Pune is an ideal vantage point from which to see the Residency's intelligence office at work. Amid the existential crisis developing within the Company during this period, the Marathas were an important threat, and serious attention was devoted to parsing their intentions. The Pune Residency records maintained during these years speak to the active role of Pune within the Deccan, as well as the Resident's struggle to monitor and control its interactions with the wider world. A few examples from Pune can therefore help illustrate how the Residents' intelligence department functioned.

---

[16] For example, H. T. Colebrooke passed on a list of reliable intelligencers to Mountstuart Elphinstone via his cousin, John Adam. BL, APAC, Mss Eur F109/88, Mountstuart Elphinstone to John Adam, 3 May 1804.

[17] For this paragraph, see Fisher, *Indirect Rule*, p. 171.

During the early years of Wellesley's regime, a key concern was to determine where the peshwa's allegiances lay, and whether he could be convinced to ally with the Company. Although Baji Rao did finally conclude a subsidiary alliance with the Company in 1802, this treaty was preceded by years of uncertainty wherein his political alignments were far from clear. For a long time, Company officials had worried about the possibility of French influence taking root at Pune. In 1776, against the backdrop of the American War of Independence and impending conflict with France, the arrival in Pune of the Chevalier de Saint-Lubin, self-identified envoy for the French king, had played an important part in exacerbating Anglo-Maratha tensions on the eve of the First Maratha War.[18] Lingering concerns of a French connection persisted into the early nineteenth century and reached their apex during the Revolutionary and Napoleonic Wars. Speculating on the likelihood of the Marathas siding with the French in the event of an invasion, Resident William Palmer remarked with perplexity that 'I have no knowledge of this Coast maintaining any direct intercourse or correspondence with the French but it is (by whatever means) well and recently informed of the situation of that nation in Egypt and Europe.'[19] Four years later, Arthur Wellesley, then commanding the Company's forces in the Deccan and southern Maratha country, was outraged to discover that the peshwa was still communicating with Frenchmen, '& has endeavoured to conceal his communications from the Agents of the British Govt & to screen the Frenchmen from their search'.[20]

In the end, this French connection was little more than a British fantasy (albeit an enduring one); Pune's more important relationships were with Indian powers. Of these, the most significant was Daulat Rao Shinde, whose adopted father, Mahadji, had secured Baji Rao's accession to the throne. For several years Mahadji had resided with his large army in the precincts of the city; Shinde Chhatri, a memorial built on the site of his cremation, remains a prominent urban landmark. Daulat Rao, Mahadji's successor, continued to exercise significant influence at Pune until he was driven from it by the outbreak of the Second Maratha War. Apart from Daulat Rao, the peshwa also maintained a regular exchange of vakils with Raja Raghuji Bhonsle at Nagpur, who was a strong advocate of forming an anti-British Maratha confederacy. As a major regional power, Hyderabad was another vital point of contact.

[18] Sen, *Anglo-Maratha Relations*, p. 86.
[19] BL, APAC, IOR/H/576, William Palmer to Richard Wellesley, 13 October 1800, p. 434.
[20] BL, APAC, Mss Eur E216, Arthur Wellesley to Lt. Frissell, 17 February 1804, p. 170.

Finally, and most troublingly from the Company's perspective, Baji Rao clearly sympathized with Tipu Sultan's anti-British activities.[21]

Resident William Palmer's attempts to expose this Pune–Mysore connection illustrate the strategies that Residents used to monitor interstate exchanges in India, and the difficulties they faced in trying to translate intelligence into action at this stage in their history. In the summer of 1798, on the eve of the Fourth Mysore War, intelligence from Madras reported that messengers from Pune had arrived at Tipu's court. The news surprised Palmer, who could find no evidence that correspondence of any kind had recently passed between Mysore and Pune, and doubted whether the peshwa would really engage in illicit communications given his apparent willingness to support the Company in the impending war.[22] Over the following weeks, Palmer's attempts to ascertain the contents of this rumoured correspondence were frustrated at every turn; his informants at court suspected 'a secret & irregular correspondence of letters with the Paishwa's approbation', but affirmed that nothing had passed through official channels, meaning that Palmer could not 'obtain the least intimation of the nature of it'.[23] In September, messengers from Tipu arrived at Pune, and a paid informant of the Residency, employed as an accountant by one of the peshwa's ministers, disclosed that the messengers brought letters relating to an alliance that had been proposed by the peshwa.[24] Palmer remonstrated with Baji Rao and refused to wait on him until Tipu's messengers had been expelled from the city. Pleased with the apparent success of this ultimatum, Palmer was dismayed to discover, via an *akhbar* issued from Shinde's durbar (or court), that the vakils remained in the area.[25] Over the succeeding weeks, Palmer observed with irritation that the vakils were industriously circulating rumours calculated to undermine the Company's military reputation and encourage the peshwa to side with Tipu, rumours amplified through their inclusion in the durbar newspapers.[26] The influence of these vakils proved illusory; the peshwa nominally sided with the Company and practically remained neutral during the war. Still, Palmer's failure to oust them over the better part of a year demonstrates the peshwa's determination to keep lines of

---

[21] PRCOP, vol. 38 (1798–1801), William Palmer to Richard Wellesley, May 1799, pp. 596–597.

[22] Ibid., 15 August 1798, pp. 175–176.

[23] Ibid., 25 August 1798, p. 188.

[24] Ibid., 2 September 1798, pp. 199–200.

[25] Ibid., 22 March 1799, p. 478; William Palmer to Richard Wellesley, 12 April 1799, p. 523.

[26] PRCOP, vol. 38 (1798–1801), William Palmer to Richard Wellesley, 26 April 1799, p. 553.

communication open in defiance of the Resident's grumbling. As Palmer himself complained, '[t]he Paishwa seems determined to risk all consequences of breach of Engagements to his Allies, rather than desist from his Intercourse with Tippo.'[27] Palmer was (eventually) able to identify illicit exchanges between courts, but not to prevent them.

For Palmer's successor, Barry Close, the problem was how to interpret and make educated predictions about Maratha politics. Though Baji Rao was clearly open to hearing proposals from Tipu, Close remained uncertain how far he was willing to go to resist Company intervention. The impossibility of really knowing what the peshwa was thinking is a common refrain in Close's correspondence. For example, the presence of one of the peshwa's trusted ministers at Hyderabad in early 1802 vexed Close because he was pessimistic about his ability to discover the real motives of the mission, or to identify where precisely Baji Rao's loyalties lay. In Close's view, it was entirely possible that the peshwa was playing both sides at once, meaning that he might be sincerely seeking a rapprochement with the Company while at the same time courting Hyderabad.[28] For Close, anything was possible 'considering how much the Mahratta Powers are given to intrigue'.[29] Similarly, despite the peshwa's frequent meetings with vakils from Berar, and the general belief at court that he intended to forge a union with Shinde and Holkar, Close was unwilling to draw any conclusions, arguing that 'the Peshwa's policy is so irregular, temporising, and capricious that it would be as difficult as useless to argue from his past to his future conduct.'[30] In Close's mind, it was just as likely that Raghuji's desire to form an anti-British alliance would have the opposite effect and push the peshwa into the arms of the Company.[31]

On the very eve of the Second Maratha War, Close was no more confident in his intelligence than before. When it came to Yashwant Rao Holkar's plans for overturning the Pune government, Close was unwilling to venture any prognostications: 'Reports circulate here in such quick succession that it is scarcely possible to procure any substantial grounds for a conclusion or a conjecture.'[32] Writing the following week, shortly before leaving for Bombay to escape the conflict that had by then erupted between Holkar and Shinde, Close maintained that '[h]ere appearances

[27] Ibid., May 1799, p. 596.
[28] PRCOP, vol. 39 (1801–1802), Barry Close to Richard Wellesley, 13 February 1802, pp. 171–173.
[29] Ibid., p. 173.
[30] Ibid., 11 April 1802, p. 247. See also 22 March 1802, pp. 221–223; 11 April 1802, pp. 240–243
[31] PRCOP, vol. 40 (1802–1803), Barry Close to Richard Wellesley, 11 April 1802, p. 248.
[32] Ibid., 7 November 1802, p. 196.

fluctuate so constantly that no inference from them, at any moment can be more substantial than mere conjecture.'[33] Close was responsible for informing the governor general of developments at Pune, but remained dubious of his ability to accurately judge the peshwa's views or intentions. The feeling was shared by Residents posted at other Maratha courts, too; around the same time, Josiah Webbe, then Resident with Shinde, described '[t]he state of uncertainty, which unavoidably from the confused politics of a Mharatta Government will always be a sufficient cause to deter any reasonable man from forming a judgement in the posture which its affairs may at a particular time appear to assume'.[34] British stereotypes of Maratha courts made Residents hesitant to ascribe any strategy to them at all, an assumption that, in turn, limited their ability to produce useful analyses of conditions at court.

The conclusion of the Second Maratha War resulted in a temporary reprieve from anti-British activities at Pune; when backdoor diplomacy did resume, Close's successor, Mountstuart Elphinstone, was more confident in his ability to gauge its ebb and flow. In 1814, the Company's early reverses in the Gurkha War had an exhilarating effect on their nominal allies. Evidence of communication between the Marathas and the Gurkhas began to accumulate. On 5 October 1814, two British officers intercepted letters from Daulat Rao Shinde to the raja of Nepal hidden inside a book, 'dexterously concealed between the cover and the leaves which were pasted down on it.'[35] Two years later, as the treaty was being negotiated, Governor General the Marquess of Hastings was perplexed to learn that leading Gurkha generals were convinced, for reasons they refused to explain, that the Company was at war with the Marathas. Their conviction led Hastings to suspect what he was never able to prove, namely, 'that each of them must have had knowledge of proposals for co-operation made by the mahrattas to his Court.'[36] Against this backdrop, the peshwa and the Resident at Pune nearly came to blows over the fate of the peshwa's favourite minister, Trimbakji Dengle. The minister had been implicated in the murder of an ambassador from Baroda under the guaranteed protection of the British government. When the peshwa refused to surrender the minister to the Resident's custody, and then appeared to give implicit support to the troops that Trimbakji rallied across the countryside, Elphinstone surrounded the capital and delivered an ultimatum.

[33] Ibid., 14 November 1802, p. 233.
[34] NAI, For. Sec. 29 November 1804, no. 131, Josiah Webbe to Richard Wellesley, 1 October 1804, p. 10.
[35] Bute, *Private Journal*, p. 216.
[36] Francis Rawdon Hastings, first Marquess of Hastings, *The Marquis of Hastings' Summary of the Operations in India, with Their Results* (London, 1824), p. 96.

To justify this act of aggression, Elphinstone produced clear evidence of the peshwa's connivance in the insurrection by tracing the journey of a fund of six lakhs of rupees from the peshwa to one of his ministers to a post office to one of Trimbakji's partisans.[37] In the face of this apparent betrayal (as Elphinstone saw it), a new treaty was concluded in 1817.

The treaty of 1817 prohibited the peshwa from intercourse of any kind with neighbouring courts, but for Elphinstone, this provision was no guarantee; to the contrary, Baji Rao would be watched more closely than ever before. In Elphinstone's mind, Baji Rao's resistance to the Company at a moment when there was not 'the smallest ground for apprehension or alarm of any Kind' meant that going forward the Company would be required to 'seek more effectual means of preventing the evil consequences of His Highness's intrigues and hostility, than a reliance on his honor or on his adherence to the most solemn engagements.'[38] By contrast, John Malcolm, the governor general's political agent, was convinced of Baji Rao's good faith; so much so, that the subsidiary force normally stationed near Pune were withdrawn to the north to serve in the impending Pindari Wars. Seeing his opening, the peshwa began to collect his forces in the city.

Perhaps the most detailed picture that we have of Residency intelligence comes from the notebooks that Elphinstone kept in these tension-ridden months leading up to the Third Maratha War. The notebooks reveal that Elphinstone employed Indian agents to monitor the residences of the peshwa and other key officials, and to follow the peshwa on his secret business, despite Baji Rao's best efforts to disguise himself.[39] The Residency also tracked the movement of *dak dauriyas*, postal-runners whose coloured spears, according to Assistant John Briggs, signalled their courtly affiliation: '[i]n this way we at Poona obtained instant information of the entry of any of the messengers of foreign Courts that might pass our postal stations, and were enabled to be on the look-out for their arrival, as well as to trace the direction of any despatched by the Peishwa.'[40] Briggs boasted that after surrendering to the Company in 1818, the peshwa reputedly complained, 'with deep emotion, that such was the espionage established by Mr Elphinstone that even the very dishes provided for his Highness's meals were described in detail every day at the Residency.'[41]

---

[37] PRCOP, vol. 44 (1817), Mountstuart Elphinstone to Marquess of Hastings, 7 April 1817, pp. 65–67.

[38] Ibid., 15 October 1817, p. 294.

[39] See notes dated 31 August 1816, 17 September 1816, and 6 December 1816, in BL, APAC, Mss Eur F88/60.

[40] Bell, *Memoir*, pp. 48–49.

[41] Ibid., p. 47.

Though Elphinstone in many ways represents the pinnacle of British intelligence activity at Pune, he also exposes the limits of what intelligence could do. His default position was to doubt much of what he learned, often because he believed it was propagated for the sole purpose of frightening him. Murder plots, for example, were dismissed as scare tactics. In February 1817, Elphinstone claimed to be flooded with intelligence, 'full of notices of plans to assassinate me'. Convinced that the rumours were 'the result of a design to try to intimidate me into listening to proposals for T's [Trimbakji's] pardon after temptations & prayers have failed', Elphinstone ignored them. As he concluded in his journal, '[n]o care could ward off such designs if really entertained & caring about them would probably harass one in the end.'[42] Similarly, when news reached Elphinstone that Baji Rao had been sending clothes to his hill forts and selling others for the gold and silver with which they were adorned, causing rumours to spread in the city of his intention to flee, Elphinstone was inclined to think that these reports were circulated deliberately by the durbar to convince him that the peshwa was on the point of a rupture. 'There certainly prevails among those about His Highness a strong opinion that the British Government will submit to anything rather than proceed to extremities with the Paishwa', he reflected.[43] Elphinstone, by contrast, was determined to show that he would make no concessions.

Even rumours that were generally believed were still ignored because acting on them might unsettle the status quo. Though aware that the peshwa was trying to recruit Company sepoys stationed near Pune, Elphinstone chose not to act or even report the attempt to government: '[m]y confidence in the sepoys and my conviction of the impolicy of shewing apprehension from attempts to corrupt them led me to neglect this information.'[44] Elphinstone seems to have worried that in recognizing this rumour, he might cast doubt on the sepoys' loyalty, thereby bringing their honour into question and undermining their attachment to the Company. Similarly, in the days leading up to the outbreak of the war, Elphinstone refused to leave the Residency, despite the threat of assassination, because he preferred not to appear in the guise of aggressor. According to his biographer, '[r]umours were rife of intended assassinations, and would appear to have been well founded; but a

[42] BL, APAC, Mss Eur F88/370, Journal of Mountstuart Elphinstone, 28 February 1817, pp. 18–19. He describes further rumours of assassinations in an entry of 22 October, p. 27.
[43] PRCOP, vol. 44 (1817), Mountstuart Elphinstone to Marquess of Hastings, 26 March 1817, pp. 49–50.
[44] PRCOP, vol. 45 (1817–1818), Mountstuart Elphinstone to Marquess of Hastings, 3 November 1817, p. 315.

high-minded man was not to be swayed by such fears, and the generosity of his nature prompted him to disbelieve them.'[45] To the contrary, Elphinstone's journals suggest that he fully believed in the likelihood of an impending conflict, but wanted to maintain the moral high ground by keeping lines of communication open. He was particularly determined not to unsettle Hastings's ongoing negotiations with Shinde by allowing conflict to break out at Pune. Remarking on 'the necessity of seeming friendly here', Elphinstone described his position as 'the most embarassing situation I have ever been placed in'; he burned his most sensitive papers and prepared for the worst.[46]

Though Elphinstone was prepared to dismiss rumours relating to his own safety, he was very active in combating rumours about the Company then spreading through Pune. The stakes were high; he seems to have feared that rumours of this kind were being used by the peshwa to provoke general resistance to the Company's encroachments. Elphinstone noted the rising popularity of the peshwa's cause, and that 'H H [His Highness] spared no arts to foster these feelings, and excite an odium against us'. To Elphinstone, the peshwa's success was evident 'in the facility with which all rumours disadvantageous to the British Government were received, continual reports of combinations in Hindostan of defeats of our armies, disaffections of our troops, and defection of our allies were studiously circulated and readily believed.' In response, Elphinstone promoted the Company's version of events: 'I took all the means I could, without showing an over anxiety on the subject to counteract the effect of these stories, and especially convince the Durbar of the real state of affairs in Hindoostan.'[47]

Once war had erupted, Elphinstone continued to try to shape public perceptions in the region. He was concerned to disseminate news of the peshwa's purported inhumanity, transmitting enclosures written in Marathi regarding 'the atrocious barbarity of Baji Rao's troops towards the defenceless inhabitants of a village near Purtoor [Partur, in the peshwa's line of flight]', which he requested be given 'the utmost publicity' at Pune and at Hyderabad.[48] Similarly, when Satara was captured, Elphinstone issued proclamations presenting a British narrative of events, justifying the Company's reason for going to war and for removing the

---

[45] T. E. Colebrooke, *Life of the Honourable Mountstuart Elphinstone* (London, 1884), p. 258.

[46] BL, APAC, Mss Eur F88/370, Journal of Mountstuart Elphinstone, 27 October 1817, p. 27.

[47] PRCOP, vol. 45 (1817–1818), Mountstuart Elphinstone to Marquess of Hastings, 3 November 1817, p. 314.

[48] PRCOP, vol. 52 (1818), Mountstuart Elphinstone to Captain Robertson at Pune, 13 May 1818, p. 85; Mountstuart Elphinstone to Henry Russell, 9 April 1818, p. 5.

peshwa from power. Later, when the raja of Satara was seated on the musnud (or throne), Elphinstone encouraged him to issue proclamations in his own name, sanctioning the political agent that Elphinstone had chosen for him, and publicizing his intimacy with the Company. In describing this relationship, the raja of Satara emphasized the injuries that had been done him by Baji Rao, particularly an order he claimed had been issued to the commandant of the fortress at Vasota to put the whole family to death rather than suffer them to fall into the hands of the British.[49]

Even the most seemingly trivial reports were followed up and discountenanced. Elphinstone did everything in his power to discourage the circulation of a prophecy, which, though its contents were not disclosed in the Residency records, clearly contravened the image he desired to cultivate across the countryside. Noting that the prophecy was circulating around Sirur and Satara in manuscript form, Elphinstone wrote to John Briggs requesting him to prohibit the transmission of the papers from village to village. If the paper was discovered, Briggs was instructed to impose a fine on the village where it was found, which the inhabitants were then authorized to transfer to the village from whence the report had been received, thereby enabling Briggs to trace the passage of the prophecy from place to place.[50]

This narrative of events from Pune contains within it several important themes that will be elaborated in the following analysis. Residents used existing institutions and expertise at Indian courts to amass intelligence and identify potential threats to their authority. Yet, the seriousness with which Residents invested this intelligence was undermined by assumptions about the Indian courtly elite, as well as Residents' awareness of the strategies used by their enemies to resist or to confuse them. Residents were keen to maximize the quality and quantity of their intelligence as well to promote the Company's own version of events at their respective courts, but in practice found that, far from prescribing a straightforward line of action, the intelligence they collected sometimes complicated rather than clarified their position at court. Some rumours were derided or ignored, while others, particularly those relating to the Company's public image, were taken very seriously. The following sections explore in greater depth how Residents tried to authenticate and use intelligence, focusing on letters and rumours, respectively.

---

[49] James Grant Duff, *A History of the Mahrattas*, 3 vols (London, 1826), III, p. 482.
[50] PRCOP, vol. 54 (1818–1819), Mountstuart Elphinstone to John Briggs, 19 February 1819, pp. 391–392.

2.2   Deception, Decorum, and the Epistolary Arts

For the Residents, perhaps no single document was more tantalizing than an intercepted letter. Intercepted letters provided valuable confirmation of illicit connections and subversive schemes; they were tangible proof of the connections between courts that the policy of subordinate isolation was designed to repress. The testimony of one of William Palmer's sources from 1800 demonstrates that those in and about court knew what this evidence was worth, and who would pay the best price for it. Nagoji Pandit was employed as an emissary for a vakil at Pune. When the nizam of Hyderabad's second son authorized Nagoji's employer to negotiate with Shinde on his behalf, Nagoji delivered their letters. The work was delicate since the negotiations related to a prospective coup at Hyderabad as Nizam Ali Khan declined into old age. Nagoji had been promised a reward of 500 Rs and a salary increase of 100 Rs monthly; when he insisted on the fulfilment of this promise, however, his employer balked. Learning that the vakil intended to hold him in confinement for his 'Importunity', Nagoji hid the relevant papers in his clothes and asked permission to return home, intending to make his escape. Once Nagoji's safety was secured, he informed a friend of his plan to reveal all to the peshwa. Nagoji's friend discouraged it, however, and 'advised me to disclose it to the English Resident from whom I might expect a suitable Reward.' Nagoji brought the compromising letters to Resident William Palmer and placed himself under Palmer's protection.[51] Nagoji's objective was profit, as well as security from his former employer. People like Nagoji, middlemen precariously employed at the peripheries of courtly society, had both the motive and the means to become Company informants. Residents sometimes described this kind of behaviour as 'treachery', but without it, they would have been in the dark about much of what passed at court.[52]

Evidence like this was not taken at face value. Residents were wary of being duped by astute forgers, knowing that stolen seals or old envelopes could be used to produce convincing counterfeits.[53] There was, after all, a financial incentive to fake political intelligence. James Anderson, one of the first Residents at Shinde's court, observed that '[a]t every Durbar in Hindostan the furnishing of [intelligence] has become a fixed Trade & I have in general observed that the agents employed in

---

[51] PRCOP, vol. 38 (1798–1801), 'The Declaration of Nagojee Pundit Made to the Resident at Poona', 22 December 1800, pp. 1090–1091.
[52] BL, APAC, IOR/H/241, Extract of letter from H. T. Colebrooke to governor-general-in-council, 8 May 1801, p. 653.
[53] BL, APAC, IOR/L/PS/6/20, 27 September 1808, pp. 239–240.

it suit their Intelligence in some shape or other to the disposition of their Constituents.'[54] There was also a risk of forged letters being produced by courtly factions; Residents feared becoming the instruments of plots whose contours they could only vaguely discern. Evidence produced by royal family members was subject to special scrutiny for this reason. Their place at the centre of courtly life made them both invaluable and fundamentally suspect as sources (as Chapter 6 will show). When in 1806 Munir Bakht, one of the younger princes at Delhi, supplied Resident Archibald Seton with a letter purportedly received by the heir apparent Akbar Shah from Yashwant Rao Holkar, the letter was treated with suspicion. The governor general doubted that Munir Bakht could have acquired a document containing such damning evidence of collaboration with the enemy, especially given his known sympathy for the British. The council speculated that 'such a letter might be fabricated by those who were interested in occluding Akber Shah from the succession to the Throne' and that the prince 'might have been rendered the unconscious instrument of such a project.'[55]

To identify fraudulent papers, Residents relied on Indian experts. The way intercepted letters were handled illustrates how technical knowledge of Persianate conventions, acquired through patronage of Indian scribes, was put to practical use. Every detail was considered for evidence of forgery, with special attention paid to format, seals, signatures, and superscriptions.[56] Residents fastidiously preserved letters from Indian dignitaries that were later used as models against which to examine suspected forgeries, confirming which intercepted letters carried authentic information and which did not. For instance, when in 1807 the Resident at Hyderabad Thomas Sydenham intercepted a letter addressed to a Hyderabadi courtier that appeared to have come from Yashwant Rao Holkar, the handwriting and seal were compared with other letters in the Resident's possession to test its authenticity; the Resident even compared the paper and the manner of enclosing and fastening it with a paper band.[57]

Despite differences in form and style, Indians and Britons shared certain fundamental similarities with regards to the nature and function of

---

[54] BL, APAC, IOR/H/241, James Anderson to William Kirkpatrick, 5 December 1786, p. 26.

[55] BL, APAC, IOR/L/PS/5/30, governor-general-in-council to directors, 18 September 1806, p. 417.

[56] BL, APAC, IOR/F/4/311/7097, N. B. Edmonstone to Earl of Minto, note to letter of 29 July 1809, pp. 165–167; BL, APAC, IOR/F/4/619/15425, Richard Jenkins to John Adam, 25 September 1818, p. 173; NAI, HRR, series 35, file 29, Thomas Sydenham to N. B. Edmonstone, 23 January 1809, p. 1; BL, APAC, Mss Eur D514/1, Richard Strachey to E. W. Blunt, 15 August 1812, p. 115.

[57] HRR, box 2, vol. 34, J. Monckton to N. B. Edmonstone, 4 June 1807, pp. 273–280.

letters that facilitated this process. The materiality and format of letters spoke to their nineteenth-century recipients, whether British or Indian, in ways that would not be immediately obvious to us. As historian Giora Sternberg has pointed out, 'early modern letters were not only a vehicle for narrated information, but also a formal social act, a statement by the addresser about his or her status relative to the addressee.'[58] Sternberg proposed the concept of 'epistolary ceremonial' to encompass the many ways in which letter form signified status relationships between correspondents.[59] Thinking about letters in this way alerts us to terms of address, salutations, and modes of signing off which, alongside page layout and the size of quality of the paper, would have been imbued with meaning.

Residents scrutinized prose style as well as format. C. A. Bayly has observed how the flowery Persian of Indian royal letters was tied to fine gradations of rank, suggesting that literal-minded British officials, who omitted these verses in their records, missed their underlying messages.[60] While officials might have condensed their handwritten copies to facilitate fact-checking, often omitting the lengthy Arabic invocations and honorifics that prefaced royal letters, we should not assume that they were blind to the significance of epistolary etiquette. After all, the British elite had an equally sophisticated, though stylistically opposed, letter-writing culture; in Britain, as in India, there was an extensive body of prescriptive literature on the subject.[61] Similarly, in Europe as in India composition was accorded a central place in interstate diplomacy; nearly the entire second volume of Karl von Martens' classic diplomatic manual was devoted to the conventions appropriate to different kinds of letters, instructing readers on how to make written complaints, how to address memorials to sovereigns, and how to offer congratulations.[62]

---

[58] Giora Sternberg, 'Epistolary Ceremonial: Corresponding Status at the Time of Louis XIV', *P&P* 204 (2009): 36.

[59] Sternberg, 'Epistolary Ceremonial', p. 35. For the ways in which social stratification was reflected in the Persian *insha* tradition, see Momin Mohiuddin, *The Chancellery and Persian Epistolography under the Mughals* (Calcutta, 1971), pp. 19, 66. For the ways in which status differentials were encoded in superscriptions and subscriptions during this period, as well as the 'semiotics of blank space', see Eve Tavor Bannet, *Empire of Letters: Letter Manuals and Transatlantic Correspondence, 1688–1820* (Cambridge, 2005), pp. 64–69.

[60] Bayly, *Empire and Information*, pp. 77–78.

[61] Linda C. Mitchell, 'Letter-Writing Instruction Manuals in Seventeenth- and Eighteenth-Century England', in *Letter-Writing Manuals and Instruction from Antiquity to the Present: Historical and Bibliographic Studies*, eds. Carol Poster and Linda C. Mitchell (Columbia, SC, 2007), p. 196. For Persian *insha*, see Colin Mitchell, 'Safavid Imperial *Tarassul* and the Persian *Insha* Tradition', *Studia Iranica* 26, no. 2 (1997): 180–181.

[62] Karl von Martens, *Le guide diplomatique* (Leipzig, 1832), II, pp. 318, 355, and 373, respectively.

Thus, while the specific formulae used in India might be unfamiliar, British officials were predisposed to consider details that we might dismiss as trivial. For instance, in 1821 Charles Metcalfe contrasted the injustice of Sikander Jah's refusal to embrace him in open court (which he termed 'the only ostensible Compliment paid by the nizam to the British Representative') with his own willingness to adhere to the conventions governing their relationship, among which he numbered certain epistolary habits. 'In other respects generally the forms of Royalty are assumed by the Nizam, and admitted by the Resident', Metcalfe wrote. 'Such as the application of the Title Hoozoor I poor noor to His Highness. The placing of his designation at the top of any written communication, and not where the sense of the Text would require it, with other similar forms'.[63] The modes of address and salutation employed in letters were thus recognized to form part of an array of practises through which relationships were made manifest, alongside other forms of ceremonial like the exchange of khilat and *nazr* (to be discussed in Chapter 4). Understanding the etiquette of letter-writing was just as important as knowing the protocol to be followed in open court.

At the same time as Residents were familiarizing themselves with these Indian epistolary forms (with the guidance of munshis, to be discussed in Chapter 5), Indians too were becoming acquainted with British letter-writing and using this knowledge for their own purposes. At Delhi in 1811, a few enterprising courtiers succeeded in forging letters purporting to be from the Calcutta chief justice, Henry Russell. The letters, which were addressed to Emperor Akbar Shah II, suggested that Resident Archibald Seton's activities did not conform with Company policy. By casting doubt on Seton, these men undermined his influence at court, creating a power vacuum to be filled with their own counsel and advice. The letters reflect the writers' cognizance of the English language and the conventions of British letter-writing. The secretary to government, on reviewing them, noted that the letters bore 'a subscription in the English character meant to appear as an English paper with an English superscription', where 'the imitations of the English signature are written by a person who could write bad English'. Beyond using English epistolary forms, the letters used the reputation and status of British information networks to their advantage to encourage Akbar Shah not to consult with anyone who might expose their plot: 'let no one else be privy to your Majesty's secrets, for I learned from Mr. Elphinstone

---

[63] BL, APAC, Mss Eur F109/9, Charles Theophilus Metcalfe to George Swinton, 13 February 1821.

[the Resident at Pune], that all your Majesty's servants are traitors, and very worthless.'[64] The Company's reliance on the circulation of letters meant that the whole system was open to subversion; it presented an opportunity for people outside the Company to appropriate its authority by writing letters in the Company's name.

To eliminate this subversive potential, and to promote their own views at court, Residents tried to orchestrate the composition, transmission, and delivery of official letters. Dispatches from the governor general were invariably submitted to the ruler through the channel of the Resident, thereby enabling him to influence how the letter was received and understood, and by whom. Although Thomas Sydenham did at one point make a copy of the governor general's address for Sikander Jah's perusal, to give him 'an opportunity to examine, and comprehend, the nature, Tendency, and object of your Lordships Remonstrances and advice' (in this case, relating to the nizam's suspected secret correspondence with a former minister then in open rebellion against the Company), Sydenham averred that this practice was the exception rather than the rule. 'On many occasions, I have declined furnishing the minister, or the Nizam, with copies of the Governor Generals Letters, in order that the contents of them might not become public amongst a Description of persons, who are ready to prepare the Nizam for resistance against every proposal from the British Government.'[65] The information communicated in letters was liable to be used by ministers antipathetic to the Company in ways unintended by the author. Accordingly, the Resident consciously couched the messages conveyed by official letters in terms that left little room for misinterpretation.

For the Residents, the problem was thus not simply to collect and communicate intelligence, but to determine how best to present and use it. Miles Ogborn has made a similar observation regarding the royal letters that were so vital to the Company's early commercial strategy within the subcontinent; however, whereas Ogborn focuses on the contingency of first encounters, the dynamics at work in the late eighteenth century were very different.[66] The relationships that these letters were designed to sustain were both far more intimate, and far less equal.

In this context, a few patterns emerged. Points of policy were usually delivered via a written memorandum, ensuring that every detail was

---

[64] BL, APAC, IOR/F/4/393/1009, Charles Theophilus Metcalfe to N. B. Edmonstone, 11 July 1811, pp. 59–62.

[65] BL, APAC, IOR/F/4/296/6833, Thomas Sydenham to Earl of Minto, September 1809, pp. 78–79.

[66] Miles Ogborn, *Indian Ink: Script and Print in the Making of the English East India Company* (Chicago, 2007), pp. 38–39.

communicated with precision.[67] Reprimands or peremptory instructions were, at least initially, delivered verbally and in private out of delicacy to the ruler in question (though continued resistance to the governor general's commands might elicit a public reproach).[68] The 'delicacy' that Residents avowed to be their guiding principle in these circumstances was motivated by more than mere politeness; discretion could have strategic value. When the governor-general-in-council sent a letter to Sikander Jah urging him to cease corresponding with the rebel Mahipat Ram, for example, Resident Thomas Sydenham was advised to present the letter in private. 'By thus rendering the interposition of the British Government less apparent', it was thought, 'His Highness would be enabled to adopt the course of conduct recommended to him with more credit and dignity than if the compulsory motives of it were publicly exposed.'[69] Handling these points of contention privately allowed the ruler to cede to the Company without losing face in the eyes of the court.

Try as they might, however, Residents were not always able to control the wider reception of letters, particularly given that the receipt of important dispatches usually occasioned a public, ceremonial event. Under these conditions, it was possible for the ruler to create public impressions about the import of the letters being delivered. This subversive potential is illustrated by an incident at Lucknow in 1816, when Nawab Vizier Ghazi ud-Din Haidar Khan was in the process of appealing to the governor general for control of a deceased relative's property. When the nawab received an official letter from the governor general ratifying, in no uncertain terms, the Resident's earlier denial of the nawab's claim to Bahu Begum's vast wealth, Resident Richard Strachey was unsettled to witness how the news was handled. Rather than expressing his disappointment or resentment, as Strachey had perhaps expected,

---

[67] For instance, Elphinstone issued his complaints about the peshwa's minister in a written memorandum, as it 'might by a little misconstruction be so represented as to excite much alarm and jealousy in the Peshwa's mind'. Mountstuart Elphinstone to Earl of Minto, 7 July 1812, in *PRC*, XII, p. 224.

[68] When Richard Jenkins issued a memorandum to Raghuji Bhonsle he omitted in the Persian translation the governor general's doubts about Raghuji's loyalty to the Company, which he thought 'it would be more delicate towards the Rajah as well as more consistent with propriety in other respects to confine Entirely to a verbal form.' BL, APAC, IOR/H/600, Richard Jenkins to Marquess of Hastings, 12 May 1815, p. 738. Meanwhile, Richard Strachey thought it best to prepare a paper on the Company's policy towards Bhopal. BL, APAC, IOR/H/600, Richard Strachey to Marquess of Hastings, 13 May 1815, p. 764.

[69] NAI, HRR, box 2, vol. 33, N. B. Edmonstone to Thomas Sydenham, 23 October 1806, pp. 359–360.

Ghazi ud-Din instead made a public display of satisfaction by honouring, with ceremonial robes, the person who had delivered the dispatch and the munshi who had transcribed the original letter. According to the bewildered Resident,

> public rejoicings also took place, and His Excellency's satisfaction has been so unequivocally manifested that I cannot but believe his Excellency to have countenanced the report which has gained universal Currency, that he has received the Authority of the Governor General to the fullest extent of his wishes regarding Fyzabad.[70]

By handling the letter publicly in the way that he did, the nawab vizier negated, to some extent, the message it contained and the intention with which it was dispatched. Through public celebration, he cultivated the impression that his claim was condoned by the begum's executors, giving an aura of legitimacy to his subsequent seizure of the begum's household. The Resident might do everything in his power to orchestrate, to the smallest degree, the communications between Calcutta and the court, but the marks on the page sometimes meant very little in practice.

While Residents could exert some control over the letters traversing the subcontinent, news passed by word of mouth sometimes proved more ungovernable. In 1801, shortly before the French residents of the city were deported to Puducherry, Resident at Hyderabad James Achilles Kirkpatrick remarked in Mountstuart Elphinstone's hearing that 'the secrets of govt are so ill kept that the resolutions of govt about the French here were known to Gardner an officer in the nizam's service before they were known to the resident.'[71] Tellingly, when the minister of Travancore was requested to write a letter to the governor general expressing his willingness to cooperate with the Company's proposed administrative reforms, the minister refused on the grounds 'that in less than Three Days the contents would circulate through every corner of the Country'.[72] As the import of official letters spread through conversation, their intended meanings could be lost or superseded. Yet, Residents were often uncertain how to act in response to the rumours snaking through the streets of their respective capitals.

---

[70] BL, APAC, Mss Eur D514/3, Richard Strachey to John Adam, 21 March 1816, p. 132.
[71] BL, APAC, Mss Eur F88/368, Journal of Mountstuart Elphinstone, 25 August 1801, p. 94.
[72] BL, APAC, IOR/H/589, Colin Macaulay to Earl of Minto, 16 September 1808, pp. 395–396.

2.3   'The Tattle in the Suburbs of the City'

Rumour, as the circulation of unverified information, has traditionally carried a pejorative connotation. Early analyses of the phenomenon identified untruth as its essential feature and were concerned primarily to detect and explain patterns of distortion.[73] Yet, as social science studies became increasingly sensitized to the conditions in which rumours emerge, anthropologists and sociologists have recognized the practical importance of rumour as a way for people to pool resources and make sense of ambiguous situations. In his classic analysis, sociologist Tamotsu Shibutani illustrated how rumours are developed deliberatively and collaboratively in situations where the news provided by institutional channels is lacking or unsatisfactory.[74] Considering these insights, historian Luise White, based on her reading of vampire stories circulating in colonial and postcolonial Africa, has suggested that we think of rumour differently, 'not [as] events misinterpreted and deformed, but rather events analyzed and commented upon'.[75] Like Shibutani, White sees rumour as a sign of a critically engaged public seeking to understand their world and stake their place in the political discourse of the day. Similarly, anthropologist Glen Perice has suggested that rumour, as a form of unauthorized speech, can be a way of taking action and registering opposition, albeit without publicly resisting oppressive regimes; these findings reflect, in moderated form, James Scott's famous depiction of gossip as a 'weapon of the weak'.[76]

Many of these general observations about rumour are applicable to the Indian context. In Indian society news and conjecture proliferated swiftly, passed through word of mouth at mosques, markets, pilgrimage sites, and army encampments; this was the sphere of political debate that C. A. Bayly dubbed the Indian ecumene.[77] Oral culture of this type was important before the advent of print, and in a context where illiteracy was widespread, but acquired additional significance given British policies of subordinate isolation. However resilient their networks might be, Indian elites were still conscious of the Company's endeavours to extinguish

[73] Gordon W. Allport and Leo Postman, *The Psychology of Rumor* (New York, NY, 1947), p. 134.
[74] Tamotsu Shibutani, *Improvised News: A Sociological Study of Rumor* (Indianapolis, IN, 1966), p. 17.
[75] Luise White, *Speaking with Vampires: Rumor and History in Colonial Africa* (Berkeley, CA, 2000), p. 58.
[76] Glen A. Perice, 'Rumors and Politics in Haiti', *Anthropological Quarterly* 70, no. 1 (1997): 1–10; James C. Scott, *Weapons of the Weak: Everyday Forms of Peasant Resistance* (New Haven, CT, 1985), p. 282.
[77] Bayly, *Empire and Information*, p. 82.

these channels of communication, leading them to speculate about what the Resident might be trying to keep from them. The Resident's inability to comment on or confirm Indian sources intensified these suspicions. James Achilles Kirkpatrick was harangued by Nizam Ali Khan and his ministers for what they perceived to be a failure on his part to transmit crucial information about a reported Afghan invasion of north India at the turn of the century. As Kirkpatrick himself expressed it in a letter to his brother in February 1799, 'Edmonstone and his Deputy in Calcutta have discontinued for sometime past sending me the Delhi Papers, which frequently places me in an awkward predicament'. The minister seems to have suspected that Kirkpatrick was being disingenuous, and, in hopes of drawing him out, presented the Resident with letters from his own informants abroad, the contents of which Kirkpatrick was unable to confirm or contradict until he received news from Calcutta.[78] This atmosphere of mistrust, combined with the slow pace of official communications from Calcutta, meant that rumours could take root at Indian courts, where the general public as well as the political elite were keen to pull back the veil of concealment and discover the Company's real intentions.[79]

British contemporaries commonly made light of what they considered to be an Indian predisposition towards gossip and were disposed not to take it seriously. Thomas Williamson's best-selling handbook *The East India Vade-Mecum* reflected popular British opinion when it disparagingly described the contents of *akbharat* as 'the mere tattle in the suburbs of a city'.[80] Residents were leery about forwarding this kind of news to government, fearing that it would bring their personal credit, that is, their reputation for truthfulness and accuracy, into question. In the eighteenth century, personal credit, as Margot Finn has illustrated, operated as 'a broader social and cultural measure of personal worth.'[81] In the interests of caution, Residents were careful to preserve their credit by couching their information with phrases like 'my information adds' or 'I have heard through confidential channels' or 'it is said'. Only rarely did Residents communicate these kinds of rumours with confidence, and then only when the opinion of the court was unanimous. For instance,

---

[78] BL, APAC, Mss Eur F228/1, J. A. Kirkpatrick to William Kirkpatrick, 3 February 1799, p. 59.

[79] The movement of troops was particularly subject to speculation. See for example BL, APAC, IOR/H/599, Richard Jenkins to Marquess of Hastings, 11 December 1814, p. 462, on speculation regarding the advance of Colonel Doveton's force to Achalpur.

[80] Williamson, *East India Vade-Mecum*, II, pp. 471–472.

[81] Margot Finn, *The Character of Credit: Personal Debt in English Culture, 1740–1914* (Cambridge, 2003), p. 19.

on the eve of the Third Maratha War, Richard Jenkins laid out several points of mutually reinforcing intelligence that substantiated his theory that the raja of Berar was conspiring with Shinde against the Company. He concluded: 'the principal circumstances above mentioned [that the raja is corresponding secretly with Shinde] I hear from so many quarters that I cannot doubt their correctness and I am constantly receiving warnings from the principal persons in our interest in the Durbar.'[82]

The Residents' circumspection about forwarding information acquired through word of mouth was due in large part to the misinformation disseminated by rival Indian powers, who thereby hoped to confuse and misdirect Company policy, as well as to rally support among the general population. The rumours circulated by the Company's enemies generally involved exaggerations concerning the number and movement of Indian troops, or the formation of hostile coalitions. For example, during their war with Yashwant Rao Holkar, Residents reported that his agents regularly publicized his planned assaults against the Company, attacks that in fact rarely materialized. In the Company's view, these rumours were used as 'an instrument for the support of his consequence, and the maintenance of his military reputation and political ascendancy', and promulgated 'through the industry of those who have an interest in reviving scenes of turbulence and disorder'.[83] Later, during the Third Maratha War, Richard Jenkins, monitoring the raja of Berar's troops for signs of incipient attack, made note of 'false reports propagated regarding Pindarries, which are made the instruments of exciting alarm, and the pretence of keeping the Rajah's troops in a continued state of readiness for movement'.[84] The strategic use of rumour is a common feature of the information warfare that often accompanies large-scale conflict, forming a vital part of the arsenal of governmental power in India as in Europe.

Because of this instrumental quality, Company officials were liable to attribute budding rumours to the machinations of their enemies.[85] When in 1807 Archibald Seton alerted the governor general to rumours of an alliance between Shinde and Holkar, the report was dubbed

---

[82] BL, APAC, Mss Eur F311/10, Richard Jenkins to Thomas Hislop, 14 November 1817, p. 10.

[83] NAI, HRR, box 2, vol. 33, N. B. Edmonstone to W. C. Bentinck, 21 October 1806, pp. 328–329.

[84] BL, APAC, Mss Eur F311/10, Richard Jenkins to Thomas Hislop, 24 November 1817, p. 14. Jenkins also suspected that Raghuji Bhonsle used the occasion of the Marquess of Hastings's tour of the upper provinces to sow rumours about an impending war and to spur the Maratha chiefs to unite against the Company. BL, APAC, IOR/H/599, Richard Jenkins to Marquess of Hastings, 26 September 1814, pp. 21–22.

[85] Anand A. Yang, 'A Conversation of Rumors: The Language of Popular "Mentalités" in Late Nineteenth-Century Colonial India', Journal of Social History 20, no. 3 (1987), p. 488.

'absurd', and Seton was warned against relying on 'the credit of common Newspapers', or on his Indian informant, who was deemed to be a willing instrument in the hands of Yashwant Rao Holkar.[86] The supreme council believed that the rumour was a fabrication of Holkar, who thereby hoped to break the alliance between Shinde and the Company; the council reminded Seton that similar reports had proliferated the year before with no result, and repeated that rumours like this 'will continue to be propagated through the Channel of the daily Newspapers, in proportion to the consequence which is ascribed to them.'[87] By taking rumours seriously, Residents risked playing into the hands of their rivals. Leading Company diplomatist John Malcolm advised prospective members of the political line that given the unsettled condition of central India, 'intrigues, treasonable conversations and papers, and immature plots, must for some time be matters of frequent occurrence and growth, but such will in general be best left to perish of neglect.'[88]

Sometimes Residents were unwilling to deny even patently false information for fear of giving credence to it; because of the mutual distrust that so often existed at court, vigorously attempting to quell a rumour could be interpreted as confirmation of its truth. An incident at Hyderabad illustrates this principle at work. In the year 1808, Thomas Sydenham decided to host an entertainment for Sikander Jah as a gesture of good will, an invitation that the nizam refused despite having previously shown signs of eagerly anticipating the party. Eventually Sydenham traced the nizam's uneasiness to a rumour that the Company intended to depose him and place his brother on the musnud. The most straightforward solution would seem to be for Sydenham to confront the gossip head-on, but Sydenham was reluctant to address the problem so candidly, afraid of exciting nizam's suspicions.[89] 'If I had urged the Nizam to perform his promise his suspicions would have increased with the Earnestness of my manner. On the other Hand if I permitted the Nizam to decline my Invitation, I should have encouraged the belief of the Truth of the Report.'[90] Sydenham ultimately resorted to rumour himself. In his replies

---

[86] BL, APAC, IOR/F/4/216/4753, N. B. Edmonstone to Archibald Seton, 26 February 1807, pp. 7–8. Mountstuart Elphinstone was similarly warned against taking 'idle rumours' about Holkar too seriously. N. B. Edmonstone to Mountstuart Elphinstone, 22 December 1804, in *NRR*, I, p. 164.

[87] BL, APAC, IOR/F/4/216/4753, N. B. Edmonstone to Archibald Seton, 26 February 1807, pp. 7–8.

[88] John Malcolm, 'Notes of instruction', in John Briggs, *Letters Addressed to a Young Person in India* (London, 1828), pp. 208–209.

[89] BL, APAC, IOR/F/4/926/6833, Thomas Sydenham to Earl of Minto, 28 August 1808, p. 33.

[90] Ibid.

to 'Indirect Enquiries', Sydenham 'treated the Nizam's Fears with ridicule and expressed my compassion only that his Highness should seriously entertain such unmanly and absurd suspicions'.[91] By addressing a rumour directly Residents risked exacerbating the suspicions that had given rise to it in the first place; when the rumour was unlikely to have implications beyond the court, it was usually best for Residents to wait for it to die out of its own accord.

In an effort not to betray their mutual suspicions, then, both Britons and Indians often engaged in oblique and circuitous tactics, thereby fuelling the atmosphere of suspicion at court. How this sometimes-tortuous negotiation might have worked is illustrated by the complaints of Richard Jenkins, Resident at Nagpur. Jenkins described with contempt Raghuji's policy of 'using every endeavor to procure the most particular intelligence respecting our designs and the movement of our troops', noting that 'on one occasion his alarm was excited by a report from a person sent to Hyderabad to purchase Elephants' as well as by agents 'of still more despicable description'.[92] Having received a report warning him of the Company's plans to go war against the Marathas, Raghuji forwarded the information to Jenkins without comment. Unsure how to interpret his motive in so doing, Jenkins treated the rumour with condescension, remarking that the Company's goodwill towards the raja 'was too well established to render it necessary for me to give importance to such insignificant rumours by making any further remark'.[93] When another report about an impending Company attack was transmitted to the Resident via messenger, however, Jenkins dispatched his munshi to Raghuji to assure him 'that there was no ground for the report which I should not have noticed had I not thought it would appear disrespectful to disregard a communication directly from His Highness through whatever channel conveyed'.[94] To this Raghuji simply replied 'that he had mentioned the subject merely to shew that he did not wish to have any concealments, and that he relied perfectly on the friendship of the British Government'.[95]

When rumours were true, however, Residents were sometimes forced to acknowledge them more unequivocally, even when they might have preferred not to, to maintain a show of good faith. William Palmer avoided informing the Pune court of his recall in 1800, worried that it would

[91] Ibid., p. 36.
[92] BL, APAC, IOR/H/600, Richard Jenkins to Marquess of Hastings, 16 April 1815, pp. 717, 720.
[93] Ibid., p. 720.
[94] Ibid., pp. 721–722.
[95] Ibid., pp. 722–723.

undermine the authority remaining to him until the arrival of his successor. Not wanting to disrupt the business then underway, Palmer remained silent. Eventually, however, 'the Event being known to many of the principal Inhabitants of this Town by intelligence from various Quarters I judged it necessary to obviate the suspicions which the Peshwa might entertain of motives unfavourable to him if an appearance of Concealment should be countenanced.'[96] While in some cases it served the Resident's interests to keep information from the ruler and his ministers, he did so at the risk of damaging the Company's credit at court; generally that risk was too great to hazard, however embarrassing the information in question might be. For credit, as diplomat Abraham de Wicquefort observed, was the political representative's most valuable commodity, 'the Foundation of all the Commerce that passes among Men, of what Nature soever it may be.'[97]

Moreover, although Residents generally preferred not to acknowledge rumours relating to factional politics, opting to rise above 'the Intrigues and Squabbles of the Court', this is not to say that these rumours were practically insignificant.[98] Whispers issuing from hostile quarters could corrode the Resident's political agenda over time, attenuating his connections to key players and his ability to mobilize them in pursuit of Company objectives. For instance, in 1822, Charles Metcalfe discovered that a party hostile to him, as part of a general attempt to undermine his proceedings at Hyderabad, had succeeded in persuading the minister Chandu Lal that Metcalfe planned to remove him from office. Because of this information, which Chandu Lal described vaguely as originating in 'the neighbourhood of the Residency', the minister ceased confiding in Metcalfe and instead tried to correspond directly with the governor general without Metcalfe's knowledge. Chandu Lal later justified his actions by reasoning 'that he had been extremely alarmed by reports of Intrigues at the Court for his overthrow', an alarm compounded by Metcalfe's 'reserve and distrust towards him'. Metcalfe had been aware of these rumours but admitted that he had done nothing to dispel them, not anticipating that Chandu Lal would be swayed by 'such imaginary fears'.[99] Yet in an unstable and changing environment fears are quick to take root and, as the activities of Chandu Lal make plain, fear can be a

---

[96] BL, APAC, IOR/H/576, William Palmer to Marquess Wellesley, 6 September 1800, pp. 324–325.

[97] Abraham de Wicquefort, *The Embassador and His Functions* (London, 1716), p. 333; see also Martens, *Guide diplomatique*, p. 121; Francois de Callières, *The Art of Diplomacy*, ed. Maurice Keens-Soper and Karl W. Schweizer (New York, NY, 1983), p. 152.

[98] Bodl. Oxf., Russell Papers, MSS Eng. lett. d. 151, Henry Russell to Charles Russell, 24 May 1810, p. 84.

[99] BL, APAC, Mss Eur F109/9, C. T. Metcalfe to George Swinton, 3 September 1822.

potent spur to action, prompting individuals to take decisive measures in their own defence. The scholarship on rumour has illustrated time and again that rumour, fear, and collective tension are mutually reinforcing; where alarm and apprehension are acute, rumours can trigger dramatic reactions.[100]

The performative power of rumours is perhaps most forcefully illustrated by a violent confrontation between British soldiers and local inhabitants of Pune in 1809. Soldiers on leave were assaulted outside a garden on the outskirts of the city because of rumours that British construction workers, charged with building the peshwa a palace in the English style, were seizing, murdering, and burying local women and children under the palace's foundations. Hamilton, the Acting Resident, conceded that he had been aware of the rumour, but had decided not to communicate it to government: 'I thought the most likely way to bring it into discredit, as far as my influence went, was to treat it with contempt or ridicule.' In the wake of the confrontation, however, the Resident demanded that the ministers 'supress reports so injurious to the English name (although in themselves so incredibly absurd) and find out and punish the authors of them.' Hamilton expressed, moreover, 'the conviction that they [the rumours] were fabricated and circulated by enemies of the two Governments for the express purpose of disturbing the existing harmony.'[101] Subsequently, the English soldiers' movements were restricted to the cantonment for fear of further attacks.[102]

Events at Pune, if Hamilton's interpretation is to be believed, suggest the danger of allowing rumours to circulate unobstructed; they imply that Residents had to suppress narratives contrary to the Company's interests, and present counter-narratives favourable to its image.[103] In the aftermath of the incident, Hamilton's successor as Acting Resident, Henry Russell, did precisely that. Aware that it was rumoured in the city that the peshwa intended to blow the perpetrators from a cannon, Russell interceded, asking that their sentence be commuted to

---

[100] Rumours are generally said to flourish in conditions of disaster, social unrest, and war. See Shibutani, *Improvised News*, p. 32 and p. 46; Ralph L. Rosnow and Gary Alan Fine, *Rumor and Gossip: The Social Psychology of Hearsay* (New York, NY, 1976), p. 62. For historical illustrations of this phenomenon, see Georges Lefebvre, *The Great Fear of 1789: Rural Panic in Revolutionary France,* trans. Joan White (Princeton, NJ, 1983), pp. 210–211 or Arlette Farge and Jacques Revel, *The Vanishing Children of Paris: Rumor and Politics before the French Revolution,* trans. Claudia Miéville (Cambridge, MA, 1991), p. 10.

[101] William Hamilton to Barry Close, 30 October 1809, in *PRC,* VII, pp. 421–422.

[102] Henry Russell to Lt. Col. Lawrence, 18 November 1809, in *PRC,* VII, p. 433.

[103] A further example of the performative power of rumours is the dismissal of the peshwa's agent at the Residency, Gopal Rao, who was rumoured to be collaborating with Holkar to depose the peshwa. Barry Close to Marquess Wellesley, 3 July 1802, in *PRC,* X, p. 15.

imprisonment and hard labour. Russell reported with satisfaction that 'The whole of this conversation was heard, and would, of course, be repeated by all the persons who were present when it occurred. I took care to disseminate the purport and result of it through all those channels by which they would be likely to gain the most extensive circulation and publicity.' As a result, Russell believed, 'the rigorous severity of the Paishwa's own decision and the merciful interposition of the British Government to mitigate and restrain it, are universally known throughout Poona.'[104] Not long after, when a labourer died after being knocked down by a British officer on horseback in 1810, allegedly by accident, Russell immediately issued statements 'to prevent unpleasant reports from getting abroad'.[105] Russell knew the kind of scrutiny the Residency and its associated forces were under, and the importance of overpowering alternate interpretations with his own narrative of events.

According to this logic, Residents were quick to make public announcements following violent incidents of any kind, hoping to repress rumours that might incite the population to protest. While political gossip or rumours relating to military movements were treated with caution since attending to them could entail broader shifts in government policy and military strategy, anything that might ignite popular fears or resentments was promptly counteracted with a public statement. Following a violent confrontation at Delhi between Muslims and Hindus in 1807, Archibald Seton wrote dispatches to the other Residencies informing them of his version of events, explaining his letter as an attempt to stem 'the exaggeration and misrepresentation which generally attend the diffusion of intelligence regarding any incidental disturbance within the limits of the Company's dominions.'[106] It was for this reason too that following the mutiny at Vellore in 1807 the governor general issued immediate reports to the Residents, assuring them 'that the disturbance has been merely local and that is ceased with the recapture of the fort and the destruction of the insurgents', urging them to 'counteract any reports which may prevail inconsistent with the real facts'; apparently, the uprising in Travancore in 1809 was inspired, at least in part, by precisely such incendiary rumours about Vellore.[107] As Ranajit Guha has observed, rumour

---

[104] Henry Russell to Minto, in *PRC*, X, pp. 449–450.

[105] Henry Russell to N. B. Edmonstone, 11 August 1810, in *PRC*, VII, pp. 483–484.

[106] NAI, HRR, box 2, vol. 34, letter forwarded by N. B. Edmonstone to Thomas Sydenham, 21 May 1807, pp. 237–238.

[107] Quote from N. B. Edmonstone to Mountstuart Elphinstone, 27 July 1806, in *NRR*, I, p. 6; For events in Travancore, see BL, APAC, IOR/E/4/904, Court of Directors to Governor-in-Council Fort St. George, 29 September 1809, pp. 346–347.

often played a significant role in mobilizing popular resistance to the Company by feeding into widespread hopes and fears.[108] British officials were keenly aware of this pattern. As Charles Metcalfe phrased it, 'the Intelligence of disaster spreads like wildfire, and immediately excites the hopes and speculations of the Millions whom we hold in subjugation.'[109] Residents recognized that rumoured attacks on Company rule elsewhere in the subcontinent, whether in the form of urban riots or organized military campaigns, could undermine impressions of British inviolability. Rumour's subversive potential became especially evident following the Company's early reverses in the Gurkha War, when Residents detected a notable increase in the circulation of illicit correspondence and dangerous rumours relating to the formation of an anti-British confederacy.

Much of the Residents' time and effort was thus expended in combatting unfavourable rumours, particularly when the Company was at war; victories had to be publicized for the Company's appearance of military might to be sustained. At Nagpur, Elphinstone worried that reports of Yashwant Rao Holkar's successes against the Company in 1805 would lead the raja to abandon his stated neutrality and throw his support behind Holkar; Elphinstone blamed this tenuous state of affairs on Raghuji's vakils, who had been endowed with military offices in Holkar's army and were consequently inclined to exaggerate his successes and fabricate stories of Company defeats.[110] The following year Thomas Sydenham, Acting Resident at Pune, was similarly engaged in attempting to identify the sources of reports 'injurious to the British Government'. Again, the enemies of the British government were accused of promulgating 'the most absurd and extravagant reports of the strength, resources, success and intentions of Holkar and his adherents'.[111] The Company, then, had not only to defeat enemy forces in the battlefield, but ensure that accurate representations of these victories were communicated to rival courts. The Company sought to conjure up an aura of martial supremacy that would preclude regional powers, through intimidation, from attempting to unseat them.

News of the Company's successes could thus act as a convincing disincentive for resistance; the connections between courts could sometimes work in the Company's favour. Following his successful repression of unrest at Hyderabad in 1815, Henry Russell observed with pleasure that

[108] Ranajit Guha, *Elementary Aspects of Peasant Insurgency in Colonial India* (Delhi, 1983), p. 256.
[109] BL, APAC, Mss Eur F140/93, C. T. Metcalfe, 'Notes on Burman War'.
[110] BL, APAC, Mss Eur F109/89, Mountstuart Elphinstone to John Adam, 20 March 1805.
[111] Thomas Sydenham to Marquess Wellesley, 15 June 1805, in *PRC*, VII, p. 253.

news of the nizam's surrender of his two rebellious sons had encouraged the peshwa to submit to the Resident's demands to place his own minister into Company custody. Russell also quoted letters from Richard Jenkins at Nagpur that suggested that there too events at Pune and Hyderabad were taken as a warning against pushing the Company too far.[112] As Ann Stoler has observed with respect to gossip circulating in colonial Indonesia, 'rumor was a highly ambiguous discursive field: it controlled some people, terrorized others; it was damning and enabling, shoring up colonial rule and subverting it at the same time.'[113] Rumour could perpetuate an atmosphere of fear, persuading Indian rulers to accede to Residents' demands.

It was this slippery, polyvalent quality of rumour that Residents had to try to control. Rumour was a pervasive feature of Indian courtly society, flourishing, it would seem, in the atmosphere of suspicion produced by the Company's policy of subordinate isolation. Residents often mistrusted these rumours, and not without reason; rival factions used them to destabilize and mislead the Company, and by reacting too forcefully Residents risked playing into their rivals' hands. Still, rumours had to be considered carefully; while courtly gossip was often best ignored, some rumours carried incendiary implications and could produce destructive consequences, be they street brawls or rebellions. In these instances, the Residents were responsible for promoting their own representations of events. Publicizing the Company's victories in this way was a powerful intimidation tactic, a way of making the flow of information within and between courts work for the Company. To do all this effectively, however, Residents were reliant on the proper functioning of the Company's networks, upon which their legitimacy as a Company representative equally depended. Yet, Residents were often frustrated to discover that it was within the Company itself where information tended to fall through the cracks, and where doubt and distrust were generated.

2.4   Silences and Misrepresentations in the Official Archive

To the extent that divisions within the Company have been considered, it has usually been in terms of an 'agency problem', whereby the Court of Directors in London, and governor-general-in-council in Calcutta,

---

[112] Bodl. Oxf., Russell Papers, MS. Eng. lett. c. 151, Henry Russell to his father, 22 October 1815, p. 146.

[113] Ann Laura Stoler, 'In Cold Blood: Hierarchies of Credibility and the Politics of Colonial Narratives', *Representations* 37 (1992): 151–189.

struggled to devise ever more elaborate procedures for monitoring their distant employees.[114] Yet, as Bhavani Raman has observed, documentary practices that were supposed to make visible the exercise of colonial power, rendering it amenable to the oversight of the central administration, in fact enabled precisely the kinds of corruption they were meant to prevent: 'far from fixing, codifying, and stabilising or reconciling the contradictions of rule, acts of filing, listing, and registering generate domains for all manner of transactions at the margins of the documentary state.'[115] Given the political significance of their work, Residents were under more pressure than most to keep Calcutta apprised of their activities, even keeping daily journals that they were expected to transmit to the governor general at set intervals.[116] Still, these reams of paper did not entirely efface doubts about the reliability of the Residents' representations, nor did they succeed in creating relationships of trust between Residents and their superiors.

It is hard to know how far Residents lied or misrepresented their activities at court. To ascertain the extent of their malfeasance we are reliant on the willingness of witnesses to speak out against them. This kind of evidence is scant. For one thing, the Resident's household was often comprised of friends and kin, some of whom depended on the Resident for his patronage. Even where this was not the case, the risks of antagonizing the Resident largely outweighed the rewards, because Residents fought very hard to foreclose lines of communication between the court and the rest of the Company. Their motives for doing so were not necessarily those of concealment. Residents also stood to gain professionally by consolidating their role as mediator, and the influence and authority attendant on that position. As E. Nathalie Rothman has pointed out, though we often take the 'in-betweenness' of cultural brokers for granted, intermediaries have a vested interest in constructing cultural boundaries and strategically fashioning themselves as in-between.[117]

To justify their prerogatives as the sole channel of communication between court and Company, Residents emphasized the disruptive effects of unregulated intercourse between Indian rulers and other Europeans, particularly those outside the political line. These unofficial relationships, it was argued, might upset the Resident's finely calibrated diplomatic strategies, potentially undermining his authority at court. Colin Macaulay, the Resident at Travancore, successfully

---

[114] Bowen, *Business,* p. 151.
[115] Raman, *Document Raj,* p. 3.
[116] Fisher, *Indirect Rule,* p. 172.
[117] Rothman, *Brokering Empire,* pp. 14, 184.

applied to the Madras government to order the Commercial Resident at Anchuthengu William Augustus Handley to refrain from corresponding with the raja or diwan of Travancore, convincing the Madras government of 'the serious injury which might arise from the appearance of a divided authority in the administration of the British Interests in that part of India'.[118] Richard Strachey similarly disallowed the exchange of letters and gifts between the nawab vizier of Awadh and a certain Dr Pears, a former acquaintance of the Nawab stationed at Chitra, even though it consisted merely of minor pleasantries and the exchange of gifts.[119]

Dr Pears was a relatively marginal figure, but Residents were empowered to deny the very highest echelons of the Company the privilege of communicating with Indian sovereigns. Even the governor general was prohibited from engaging in such a private correspondence.[120] When Mary Elizabeth Frederica Stewart-Mackenzie, Lady Hood (a visitor to Lucknow) innocently forwarded a letter to the governor general directly from the nawab, the Marquess of Hastings, as he later described it 'remonstrated with Lady Hood by Letter for having forwarded even such a paper in breach of the Regulation which requires all communications from Foreign Princes to go thro' the Resident at the respective Courts.' Hastings then informed Resident John Baillie of the circumstance, 'that he might be confident no indirect correspondence would ever be allowed by me'.[121]

The limited relationship between the court and the governor general meant that Residents had the advantage when it came to courting the governor general's support over and against the appeals of the courtly elite. The exceptions prove the rule. For example, Hastings did eventually dismiss John Baillie from his post, acceding to Nawab Vizier Ghazi ud-Din Haidar's demands, but only after several years and a series of written and oral complaints from both the nawab and his predecessor Saadat Ali. Hastings, in retrospect, discovered that Baillie's association with the Company had made the nawab and his ministers loath to cross him, meaning that Baillie 'had no terms to keep with His Excellency beyond the screening himself from having direct indecorum proved against him'.[122] The nawab's resentments were therefore suppressed

[118] BL, APAC, IOR/F/4/244/5536, Government at Fort St. George to N. B. Edmonstone, 9 September 1807, p. 62.
[119] BL, APAC, Mss Eur D585, Enclosure, Richard Strachey to John Adam, 26 June 1817, p. 196.
[120] BL, APAC, IOR/F/4/510/12267, p. 47.
[121] Ibid.
[122] Ibid., p. 113.

and, concealed beneath a thin veneer of civility, allowed to fester.[123] Relations with the Resident soured to such an extent that Ghazi ud-Din declared himself willing to take desperate measures and to ally himself with any power able to take the field against the Company.[124] Although Baillie paid the price in the end, the fact that relations with the nawab were allowed to degenerate to such a point demonstrates the extent to which the Company was unable or perhaps even on occasion unwilling to monitor the Residents closely.

The epistolary exchanges between the Earl of Minto and Nawab Vizier Saadat Ali during the earlier part of the crisis make this lack of oversight amply evident. When in 1808 Saadat Ali requested a private interview with the then governor general, Minto not only refused to make a personal visit, but reprimanded the nawab for withholding his entire confidence from the Resident, reminding the nawab that nothing could be achieved outside of the designated channels. Baillie placed his own behaviour beyond suspicion, asserting in his letters that he would have been uneasy about Saadat Ali's protests 'if a minute & attentive introspect of my own proceedings at the Durbar, & of every recent discussion between his Excellency and me had not entirely precluded the possibility of my connecting the avowed distress of his mind with any part of my proceedings'.[125] In 1813, when the nawab vizier wrote to Minto again, explicitly complaining this time about the Resident's insulting tone and accusing the Resident of falsifying the nawab's words in letters to the governor general, Minto remained dismissive. Responding to the nawab's description of a particular instance of Baillie's allegedly threatening conduct, Minto referred to 'the clear and satisfactory statement' which Baillie gave in writing of that meeting, as well as the 'acknowledged integrity and veracity of that officer', on the basis of which Minto remained convinced that 'your Excellency must have entirely misapprehended the tenor, spirit and manner of his discourses to your Excellency on that occasion'.[126] Ironically, Minto concluded his letter to Saadat Ali by reprimanding him for the tone that *he,* the nawab vizier, adopted in his letters to the Resident.

Similarly, after the 1809 revolt in Travancore, the Board of Control in London were shocked to find that they had not been apprised of letters of complaint written by the raja and minister of Travancore to the governor general, and criticized the Indian government's apparent

---

[123] Ibid., pp. 113–114.
[124] Ibid., p. 116.
[125] BL, APAC, IOR/F/4/251/5632, John Baillie to N. B. Edmonstone, 14 March 1808, p. 5
[126] NLS, Minto Papers, MS 11594, Earl of Minto to Nawab Vizier of Awadh, 5 March 1813, p. 23

disregard for the appeals contained therein.[127] The raja himself provided an account, in a letter to government, of the isolation inflicted on him by the Resident during this period. Because of Company conventions, the raja was forced to entrust his letters of complaint about Lieutenant Colonel Colin Macaulay, into the hands of Macaulay himself, who delivered these letters in person to the governor general in Bengal. When Macaulay returned with letters from Wellesley, the raja was, in his own words, 'utterly astonished', remarking that 'the Colonel had impressed His Excellency's [the governor general's] mind with a belief of what I had never represented'.[128] The raja then attempted to communicate with Wellesley directly by letter, only to be reprimanded for not transmitting his epistle through the channel of the Resident. Later, when (according to the raja's account) the Resident attempted to impose a new treaty upon him by force, the raja felt that he had no option but to concede defeat, 'apprehending that if I wrote a letter to the supreme Government for the purpose of exposing my innocence I could only transmit it through the channel of Lieutenant Colonel Macaulay.'[129] Macaulay's control over the situation was, it seemed, complete.

In the end, however, Macaulay's dissimulation proved to be his undoing. He exemplifies how evasiveness and misrepresentation on the part of the Resident could lead government to doubt the truth of his reports, even where his information was accurate. Despite their earlier disregard for complaints issuing from Travancore, the government appear to have entertained a growing suspicion that Macaulay was not to be trusted in his representation of that court. This budding doubt prevented them from furnishing Macaulay with military support when the uprising at Travancore did erupt. According to the Board of Control's enquiry, government countermanded orders to march troops to the frontiers of Travancore and recalled Macaulay from the Residency. To justify this, they stated merely that they had 'received information of a private nature from different quarters which certainly impressed [them] with a belief that the rumours respecting the preparations in Travancore had been exaggerated.' Their apprehensions were founded on the 'well known' fact that the Resident was on bad terms with the minister. Meanwhile, the minister had continued to send letters to government evincing 'the strongest professions of his earnest desire and endeavour to preserve undisturbed

[127] BL, APAC, IOR/E/4/904, Board of Control to Fort St. George, 29 September 1809, pp. 284–288.
[128] NLS, Minto Papers, MS 11571, Raja of Travancore to Earl of Minto, 16 August 1807, p. 62.
[129] Ibid., p. 63.

the subsisting relations between the two Countries' (starkly contradict-
ing the Resident's descriptions of the minister's preparations for war).[130]
In this instance, distrust of the Resident had built to such a pitch that
private information from unnamed sources, corroborated by protestations from the rebellious minister, meant that Macaulay was forced
to flee when the minister led an attack on his home on the night of
27 December. By misrepresenting goings-on in Travancore, Macaulay
endangered his credit with the Company, which in turn meant that he
could not rely on their support when his very life was in danger.

Macaulay's story reminds us that while Company officials might benefit
from strategies of concealment, there were also advantages to being honest. Transparency generated trust, ensuring that the Resident could rely
on Company support when necessary. Openness with one's superiors
about an intended line of action was an important way of limiting personal liability if diplomatic relations took a turn for the worse; it meant
that the Resident could later justify his actions by pointing out that the
logic of his decision had been corroborated by senior officials. This was a
general rule of diplomatic conduct; as de Wicquefort advised his readers,
'the Minister who undertakes an Affair for which he has no Orders, is
responsible for the Success thereof; whereas he who only executes the
Orders that are given him, how unjust or unreasonable soever they may
be, charges his Master therewith.'[131] Thus, while there are notorious
instances of Residents painting an inaccurate portrait of developments at
court, they also stood to gain from presenting detailed narratives in the
interests of risk management.

At court, too, the Residents' success depended on facilitating lines of
communication with Calcutta. To be effective, Residents had to present
a convincing image of Company support. Residents regularly commissioned letters from the governor general, whether of congratulation or
remonstrance, that were presented or read aloud for strategic effect in
open court.[132] The Indian political elite were attuned to the Resident's
position within a larger hierarchy, which meant that he occasionally had
to invoke written support from his superiors to lend force to his assertions. Richard Jenkins apparently had such a difficult time convincing

---

[130] BL, APAC, IOR/E/4/904, Board of Control to Fort St. George, 29 September 1809,
pp. 284–288.
[131] Wicquefort, *The Embassador and His Functions*, p. 326.
[132] BL, APAC, Mss Eur F176/28, John Collins to Acting Governor General George
Barlow, 25 December 1805; BL, APAC, Mss Eur D585, Richard Strachey to John
Adam, 12 June 1813, p. 82; BL, APAC, IOR/H/599, Richard Jenkins to the Marquess
of Hastings, 14 December 1814, p. 474.

Raghuji Bhonsle of the Company's friendly intentions (despite the alliance then being negotiated with rival Bhopal) that he finally presented a letter to the raja in the governor general's own handwriting, 'which it is to be hoped will prevent the insinuations of interested persons from leading the Rajah into an Error respecting the designs of the British Government.'[133] Letters like these were handled with great ceremony, in the same way that the governor general's visit would have been carefully choreographed were he present in the flesh.

In addition to their symbolic power and persuasive force, letters bearing the governor general's signature were important markers of legitimacy for the Resident. The credentials that the Resident carried with him on his arrival at court were critical to his acceptance and recognition as an officially sanctioned representative of the Company.[134] The absence of written expressions of support from Calcutta could severely undermine his authority. For this reason, it was traditional for the governor general to conclude every letter to an allied ruler with a reference to the Resident, indicating that he deposited his entire confidence in the Resident, and that all opinions expressed by the Resident should be regarded as tantamount to those of the governor general himself.[135] The significance of this seemingly trivial convention is illustrated by an incident at Nagpur when Cornwallis arrived in India to replace Wellesley as governor general in 1805. Rumours had been circulating that Cornwallis planned to remove Mountstuart Elphinstone from his post at Nagpur, and Elphinstone was worried that these suspicions would only be substantiated by a letter written by Cornwallis to the raja of Nagpur in which Elphinstone was not referenced as usual. Elphinstone begged his friend and cousin John Adam, secretary to the governor general, to transmit new credentials in the governor general's name, declaring that he could 'take no step whatever without orders & consequently shall avoid the risk of being disavowed'. As a result, Elphinstone opined, 'every thing is going to ruin in consequence of the ideas occasioned by our remaining inactive (while every body else is bustling) & taking no notice of any thing that is done or doing against us.'[136] Residents could be influential figures at court, but only insofar as they were recognized to have the Company at their back;

---

[133] BL, APAC, IOR/H/599, Richard Jenkins to the Marquess of Hastings, 11 December 1814, p. 464.

[134] Letters of credence were also critical in European diplomacy. See Wicquefort, *The Embassador and His Functions*, p. 109; Martens, *Guide diplomatique*, p. 48.

[135] See for example NLS, Minto Papers, MS 11594, Earl of Minto to Daulat Rao Shinde, 4 June 1813, p. 88; Minto to Nawab Vizier of Awadh, 2 July 1813, p. 102.

[136] BL, APAC, Mss Eur F109/89, Mountstuart Elphinstone to John Adam, 27 August 1805.

the Resident's personal authority thus depended on his ability to sustain the flow of letters from the Company's administrative centres.

More often, then, it was Calcutta, and not the Resident, that failed to live up to expectations. Partly the communication gap was a product of geographical distance (with dispatches taking weeks to make their way to Calcutta). The bigger problem, however, seems to have been an overload of business that the central government struggled to keep under control, particularly in the early years of the nineteenth century. The governor-general-in-council was notorious for leaving Residents in the lurch, sometimes failing to respond to important missives for months at a time. James Achilles Kirkpatrick had to wait impatiently not just for an acknowledgment of the treaty he had signed with the nizam in 1799, but for any news or information at all from 'any one in the Calcutta Quarter'. Kirkpatrick's only consolation was that he was not alone in his state of neglect, noting 'the account Mr. Strachey gives of the extreme delay experienced in every public Department of late', further remarking that 'Scott the Lucknow Resident complains he says, that he has been half a year together without a Reply to references of the greatest importance!!'[137]

Where official communications were lacking, private contacts could become important. To revert to the previous example, Kirkpatrick was writing informally to his brother William, who was a member of Wellesley's council and could offer an insider's insight into the governor general's mood; this family connection was an important one for Kirkpatrick at a time when official contact was intermittent. Residents frequently mobilized personal correspondence networks in this way. In the late eighteenth and early nineteenth century, 'private' and 'public' were contested categories whose boundaries were shifting and pliable. Given the pervasiveness of patronage, ties of personal and occupational affiliation tended to overlap; appointments to the Company depended on nomination from the Court of Directors, meaning that most employees were connected in one way or another through ties of blood or friendship. The concept of 'friendship' itself (a generic term that encompassed people connected through kinship, sentiment, occupation, politics, and all manner of other attachments) was defined largely by reciprocal services.[138] This imbrication of public and private, personal and professional, was reflected in contemporary epistolary practice, through which

---

[137] BL, APAC, Mss Eur F228/13, J. A. Kirkpatrick to William Kirkpatrick, 25 August 1801, p. 135.

[138] On friendship and patronage, see Harold Perkin, *The Origins of Modern English Society 1780–1880* (London, 1969), pp. 44–50. See also Naomi Tadmor, *Family and Friends in Eighteenth-Century England: Household, Kinship, and Patronage* (Cambridge, 2001), pp. 167, 212–213.

enterprising individuals mobilized correspondents to help advance their careers.[139] Historians have argued that eighteenth-century letters cannot be neatly categorized as 'private' or 'public' at all; Clare Brant has suggested abandoning the concept of 'private' missives altogether, arguing that the term 'is simply inaccurate for many eighteenth-century familiar letters, which were composed in company, voluntarily circulated beyond the addressee, and frequently found their way into print.'[140] Yet, few studies of letters actually explore public/private as categories of practice as well as analysis, or examine the consequences of that distinction on a practical level.[141] For the Residents, the existence of two overlapping epistolary traditions, a public and a private, posed definite possibilities (and perils).

Rather than constituting two distinct categories, 'public' and 'private' (at least as they applied to the Residents' letter-writing practices) are perhaps most usefully envisioned as existing on either end of a spectrum. On one extreme were official dispatches, usually transcribed neatly on large sheets of paper using formal language. On the other extreme were personal epistles, scrawled messily on scraps of paper, written in intimate tones relating matters of interest only to the author and a small circle of friends and kin; in the language of the day these were usually termed 'familiar letters'.[142]

Given the Residents' remote situation, familiar letters carried profound emotional significance. Reacting to his appointment at Nagpur, Elphinstone admitted to his close friend Edward Strachey (then Assistant Resident at Pune) that 'I dread being stationed long at a place where I shall be so solitary', begging Strachey to 'write me often and long in prose and verse, and have compassion on me now that I am *door ooftadeh* [outcast].' As a counterpoint to the dry official correspondence piling up on his desk, Elphinstone requested 'long, frequent, open, wild, sentimental letters, with occasional peeps down the very abyss of your heart'.[143] In the longer term, letters like these furnished Elphinstone with an avenue

---

[139] For examples from different professions, see Alison Duncan, 'The Sword and the Pen: The Role of Correspondence in the Advancement Tactics of Eighteenth-Century Military Officers', *Journal of Scottish Historical Studies* 29, no. 2 (2009): 106–122; Ellen Gill, '"Children of the Service": Paternalism, Patronage and Friendship in the Georgian Navy', *Journal for Maritime Research* 15, no. 2 (2013): 149–165.

[140] Clare Brant, *Eighteenth-Century Letters and British Culture* (Houndmills, Basingstoke, 2006), p. 5.

[141] For this distinction see Jeff Weintraub, 'The Theory and Politics of the Public/Private Distinction', in *Public and Private in Thought and Practice: Perspectives on a Grand Dichotomy*, ed. Jeff Weintraub and Krishan Kumar (Chicago, IL, 1997).

[142] Tavor Bannet, *Empire of Letters*, pp. 43–44.

[143] Colebrooke, *Life of the Honourable Mountstuart Elphinstone*, pp. 103, 122, 143.

to his past life, which, as David Gerber has observed in his study of emigrant letter-writers in North America, was a crucial factor in helping dislocated individuals to sustain a sense of personal history.[144] Elphinstone regularly re-read old letters and journals, which, he explained, allowed him to 'recall not only the occurrences but the opinions & sensations of past times'.[145] Through these exchanges, Residents were able to stake out a personal life separate from their professional lives as Company officials. Accordingly, Residents sometimes consciously avoided writing too extensively about work, even in letters to friends in the political line. 'Enough', Metcalfe concluded after a long paragraph deploring the policies of his predecessor in office, 'this letter begins to smell of the shop.'[146]

Familiar letters could also provide a welcome venue for informal conversation, as well as a cathartic outlet for feelings that might otherwise have remained painfully pent up. James Achilles Kirkpatrick certainly viewed his letters to his brother as an outlet for resentments that could not easily be voiced in the company of his household, who were his inferiors in rank. After being rebuked by his brother for complaining about a colleague, Kirkpatrick protested 'my dear Will if I do not unbosom myself to you, and lay open to you all my weaknesses even, it will be a cruel mortification to me'.[147] Though James conceded that William was perhaps right in admonishing him for his virulence, and even thanked his brother for his counsel, he nevertheless claimed his right to 'unburthen myself so unreservedly'.[148] While it was not unusual for 'private' letters to be shared among family and friends, in cases like these when the author deemed the contents unsuitable for wider consumption (usually because they contained personally or politically sensitive material), letters were labelled 'private', 'secret', or 'most secret', occasionally underlined several times for greater effect. Sometimes these stipulations were made in the text of the letter itself; after going on at length about the defects of a colleague in a letter to Lady Hood, Mountstuart Elphinstone concluded, 'Your Ladyship will perhaps have surmised that this letter is not intended to be read at the breakfast table.'[149]

[144] David A. Gerber, *Authors of Their Lives: The Personal Correspondence of British Immigrants to North America in the Nineteenth Century* (New York, NY, 2006), p. 3.
[145] BL, APAC, Mss Eur F88/359, Journal of Mountstuart Elphinstone, 29 February 1805, p. 93.
[146] Charles Metcalfe to J. W. Sherer, 16 June 1807, in *The Life and Correspondence of Charles, Lord Metcalfe*, ed. John William Kaye, 2 vols (London, 1858), I, p. 155.
[147] BL, APAC, Mss Eur F228/10, J. A. Kirkpatrick to William Kirkpatrick, 11 November 1798, p. 132.
[148] Ibid.
[149] NRS, Seaforth Papers, GD46/17/42, Mountstuart Elphinstone to Lady Hood, 16 May 1813.

Letters like these might be cause for embarrassment if their contents became widely known, but they had little practical relevance for Company business. Where public and private correspondence converged more significantly, it was usually when Residents sought auxiliary channels of information in cases where official sources had dried up. Sometimes it was a particular colleague who proved frustratingly reticent. No single individual appears to have inspired so much ill feeling on this head as Colonel Barry Close. In 1802, tensions ran high as the governor-general-in-council reprimanded James Achilles Kirkpatrick for what was perceived to be a tone of 'dissatisfaction & of mistrust' in his official letter addressed to Close. Though Kirkpatrick apologized profusely, vowing that he was entirely unmotivated by personal resentments, he nevertheless emphasized the risk to public interests arising out of 'the ignorance under which I laboured – not only of the result of Colonel Close's Negociations but of his proceedings and intentions at large'.[150] Close's epistolary habits continued to draw complaints over the following decade. This was a man who Henry Russell deemed 'reserved and mysterious in everything he does, and everything he intends to do', and who Mountstuart Elphinstone characterized as a 'captious & fractious [...] old gentleman' who 'scarce ever answers letters'.[151] The acrimonious tone with which contemporaries described this facet of Close's personality suggests how important regular and accurate communication was in the political line. Individual idiosyncrasies could have broad ramifications given that Residents were reliant on the information contained in dispatches from colleagues at other courts. Consequently, the epistolary foibles of fellow Residents are frequently commented on in official and familiar letters of the period.[152] Historians are left with reams of letters about letters, manifesting the Residents' awareness of the finer points of what Eve Tavor Bannet describes as letteracy: 'the collection of different skills, values, and kinds of knowledge beyond mere literacy that were involved in achieving competency in the writing, reading, and interpreting of letters.'[153]

---

[150] BL, APAC, Mss Eur F228/76, N. B. Edmonstone to James Achilles Kirkpatrick, 22 November 1802, p. 13.

[151] Bodl. Oxf., Russell Papers, MS. Eng. lett. d. 164, Henry Russell to James Casamaijor, 24 March 1810, p. 141; BL, APAC, Mss Eur F109/88, Mountstuart Elphinstone to John Adam, 16 January 1804.

[152] Henry Russell, for instance, contrasted Mountstuart Elphinstone's 'manly modest Dispatches' with 'the vaunting mawkish stuff of [Richard] Jenkins.' Bodl. Oxf., Russell Papers, MS. Eng. lett. c. 151, Henry Russell to his father, 6 March 1818, p. 216.

[153] Tavor Bannet, Empire of Letters, p. xvii.

Barry Close, though in other respects a bad correspondent (if his contemporaries are to be believed), also furnishes us with an example of how a Resident might use the private epistolary form to sidestep an indiscretion. From the first sentence of his letter of 29 April 1802, Close signals the unconventionality of his epistolary choice, writing that 'the sequel of this address will explain to your Lordship [Wellesley] the motives which induce me to give it a private form.'[154] The letter describes a meeting with the peshwa, which Baji Rao himself had proposed on the condition that Close keep their conference a secret. Although Close clearly perceived the value of a private conversation with the peshwa unattended by his ministers or constrained by the formalities of open durbar, it was nevertheless obvious that he would be in serious breach of his orders if he met with the ruler without reporting it. Accordingly, Close suggested a compromise: 'I should adopt a private mode of address that would induce your Lordship to allow the subject to continue secret till disclosing it should become a matter of indifference, and that his Highness might rely that beyond your Lordship I should observe the most profound secrecy.'[155] To this the peshwa acquiesced. By resorting to a private letter, Close could make a show of confidentiality and good faith to the peshwa, without betraying his responsibility to the governor general. Private letters could thus provide a useful middle ground for the Resident, although in this case Close had nothing much to report other than that the peshwa was trying to set their relationship on a more intimate footing.[156]

Though personal and public correspondence could complement one another in this way, the intersection of the two did produce problems. Sometimes networks of information fragmented; crucial facts were channelled through private letters rather than public correspondence, becoming inaccessible to the central government who would otherwise have received copies of the letters being exchanged. Thomas Sydenham lost his position at the Hyderabad Residency because he failed to apprise government of his correspondence with a captain implicated in the 1809 mutiny in the Madras Army; although Captain Doveton had consulted Sydenham as a friend, the governor-general-in-council argued that it was Sydenham's duty to report the exchange, and charged him with having acted 'with a deliberate purpose to conceal from the knowledge

[154] Barry Close to Marquess Wellesley, 29 April 1802, in *PRR*, X, p. 7.
[155] Ibid., p. 8.
[156] Ibid.

of Government all the circumstances of that transaction'.[157] At the same time, the disclosure of personal correspondence in this fashion was not universally regarded as appropriate, even under such dramatic circumstances. When Henry Russell learned the details of Doveton's trial, where Sydenham's private letter was made public, he wrote to his brother Charles that 'if he [Sydenham] authorized Doveton to produce it upon the Court Martial, he is a Fool; and if Doveton produced it without that authority, he is a Villain. They may make the Selection between them.'[158] Where personal and professional relationships overlapped, as they so often did in India given that most Britons living there were in one way or another associated with the Company, the lines between public and private blurred and complications ensued.

Given the difficulties that could potentially erupt around the imbrication of public interests and private relationships, some Company employees considered the maintenance of a strict distinction between the two as the best defence against future animadversions. This strategy is rendered transparent in the correspondence between brothers, where older siblings advised younger ones about the desirability of disentangling political and personal topics.[159] The Resident Henry Russell was particularly keen to educate his younger brother Charles in the art of letter-writing; his missives reveal much about the epistolary conventions of the day. Henry commented on Charles' style ('where[,] did you imbibe that horrid Expression "Your Letter may hereafter perhaps *come to Hand*"? It smells so strongly of the Haberdasher') and his punctuality, or lack thereof. ('Reciprocity is the Law of Epistolary Communications'.)[160] What Henry emphasized most pointedly was the importance of differentiating between the appropriate contents of private and public correspondence, respectively. In a letter of 12 June 1805, Henry chided Charles for expressing his opinions on the Company's present administration. 'The Difference of our Opinions respecting Lord Cornwallis as a Governor', Henry reminded him, 'is a Difference of a political nature; which it is always impolite, and frequently dangerous,

[157] BL, APAC, IOR/F/4/335/7665, Fort St. George to Board of Control, 24 March 1810, pp. 30–31.
[158] Bodl. Oxf., Russell Papers, MS Eng. lett. d. 151, Henry Russell to Charles Russell, 1 April 1810, p. 38.
[159] William Kirkpatrick also regularly chided his brother James Achilles Kirkpatrick for mixing private and public business in his correspondence. See BL, APAC, Mss Eur F228/11, J. A. Kirkpatrick to William Kirkpatrick, 15 August and 15 October 1799, p. 207 and p. 275.
[160] Bodl. Oxf., Russell Papers, MS Eng. lett. c. 155, Henry Russell to Charles Russell, 12 August 1802, p. 19; Henry Russell to Charles Russell, 9 June 1802, p. 15.

to render the subject of a familiar Letter.'[161] In a communication of 4 June 1810, Russell censured the inclusion of personal details in a letter Charles had composed to the secretary to the governor general, particularly Charles's allusion to then Resident Thomas Sydenham's plans to meet Colonel Barry Close and his brother. In Henry's view, Sydenham's arrangement was 'a private Thing, [with] nothing in it either to require or deserve that it should be reported to the G.G. [Governor-General]'.[162]

In Henry's mind, the safest principle when writing official letters was to be as objective as possible; by avoiding points of dispute or questions of interpretation, it was possible to limit the likelihood of disagreement or reproach. He instructed his brother to 'confine yourself, as much as possible, to statement of Facts and Appearances. Avoid Opinions and Suggestions where you can.'[163] The same logic is evident in Charles Warre Malet's correspondence with the agent at Benares, George Cherry, in the 1790s. Malet set great store by George Cherry's letters, which, he claimed contained 'Landmarks which to a Wanderer like me in the Wide Sea of Politics must Ever be Extremely grateful & useful.'[164] Malet repaid the favour with 'my Country Intelligence which I must continue to recommend to your attentive Perusal as Containing a number of Items & Clues for Consideration which tho highly worthy of Notice are not of a nature to be introduced into my official Correspondence with Government.'[165] In the interests of avoiding reproach and maintaining their personal credit, Residents sometimes limited their official reports to concrete facts. Yet, bare accounts of developments at court were sometimes of little use without an interpretative layer to give them context and meaning. The desire to eliminate the personal or the subjective from official dispatches is an important part of the explanation for why Residents hesitated to comment on intelligence that they were incapable of proving conclusively.

Henry Russell's cautious mode of composition reflects his occasionally uneasy relationship with government; he feared and resented being made a scapegoat when things went wrong. He was outraged when, as Acting Resident at Pune, the governor-general-in-council wrote to him

---

[161] Bodl. Oxf., Russell Papers, MS Eng. lett. c. 155, Henry Russell to Charles Russell, 12 June 1805.
[162] Bodl. Oxf., Russell Papers, MS Eng. lett. d. 151, Henry Russell to Charles Russell, 4 June 1810, p. 99.
[163] Ibid., 13 August 1810, p. 206.
[164] BL, APAC, Mss Eur F149/56, C. W. Malet to G. F. Cherry, 29 June 1793, p. 220.
[165] Ibid., C. W. Malet to G. F. Cherry, 5 July 1793, p. 228.

to disclaim their earlier instructions and advise him not to intervene in conflict between the peshwa and his jagirdars, despite the fact that by that point Russell had already implemented their initial orders. Russell's reaction is worth quoting in full for what it reveals about the awkward position that the Resident was sometimes placed in because of fluctuations higher up in the political line:

> They have used me very unhandsomely; so much so that I never can feel any confidence in them again. Before I set my Foot on the Ground, I will always hereafter make them chalk out the very spot on which I am to place it. They send me a set of Instructions so plain and clear, that I will defy a Child of six years old to mistake their fair meaning; and no sooner have I begun to act upon them, and gone too far to retract with credit, then they send me another set, attempting, with the most frivolous refinement, to explain the Tone of the former ones entirely away, and insinuating pretty plainly, 'if you act upon our Instructions, and are successful, well and good; but if, in consequence of your acting upon them, any Expense or temporary Inconvenience is incurred, the Blame will rest with you.' This is not the way a government ought to act in.[166]

Residents might have been forced to tread lightly at court for fear of playing into their enemy's hands or exacerbating latent suspicions, but their relationship with their superiors in Calcutta was not necessarily trusting, either. After all, as Russell's experience demonstrates, seemingly clear instructions could be disavowed; the written record could be interpreted to mean something else altogether. Words might be inscribed in ink and paper, but that did not fix their meaning in perpetuity. In the political line, instructions had to be implemented with caution, and official reports composed with circumspection.

2.5   Conclusion

To operate effectively, the Company depended upon pen and paper. Residents corresponded with Indian rulers through handwritten notes and memoranda and coordinated their activities with fellow officials through the regular exchange of public and personal letters. This reliance on paper created the potential for misrepresentation, forgery, and fraud. In response, Residents developed sophisticated strategies for authenticating the documents that passed through their hands. Where word of mouth was concerned, however, the problem was less about determining truth or credibility than about predicting motives and possible impact. While Residents were wary of being manipulated, there was a danger in

---

[166] Ibid., Henry Russell to James Casamaijor, 9 February 1811, p. 146.

allowing untruths to gather momentum, particularly when the Indian population had obvious reasons to believe allegations of violence, and to hope that rumours of British defeat were true. To offset the stories percolating through the streets and bazaars of royal capitals, Residents relied on their Company connections, but these networks did not always come through. Via the Resident, we see how suspicion, doubt, and mismanagement proliferated within the Company itself, where essential information was liable to fall through the cracks. Partly the Residents were to blame for creating barriers to free communication, but the problem was not solely of their making. If anything, Residents relied on keeping lines of communication open, and it was the governor-general-in-council who more often than not let them down. Tensions erupted because of distance, an overload of paperwork, neglect, and fragmentation as well as strategies of explicit misrepresentation. C. A. Bayly argued that there was an information crisis within the nineteenth-century Company arising from its inability to fully exploit Indian networks, but overlaying these networks were European relationships that were sometimes equally hard to sustain.

This aspect of the Resident's work brings to light more general themes relating to his place in courtly society as well as his position within the Company's official hierarchy. Contemptuous attitudes to Indian news media reflect the cultural arrogance we might expect of British imperial officials, but the ways that Residents managed the exchange and interception of letters suggests how certain basic similarities between Indian and British political culture facilitated the consolidation of British influence at court. The British and Indian elite had in common a highly sophisticated epistolary culture that valued subtleties of prose and address as well as the materiality of seals, ink, and paper. With the aid of skilled scribes and translators, Residents were well equipped to penetrate, and make sense of, the stream of letters flowing from court to court. At the same time, the Resident's trustworthiness as a reliable conduit of information was, from a Company perspective, ever in doubt. Not only did administrators in London and Calcutta fear that Residents were being taken in by Indian informants with agendas of their own, they also worried that Residents were using private letters to forward information that ought, by rights, to have been accessible to their scrutiny and supervision. Residents, meanwhile, saw the governor general's support as contingent and unreliable, as something that had to be cultivated through carefully worded letters rather than trusted implicitly.

This chapter has focused more on the use of the pen than the sword, but based on the letters and rumours discussed here, it should already be apparent that violence or the threat of violence was an important aspect of the Residency system. Most of the political intelligence that Residents noted in their journals and forwarded in their letters related to the threat of war or local revolt, while much of the gossip circulating in the streets involved alleged incidents of British brutality. The next chapter considers the role of violence in the developing Residency system, both as an ideological justification for Company intervention and as a mode of imperial authority.

3   Warfare and 'Wanton Provocations'

If the classic diplomatic manuals of ancien régime Europe shared one argument in common, it was this: that aspiring diplomats ought, above all things, to be accommodating and adaptable. To borrow François de Callière's Classical allusion, 'he ought to be as Proteus in the fable: always ready to put on all sorts of shapes, according as occasion and necessity may require.'[1] It was with this expectation in mind that the newly appointed Governor General the Marquess of Hastings turned his attention to the political line upon his arrival in India in 1814, and it was according to this standard that Hastings made his assessment: that '[i]nstead of acting in the character of ambassador, he [the Resident] assumes the functions of a dictator'. By this, Hastings meant that the Resident 'interferes in all their [meaning the allies'] private concerns; countenances refractory subjects against them; and makes the most ostentatious exhibition of this exercise of authority'.[2] To the extent that Indian sovereigns were dissatisfied with the alliance system, it was largely, in Hastings's view, owing to such 'wanton provocations'.[3] Henry Thomas Colebrooke, who had served on the supreme council under Minto's administration (and was himself a former Resident at Nagpur), was inclined to agree. When Hastings consulted Colebrooke in 1815, the former Resident declared that the Company's objectives would be more readily attained were the Residents 'duly impressed with the importance attached by Government to a conciliatory conduct'.[4] The Residents' responsibilities closely approximated those of a resident diplomat, but their views and tactics, according to this contemporary portrait, differed markedly.

---

[1] de Callières, *Art of Diplomacy*, p. 88.
[2] Bute, ed., *Private Journal*, pp. 47–48.
[3] Ibid., p. 44.
[4] BL, APAC, Cleveland Public Library Papers, IOR Neg 4226, wq091.92 Ea77p5, Report appended to H. T. Colebrooke to Marquess of Hastings, 15 October 1814, pp. 23–24.

It had not always been this way. Seen through the eyes of Resident William Palmer, the transformation within the political line at the turn of the nineteenth century seems clear. Palmer (1740–1816) had served the Company for over thirty years prior to Richard Wellesley's arrival. Palmer had found Wellesley's predecessor, Sir John Shore, highly congenial to his views, and had approved of Shore's plans in favour of 'mild & gradual Reforms to be effected by friendly advice & influence without any appearance of indeed exercise of degrading interference.'[5] The change in administration, however, wrought an abrupt change in Palmer's fortunes. According to Wellesley, the point at issue was clear; Palmer had botched the negotiations for a subsidiary alliance with the peshwa by opening the subject first with Baji Rao's minister instead of directly with Baji Rao himself, thereby exciting the peshwa's jealousy. Wellesley was convinced that Baji Rao had been on the verge of agreeing to his demands and that 'nothing but mismanagement could have checked the success of my propositions.'[6] Palmer saw the matter differently. Palmer might have railed against Baji Rao privately, but he had always, he insisted, treated Baji Rao publicly with deference and respect. For Palmer, the reasons for his dismissal from Pune were not at all those postulated by Wellesley. 'Perhaps my Disposition is not thought suitable to the management of our concerns, with so perverse & faithless a Court as this', Palmer mused to his former patron, Warren Hastings. 'And if Alliances are to be obtained by Menace & Intimidation instead of Argument persuasion & conciliation it is certain that a fitter person than I am may easily be found.'[7] Taking these observations as a starting point, this chapter explains why a new generation of Residents were inclined to prefer intimidation to accommodation.

To some extent, this shift towards more coercive tactics was part of a wider trend affecting the Company at large. One distinctive feature of the Company in the early nineteenth century was its militarism: its employees' high valuation of, and persistent reliance on, military measures. Writing to *The Times*, a Company officer affirmed that 'the influence we have acquired in India is by arms and can be preserved by victory alone. Public opinion follows our successful standards, but would speedily quit them in the first moment of defeat.'[8] While there were undoubtedly dissenters, Douglas Peers has shown how Anglo-Indian militarism united conservatives, orientalists, and liberal imperialists who, though

---

[5] BL, Add. MS 29173, William Palmer to Warren Hastings, 10 July 1801, p. 63.
[6] Mornington to Dundas, 11 October 1798, in Ingram, ed., *Two Views*, p. 93.
[7] BL, Add MS 29173, William Palmer to Warren Hastings, 10 July 1801, p. 63.
[8] Anonymous, 'To the editor of the Times', 7 January 1817, *Times* (London).

they might have different visions of the kind of empire they aspired to in India, nevertheless agreed that the threat of punitive measures was the only means of securing them.[9]

Shared convictions regarding the importance of military might did not, however, guarantee that contemporaries always agreed on the meanings of violence or its appropriate forms and uses. The wider context of war and resistance seems to have predisposed the Residents to the use of brute tactics in pursuit of their political agendas, but this was, in the minds of their superiors, a troubling affinity that contradicted the very purpose for which the Residency, as an institution, had been created. The use of physical force therefore became a significant point of tension between the Residents on the ground and their superiors in London and Calcutta. Many Residents could not envision a form of political influence in India that did not manifest itself through violence or the threat of violence, while their superiors were, to the contrary, determined to preserve a sharp, if artificial, distinction between their military and political arms. An analysis of the Residents therefore highlights the ways in which war and diplomacy, violence and politics, intermingled in an imperial context, flying in the face of a contemporary discourse that justified imperial influence by emphasizing its civilizing and peace-bringing effects. The Residencies have often been described as oases sheltered from the wider currents of Company politics, but the testimony left behind by leading Residents suggests that, to the contrary, violence or the threat of violence was a prominent feature of Residency life.[10]

This chapter considers the causes and consequences of these attitudes about the use of force within the political line, as well as how the governor-general-in-council and the Court of Directors in London endeavoured to contain them. The chapter begins by describing the conceptual frameworks through which the Residents understood and ascribed meaning to the disorders they witnessed in the subcontinent, and shows how, out of these raw ideological materials, Residents constructed an argument in favour of unequal alliances backed by force. The remainder of the chapter examines how this emergent strain of hawkishness translated into practice, first, in terms of diplomatic negotiations and the role of subsidiary forces, and second, in strategies of discipline and punishment. To some extent, the Residents exemplify the link that historian Mark Condos has drawn between feelings of insecurity and the emergence of authoritarian tendencies during this period; many Residents did consider themselves to be stationed behind enemy lines, thereby

---

[9] Peers, *Between Mars and Mammon*, p. 7.
[10] Spears, *Nabobs*, pp. 82–83; Travers, *Ideology*, p. 28.

justifying the use of force to preserve their personal safety as well as the interests of the Company.[11] Just as important, however, were the ordering, disciplining, and civilizing functions that violence on different scales was perceived to have, from military campaigns to floggings. The Company's executive were not immune to these arguments about the value of intimidation; instead, disagreement centred on the question of how far and under what circumstances the Residents themselves should employ these tactics.

3.1   The Cultural Coordinates of the Subsidiary Alliance System

One of the ostensible objectives of the subsidiary alliance system, as engineered by Wellesley, was 'tranquillity'. India was viewed as a land of turmoil that the Company had an obligation to settle. Ongoing conflicts between Indian powers were understood to require the Company's pacifying influence and were seized on as a legitimation for increasing the Company's military presence. British paramountcy, in other words, was framed as the most efficient means of restoring order to a disorderly land.[12] Wellesley's explicit policy was to 'convince the several powers of India that their real interest consists in respecting the rights of their neighbours, and in cultivating their own resources within the limits of their several territories'.[13] By imposing clear borders, British officials claimed to be civilizing and disciplining the Indian landscape, curbing 'the lawless ambition, predatory habits, and restless violence of the native states of Hindostan and the Dekan'.[14] Parallels were drawn with Britain's perceived role in European politics, and its opposition to the rise of French or Spanish land-based empires; similarly, in India the Company identified itself as the champion of smaller kingdoms, particularly the Rajputs, against the depredations of the rival Maratha empire.[15] Many prominent officials within the political line viewed Barlow's withdrawal from beyond the Yamuna as a betrayal, and when Hastings defended his

---

[11] Mark Condos, *The Insecurity State: Punjab and the Making of Colonial Power in British India* (Cambridge, 2017), p. 25.

[12] BL, APAC, Cleveland Public Library Papers, IOR Neg 4226, wq091.92 Ea77p5, Richard Jenkins to Marquess of Hastings, 5 September 1816, pp. 457–458.

[13] Marquess Wellesley to J. A. Kirkpatrick, 8 July 1798, in *Wellesley Despatches*, I, p. 104.

[14] Anonymous, *Notes Relative to the Peace Concluded between the British Government and the Marhatta Chieftains, and to the Various Questions Arising Out of the Terms of the Pacification* (London, 1805), p. 37.

[15] Richard Whatmore, '"Neither Masters nor Slaves": Small States and Empire in the Long Eighteenth Century', in *Lineages of Empire: The Historical Roots of British Imperial Thought*, ed. Duncan Kelly (Oxford, 2009), p. 754.

administration to parliament upon his return to Britain, he emphasized how he had saved the Rajput states from the 'devastation' inflicted on them by Daulat Rao Shinde and Yashwant Rao Holkar.[16]

Where the Marathas were concerned, convictions about the need for Company mediation were partly a product of what might be described as a clash of military cultures. Conceptions of legitimate violence are historically contingent and culturally conditioned; ideas about what forms of violence are appropriate or necessary in different contexts differ across space and time.[17] The Residents' reactions to Indian warfare were shaped by their own models of how conflicts should be conducted, leading them to classify the Marathas in particular as outlaws and brigands.[18] From a European perspective, pitched battles limited damage, constituting a relatively civilized means of resolving conflicts; the Marathas' preference for mobile, 'irregular' warfare, their reliance on light cavalry, and their use of tactics like cutting supply lines and ravaging surrounding territories thus elicited the condemnation of prominent Company officials.[19] Particularly problematic, in the Company's view, were escalating incidences of armed plunder within Maratha domains. Pillaging was, as historian Stewart Gordon has argued, a key method of accumulating resources and maintaining standing armies in central India; in a context where many Indian kingdoms were critically underfunded owing to bad harvests and Company debts, it was difficult to pay for military support in any other way.[20] Company officials, however, condemned Indian rulers for their seeming indifference to banditry within their borders, arguing that the Marathas sacrificed the well-being of their subjects to keep a pool of mounted military labour close at hand without having to pay directly for the privilege. In 1813, Resident Richard Jenkins observed censoriously that Nagpur and surrounding regions were hard hit by plunderers: 'indeed all these territories are overrun by them, and never free from their parties so great is

---

[16] 'The Marquis of Hastings' Summary of the Operations in India, with their Results; from the 30th April 1814 to the 31st January 1823', in the General Appendix to House of Commons, *Report from the Select Committee on the Affairs of the East India Company* (London, 1832), p. 100.

[17] See introduction to John Smolenski and Thomas J. Humphrey, eds., *New World Orders: Violence, Sanction, and Authority in the Colonial Americas* (Philadelphia, PA, 2005), p. 12.

[18] According to Barry Close, the Marathas 'lead rather bands of robbers, than collected and substantial armies'. NLS, Minto Papers, MS 11323, Memorandum of Colonel Barry Close, p. 31. See also BL, APAC, Mss Eur F88/219, Report on the Deckan, p. 11.

[19] For European perspectives, see James Q. Whitman, *The Verdict of Battle* (Cambridge, MA, 2012), pp. 3–17. On Indian tactics, see Kaushik Roy, *The Oxford Companion to Modern Warfare in India: From the Eighteenth Century to Present Times* (Oxford, 2009), pp. 19–21.

[20] Gordon, 'Scarf and Sword', in *Marathas, Marauders, and State Formation*, pp. 19–20.

their confidence of not being attacked, and so little are the Exertions of the Government to protect its miserable subjects'.[21]

This behaviour was perceived to warrant forceful intervention. British attitudes on this point were heavily informed by classical understandings of 'tyranny', a concept that encompassed various forms of misgovernment but generally implied either active brutality or a passive disregard for popular well-being.[22] In a European context, 'tyranny' was historically a powerful justification for military intervention.[23] In Thomas More's *Utopia*, the Utopians 'go to war only for good reasons: to protect their own land, to drive invading armies from the territories of their friends, or to liberate an oppressed people, in the name of humanity, from tyranny and servitude'.[24] For British officials who espoused these views, the logical conclusion was that the Company would be doing the population a service by intervening. Resident Thomas Sydenham, describing conditions in Hyderabad in 1810, proclaimed that 'the cultivators of the soil, the manufacturers, artisans and merchants groan under a load of exactions and oppressions, and would willingly be transferred to the British government'.[25] In even more moralizing terms, William Palmer condemned Shinde and the peshwa for being 'wholly regardless of the happiness of the people committed to their charge, & destitute of any sense of moral Obligation', while Mountstuart Elphinstone, then at Nagpur, proclaimed that 'it is a satisfaction to think that we are engaged in a holy war against violence and rapine & there is not one of our enemies whose destruction will not be a blessing to India as it relieves the country from his crimes.'[26]

Historical narratives were mobilized to support this view and justify violence against Indian rulers.[27] British commentators emphasized that

---

[21] BL, APAC, Mss Eur E111, Richard Jenkins to Capt. Roughsedge, 29 December 1813, p. 203. See also BL, APAC, IOR/H/576, William Palmer to Marquess Wellesley, 13 February 1801, pp. 590–591.

[22] On 'tyranny' see Emer de Vattel, *The Law of Nations, or, the Principles of the Law of Nature, Applied to the Conduct and Affairs of Nations and Sovereigns*, eds. Béla Kapossy and Richard Whatmore (Indianapolis, IN, 2008), book I, chapter IV, section 49.

[23] David Trim, 'Intervention in European History, c. 1520–1850', in *Just and Unjust Military Intervention: European Thinkers from Vitoria to Mill*, eds. Stefano Recchia and Jennifer M. Welsh (Cambridge, 2013), p. 26.

[24] *Utopia*, eds. George M. Logan and Robert M. Adams (Cambridge, 1997), pp. 89–90, quoted in Richard Tuck, *The Rights of War and Peace: Political Thought and the International Order form Grotius to Kant* (Oxford, 1999), p. 42.

[25] NAI, For. Sec., file no. 1, Thomas Sydenham to Minto, 21 April 1810, p. 24. Sydenham made exception for 'the lower orders of Mussulmans', who he claimed 'detest us and abuse us, because we are Christians and are powerful.'

[26] BL, Add MS 29178, William Palmer to Warren Hastings, 10 July 1801, p. 63; BL, APAC, Mss Eur F109/88, Mountstuart Elphinstone to John Adam, 29 March 1805.

[27] For a discussion of history-writing and imperial ideology, see Alix Chartrand, 'Comparing Comparisons: The Role of Religion in British-Produced Histories of Ireland and India, c. 1650–1800', *Journal of Colonialism and Colonial History* 18, no. 3 (2017).

many Indian rulers then dominant in India had come to power through conquest, contending that the subcontinent was a land governed by the rule of the sword rather than the rule of law. To quote two contemporary observers, 'all the Mahomedan [powers] have been founded in rebellion, crime and usurpation', while the Marathas were 'an empire which has arisen on the basis of injustice, falsehood, and treachery'.[28] Visions of Indian brutality were reinforced by widely circulated horror stories about the Black Hole of Calcutta and Tipu Sultan's treatment of British captives.[29] Drawing on theories of the law of nations elaborated by influential thinkers like Emer de Vattel, many Britons (the Residents among them) felt that their common humanity authorized them to combat the oppressions of tyrants.[30]

The concept of 'humanity' was regularly invoked as a motive for and vindication of the use of force. One might expect that ideas of shared humanity would mitigate against violent or coercive measures, and indeed natural law has traditionally been associated with a more open and inclusive notion of the international community, in contrast to the state-centred, positivist tradition of the nineteenth century.[31] Yet, 'humanity' could also function as an exclusionary category, and the idea that Indian enemies were for one reason or another 'inhuman' was used to legitimate extra-legal forms of justice. This was a common motif of European political propaganda of the period, wherein the enemies of the state were constructed as morally deficient barbarians excluded from the civilized European community.[32] Dan Edelstein has illustrated how conceptions of the laws of nature could entail this idea of outlaws and enemies of humanity which in turn laid the ideological groundwork for

[28] John Clunes, *An Historical Sketch of the Princes of India, Stipendiary, Subsidiary, Protected, Tributary, and Feudatory; with a Sketch of the Origin and Progress of British Power in India* (Edinburgh, 1833), p. 18; An Officer in the Service of the Honourable East India Company, *Origin of the Pindaries; Preceded by Historical Notices on the Rise of the Different Mahratta States* (London, 1818), p. 34.

[29] Partha Chatterjee, *The Black Hole of Empire: History of a Global Practice of Power* (Princeton, NJ, 2012), pp. 47, 95; Kate Teltscher, '"The Fearful Name of the Black Hole": Fashioning an Imperial Myth', in *Writing India 1757–1990: The Literature of British India*, ed. Bart Moore-Gilbert (Manchester, 1996), p. 40; Kate Teltscher, *India Inscribed: European and British Writing on India 1600–1800* (Delhi, 1995), pp. 229, 233.

[30] Jennifer Pitts, 'Empire and Legal Universalisms in the Eighteenth Century', *AHR* 117, no. 1 (2012): 100.

[31] Famously in the South Asian context by C. H. Alexandrowicz, *An Introduction to the History of the Law of Nations in the East Indies (16th, 17th, and 18th Centuries)* (Oxford, 1967), p. 2.

[32] Renaud Morieux, 'Patriotisme humanitaire et prisonniers de guerre en France et en Angleterre pendant la Révolution française et l'Empire', in *La politique par les armes. Conflits internationaux et politisation, XVe-XIXe siècles*, eds. Laurent Bourquin et al. (Rennes, 2014), pp. 301–316; David A. Bell, *The Cult of the Nation in France: Inventing Nationalism, 1680–1800* (Cambridge, MA, 2001), p. 84.

brutal acts of summary justice. In France, he argued, these categories were used to justify the violence meted out during the Terror and the war in the Vendée.[33] Philip Dwyer has similarly observed how massacres during the Revolutionary and Napoleonic Wars were accompanied by dehumanizing rhetoric that labelled the enemy as vagabonds, brigands, bandits, and beasts, categories that exempted them from the normal rules of warfare.[34] The same logic applied in India, particularly with regards to the Pindaris, who, during the upheavals of 1816–1818, were subject to summary trial and execution in the field if found guilty of 'depredations'.[35] These disciplinary measures were considered necessary to curb the 'inhuman barbarities' of the Pindaris, 'whose progress is generally marked by the smoking ruins of villages, the shrieks of women, and the groans of their mutilated husbands.'[36]

Alongside these moral imperatives, Residents posited practical reasons for their asymmetrical alliance system. The disorganized state of Indian governments was said to make them practically ineffective as allies, meaning they had to be actively controlled rather than passively trusted. Indian armies were, Residents argued, ill-administered and unruly; they complained that Company armies were forced to do the worst of the fighting, with little or no assistance from their Indian allies.[37] Ongoing unrest in Indian states, which rulers were apparently unwilling or unable to control, brought their military capabilities further into question. The Company routinely resorted to military measures to quell rebellions in neighbouring territories that threatened to spread to their own subjects.[38] The general feeling was that the impotence of Indian states was more dangerous to the Company than direct attack; 'the ills arisen from their weakness, and bad policy, have not been much less than those which we might have feared from their hostility', according to Richard Jenkins (writing in 1816).[39]

---

[33] Dan Edelstein, *The Terror of Natural Right: Republicanism, the Cult of Nature, and the French Revolution* (Chicago, IL, 2010), pp. 15–21.
[34] Philip G. Dwyer, 'Violence and the Revolutionary and Napoleonic Wars: Massacre, Conquest and the Imperial Enterprise', *Journal of Genocide Research* 15, no. 2 (2013): 117–131.
[35] BL, APAC, Mss Eur E111, Richard Jenkins to Alexander Walker, 23 December 1816, p. 367; BL, APAC, Mss Eur F88/57, p. 5.
[36] An Officer, *Origin of the Pindaries*, p. 121.
[37] BL, APAC, Mss Eur F88/405, Henry Russell to C. T. Metcalfe, 15 May 1819, p. 62; BL, APAC, IOR/H/600, Mountstuart Elphinstone to Thomas Hislop, 30 March 1815, p. 54; BL, APAC, IOR/H/620, N. B. Edmonstone to Barry Close, 23 June 1802, p. 53.
[38] BL, APAC, Cleveland Public Library Papers, IOR Neg 4226, wq091.92 Ea77p5, Richard Jenkins to Marquess of Hastings, 5 September 1816, pp. 408–409.
[39] BL, APAC, IOR/H/603, Marquess of Hastings, 'Political State of India 1815', p. 50. See also BL, APAC, Cleveland Public Library Papers, IOR Neg 4226, wq091.92 Ea77p5, Richard Jenkins to Marquess of Hastings, 5 September 1816, p. 407.

Residents also argued that the Company had no choice but to actively enforce its treaties since Indian rulers were fickle, liable to be swayed by the insinuations of conniving ministers. Thomas Sydenham was 'not disposed to place any Confidence in the Friendship or Constancy of the present Nizam [Sikander Jah]', observing that 'his sentiments and Feelings, on all subjects, are generally directed by those who surround him'.[40] John Malcolm was similarly convinced that Baji Rao lacked the 'firmness to resist any bold or wicked counseller', and even went so far as to speculate that it was 'this prominent defect in his character which has rendered him from the first, so uncertain and dangerous an Ally to the British Government'.[41] Credulous rulers of this type could turn against the Company at a moment's notice, or so the argument ran.

Allegations like these were, to some extent, a common feature of courtly politics the world over. When Residents focused their ire on unfit advisors, they echoed complaints from centuries past; the 'evil counsellor' is a common archetype in European political history. In England in the thirteenth and fourteenth centuries, medieval baronial rebellions were conventionally justified with reference to the need to remove wicked advisors who had led the king astray. By directing their complaints against royal advisors, the barons preserved the monarchy intact and avoided undermining the basic social structure of the state upon which their own authority rested.[42] For the Residents, scapegoating the minister fulfilled a similar function.

Still, Residents also seem to have shared the assumption, often repeated but rarely explained, that the Indian courtly elite were somehow uniquely deceitful. Based on these presumptions, many contemporaries were convinced that Indian intrigues could only be held in check by the threat of violence. This stereotype was particularly associated with the Marathas. As an anonymous author put it in a contemporary text, 'no power ever placed confidence in them, without ultimately having reason to repent of its credulity.'[43] This was an opinion regularly expressed by the Residents, too.

---

[40] NAI, For. Sec., file no. 1, J. A. Kirkpatrick to Minto, 21 April 1801, p. 19.

[41] BL, APAC, IOR/L/PS/19/2, John Malcolm to John Adam, 31 August 1818. Daulat Rao Shinde was also described as having a 'weak and wavering mind' under 'the entire ascendancy of Sirji Rao Ghautka, his father-in-law.' BL, Add MS 13603, N. B. Edmonstone to Barry Close, 4 December 1804, p. 19.

[42] Joel T. Rosenthal, 'The King's "Wicked Advisers" and Medieval Baronial Rebellions', *Political Science Quarterly* 82, no. 4 (1967): 595–618. See also John Watts, 'The Problem of the Personal: Tackling Corruption in Later Medieval England, 1250–1550', in *Anti-Corruption in History: From Antiquity to the Modern Era,* eds. Ronald Kroeze, André Vitória, and Guy Geltner (Oxford, 2017), p. 96.

[43] Mundy, *Pen and Pencil Sketches,* II, p. 47. See also Thomas Duer Broughton, *Letters Written in a Mahratta Camp during the Year 1809* (London, 1813), pp. 104–105.

William Palmer, Resident at Pune, alleged that 'violence and perfidy are the usual means employed and injustice the end proposed in all the transactions of the Mahratta people.'[44] Mountstuart Elphinstone, one of Palmer's successors, described at length in his private journal his 'hatred of the Marattas perhaps of the Indians in general & my disgust at their [...] want of faith & principles'.[45] As this complaint attests, British officials viewed faithlessness as a key attribute of the Maratha political elite. When the Earl of Minto asked Colonel Barry Close, then Resident at Pune, to report on the likelihood of Indian rulers supporting the British in the event of a French invasion, Close responded by asking 'what reliance could be placed on a *Maratha* chief [...] totally ignorant of the principles of Government, and of the use of probity, faith, or credit, and who knows no policy but that of violence, fraud, deceit, & monetary gain'.[46]

These accusations of bad faith had serious implications, for in the European tradition public faith was the very cornerstone of the law of nations itself, without which, as Emer de Vattel put it, 'treaties are no better than empty words'.[47] Public faith made negotiation, and by extension peaceful coexistence, possible. Grotius concluded his influential text on the laws of war and peace by admonishing princes to keep their faith: 'wherefore take away Faith, they will be like wild Beasts, whose Rage all Men dread.'[48] British perceptions of Indian lack of public faith meant that political negotiations with Indian powers were apt to be viewed as empty exercises, since Indian elites were not trusted to follow through on anything that they might, in principle, agree to.

There was a parallel line of interpretation, however, that attributed Indian 'lack of faith' less to an inherent Indian character, than to the unequal power dynamic embodied in Anglo-Indian relationships. Divided opinion on this question reflected broader uncertainties in eighteenth- and early-nineteenth-century legal theory, particularly on the question of whether states were obliged to keep promises made under duress.[49] It was not infrequently conceded or implied that the reason why

---

[44] William Palmer to Marquess Wellesley, 25 March 1799, in *PRC*, VI, p. 375.

[45] BL, APAC, Mss Eur F88/370, Journal of Mountstuart Elphinstone, 4 February 1817, p. 17.

[46] NLS, Minto Papers, MS 11323, Memorandum of Colonel Barry Close, 31 August 1808, pp. 31–32.

[47] Vattel, *Law of Nations*, book II, chapter XV, section 219.

[48] Hugo Grotius, *The Rights of War and Peace*, ed. Richard Tuck, 3 vols (Indianapolis, IN, 2005), vol. III, chapter xxv, section I.

[49] Samuel Pufendorf, *De jure naturae et gentium libri octo*, 1688 ed., 2 vols, trans. C. H. Oldfather and W. A. Oldfather (Oxford, 1934), book III, chapter VI, section 272; Christian Wolff, *Jus gentium method scientifica pertractatum*, 3 vols, trans. Joseph H. Drake (Oxford, 1934), vol. II, chapter IV, sections 434–435.

Indian rulers could not be trusted was that they had been coerced into alliances in which they were subordinate partners. This was an opinion commonly expressed by critics of the Company during the parliamentary inquiry into Wellesley's activities in India, which focused on his alliance with the peshwa and his subsequent conflict with the Marathas. In a pamphlet commenting on Wellesley's system of subsidiary alliances, the anonymous author argued that 'where one party enters into such engagements with reluctance or by constraint, the advantages to be expected from such an alliance will not be realized, because the reluctant or the constrained party can never be relied upon in the hour of danger', and that the inferior partner in such an alliance would, moreover, be 'constantly upon the watch for an opportunity of emancipating themselves whenever the tide of affairs should chance to turn against us'.[50]

In line with this interpretation, some Residents conceded that it was natural for Indian rulers to seek to free themselves of unwanted alliances that impinged on their sovereign status. Writing on the eve of the Second Maratha War, William Scott (Resident at Lucknow) anticipated that the peshwa would either abandon his British alliance in favour of joining the enemy Maratha alliance, or that he would be deserted by his troops and followers. Scott's fears were founded in the belief, apparently 'generally admitted', that Indian rulers who allied with the Company did so out of fear of Holkar and Shinde's depredations, but might recognize with the passage of time 'that these oppressions were temporary and may be rescinded, whilst our authority and influence when once established become permanent and our encroachments progressive'.[51] Similarly, in a memorandum responding to Governor General the Earl of Minto's query about whether or not the Maratha powers were likely to ally with the French, Colonel Close admitted that 'it might betray a want of knowledge of human nature, to suppose that the Maratta Chieftains [...] do not regret their heavy losses from the late war, are not jealous of our superior power, and anxious to regain the relative levels, from which they have respectively fallen.'[52] Richard Jenkins echoed this sentiment in a report written on the eve of the Pindari War; describing the Marathas' humiliation at their loss of independence, Jenkins concluded that 'it is not in human nature for such feelings to be subdued, by any show, or reality of moderation, by any thing, in fact, short of a thorough conviction of the hopelessness of ever recovering their former dominion'. Jenkins believed

[50] BL, APAC, IOR/H/481, S. J., 'Cursory Remarks on the Late Proceedings with Respect to the Marhattas', 26 February 1806, pp. 907–908, 923.
[51] BL, APAC, Mss Eur F142/8, William Scott to Robinson, 24 August 1803.
[52] NLS, Minto Papers, MS 11323, Memorandum of Colonel Barry Close, 31 August 1808, p. 28.

that the Marathas would always be willing to rebel, however minimal their chances; if 'they can shake the pillars of the edifice, which overshadows them, they will overlook the chance of being buried in its ruins', he affirmed.[53] Far from being somehow 'inhuman', the Marathas were, to the contrary, deeply human in their desire to preserve their freedom of action.

These opposing perspectives on the issue of Indian public faith reflected a deeper ambiguity at the heart of contemporary understandings of the law of nations, which was in brief that the dictates of the law of nature and the self-interest of sovereign states were not always in alignment. Given that the preservation of the state was agreed to be of primary importance according to natural law, how far were governments allowed to go in pursuit of that end, and to what extent were they permitted to break with other tenets of the law of nations? Isaac Nakhimovsky has identified this tension in Emer de Vattel, a paradox which, he argues, has led to opposite interpretations of *The Law of Nations*. According to Vattel, states were authorized to punish inhumanity and injustice. Yet, sovereign states were also supposed to be equals with no right to sit in judgement of one another, since their self-interests might bias their verdict.[54] To quote Vattel, 'each party asserting that they have justice on their own side, will arrogate to themselves all the rights of war, and maintain that their enemy has none, that his hostilities are so many acts of robbery, so many infractions of the law of nations, in the punishment of which all states should unite.'[55] As Stefano Recchia and Jennifer Welsh observe, military interventions always, to some extent, contravene ideals of self-determination and political independence that have historically been central to the law of nations. Interventions bring into question, not just motives and means, but also right authority, in other words, who has the right to determine the legitimacy of an intervention?[56] Many senior British officials certainly presumed this right to declare the justice or injustice of Indian acts of war, which they impugned as 'depredations', but this interpretation did not go uncontested. Charles Grant, a vocal opponent of military conquest within the Court of Directors,

---

[53] BL, APAC, Cleveland Public Library Papers, IOR Neg 4226, wq091.92 Ea77p5, Richard Jenkins to Marquess of Hastings, 5 September 1816, pp. 442–443.
[54] Isaac Nakhimovsky, 'Carl Schmitt, Vattel and the Law of Nations: Between Enlightenment and Revolution', *Grotiana* 31, no. 1 (2010): 141–164.
[55] Vattel, *Law of Nations*, book III, chapter XII, section 188. On the limits to Vattel's formal universalism, see Jennifer Pitts, *Boundaries of the International: Law and Empire* (Cambridge, MA, 2018), p. 92.
[56] Stefano Recchia and Jennifer M. Welsh, 'Introduction: The Enduring Relevance of Classical Thinkers', in *Just and Unjust Military Intervention: European Thinkers from Vitoria to Mill*, eds. Stefano Recchia and Jennifer M. Welsh (Cambridge, 2013), p. 2.

underscored the subjective nature of these assessments when he pointed out that, though in the eyes of the Company the Marathas 'were immediately the aggressors, and they little scrupled the violation of treaties', the Marathas might for their part 'consider us the first aggressors, and themselves as originally the injured parties'.[57]

Not everyone accepted prevailing stereotypes of Indian misgovernment, either. At least one Resident did draw the connection between the Company's encroachment and the apparently disordered state of its Indian allies. Henry Russell was explicit on this subject, observing that 'an alliance with us, upon the subsidiary system, however it may contribute to the advancement of our own Power, leads inevitably to the ultimate Destruction of the state which embraces it'. Specifically, Russell complained that the Company's intervention stifled competition among the Indian courtly elite, precluding the development of political expertise and administrative know-how. Residents were instructed to shore up the authority of pliant ministers to perpetuate the Company's influence, but in so doing, Russell felt, the Company were in fact creating the very conditions of disorganization and political stagnation at Indian courts that they so vociferously condemned. At the same time, even Russell believed the Company's withdrawal from Hyderabad would, in his words, 'be productive of the Subversion of the Government'. As he put it, 'all the Functions of Administration would be dissolved, the Fabrick of Government would sink under its own weakness, and the Nizam himself would probably become the victim of an insurrection of his subjects, and the country be made a scene of anarchy & outrage'.[58] In Russell's opinion, only the direct intervention of the Resident could prevent Hyderabad from descending into chaos.

To some extent, then, even Residents who seem to have eschewed the language of tyranny nevertheless felt they had a moral imperative to intervene. After all, they pointed out, the Company had long meddled in Indian governments to serve its own interests; given these precedents, how could they not intervene to serve the greater good, as they saw it? As Charles Metcalfe put it in his defence of the Company's involvement in revenue collection at Hyderabad, 'if it be right to interfere, in behalf of our own Interests, by imposing a Minister on the country, it cannot surely be wrong, to interpose for the Interests of the People with a view to their protection against his Rapacity.'[59] Jenkins asserted that the Marathas, at least, 'have been injured from whatever circumstances,

---

[57] 'Debate at the East-India House, February 3 1819', *Asiatic Journal and Monthly Register* (1819), VII, p. 276.

[58] All quotes in this paragraph from BL, APAC, Mss Eur F109/9, Henry Russell's report, 24 November 1819.

[59] BL, APAC, Mss Eur F109/9, C. T. Metcalfe to George Swinton, 31 August 1822.

beyond the possibility of reparation, or of reconciliation'.[60] As sociologist Charles Maier observed, 'empire does not emerge as a fit of absence of mind. Instead it represents a fit of what social scientists call path dependency, that is, clinging to choices made early on whose reversal seems unthinkable.'[61] Rather than being entirely in favour of sustaining or further expanding the Company's empire in India, some Residents suggested that the Company had to continue along its set trajectory simply because they saw no way in which it could responsibly withdraw from the crisis of states it had created in India.

There was, at times, a note of melancholy in the Residents' assessment of their future in India. Many prominent members of the political line, perhaps consonant with the cyclical understanding of history prevalent during this period, anticipated the Company's ultimate downfall, which, though perhaps not imminent, they nevertheless considered inevitable.[62] In 1805, following the Company's victory in the Second Maratha War, Mountstuart Elphinstone predicted that 'India will most likely go as France & America did before'.[63] As William Palmer remarked in a private letter to Warren Hastings around the same time, '[t]hat an Empire so extensive including many Millions of men to whom our Religion, Laws, Manners & even our very Faces are abhorrent, can be governed to the effects of augmenting the National Wealth & power, [...] I have met with no man so sanguine as to expect.'[64] In his private letters to his father almost fifteen years later, Henry Russell agreed that 'our Power in India, like the ripple of a stone thrown into the water, is destined to be lost in its Expansion', remarking that 'I do not believe that our vast Indian Empire will form a single Exception to the Rule of all the Empires since the world began.'[65] In the nineteenth century, even as visions of history became more firmly yoked to the idea of progress, empires continued to be associated with decline. As Russell's letter to his father suggests, empires were assumed to carry within themselves the seeds of their own demise. After all, contemporaries had only to look to

---

[60] BL, APAC, Cleveland Public Library Papers, IOR Neg 4226, wq091.92 Ea77p5, Richard Jenkins to Marquess of Hastings, 5 September 1816, p. 442.

[61] Charles Maier, *Among Empires: American Ascendancy and Its Predecessors* (Cambridge, MA, 2007), p. 21.

[62] David Spadafora, *The Idea of Progress in Eighteenth-Century Britain* (New Haven, CT, 1990), pp. 14–15.

[63] BL, APAC, Mss Eur F109/89, Mountstuart Elphinstone to John Adam, 5 November 1805.

[64] BL, Add MS 29180, William Palmer to Warren Hastings, 29 December 1804, p. 76.

[65] Bodl. Oxf., Russell Papers, MS. Eng. lett. c. 151, Henry Russell to Henry Russell Sr., 6 March 1818, p. 215; Henry Russell to Henry Russell Sr., 22 August 1818, p. 241.

the historical example of ancient Rome, an important reference point for Britons speculating about the future of their empire in India.[66]

Although Residents were thus not necessarily optimistic about their expanding empire in India, a few key assumptions nevertheless convinced them of the desirability of using coercion to reshape the politics of ostensibly independent Indian states. Not only were British and Indian military cultures starkly opposed, but British conceptions of 'tyranny', 'inhumanity', and the 'balance of powers' combined to form a potent moral justification of the Company's military presence. These concerns were overlaid with pragmatic considerations about the perceived ineffectiveness and untrustworthiness of Indian states as allies, even though some Residents conceded that the apparent weaknesses they observed in Indian administrations were a direct product of the Company's intervention. Although the Company's role in Indian states raised difficult questions about the laws of nations, for instance, about the binding power of treaties made under duress, and the relative priority to be accorded to raison d'état over the law of nature, Residents were generally satisfied with the rectitude of the Company's interference. Richard Jenkins for one felt that an article of 'authoritative interference' ought to be introduced into any future treaties, arguing in 1816 that 'we must almost Entirely new model the Marhatta Governments if we wish to make anything of them, conducive to the settlement & peace of India.'[67] Interventions backed by the threat of force were considered the most efficacious, indeed only means of safeguarding the Company's position in the subcontinent. Mountstuart Elphinstone was convinced that the alliance system could not be substantially improved and said as much when the Marquess of Hastings approached him about the possibility of reform. In an ideal world, according to Elphinstone, these relationships would be an alliance of equals, founded in mutual trust, without political intervention on either side. Yet the character of the Indian rulers in question, as Elphinstone saw them, appeared to make such an arrangement impracticable:

their restlessness, their rapacity, their weakness and the general want of confidence in them that results from their want of faith, continually bring them into situations where we are forced to interfere, either to save them from utter ruin or to prevent their making our power instrumental to their injustice and oppression.[68]

---

[66] Duncan Bell, 'From Ancient to Modern in Victorian Imperial Thought', *HJ* 49, no. 3 (2006), pp. 736–738; C. A. Hagerman, *Britain's Imperial Muse: The Classics, Imperialism, and the Indian Empire, 1784–1914* (Houndmills, 2013), p. 109.

[67] BL, APAC, Mss Eur E111, Richard Jenkins to Mountstuart Elphinstone, 22 January 1816, p. 270.

[68] All quotes BL, APAC, Mss Eur F88/403, Mountstuart Elphinstone to Marquess of Hastings, 17 July 1815, p. 156.

The traits that Elphinstone identified, namely, rapacity, weakness, and want of faith, are implicit in many of the Residents' descriptions of the Indian elite.[69] According to this vision, Indian administrations had to be controlled if they were going to make for effective instruments of British imperial interests, or even for peaceful neighbours.

To the extent that these ideas were made explicit in writing, they were rarely disputed by the Residents' superiors in London and Calcutta. To the contrary, Hastings consulted with Henry Russell, Mountstuart Elphinstone, and Richard Jenkins on whether to risk war with the Marathas by opening a military campaign against the Pindaris; his decision to enter the field appears to have been influenced by their ready assent to the plan.[70] Where Residents and their superiors differed, it seems, was the question of how far Residents themselves should resort to the use of force as an instrument of influence at court. Evidence from the Residency records suggests that some of the Residents, at least, saw themselves less as diplomats bound by the usual rules of comportment, than as mavericks operating in lawless spaces. As the following section will show, Residents clearly felt most comfortable when capable of wielding military force.

3.2   Armed Diplomacy

The years 1798–1818 were years of war: against Mysore, the Marathas, the Gurkhas, and the Pindaris. Despite spending more time at their desks than on the battlefield, this wider atmosphere of conflict seeped into Residents' routine business and coloured their perceptions of, and engagement with, Indian courts. Residents, though confident in the Company's military's might, were still far from complacent about its hold over the subcontinent. The Company might have been a dominant military power by this stage, but 'the transference of power in South Asia was not analogous to passing the baton of governance in a relay race', as historian Randolf Cooper phrased it.[71] Indian regional powers had access to military technologies not dissimilar to those employed by the Company, and were able to muster the expertise and insider knowledge of European mercenaries.[72] Some capitalized on their intimate knowledge of the landscape, eluding the grasp of

---

[69] See also for example BL, APAC, Mss Eur F88/405, Henry Russell to C. T. Metcalfe, 15 May 1819, p. 61.

[70] See letters contained in BL, APAC, Cleveland Public Library Papers, IOR Neg 4226, wq091.92 Ea77p5.

[71] Randolf G. S. Cooper, *The Anglo-Maratha Campaigns and the Contest for India: The Struggle for Control of the South Asian Military Economy* (Cambridge, 2003), p. 1.

[72] Mahadji Shinde notoriously adopted European military tactics; see Cooper, *Anglo-Maratha Campaigns*, p. 10.

European detachments who longed for the familiar conventions of pitched battles.[73] Although a secure line of credit gave the Company the advantage when it came to control of the military labour market, their expanding presence in the subcontinent did not go unchallenged, leading some prominent members of the political line to fear that 'From the Pinacle to the Abyss might be only one step'.[74]

Residents also had more immediate reasons to fear for their safety in the form of violent opposition at court. Resistance emanated from several quarters. Often it was incited by royal family members, as at Delhi when Prince Mirza Jahangir occupied the palace, or at Hyderabad when Prince Mubariz ud-Daula assembled disaffected troops at his house in the city (to be discussed in greater detail in Chapter 6).[75] Just as frequently resistance was spearheaded by former ministers: as when Mahipat Ram united angry landowners in the hinterlands of Hyderabad; when the diwan of Travancore led an attack on the Resident's household in the middle of the night; or when Trimbakji Dengle formed an army with the implicit support of the peshwa.[76] These moments of agitation were short-lived and violently repressed, but, taking a broad view of the period, they cropped up persistently, reminding Residents, should they doubt it, that their presence was unwelcome. There were even accounts of peasants attacking Company troops passing through the countryside; during the upheaval of 1818 an army officer in the Nagpur area reported 'there can be no doubt of the Inhabitants being much disaffected towards us'.[77] For the Residents, this disaffection sometimes manifested itself more personally in assassination attempts. In Travancore, the life of the Resident was regularly rumoured to be at risk.[78] The mutinous Nair battalions in the raja's service threatened to assassinate him in 1804, and in 1806 the minister allegedly planned to poison him.[79]

In this unstable atmosphere, the military support available to the Resident varied from court to court. Kingdoms bound to the Company by

[73] Anonymous, *Considerations Relative to the Military Establishments in India Belonging to the British, and Those of the Native Princes* (London, 1803), pp. 10–11.

[74] BL, APAC, Mss Eur F140/93, C. T. Metcalfe, Notes on the Burman War, 8 June 1824.

[75] NRAS, Fraser of Reelig Papers, vol. 33, Alexander Fraser to his mother, 23 December 1810, p. 219.

[76] For Mahipat Ram, see NAI, For. Sec., file no. 1, Thomas Sydenham to Earl of Minto, 17 April 1808, p. 1; for *diwan* of Travancore, see BL, APAC, IOR/E/4/904, Court of Directors to the Government at Fort St. George, 29 September 1809, p. 203.

[77] BL, APAC, IOR/F/4/619/15425, A. Cumming to R. Becker, 30 July 1818, pp. 107–108; BL, APAC, IOR/F/4/619/15425, Richard Jenkins to John Adam, 29 July 1818, pp. 27–28.

[78] BL, APAC, IOR/E/4/914, Fort St. George Political Department to John Munro, 10 August 1814, pp. 178–179.

[79] For attempted poisoning of Colin Macaulay see BL, APAC, IOR/E/4/904, pp. 235, 282.

subsidiary alliances were required to pay for and accommodate thousands of Company troops. By 1813, this ranged from the 6,464 men stationed in Awadh (1,947 of them at Lucknow) to the 9,591 men stationed in Hyderabad (3,974 of them stationed in the vicinity of the capital).[80] Although these battalions ostensibly served the interests of allied rulers, their loyalty was without question to the Company, who continued to dictate where and how they might serve. These men were available to the Resident to quell resistance where necessary, meaning that in places like Lucknow, Pune, Hyderabad, or Travancore, the threat of Company coercion was palpable. The same was not true everywhere, however. Prior to 1818, the Residents attached to Daulat Rao Shinde and the raja of Berar had, at best, only small escorts for their personal protection.

Residents without armed forces close at hand seem to have regretted their absence. This sentiment emerges most clearly at Nagpur. Following the conclusion of a subsidiary alliance in 1817, Nagpur would become a major military station at the heart of the subcontinent, but during the period under study, it was notorious within the Company both for its isolation from European settlements and for its vulnerability to armed marauders. After he was appointed Resident there in 1804, Mountstuart Elphinstone engaged in a long and increasingly petulant campaign to secure a military escort for his Residency. In March of 1805, as Pindaris raided deeper into the raja's territory, Elphinstone requested his friend and cousin in Calcutta John Adam to put in a word for him. As Elphinstone put it, '[y]ou can't think what a bore it was to be without any defence against them'.[81] In typical fashion, Elphinstone downplayed the danger of his situation; his objection, instead, was to the powerlessness he felt, trapped within the Residency, unable to act. With time, however, Elphinstone's letters to his cousin acquired the distinct tinge of desperation. The impatience with which he awaited the escort's arrival seems to be a testament to how much he felt the need of it. In Elphinstone's eyes, if war broke out with the Pindaris he could not depend on the raja for his defence; rather, 'I shall consider myself as placed close to the enemy's camp & shall trust only to my own vigilance for my safety.'[82] In Elphinstone's eyes the Company's failure to respond to his request betrayed a marked indifference to his personal interests, indeed his very safety. As he remarked resentfully to Adam, 'I wonder there is no "Censor of small wares" about the Govt House to wipe off things that are of no importance but to individuals & of great to them.'[83] Because Elphinstone believed that he fundamentally

[80] House of Commons, 1831 Select Committee Report, Appendix, vol. 5, pp. 266–278.
[81] BL, APAC, Mss Eur F109/89, Mountstuart Elphinstone to John Adam, 3 March 1805.
[82] Ibid., 6 April 1805.
[83] Ibid., 19 May 1805.

could not rely on Raghuji's protection, he resented any limitation to his access to, and deployment of, armed forces.

Elphinstone's successor did have an escort; what he wanted, however, was a battalion. For Richard Jenkins, the issue was less one of personal safety than of local authority. This equation of political and military power was made explicit when Jenkins was set the task of inquiring into the competing claims put forward by the raja of Nagpur and the nizam of Hyderabad to territories in Bhopal in 1811, shortly after Elphinstone's departure from the Residency. After fruitlessly interviewing people at court and trawling the Residency archives for information, Jenkins reflected in a letter to his predecessor that if 'a British force [were] established in the Raja's territories [in Nagpur] many difficulties which now impede such researches would be removed, and probably many superior sources of information now closed by fears of the raja's jealousy, would of their own accord become accessible.'[84] Without the threat of military force, Jenkins felt unable to use either intimidation or the promise of protection to offset Raghuji's authority.

Jenkins's attitude can be explained in part by his personal history. As a nineteen-year-old, he assumed the mantle of Acting Resident at Shinde's camp after his superior, Josiah Webbe, died unexpectedly. The timing could not have been worse since Shinde and the Company were deeply embroiled in territorial disputes over Gohad and Gwalior. After leaving camp in response to what he conceived to be Shinde's hostility, Jenkins was approached by a conciliatory mission from Daulat Rao inducing him to return. Yet, on rejoining the camp, Jenkins's household was attacked, and his property plundered, by a large body of Shinde's irregular troops. Members of Jenkins's entourage were severely wounded, including several sepoys, his surgeon, Dr Wise, and the head of his escort, Lieutenant Greene. Although general opinion was that Shinde was not directly responsible for the attack, he also made no effort to find and punish the offenders, nor did he make reparations for Jenkins's loss of property. Jenkins was subsequently held a virtual prisoner as Wellesley and Shinde negotiated over the status of Gwalior and Gohad, both of which were later conceded by the Company.[85]

Jenkins's initial departure from the camp met with reproof from the administration in Calcutta, reflecting their desire for conciliation over confrontation. According to a sternly worded letter from the governor-general-in-council, 'an extreme case alone could justify your

[84] BL, APAC, Mss Eur E111, Richard Jenkins to Mountstuart Elphinstone, 27 October 1811.
[85] Marquess Wellesley to Daulat Rao Sindhia, 23 February 1805, in *Wellesley Despatches,* IV, p. 297.

abdication of your representative character without the positive orders of your Government'.[86] Major General Arthur Wellesley, commanding Company forces in the vicinity, was also privately of the opinion that Jenkins had acted 'in too great a hurry'. He believed that Shinde was open to restoring good relations with the Company, and considered it 'unlucky that Mr. Jenkins has brought affairs to such a crisis that it is absolutely necessary to interfere with a strong hand to save Mr. Jenkins and our Honour' (though all Wellesley actually had in mind, in this instance, was a strongly worded letter from the governor general).[87] Similarly, though Governor General Richard Wellesley subsequently reprimanded Shinde for the injury to the Resident and his escort, in the end he was more than willing to forgive. Wellesley might have viewed events at Shinde's camp as an 'atrocious act of violating the sacred person of the British minister at your Highness's court', but he nevertheless claimed to be 'disposed to limit the measures to be adopted by the British Government upon this occasion'.[88] He did not enforce his demands for a full restoration of the Resident's property, or the punishment of the thieves. Jenkins was, moreover, strictly ordered to avoid 'severe remonstrations', or 'any harsh or irritating language which is always undignified and inconsistent with true Policy.'[89] Wellesley's tenure is usually remembered as an era of overt aggression on the part of the Company, but as governor general he reserved the right to decide when to intimidate, and when to conciliate. In European diplomatic practice, the expectation was for ambassadors to avoid domestic political entanglements and leave their principals room for manoeuvre; this was very much what Wellesley demanded of his Residents.

The Residents viewed the incident with Shinde rather differently, indicating their different ideas of their own role in the subcontinent. Jenkins interpreted Wellesley's concessions as a damning display of weakness. Two years later, he wrote to a colleague at Hyderabad that the whole incident was interpreted at Nagpur 'as the effects of fear'. Jenkins concluded that 'we have lost the respect and confidence of the native powers, and those barriers once removed, when they find they can insult, they will think it possible even to attack us with impunity'.[90] Though not present himself, the incident similarly lingered in Mountstuart Elphinstone's

---

[86] BL, Add MS 13603, N. B. Edmonstone to Richard Jenkins, 2 April 1805, p. 62.

[87] BL, APAC, Mss Eur F228/79, Arthur Wellesley to Colonel Barry Close, 4 March 1805, p. 1.

[88] Marquess Wellesley to Daulat Rao Sindhia, 23 February 1805, in *Wellesley Despatches*, IV, p. 297.

[89] BL, Add MS 13603, N. B. Edmonstone to Richard Jenkins, 2 April 1805, p. 66.

[90] BL, APAC, Mss Eur E111, Richard Jenkins to Charles Russell, 22 February 1807, p. 11.

mind, perhaps because of the close friendship he formed with Jenkins while the two were stationed together at Nagpur. Three years after the event, Elphinstone visited the site of the incident and 'speculated' with his companions 'about the scene of the destruction of Jenkins' escort'. 'It is humiliating to reflect on that transaction', Elphinstone wrote, and 'to remember that Sindia is now within 30 miles of the spot increased in power & reputation by that very act when 3 corps of infantry & 2 of cavalry would have completely protected or avenged this city & recovered our honour'.[91] Almost ten years later, in the midst of the difficult negotiations for the surrender of Trimbakji Dengle, Elphinstone suspected that Baji Rao was emboldened to hold out because his ministers invoked the example set by Shinde's attack on Jenkins. 'These counsellers allow none of our political mistakes however old to be forgotten and reason from them that the true way to carry a point with us is to meet us with a resolute opposition.'[92] Elphinstone was constantly working against the impression which, he believed, this incident had cultivated in the minds of Maratha courtiers, determined to show that he, at least, would never cede ground. While administrators in London and Calcutta expected Residents to adhere to diplomatic conventions of behaviour usually characterized as conciliatory, Residents themselves thus had rather different ideas about how to secure Company interests.

The presence of a subsidiary force had a notable effect on Residency life, one that emerges especially clearly at Hyderabad (where the largest number of men was concentrated). Here we see both the importance invested in these forces by the Resident, and the frictions that Residents encountered in attempting to deploy them. This tension is clearly illustrated by an incident that occurred in 1815, when Prince Mubariz ud-Daula and his brother took Henry Russell's tailor hostage. After a small party of infantrymen was fired upon while attempting to capture the prince's house (resulting in the death of a member of the Resident's personal escort), the entire force from the cantonment of Secunderabad, along with reinforcements from neighbouring stations, were called in to settle the city.[93] The subsidiary force alone was considered too weak to control Hyderabad in the event of a general insurrection, hence the need to await forces requisitioned from Bellary and the northern frontier. By summoning troops from Madras and refusing to authorize their

[91] BL, APAC, Mss Eur F109/89, Elphinstone to John Adam, 18 May 1808.
[92] MSA, PRCOP, vol. 44 (1817), Mountstuart Elphinstone to Marquess of Hastings, 26 March 1817, pp. 49–50.
[93] Central Records Office, *Chronology of Modern Hyderabad*, pp. 154–155; Prinsep, *History*, p. 262.

return, Russell got himself into trouble with the government at Fort St. George.[94] In his defence, Russell argued that Hyderabad was a city exposed to danger at all times 'from sudden & unexpected movements of sedition of violence', 'and the only security against that species of danger is to be found in the actual presence on the spot of an efficient body of Troops.' Russell underlined the 'alarmingly insufficient' state of the subsidiary force at Secunderabad and contended that only the Resident was in possession of 'those facts & circumstances' that determined the number of troops that were requisite there.[95]

This raises an ongoing issue that plagued the Residency system, namely, the tension between political and military authority. On assuming the office of Resident at Hyderabad in 1798, James Achilles Kirkpatrick recorded the difficulty he was having in bringing the officers of the detachment 'to pay me that kind of deference due to my station'.[96] In a letter to his brother, he worried, 'Will it not be proper to draw some line for General Harris's guidance with respect to the degree of command or control he may exert over his Highness's subsidiary Force? [...] Am I to be at all subordinate to General Harris?'[97] The quandary arose in part because of Kirkpatrick's own military background; as a captain, he ranked relatively low within the military hierarchy, but as a Resident, he embodied the authority of the governor general. What, then, was his position relative to the officer commanding the subsidiary force at Hyderabad? A succession of Residents struggled to assert their control over these bodies of armed men. In 1808, the arguments between Thomas Sydenham and Lieutenant Colonel Thomas Montresor over their respective authority reached such a pitch that Sydenham was forced to refer to the governor general to establish a rule to obviate such misunderstandings in future. Montresor objected to the fact that Sydenham had been corresponding with Colonel Doveton, commanding a corps in Berar. Montresor viewed this correspondence as a breach of his military authority, while Sydenham argued that the letters exchanged, and the instructions issued, were political in nature and therefore fell within the Resident's purview, relating, as they did, to the rebellion of a *mansabdar* (nobleman and officeholder) closely connected with the nizam's court. It was Sydenham's view that, given his political experience and responsibilities, only he was able to issue certain commands to the subsidiary force. In a private letter

---

[94] BL, APAC, IOR/F/4/592/14290, Extract political letter from Bengal, 1 January 1817, p. 14.
[95] Ibid.
[96] BL, APAC, Mss Eur F228/10, James Achilles Kirkpatrick to William Kirkpatrick, 11 November 1798, p. 122.
[97] BL, APAC, Mss Eur F228/10, James Achilles Kirkpatrick to William Kirkpatrick, 7 December 1798, p. 174.

to Sydenham, Montresor voiced quite a different opinion, complaining that 'from the length of time you have been acting in a political capacity you are not aware what must be the feelings of an Officer' when information about orders being issued to his subordinates was being systematically withheld from him. The governor-general-in-council ultimately acknowledged Sydenham's right to correspond with officers when circumstances appeared urgently to demand it, but Sydenham was nevertheless advised to communicate through the commanding officer whenever possible. This decision did not resolve the issue, however, as it did not define what constituted an urgent situation.[98] During his tenure Sydenham's successor Henry Russell similarly came into conflict with the commanding officers of the Hyderabad subsidiary force.[99]

A large military presence within close range of the city could cause other kinds of problems, too. To be sure, relations between the military and the Residency, though occasionally tense, were also convivial. The proximity of large numbers of officers transformed the Residency into a space of gentlemanly sociability. The Residents record sizeable purchases of liquor and food for dinner parties. Balls, horse races, and cricket matches were staples of life at Pune and Hyderabad, where the Residents' household mixed and mingled with members of the European officer class.[100] Yet, their activities within the city also created problems that the Resident was required to manage. In the previous chapter, allusion was made to the attack on Company soldiers at Pune, and the death of a local knocked down by an army officer on the road. At Hyderabad James Achilles Kirkpatrick recorded a series of unpleasant encounters. The incidents were, for the most part, trivial: one of Nizam Ali Khan's brothers forced his way through a narrow passage, his chobdars (staff-bearing attendants) pushing European officers aside to make room; another British officer stationed at the house of Akbar Jah, the nizam's son, complained of having 'received insulting and menacing messages from that Prince for some supposed mark of disrespect'; a captain commanding a British guard over the nizam's house created confusion and resentment by prohibiting the beating of the *naubut* (a kettle-drum struck at specified hours); the officer commanding the guard in front of Prince Feridoon Jah's palace was accused of beating household servants and attendants; another almost marched his sepoys through an area where

---

[98] BL, APAC, IOR/F/4/247/5583, Extract political letter from Bengal, 2 February 1808, p. 4.
[99] Bodl. Oxf., Russell Papers, MSS. Eng. lett. d. 151, Henry Russell to Charles Russell, 26 June 1810, p. 131.
[100] See for example descriptions of horse races and cricket in Bodl. Oxf., Russell Papers, MSS. Eng. lett. d. 152, Henry Russell to Charles Russell, 1810–1813.

the women of the royal household were encamped.[101] In all these cases, the officers' ignorance of the language exacerbated the issue; attendants who tried to intervene found themselves misunderstood, dismissed, even physically attacked. As time passed, these tensions appear to have eased. Possibly this was a genuine improvement resulting from increased institutional knowledge as the officers of the subsidiary force became more familiar with the city. Possibly the absence of these incidents within Residency records reflects the changing attitudes of the Residents themselves, who seem to have been less concerned than Kirkpatrick to treat the courtiers of Hyderabad with due delicacy.

In 1809, however, the officers at Hyderabad created an even greater problem for Resident Thomas Sydenham in the form of open mutiny. The immediate cause of the wave of disobedience that swept through the Madras Army in that year, namely, the purportedly unjust suspension of two officers by an unpopular commander-in-chief, was simply the spark that ignited smouldering disaffection around issues of pay, promotion, and perquisites.[102] The mutiny at Hyderabad was over within less than a month, but the anxiety that it unleashed exposes the reliance that the Company placed upon its forces to impose control over allied courts. In his narrative of events, Lieutenant Colonel Montresor, commanding the subsidiary force at Hyderabad, explained his unwillingness to punish the mutinous officers with reference to the nature of the city itself. The need to maintain good relations with his troops was made the more urgent by what he described as 'the critical situation of this Force, in the vicinity of a populous city, where the ill governed and turbulent Inhabitants would eagerly seize the first moment to destroy the British Interests'.[103] The loss of a few European officers would, in Montresor's view, have catastrophic effects by undermining the structure of military discipline that held the subsidiary force together. In such a situation, 'a daring leader, or fanatic Mussulman, might incite the troops to rid themselves of their European masters'. Montresor described the worst case scenario in the following terms:

Thousands of Intrigues and disaffected persons in the City would also irritate the Sepoys against their officers, and urge them on to mutiny, whilst others would endeavour by lavish rewards, and splendid promises, to make them desert the service, and enter into that of the discontented omrahs [high-ranking nobles], the consequence of which would be a revolution at this Court, the loss of a great part of our Troops, and probably of our influence in the Deckan.[104]

[101] NAI, FSC, 21 June 1804, no. 152–167.

[102] For a more detailed account of their grievances, see W. J. Wilson, *History of the Madras Army*, 4 vols (Madras, 1883), III, 235–296.

[103] NLS, Minto Papers, MS 11658, Lieut. Col. Montresor's Narrative of Transactions at Hyderabad, 29 July 1809, p. 9.

[104] NLS, Minto Papers, MS 11658, Lieut Col Montresor's Narrative of Transactions at Hyderabad, 28 August 1809, p. 75.

A mutiny of European officers, though dangerous in and of itself, would thus create the potential for a much greater problem: loss of control over the Indian rank and file. One of the most notorious features of the Company in the nineteenth century was its reliance on the military service of Indians. Their contingent loyalty presented a major existential threat. John Malcolm affirmed that 'among the many political considerations likely to affect the future prosperity and security of the British empire in India, there appears hardly one of more magnitude than the attachment of the natives of our army.'[105] Henry Russell agreed; when giving evidence before a parliamentary select committee, Russell argued that the greatest danger to the Company's survival came from the native army, based on the assumption that, in his words, 'our military force is the sole and exclusive tenure by which we hold the government, and that the fidelity of the troops of whom that force is composed is necessarily precarious'.[106] Sepoys employed in princely states, stationed in the vicinity of large urban centres, were perceived to be under greater temptation than most to change allegiance. Whereas the language barrier created problems between European officers and the inhabitants of the city, where the sepoys were concerned, the issue was precisely the opposite from the Residents' point of view. The entanglement of the cantonment and the urban population, the exchange of news, goods, and ideas between locals and Company soldiers, was a source of recurring disquiet. For one thing, the cantonment was seen as a weak point from which leaks of intelligence could flow.[107] For another, there was a danger that the Company's enemies at court might take advantage of unrest within the army, whether by rallying sepoys to their cause or simply by exploiting the Company's inability to deploy its own troops. Though the Company's subsidiary forces were seen as an important tool of intimidation to be wielded by the Resident at court, they were also, to some extent, a danger in and of themselves.

Two revolts cemented this impression. In 1806, a mutiny broke out among the sepoys at Vellore, then a major military station in the Madras Presidency. The catalyst was a change in uniform, specifically, the introduction of a new style of turban; the unwelcome imposition seemed to contravene caste and status, sharpening fears about the Company's intention to convert its Indian forces to Christianity. Discontent was widespread, but at Vellore, where two sepoys were flogged and dismissed

---

[105] Malcolm, *Political History of India,* II, p. 224.

[106] House of Commons, *Report from the Select Committee on the Affairs of the East India Company* (London, 1831), V, p. 160.

[107] NAI, Foreign Department, file no. 76, Thomas Sydenham to N. B. Edmonstone, 19 July 1806, pp. 1–2.

from the service, this disaffection erupted into open revolt (abetted, many believed, by the family of the late Tipu Sultan, who were confined there). Over a dozen European officers and ninety-nine rank and file were killed in the struggle. Discontent at Hyderabad was, by contrast, repressed relatively quickly. On the night of 12 July groups of sepoys assembled to the rear of the cantonment, to the extent that preparations were made by their European officers for open conflict; however, the anticipated outbreak never materialized and discontent seemingly evaporated when Sydenham revoked the regulations on 23 July. In some ways, events at Hyderabad provided a comforting contrast to the violence at Vellore; whereas officers there had no inkling of the mutiny until it was too late, at Hyderabad the Resident, Thomas Sydenham, identified growing unrest and acted to eradicate it. Sydenham was commended for his actions; the events of 1806 were interpreted by contemporaries as a demonstration of the Residents' knowledge of, and sympathy with, the sepoys stationed in his vicinity. Yet, it also reminded contemporaries of the fragility of the contract between the Company and its sepoys.[108]

In 1812, another sepoy mutiny broke out at Hyderabad with more significant local consequences. Beginning in 1811, Henry Russell had started to reform parts of the nizam's army and place Company officers in positions of command. In November 1812, one of these regiments, commanded by a European officer, Major Edward Gordon, mutinied because of arrears in pay. To compel the Resident to take their claims seriously, the mutineers tied Major Gordon to the muzzle of a gun and threatened to blow him away unless their pay and a free pardon were issued. The mutiny was severely repressed, and the battalions re-formed; Russell took direct control of their operations, earning them the designation 'the Russell Brigade'. For Russell, the danger was that dissension within the troops might spread to the city, where the inhabitants would take the opportunity to act against the Company. As Russell put it, 'there was at one Time a good deal of Agitation in the City, and I am convinced that if the Mutiny had not been put down with a strong Hand, some very unpleasant Consequences would have ensued from it.'[109] By a 'strong hand', Russell was referring to summary executions, as the following section will show.

The case of Hyderabad demonstrates that subsidiary forces were a potential problem for the Resident to manage as well as a tool for him to wield. Describing the early failures of the alliance system at Lucknow,

[108] Wilson, *History of the Madras Army*, III, pp. 169–202; BL, APAC, IOR/E/4/900, pp. 56–57.
[109] Bodl. Oxf., Russell Papers, MS. Eng. lett. d. 163, Henry Russell to J. H. Casamaijor, 1 December 1812.

Richard Barnett observed that '[t]he English were quick to realize that mutiny within the forces they commanded was the Achilles' heel of the subsidiary alliance system.'[110] This continued to be true of the nineteenth-century Residency system, where Residents faced not only mutiny and unrest but also local tensions and squabbles over precedence. The anxieties elicited by these different issues speak to the importance of the subsidiary force as a pillar of the Company's influence at court; Residents like Thomas Sydenham and Henry Russell doubted their ability to maintain their position at court if the forces stationed at Hyderabad displayed signs of weakness and disorder. The connection that they drew between political and military power led them to assert control over subsidiary forces, even in the face of contestation from commanding officers. As Henry Russell phrased it, 'a political Rule is of little avail without a military Force to sustain it.'[111] Residents viewed control over the subsidiary forces as key to their influence and believed in the necessity of taking a strong stand when their perceived rights were infringed. Though Residents' military interventions might have been contested by commanding officers, however, the greatest controversy attached to Residents' use of judicial violence, as the following section will show.

3.3   Debating the Pedagogical Value of Violence

On 30 October 1827, *The Times* printed an excerpt from a pamphlet called *An Appeal to the British Nation against the Honourable the East India Company* authored by a former officer in the Bengal Army, Captain William White. The excerpt told a troubling story. White alleged that a 'Resident at the Court of a powerful native Prince' had ordered an Indian soldier flogged to death, despite the remonstrances of the local surgeon. According to White, the surgeon reported the incident, and the government replaced the Resident with 'no less a personage than their Chief Secretary', who was instructed to investigate. Despite the formation of a court of inquiry, however, the crisis reached an anticlimactic end:

[P]ending their proceedings, the Government allow of the late resident to embark for England with a splendid fortune (800,000£!) The civilian reaches England in safety, purchases a splendid estate, and becomes a large proprietor of India stock. After a length of time has been allowed to transpire, to forget the wicked affair, the proceedings of the Court of Inquiry are transmitted to England; they are deposited in the archives of Leadenhall-street; and here the transaction ends!

---

[110] Barnett, *North India*, p. 116.
[111] Bodl. Oxf., Russell Papers, MS. Eng. lett. c. 151, Henry Russell to his father, 10 December 1817, p. 204.

White never named the Resident, or the court, in question. To the editor of *The Times*, such an injustice seemed 'quite incredible'; 'that murder, preceded and produced by torture, should [...] have been perpetrated by a civil functionary, and left, not only unpunished by the Government, but for many years neglected, even as a subject of inquiry.' He had decided to publish these complaints as a 'fit matter for examination' but did not vouch for their truth.[112]

The anonymous Resident does, however, bear a striking resemblance to Henry Russell, who was replaced by the political and private secretary to the governor general and permitted to retire on his own initiative. In Russell's case, however, it was two men who died of a brutal flogging by his order, not one. The men had been caught robbing the Residency bazaar, and Russell had ordered them flogged almost to death, that is, just short of what the doctor on hand predicted would kill them. The Directors condemned Russell for failing to allow the two men the benefit of a trial, and for punishing them so ruthlessly. In the Court's view, 'such a proceeding must have impressed the people of Hyderabad with a strange idea of British justice'.[113] The consequences were perceived to be serious, since the Company relied on the introduction of rule of law as a powerful justification for imperial intervention. India was perceived, or at least was described as, a lawless place where tyrants ruled by whim. Some of the most triumphant language of the period celebrated the fact that Britons had moderated what they believed to be the brutality of Indian law, particularly punishment by mutilation.[114] Russell's actions were therefore starkly opposed to the public image Britons sought to cultivate in India and across the empire, as illustrated by James Epstein's study of a similarly scandalous instance of corporal punishment in Trinidad around the same period.[115] Russell was considered to have acted contrary to the very principles that were supposed to distinguish him as a Briton; for, as Colin Kidd has emphasized, in the eighteenth century 'Britishness' was seen to derive particularly from the enjoyment of rights and liberties, including government by consent and trial by jury.[116] British justice was supposed to be the best and fairest in the world, so it was particularly galling to

[112] For this paragraph, see *Times*, 30 October 1827, pp. 3–4.
[113] BL, APAC, IOR/E/4/700, Court of Directors to Bengal Political Department, p. 241a.
[114] Jörg Fisch, *Cheap Lives and Dear Limbs: The British Transformation of the Bengal Criminal Law 1769–1817* (Wiesbaden, 1983), p. 130.
[115] James Epstein, *Scandal of Colonial Rule: Power and Subversion in the British Atlantic during the Age of Revolution* (Cambridge, 2012), pp. 17, 20.
[116] Colin Kidd, *British Identities before Nationalism: Ethnicity and Nationhood in the Atlantic World, 1600–1800* (Cambridge, 2006), pp. 79–80. See also Peter Mandler, *The English National Character: The History of an Idea from Edmund Burke to Tony Blair* (London, 2006), pp. 37–38.

the Directors that a Briton should behave in such a cruel and arbitrary manner when in a position of public authority abroad.

The Company's stance on corporal punishment can be understood in part by situating it against a backdrop of changing attitudes in Britain. In the early modern period, violent forms of discipline and punishment were central to the exercise of power. This power was diffuse throughout society, belonging, in varying degrees, to heads of households, local authorities, and the state. Violence, and the shaming rituals and public spectacle that often accompanied it, was regarded as a legitimate disciplinary tool so long as it was judged commensurate with the offense.[117] By the late eighteenth century, however, transportation and imprisonment were increasingly preferred to whipping, branding, and hanging. When physical punishments were administered, there was a greater likelihood that they would be carried out in the privacy of the prison or immediately outside its walls.[118] Growing numbers of commentators denounced the brutalizing effect that public displays of judicial violence might have on the population, and questioned whether crowds were extracting the intended meanings from these performances.[119] These changing attitudes to corporal punishment were informed by changing ideas about the body.[120] As Lynn Hunt has argued, a more recognizable notion of human rights was emerging as greater value was placed upon bodily integrity, and as a culture of sensibility urged an ever greater sense of identification with other human beings and their experiences both physical and spiritual.[121] At the same time, the development of the modern penitentiary promised alternative means of social control.[122] This is not to suggest, though, that the change was instant or total; public executions continued to have their vocal supporters well into the nineteenth century, when they were finally abolished in Britain in 1868.[123]

Opinions in India were also divided, though the tenor of the debate was slightly different, inflected as it was by racial and civilizational discourses. To revert to the previous example, whereas the Court of Directors in London were unanimous in their condemnation of Russell's

---

[117] Susan Dwyer Amussen, 'Punishment, Discipline, and Power: The Social Meanings of Violence in Early Modern England', *JBS* 34, no. 1 (1995): 1–34.

[118] J. A. Sharpe, *Judicial Punishment in England* (London, 1990), p. 47.

[119] V. A. C. Gatrell, *The Hanging Tree: Execution and the English People 1770–1868* (Oxford, 1994), p. 328.

[120] Randall McGowen, 'The Body and Punishment in Eighteenth-Century England', *The Journal of Modern History* 59, no. 4 (1987): 652–679.

[121] Lynn Hunt, *Inventing Human Rights: A History* (New York, NY, 2007), p. 82.

[122] Michael Ignatieff, *A Just Measure of Pain: The Penitentiary in the Industrial Revolution, 1750–1850* (London, 1978), p. 210.

[123] Gatrell, *Hanging Tree*, p. 591.

actions, the governor-general-in-council in Calcutta seem to have been in serious disagreement about the justice and 'humanity' of Russell's decision to flog the thieves in the Residency bazaar.[124] Public punishments including execution, gibbeting, and flogging had traditionally formed part of the Company's penal repertoire, but were beginning to come under increased scrutiny.[125] In contrast to Britain, however, arguments concerning the public benefits of corporal punishment were given new life in a context where the populace was believed to respond particularly well to vigorous rule as well as visual display (a theme that will be picked up in Chapter 4). This argument was commonly used by Residents, who defended aggressive measures by suggesting that public displays of force were uniquely appropriate in an Indian context. Indians, they declared, responded best to coercive tactics. Some Residents argued that clemency and conciliation, which in Britain might be considered virtues, were entirely lost on the Indian populace, 'whose barbarous pride makes them bad judges of dignified moderation', to quote Mountstuart Elphinstone.[126] In India, it was sometimes argued, the usual rules for civilized behaviour did not apply at all. Russell, for instance, defended the brutal flogging meted out at Hyderabad based on the purportedly lawless and violent nature of the city itself. As he put it, 'illegality is a breach of law. Where there is no law there can be no illegality.'[127] This statement reflected a strand of European thought which held that the laws of nations did not operate in the non-European world in the same way as in Europe.[128] Thus, while there was certainly a rival strand that emphasized Britain's responsibility to mitigate what Britons considered to be the vicious extremes of Hindu and Muslim law, particularly the punishment of mutilation, there were equally British officials who believed that such acts of state violence were entirely appropriate, even necessary, in an Indian context.

These acts of judicial violence were primarily intended to deter resistance rather than punish the guilty. This conviction, rooted in eighteenth-century European understandings of 'salutary' terror, was given added traction in

---

[124] A member of council decided to issue his own minute expressing his censure of Russell. BL, APAC, IOR/F/4/588/14274, Minute of Mr. Dowdeswell, 12 September 1818, pp. 38–43.

[125] Singha, *Despotism of Law*, p. 231.

[126] BL, APAC, Mss Eur F109/89, Mountstuart Elphinstone to John Adam, 6 May 1805. Henry Russell agreed that 'they mistake for weakness what we practice as forbearance', Bodl. Oxf., Russell Papers, MS. Eng. misc. c. 324, Henry Russell to Marquess of Hastings, 'The Condition and Resources of the Nizam's Government', p. 6.

[127] Bodl. Oxf., MSS. Eng. lett. c. 172, p. 141.

[128] Eliga Gould, 'Zones of Law, Zones of Violence: The Legal Geography of the British Atlantic, circa 1772', *The William & Mary Quarterly* 60, no. 3 (2003): 474.

a colonial context.[129] Residents saw the spectre of opposition everywhere, and the breadth of the perceived threat led them to believe in the necessity of exemplary acts of violence. Henry Russell speedily tried and executed several Indian officers in the Hyderabad subsidiary force who had mutinied in 1812, because 'the Populace of Hyderabad are made of very combustible Materials, and a little Spark is at any time sufficient to occasion an Explosion'.[130] Similarly, when the dethroned raja of Nagpur Appa Sahib attempted to lead a revolt against the Company in 1818, Richard Jenkins was quick to identify and publicly hang his supporters; in his view,

there will be no want of turbulent and disaffected people to second any sinister views of our enemies and those of the new Government, if they are not overawed by the presence of a sufficient body of our troops and the vigor of the measures adopted by the Government to repress and punish all treasonable attempts.[131]

Because resistance and ill feeling were seen as pervasive, the guilt of any one individual was less important than the effects that a visibly ruthless punishment would have on the broader population.

Because of this emphasis on deterrence, the best punishments were believed to be those that were locally specific and intelligible to Indian audiences. When Mountstuart Elphinstone was asked to report on the desirability of introducing British criminal justice into the peshwa's former dominions following the Third Maratha War, he argued against it since 'the whole of this [British] system is evidently better calculated for protecting innocent from punishment and the guilty from undue severity, than for securing the community by deterring from crimes', whereas Indian forms of punishment, 'although they were inhuman (or rather because they were inhuman) were effectual in striking terror'.[132] Blowing perpetrators from a cannon, for instance, was identified as an ideal form of punishment both because it drew from Indian precedents, inspired terror in those who witnessed it, and perhaps unexpectedly, could be argued on humanitarian grounds to constitute a quicker and more painless death than decapitation.[133] Accordingly, when three men were arrested and executed for treason at Pune for their association with the rebel Chittoor Singh in 1817, Mountstuart Elphinstone chose to blow them from a cannon, a choice that was later justified on the grounds

---

[129] Ronald Schechter, *A Genealogy of Terror in Eighteenth-Century France* (Chicago, 2018), pp. 59–76.
[130] Bodl. Oxf., Russell Papers, MS. Eng. lett. d. 163, Henry Russell to James Casaimaijor, 1 December 1812, p. 184.
[131] BL, APAC, IOR/F/4/619/15425, Richard Jenkins to John Adam, 29 July 1818, pp. 27–28.
[132] BL, APAC, Mss Eur F88/219, Report on the Deckan, pp. 98–99.
[133] Ibid., p. 199.

that the threat of rebellion following the Company's conquest 'could only be repressed by severe examples'.[134] The crucial point, then, was the spectacle. Kim Wagner has traced this mentality to the Uprising of 1857 and has identified it at work following outbreaks of resistance in late nineteenth-century India; yet, as the example of the Residents makes plain, this logic is evident in much earlier sources.[135] Residents did not need the example of 1857 to justify what they explicitly described as acts of terror.

The execution of rebels was for the most part approved of by the governor-general-in-council in Calcutta; the fear of a general uprising was so acute that everyone seems to have agreed on the necessity of severe punitive measures to repress incipient revolt. The point at which consensus splintered was on the question of whether acts of summary justice should be employed in other scenarios where the threat of general rebellion was less apparent or indeed non-existent; in other words, whether judicial violence should become an accepted part of the Resident's repertoire. Thus, Henry Russell viewed the pitiless flogging of the thieves who encroached on his domains as a mandatory display of his power and authority, while his superiors questioned the necessity and indeed the ethics of such a measure given that it was elicited by what appeared to be an isolated and ordinary criminal act.[136]

Russell's attitude was not unusual, however. He was a believer in accommodating to Indian political norms (as Britons understood them); following this conviction to its logical conclusion, he believed in the necessity of summary punishment. At the same time, it was possible for a Resident possessing very different values to make the same estimation. Colin Macaulay, for example, was raised in a clergyman's household; his brother, Zachary Macaulay, was a noted evangelical and abolitionist, and Colin shared his brother's religious convictions. Yet, Macaulay's actions following the uprising at Travancore in 1809, and the reactions that they elicited, closely parallel Russell's scandalous behaviour at Hyderabad. After the revolt was repressed, Macaulay sent the executed minister's body to the capital city of Thiruvananthapuram where his body was strung up on a gibbet for public viewing.[137] The governor-general-in-council responded to news of this public exposure with horror. While

[134] BL, APAC, Mss Eur F88/57, p. 8.

[135] Kim A. Wagner, '"Calculated to Strike Terror": The Amritsar Massacre and the Spectacle of Colonial Violence', P&P 233, no. 1 (2016): 189.

[136] BL, APAC, IOR/F/4/588/14274, Minute of Mr Dowdeswell, 12 September 1818, p. 42; BL, APAC, IOR/F/4/626/16088, Court of Directors to Governor-General-in-Council, 12 July 1820, pp. 5–6.

[137] BL, APAC, IOR/F/4/338/7687, Colin Macaulay to Government at Fort St. George, 14 April 1809, p. 8.

such a revolt was taken very seriously, hanging up the minister's body was considered 'adverse to the common feelings of humanity and to the principles of a Civilised Government.' The governor-general-in-council firmly refused to admit the necessity of the measure and regretted immensely that a British official had been involved in it. To them it seemed apparent that the act was savage and uncivilized, and Macaulay's apparent acquiescence in it raised questions about his ability to properly represent the Company in Travancore. Residents, as government representatives, were supposed to embody all the virtues that Britain allegedly stood for. They were meant to exhibit self-control, reason, judgement and understanding, not the kind of vindictiveness that appeared to be the driving force behind Macaulay's treatment of the minister's corpse. Macaulay, on the other hand, regarded the degrading display of the minister's remains as nothing short of a practical necessity. In his words:

It cannot but be of importance, that in India more than any where, men should be taught that he, [...] who utterly disregards and boldly discards from his breast, every sentiment of humanity, [...] that such a man cannot be too ignominiously punished and exposed.[138]

The conduct of Colin Macaulay, and the reaction of the governor-general-in-council, expose the contradiction underlying Company policy in India. Macaulay defended his actions by arguing that the 'inhumanity' of the minister could not be too harshly punished, but in so doing Macaulay exposed himself to accusations of inhumanity from concerned administrators in Calcutta and London. This is a potent illustration of a process that Michael Taussig dubbed 'colonial mimesis', 'a colonial mirroring of otherness that reflects back onto the colonists the barbarity of their own social relations, but as imputed to the savagery they yearn to colonize.'[139] In their efforts to control what they perceived to be Indian savagery, imperial officials were liable to resort to precisely the kinds of violent acts for which Indian rulers were condemned. Such displays of cruelty on the part of some Residents inspired unease within the central government. The Company's claim to a civilizing mission was predicated on the moral and intellectual qualities of its agents, and their essential difference from the Indians they were meant to regulate and improve through example.[140] The behaviour of Residents like Henry Russell and Colin Macaulay, though it resonated with contemporary devaluations

---

[138] Ibid., p. 19.
[139] Michael Taussig, *Shamanism, Colonialism, and the Wild Man: A Study in Terror and Healing* (Chicago, IL, 1986), p. 134.
[140] Carey A. Watt, 'The Relevance and Complexity of Civilizing Missions c. 1800–2010', in *Civilizing Missions in Colonial and Postcolonial South Asia: From Improvement to Development*, eds. Carey A. Watt and Michael Mann (Cambridge, 2012), p. 1.

of Indians and Indian political culture, nevertheless undermined the Company's claims to moderate the inhumanity of allied states.

These incidents of brute display within the political line were not an everyday occurrence, but although the acts themselves were unusual, the logic underlying them was not. From the Residents' perspective, such displays of force were the best, perhaps even the only way of visibly expressing their authority. In their view, the European in India had to learn to suppress his natural aversion to violence if social and political stability were to be maintained. Mountstuart Elphinstone ventured that 'it is possible that a very civilized Government may not be suitable to a society in a less advanced stage and that coarse expedients at which our minds revolt may be the only ones likely to check those evils which originate in the barbarism of the people'.[141] While imperial rhetoric posited the 'civilization' of Britain as its distinguishing feature and the foundation on which its empire rested, many of these men, to the contrary, viewed 'civilization' as a hindrance to be cast aside.

3.4   Conclusion

As a growing body of literature has begun to show, violence continued to form part of the everyday experience of empire in India in the nineteenth and twentieth centuries.[142] To the extent that change occurred, it was in the growing consensus that formed around the use of force in imperial settings. The Residents of the generation studied in this chapter could and did excite outrage when they pushed their discretionary authority too far. When corporal punishment was temporarily abolished in British India in 1834, one of Bentinck's arguments in favour of the measure was his desire to set a good example to the Company's Indian allies and to inspire them to reform their penal systems. Radhika Singha has suggested that humanitarian discourses that accompanied penal reform, thuggee, and the abolition of sati formed part of an 'endeavour to install British paramountcy as the source of norms and standards for just and benevolent rule.'[143] Yet, the opposition to flogging that emerged in the 1820s and 1830s in British India, culminating in its abolition as a judicial punishment in 1834, was succeeded, in the aftermath of 1857, by the reintroduction of corporal punishment in 1864, justified according to a renewed emphasis on India's alleged civilizational inferiority in terms that closely

---

[141] BL, APAC, Mss Eur F88/219, Report on the Deckan, p. 196.

[142] Taylor Sherman, *State Violence and Punishment in India* (Abingdon, 2010); Deana Heath, *Colonial Terror: Torture and State Violence in Colonial India* (Oxford, 2021).

[143] Singha, *Despotism of Law*, p. 234.

echoed the arguments articulated by Mountstuart Elphinstone, among others.[144] In the late nineteenth century, as historians like Mark Condos and Elizabeth Kolsky have shown, the introduction of legal mechanisms like the Murderous Outrages Act gave colonial officials 'licence to kill' in frontier areas deemed dangerous or unstable.[145] While these acts were not entirely uncontroversial, they did reflect general acceptance of the idea that officials stationed along the borders of British India should be given free rein to defend themselves and assert their authority by whatever means necessary in what was perceived to be a zone of perpetual warfare. The assumptions enshrined in these laws were in many ways the same as those articulated by the Residents examined in this chapter, who certainly saw themselves as men under siege.

In the early nineteenth century, however, when paramountcy was in its infancy, there was no such agreement with within the Company and among the British public about the Residents' discretionary authority. Though Residents invoked widespread ideas of Indian warfare, political culture, and the law of nations to argue for the necessity of unequal alliances backed by force, their superiors remained unconvinced of the appropriateness of diplomatic agents resorting to coercive measures. While administrators in London and Calcutta emphasized the Residents' responsibility to conciliate, Residents' rather different interpretation of their role at Indian royal courts led them to try to assume military powers and occasionally even to engage in acts that contemporaries deemed savage. The presence of large subsidiary forces might have created problems of their own, not least open mutiny; still, they were clearly seen by Residents as essential to upholding British influence. The governor-general-in-council sought to impose a strict division between the military and diplomatic branches of the Company, but in an imperial context situations of war and routine questions of law and order blurred together.[146] Given that the Company's wars against Indian states were regularly justified on the grounds of the violent and untrustworthy nature of the Indian population, it was perhaps inevitable that such thinking would inform

---

[144] Alastair McClure, 'Archaic Sovereignty and Colonial Law: The Reintroduction of Corporal Punishment in Colonial India, 1864–1909', *MAS* 54, no. 5 (2020): 1716, 1726.

[145] Mark Condos, 'Licence to Kill: The Murderous Outrages Act and the Rule of Law in Colonial India, 1867–1925', *MAS* 50, no. 2 (2016): 479–517; Elizabeth Kolsky, 'The Colonial Rule of Law and the Legal Regime of Exception: Frontier 'Fanaticism' and State Violence in British India', *AHR* 120, no. 4 (2015): 1218–1246.

[146] For this point, see Anupama Rao and Steven Pierce, 'Discipline and the Other Body: Humanitarianism, Violence, and the Colonial Exception', in *Discipline and the Other Body: Correction, Corporeality, Colonialism* (Durham, NC, 2006), p. 2.

the activities of the Company's civilian officials, from their high valuation of the army to their use of corporal punishment.

These debates also speak to contemporary concerns about the adoption of purportedly 'Indian' styles of rule. As Britons perceived it, Indian political legitimacy was rooted in the ability to protect one's clients and punish infractions with dramatic shows of force, and it was certainly considered desirable for the Residents to possess this aura of authority. At the same time, this principle not only directly contravened the conventions governing traditional diplomatic activity, it also brought into question the Company's claim to be curbing the brutality of Indian rulers. Thus, controversies over displays of force were galvanized by the question of how far the Company officials should assimilate to Indian political culture.

The same basic problem animated controversies over Residency expenditures. Though we might not usually connect debates over the appropriate use of violence with seemingly petty disputes over money, there is a common thread running through these discussions. The core issue that contemporaries were grappling with was the question of what constituted legitimacy in an imperial setting. To establish themselves at Indian courts British officials had to engage with Indian culture, but in what ways, and to what extent? The following chapter will show how these questions manifested themselves in recurring disagreements over Residency budgets, particularly concerning money spent on gift exchange and display.

4   The Price of Pageantry

Scattered across the Indian landscape, a few telling traces of the Residents remain. In Lucknow, the Residency's imposing ruins are a popular tourist destination because of their association with the Uprising of 1857, when the British inhabitants of the area sheltered within the fortifications for close to three months. In Hyderabad, the splendid Palladian villa commissioned by James Achilles Kirkpatrick, once used as a university building, has recently been renovated and opened to visitors who marvel at the double staircase and grand ballroom. Further south, in Kollam (formerly Quilon, the Resident's headquarters in Travancore), a large building with Italian architectural influences, now a government guest house, represents the legacy of John Munro (1810–1820) in the area. Though in varying states of repair, these buildings nevertheless convey one unmistakable message: someone important lived here. With their lofty domes, marble columns, and clean, classical lines, these mansions represent the last vestiges of the Residents' carefully cultivated aura of pomp and circumstance. They are a visible reminder of the magnificence that both reflected and reinforced the authority of the political representatives of the East India Company in the far corners of the subcontinent. That magnificence is the subject of this chapter.

Recent scholarship has, for good reason, foregrounded theatricality, performance, and display as essential components of diplomatic practice.[1] As de Wicquefort observed in his famous diplomatic manual, 'There is not a more illustrious Theatre than a Court; neither is there any Comedy, where the Actors seem less what they are in effect, than Embassadors do in their Negotiation'.[2] Of these performances, gift-giving has attracted the most attention, reflecting a wider scholarly fascination with 'things'.[3] By focusing

---

[1] Karina Urbach, 'Diplomatic History since the Cultural Turn', *HJ* 46, no. 4 (2003): 991.

[2] Wicquefort, *The Embassador and His Functions*, p. 294.

[3] For a review of recent historiographical trends in the study of 'things', see Kate Smith, 'Amidst Things: New Histories of Commodities, Capital, and Consumption', *HJ* 61, no. 3 (2018): 841–861. For an introduction to diplomatic gifts in cross-cultural contexts, see Zoltán Biedermann, Anne Gerritsen, and Giorgio Riello, eds., *Global Gifts: The Material Culture of Diplomacy in Early Modern Eurasia* (Cambridge, 2017).

on interactions circumscribed in space and time, however, historians have tended to reduce gift exchange to a bilateral encounter between giver and receiver, diplomat and ruler. Yet, these forms of ceremonial and display sparked vitriolic and long-running debates that pitted colonial officials against each other. This is because consumption and exchange are about more than performance; they are also about the money required to purchase objects in the first place.

This chapter examines recurring disagreements surrounding the Resident's expense claims, particularly money spent on gifts, accommodation, and equipment. To the extent that they have been addressed, these debates have been described as the inevitable consequence of a basic conflict of interests: put crudely, the Company's hunger for profits was antithetical to the self-interest of the Residents, who endeavoured, for their part, to claim as much money as they could for themselves.[4] This chapter, however, is premised on the idea that the problem of what to spend money on, and how much to spend, is also the problem of what we value, and how much we value it. Rather than treating budgetary concerns as a politically neutral issue, this chapter argues that the quandaries surrounding Residency budgets are suggestive of the ideological uncertainties endemic to Company policy in the late eighteenth and early nineteenth century.

The chapter begins by describing how gift-giving operated at Indian royal courts and how the Residents fit into this pre-existing gift-giving regime; it then explains how and why Company auditors tried to constrain these exchanges. Although fears of overspending and corruption played their part, this should not be interpreted to mean that gift exchanges were dismissed as bribery. Historians of the early modern Company have demonstrated that from the very beginning its agents both recognized and exploited gift-giving's symbolic dimensions. Section 2 shows that even after dynamics within the subcontinent had shifted in the Company's favour, Residents continued to take gift-giving seriously. Auditors' attempts to reduce spending on gifts should not be read as evidence of ignorance, but instead as an anxious desire to delimit relationships between court and Company. Likewise, Section 3 suggests that while bureaucratizing impulses within the Company no doubt helped generate disagreements about money spent on consumption and display, the prevalence of corruption within the Company's history has led us to overlook other kinds of divisions about how money was spent. By taking seriously the squabbles surrounding expense claims, this chapter exposes

---

[4] Fisher, *Indirect Rule,* p. 101.

inconsistencies and ambivalences that previous studies have elided and challenges the stark oppositions that are sometimes drawn between British and Indian political culture during this period.

4.1   The Symbolism and Mechanics of Gift Exchange

Gift exchange occupies a prominent place within the historiography of South Asia because of the centrality of beneficence to early modern understandings of kingship. The provision of gifts and patronage suffused the sovereign with an aura of generosity, a quality emphasized and encouraged in both Hindu and Muslim religious culture. Through gifts of land, titles, and cloth, Indian monarchs positioned themselves as the ultimate wellspring of good fortune relative to their subjects.[5] Gifts also performed an incorporative function, establishing an almost organic relationship between people.[6] Through gifts, rulers created and renewed relationships, whether with subjects, feudatories, or regional allies. On both a symbolic and instrumental level, then, the flow of gifts bound together the multiple political communities that made up the various Hindu and Muslim polities of eighteenth- and nineteenth-century India.[7]

Some objects were more efficacious than others at creating and reproducing relationships. Cloth was considered especially suited to capturing and retaining the essence of its owner.[8] For this reason, gifts of cloth formed a routine part of Mughal court ritual. Visitors, subjects, and supplicants offered *nazr* (gold coins, the presentation of which symbolized a recognition of the ruler as the source of all wealth) and *peshkash* (in this context, assorted valuables such as elephants, horses, or jewels), and in turn accepted *khilat* (ceremonial cloths that symbolically incorporated the recipient into the body of the monarch).[9] Gifts of food performed a similar function, and Indian rulers routinely sat down to dinner with

---

[5] John R. McLane, *Land and Local Kingship in Eighteenth-Century Bengal* (Cambridge, 1993), pp. 96–98.

[6] Bernard S. Cohn, 'Representing Authority in Victorian India', in *The Invention of Tradition*, ed. Eric Hobsbawm and Terence Ranger (Cambridge, 1983), pp. 168–169.

[7] Lloyd I. Rudolph and Susanne Hoeber Rudolph, 'The Subcontinental Empire and the Regional Kingdom in Indian State Formation', in *Region and Nation in India*, ed. Paul Wallace (New Delhi, 1985), p. 51; J. F. Richards, 'The Formulation of Imperial Authority under Akbar and Jahangir', in *Kingship and Authority in South Asia*, ed. J. F. Richards (Madison, WI, 1978), p. 315.

[8] C. A. Bayly, 'The Origins of Swadeshi (Home Industry): Cloth and Indian Society, 1700–1930', in *The Social Life of Things: Commodities in Cultural Perspective*, ed. Arjun Appadurai (Cambridge, 1986), p. 287.

[9] Cohn, 'Representing Authority in Victorian India', pp. 168–169.

their ministers, distributing meals that were carefully differentiated to signal the respective status of the men who would consume them.[10] While cloth and food occupied a special place as particularly symbolic gifts, gift exchanges of all kinds could be understood, to some extent at least, as having these kinds of social and symbolic connotations. Robes of honour formed part of a wider corpus of 'transactional' symbols, objects that, according to historian Stewart Gordon, affirmed the sovereign's royal legitimacy by being given away.[11]

From the first, Europeans were readily incorporated into this gift economy. Studies of the English, Dutch, and Portuguese in the seventeenth century have shown that they recognized the importance of gifts for forming and maintaining relationships within the subcontinent.[12] For the English in particular, Guido van Meersbergen has highlighted how the exchange of objects and cash was used to enfold the Company within structures of imperial patronage and protection; facilitate good relationships with provincial authorities and local officials; and promote English trade. The gifts given conformed closely to Mughal tastes and precedents, and functioned, van Meersbergen argues, 'as the material expression of notions of submission, loyalty, and service, as well as patronage, honor, and reward.'[13]

The events of 1757, in altering power dynamics in Bengal, expanded opportunities for Company agents to profit from these exchanges. In the 1760s, as Bengali courtiers jostled for control, they made presents to council members in Calcutta to accrue influence and favour. In response, in 1764 the Court of Directors in London prohibited the receipt of presents. Henceforth, the Company's civil servants were required to sign covenants promising to eschew the practice. Almost ten years later, however, disclosures made to a parliamentary select committee suggested that the habit of taking presents persisted in

---

[10] Kate Brittlebank, *Tipu Sultan's Search for Legitimacy: Islam and Kingship in a Hindu Domain* (Delhi, 1997), p. 99.

[11] Stewart Gordon, 'Robes of Honour: A "Transactional" Kingly Ceremony', *IESHR* 33, no. 3 (1996): 241.

[12] Joao Melo, 'Seeking Prestige and Survival: Gift-Exchange Practices between the Portuguese Estado da India and Asian Rulers', *Journal of the Economic and Social History of the Orient* 56, no. 4/5 (2013): 672–695; Kim Siebenhuner, 'Aproaching Diplomatic and Courtly Gift-Giving in Europe and Mughal India: Shared Practices and Cultural Diversity', *The Medieval History Journal* 16, no. 2 (2013): 525–546.

[13] Guido van Meersbergen, '"Intirely the Kings Vassalls": East India Company Gifting Practices and Anglo-Mughal Political Exchange (c. 1670–1720)', *Diplomatica* 2, no. 2 (2020): 289.

Bengal, resulting in a further prohibition as part of the Regulating Act of 1773.[14] By this time, the return of growing numbers of wealthy Company officials was beginning to stoke fear and resentment in Britain. The impeachment trial of Warren Hastings, wherein allegations of present-taking loomed large, further cemented the image of civil servants on the take. Pitt's India Act of 1784 forbade the acceptance of presents in even stronger terms.[15] Whereas the Regulating Act of 1773 had implied that presents might be accepted on behalf of the Company, the 1784 Act included within its compass the demanding or receiving of presents 'for, or pretended to be for, the use of the said company, or of any other person.'[16]

The practice of buying the Company's favour persisted during the period 1798–1818, but more often in the guise of loans or donations than gifts. This was particularly true of Awadh. In some instances, we know that the loans were coerced. When the Marquess of Hastings claimed, on his return to Britain, that the loans advanced by Ghazi ud-Din Haidar during the Gurkha War had been made willingly as a mark of the nawab's gratitude for the dismissal of Resident John Baillie, Baillie revenged himself by publicizing that the loan 'was by no means voluntary nor spontaneous, but was negotiated [...] under most arduous and difficult circumstances'.[17] Michael Fisher has confirmed that Ghazi ud-Din was convinced, against his will, to supply the Company with horses, bullocks, and substantial loans at low interest rates.[18] Similar pressures may have been at work when his predecessor Saadat Ali Khan advanced thirty lacks of rupees on loan during the Second Maratha War, and urged his courtiers to do the same.[19] The Company's growing political influence and military presence framed the exchange of gifts; they cannot be assumed to have been voluntary.

It is difficult to determine to what extent Residents personally profited from gift exchange with the Indian political elite during the period

---

[14] Vinod Pavarala, 'Cultures of Corruption and the Corruption of Culture: The East India Company and the Hastings Impeachment', in *Corrupt Histories*, ed. Emmanuel Kreike and William Chester Jordan (Rochester, NY, 2004), pp. 293–295.

[15] P. J. Marshall, *The Impeachment of Warren Hastings* (Oxford, 1965), pp. 130–162.

[16] East India Company Act, 1784, sections 45–46.

[17] 'Debate at the East India House, 23 March 1825', *Asiatic Journal* 19 (London, 1825), p. 745. See also 'Debate at the East India House, 22 December 1824', *Asiatic Journal* 19 (London, 1825), pp. 60–61.

[18] Fisher, *Clash of Cultures*, p. 181.

[19] NAI, FSC, 31 January 1805, no. 152–154, John Collins to Richard Wellesley, 6 December 1804, pp. 1–2; further loans were made over the following days, see NAI, FSC, 31 January 1805, no. 157, John Collins to Richard Wellesley, 10 December 1804.

1798–1818. On one occasion, at least, James Achilles Kirkpatrick was presented with a valuable diamond ring as a sign of Nizam Ali Khan's favour that he appears to have kept for himself.[20] The Lucknow jewels supposedly acquired by John Baillie during his time as Resident became part of the local lore of Inverness after his return.[21] These kinds of gifts are almost never mentioned in the Residents' official or unofficial correspondence, but then Company regulations would have dictated against Residents reporting these gifts if they had sought to profit from them, and it is possible that Residents would have felt reticent about mentioning them to family or friends.

Perhaps as a result, to the extent that gifts of this nature are discussed in the Residents' correspondence, it is normally to say that they have been rejected. For example, Henry Russell mentions in a letter to his brother Charles that he has accepted a pair of shawls sent by Azizullah (the Residency munshi at Hyderabad), but has rejected the offer of a horse; in his words, 'it is hardly the sort of Present that suits our relative situation; and is besides, in Point of Value, more than he ought to give with Prudence or I to accept with Propriety'.[22] In this case the gift was probably mentioned because Charles (then Assistant Resident at Hyderabad) was the channel whereby the gift reached Russell; the horse was likely considered inappropriate because Azizullah, as an employee of the Residency, was subordinate to Russell (who had just been appointed to a post there). To accept such an expensive gift would have invested Azizullah with a dignity above his station, while placing Russell in a position of debt. Similarly, when Mountstuart Elphinstone was offered a piece of land by Raghuji Bhonsle, he interpreted the gift to mean that 'the Raja thought it material to have favorable representations given of his conduct'. Elphinstone claimed to treat the offer with 'ridicule & contempt', mentioning it only because, in the context of Elphinstone's attempts to negotiate a treaty with the raja, the offer seemed to suggest that the raja was inclined to a rapprochement with the Company.[23] In both cases, the acceptance of the gift would have been onerous to the Resident, whether by conferring prestige on an inferior (as in Russell's case) or by placing an obligation on the Resident to reciprocate in some way (as with Elphinstone). Residents might have preferred to maintain their

[20] J. A. Kirkpatrick estimated the value of the diamond ring at a thousand pounds. BL, APAC, Mss Eur F228/12, J. A. Kirkpatrick to William Kirkpatrick, 12 October 1800, p. 215.

[21] Joseph Mitchell, *Reminiscences of My Life in the Highlands* (Newton Abbot, repr. 1971), p. 60.

[22] Bodl. Oxf., Russell Papers, MSS. Eng. lett. d. 152, Henry Russell to Charles Russell, 18 December 1810, p. 62.

[23] BL, APAC, Mss Eur F109/89, Mountstuart Elphinstone to John Adam, 1 January 1805

status and freedom of action rather than to accept gifts that would have placed them in a difficult position at court or contravened Company regulations.

Residents might, however, just as easily have taken advantage of their position at court, endeavouring to make their fortune and return home in the shortest possible time frame. Writing to a family friend in Scotland, Archibald Seton alluded to the nabob's reputation for corruption and noted that 'it had been easy for me, had I been that which Indeans are frequently said to be, to have brought home with me as many pounds as I shall bring rupees'. According to Seton, 'the law could not have checked me discovery could not have followed, but *in foro conscientiae* that most just and most formidable of all tribunals I should have stood condemned'. In Seton's view, all the money in the world was not worth 'the sad sacrifice of a mans own esteem', but it is hard to say how many Residents came to a similar conclusion given that, according to Seton, they had only their own consciences to answer to.[24] Family correspondence reveals that many Residents, including Seton himself, were under pressure to provide for their relations or buy back family estates. Seton's friends in Inverness speculated that he lacked the 'vigilance & activity' to make the most of his situation, and worried that he 'never will collect a fortune to return home'.[25] By contrast, John Baillie, Resident at Lucknow and part of the same Inverness circle, was known to be 'a liberal man and is very rich'.[26] At Lucknow, visitors reported that Baillie lived in 'a sumptuous style'.[27] On returning to Scotland, he made a great splash by travelling to church in 'a very ornate and striking' carriage, 'the handsomest ever seen in the North'.[28] In addition to enlarging and improving the house inhabited by his sisters, Baillie also used his profits to build Leys Castle, a palatial country house, reminding us that the grand Residency buildings that left their mark on the Indian landscape found their parallel in manor houses across Britain and Ireland.[29]

While the exchange of illicit gifts is difficult to detect, we do know that Residents regularly exchanged gifts on the Company's behalf. In addition to exchanging nazr for khilat, Residents also gave less ritualized presents.

---

[24] NLS, Seton of Touch Papers, MS 19208, Archibald Seton to Henry Steuart, 18 December 1808, p. 100.

[25] NRAS, Fraser of Reelig Papers, B333, to William Fraser from his parents, 20 November 1807, p. 3.

[26] NRAS, Fraser of Reelig Papers, B65, Edward Fraser to his father, 31 July 1812, p. 9.

[27] NRAS, Fraser of Reelig Papers, B65, Edward Fraser to Jane Anne, May 1813, p. 6.

[28] Mitchell, *Reminiscences,* p. 58.

[29] Ibid., p. 60. On East India Company fortunes and British country houses, see Margot Finn and Kate Smith, eds., *The East India Company at Home 1757–1857* (London, 2018).

New Residents usually presented gifts to the ruler upon arrival. Mountstuart Elphinstone turned up at Nagpur loaded down with offerings for Raghuji Bhonsle, his family, and his ministers, including 'two of the largest and most ornamented mirrors', a number of pistols and fowling pieces, 'a most elegant & various assortment of cutlery', 'two or three richly embroidered saddles & trappings, for horses', and 'a few illuminated & elegantly bound Hindoo books'.[30] Holidays and major events such as weddings, births, and circumcisions all prompted further gifts.[31] Outside of special occasions, gifts were also sometimes given on a more spontaneous and informal basis, as Residents used their Company networks to secure rare and desirable items for the pleasure of the ruler or his ministers.[32]

Gifts given in informal contexts might vary subtly according to the tastes of the recipient, but there was an overwhelming continuity in the kind of gifts exchanged in official and ceremonial contexts. Gifts of cloth, jewels, elephants, and horses were traditional Indian political presents, with recognized meanings, that figured prominently in these exchanges. Whereas cloth was perceived to retain something of the essence of the giver, jewels were believed to possess talismanic qualities.[33] Elephants and horses, while practically useful for travel and warfare, were also symbolically associated with kingship and authority, and were usually presented heavily laden with jewelled saddles and trappings.[34] These key presents were supplemented with European specialties. According to Archibald Seton, it was 'to foreign articles, from their superior beauty, their greater scarcity, and their consequent difficulty of procurement, that the natives attach the highest value.'[35] Standard items included dishware, guns, telescopes, and timepieces.[36]

---

[30] BL, APAC, Mss Eur F109/88, Mountstuart Elphinstone to John Adam, 18 April 1804.

[31] See for example BL, APAC, Mss Eur D514/1, Richard Strachey to J. H. Sherer, Civil Auditor, 16 October 1811, p. 51; Richard Strachey to J. H. Sherer, Civil Auditor, 26 August 1812, p. 171.

[32] For example, James Achilles Kirkpatrick collected game cocks and pigeons for the Nizam and his ministers; see BL, APAC, Mss Eur F228/11, J. A. Kirkpatrick to William Kirkpatrick, 21 February 1799, p. 80; Mss Eur F228/13, J. A. Kirkpatrick to William Kirkpatrick, 29 June 1801, p. 83.

[33] Brittlebank, *Tipu Sultan*, p. 137.

[34] Sujit Sivasundaram, 'Trading Knowledge: The East India Company's Elephants in India and Britain', *HJ* 48, no. 1 (2005): 27–53; Jagjeet Lally, 'Empires and Equines: The Horse in Art and Exchanges in South Asia, c. 1600–1850', *Comparative Studies of South Asia, Africa, and the Middle East* 25, no. 1 (2015): 96–116.

[35] BL, APAC, Cleveland Public Library Papers, IOR Neg 4227, wq091.92 Ea77p9, Archibald Seton to Marquess of Hastings, 6 June 1814, p. 111.

[36] When the peshwa's palace was seized following the final Maratha War, soldiers discovered 'many very fine gold watches' along with globes, an orrery, and a sundial. BL, APAC, Mss Eur F311/6, Private Journal of an Officer in the Deccan during AD 1817–1818, p. 8.

These items of European manufacture were incorporated into Indian royal collections comprising objects from distant parts of the world; their acquisition was viewed as a manifestation of a ruler's global reach.[37] Some Indian rulers became enthusiastic collectors of European goods, and British visitors to Indian courts were sometimes surprised and unsettled to encounter material reminders of home in very unexpected settings. George Annesley, Viscount Valentia, described in detail his bewilderment on attending an entertainment hosted by Nawab Vizier Asaf ud-Daula, a particularly ardent collector:

The scene was so singular, and so contrary to all my ideas of Asiatic manners, that I could hardly persuade myself that the whole was not a masquerade. An English apartment, a band in English regimentals, playing English tunes; a room lighted by magnificent English girandoles, English tables, chairs, and looking glasses; an English service of plate; English knives, forks, spoons, wine glasses, decanters and cut glass vases – how could these convey any idea that we were seated in the court of an Asiatic Prince?[38]

The nizam of Hyderabad's royal magazine was similarly packed with English woollens, plate, glassware, china, clocks and 'every other article of European manufacture, both of France and of England', though the only item that Sikander Jah ever made any personal use of, according to Thomas Sydenham, was a silver teapot.[39]

The money spent on these gifts was closely regulated. While sanctioning the exchange of presents in cases where the precedent of gift exchange had been inarguably set, the governor-general-in-council nevertheless encouraged the Residents to avoid displays of generosity where possible. For instance, they approved the expenses necessary for Richard Jenkins to host entertainments at the Nagpur Residency upon the marriage of the raja's daughter, because 'this compliment would be expected in conformity to the usage observed on former occasions of a similar nature', but nevertheless cautioned him that such expenses, 'should, if possible, be avoided in future', urging Jenkins consider 'in what manner our intentions in this respect can be effected [...] without subjecting our public Residents to the imputation of being deficient in the usual forms

---

[37] Brittlebank, *Tipu Sultan*, p. 119. See also Indira Viswanathan Peterson, 'The Cabinet of King Serfoji of Tanjore: A European Collection in Early Nineteenth Century India', *The Journal of the History of Collections* 1, no. 1 (1999): 71–93.

[38] Viscount George Valentia, *Voyages and Travels in India, Ceylon, the Red Sea, Abyssinia, and Egypt*, 2 vols (London, 1809), I, p. 144. Rosie Lewellyn-Jones describes the collections of Asaf ud-Daula and his successors in *Fatal Friendship*, pp. 59–61 and *Engaging Scoundrels*, p. 34.

[39] HC Papers (1812–1813), no. 122, vol. 7, pp. 313–314.

of civility and attention.'[40] Residents were expected to keep detailed records of the presents that were disbursed, their value, and the reasons for their conferment. If they failed to satisfy the civil auditor of the political necessity of the gift, the Company would refuse to cover the cost.[41]

When it came to the receipt of gifts, the Company's position was equally strict. The items that Residents were given in return were not kept by them personally (at least in principle). Instead, the Residents compiled records of the objects they received and their monetary value; these items were then added to the *toshakhana*, a public treasury of ritual presents. These presents could be given again to a different person or could be auctioned off at Calcutta so the proceeds could fund the purchase of future presents.[42] If Residents did wish to keep a present for personal reasons, they might credit the estimated value of the gift to the Company. For example, when one of the peshwa's munshis slipped a diamond ring onto William Palmer's finger, 'saying that the Paishwa requested I would wear it in remembrance of his Friendship & Esteem', Palmer, according to 'custom', gave credit for the sum in his public accounts.[43]

One obvious rationale behind this policy of stringent account-keeping was the desire to eliminate unnecessary expense. By the turn of the nineteenth century, the Company was mired in debt. The ever-increasing deficit was largely the product of recurring warfare with Indian regional powers dating back to the mid-eighteenth century. It was not helped, however, by the wider context of the Revolutionary and Napoleonic Wars then raging across the globe. The wars not only limited trade with Europe but created a steep upswing in French privateering. The British government could usually be relied upon to bail the Company out, when necessary, but by this time the government too was feeling the strain of wartime expenditures. Consequently, its financial aid had to be bought with concessions, namely, surrendering trading privileges, or allowing the navy the use of Company ships. In this position of financial embarrassment, the Company sought to institute a policy of the strictest economy when it came to the purchase of political gifts.[44]

While financial concerns were an important factor shaping Company policy towards gift-giving, however, there is more to the story than mere

[40] BL, APAC, IOR/F/4/308/7060, Extract Political Letter to Bengal, 14 September 1808, p. 1.
[41] BL, APAC, IOR/F/4/527/12633, William Morton to Arthur Henry Cole, 5 February 1816, p. 30.
[42] Cohn, 'Representing Authority in Victorian India', pp. 639–640.
[43] MSA, PRCOP, vol. 38 (1798–1801), William Palmer to Richard Wellesley, 14 November 1800, p. 1060.
[44] For this paragraph, see C. H. Philips, *The East India Company 1784–1834* (Manchester, 1961), pp. 151–155.

parsimony. Bernard Cohn famously contended that Britons dismissed gifts as bribery, viewing these exchanges as purely economic in nature and function, construing the goods thus exchanged as empty commodities lacking social or symbolic overtones.[45] Practically speaking, however, one could hardly expect Residents to be ignorant of the significance of gifts given the Company's long history of exchange. What's more, Cohn's interpretation postulates a radical difference between Britons and Indians, identifying the former as modern and capitalist, the latter, implicitly, as something other. This dichotomy has a long history within the anthropological discipline.[46] Beginning with Marcel Mauss, anthropologists have drawn sharp distinctions between gifts and commodities and the theatres in which these exchanges take place, associating gift-giving predominantly with small-scale, pre-industrial societies.[47] Yet, recent studies of gift-exchange in Europe have made this polarity increasingly untenable, while the broader literature on consumption and exchange has suggested that even apparently straightforward economic transactions can still be and often are symbolic, culturally contingent, and highly social.[48]

4.2   A Fake Circulation of Fake Coin?

Although Britons in India might have treated particular instances of gift-giving with disdain, this by no means signified their disregard for the social and symbolic dimensions of these exchanges in general. To the contrary, Company officials were very sensitive to questions of etiquette. In his published account of his time as escort to the Resident at Shinde's camp, Thomas Duer Broughton grumbled that the presentation of gifts, and particularly khilats, 'is considered more as a matter of bargain and sale than as a compliment'. For Broughton, '[t]here is something very repugnant to European ideas of delicacy in the mode of conducting this part of an entertainment [the exchange of khilats]; especially at a Mahratta Durbar'. Broughton proceeded to complain that 'at this court the *Khiluts* are notoriouosly bad; the Muha Raj always seizes the opportunity to get rid of a lame horse or a foundered elephant', while at the same time noting with contempt how 'some of his Surdars

---

[45] Cohn, 'Representing Authority in Victorian India', p. 163.
[46] Natasha Eaton 'Between Mimesis and Alterity: Art, Gift, and Diplomacy in Colonial India, 1770–1800', *Comparative Studies in Society and History* 46, no. 4 (2004): 17.
[47] Marcel Mauss, *The Gift: The Form and Reason for Exchange in Archaic Societies* (London, repr. 1990), p. 3.
[48] Jonathan Parry and Maurice Bloch, eds., *Money and the Morality of Exchange* (Cambridge, 1989), pp. 1–2.

return a pair of shawls, which they did not like, and desire that they might be changed; with as little delicacy as if they had purchased them at a shop'[49] Contrary to Cohn's thesis, here it is a Company official who accuses Indian ministers of confusing gifts, imbued with sentimental and symbolic value, with commodities. For Broughton, at least, gifts were more than commodities to be bartered for.

Some Residents imply in their letters that they regarded the exchange of gifts as a particularly Indian phenomenon, but they should not be taken at their word. These men were effectively engaging in what Anthony Anghie has termed the 'dynamic of difference', the 'process of creating a gap between two cultures, demarcating one as universal and civilized, and the other as particular and uncivilized'.[50] Mountstuart Elphinstone, for instance, claimed that Indians invested gifts with an importance 'of which a man of sense could have no idea'. In his opinion, 'a few such gifts conciliate the natives more than a long course of fair & honourable conduct joined to the gentlest behaviour. They are all fools & children to a man.'[51] Yet Elphinstone himself regularly exchanged gifts with friends, and never reacted with anything less than delight when favoured with a present; he lauded his friend Edward Strachey as 'the prince of good fellows & pride of old men' for having sent a pair of boots, though he opined that no half boots were to be had, he being 'now under the mortifying necessity of going to dinner in silk stockings which I fancy is rather scandalous.'[52]

As the example of Mountstuart Elphinstone suggests, British men (and women) routinely exchanged gifts as a means of marking out relationships. Historians of eighteenth-century Britain have convincingly demonstrated the important social functions that gifts were recognized to have. Charitable giving endowed the giver with status and strengthened vertical ties within the community, while the exchange of presents between friends and kin created and consolidated horizontal connections.[53] Recipients might be aware of a gift's financial worth, but its value just as often inhered in its social or sentimental connotations; portraits,

[49] Broughton, *Letters Written in a Mahratta Camp*, pp. 95–96.
[50] Anghie, *Imperialism, Sovereignty, and the Making of International Law*, p. 4.
[51] BL, APAC, Mss Eur F109/88, Mountstuart Elphinstone to John Adam, 18 April 1804.
[52] BL, APAC, Mss Eur F128/163, Mountstuart Elphinstone to Edward Strachey, 23 August 1803.
[53] Ilana Krausman Ben-Amos, *The Culture of Giving: Informal Support and Gift-Exchange in Early Modern England* (Cambridge, 2008), p. 195; Amanda Vickery, *The Gentleman's Daughter: Women's Lives in Georgian England* (New Haven, CT, 1998), p. 209; Margot Finn, 'Men's Things: Masculine Possession in the Consumer Revolution', *Social History* 25, no. 2 (2000): 146, 148; Margot Finn, 'Colonial Gifts: Family Politics and the Exchange of Goods in British India, c. 1780–1820', *MAS* 40, no. 1 (2006): 203–231.

for example, were particularly valued for bridging the geographical distance separating friends and relatives.[54] In diplomatic and mercantile contexts, as well, there was a long tradition of establishing relationships through gifts, signalling mutual respect and the desire for mutual benefit.[55] Gift-giving, then, operated in a broadly similar way, in British as in Indian society, as a kind of social and political glue, imbued with meanings that were not strictly tied to the economic value of the object changing hands.

Even where British and Indian gifting conventions differed, givers and recipients were both highly motivated to make sense of the meanings being communicated. Past experience could be mobilized to these ends; a long history of political transactions with Indian royalty meant that members of the Company's political line had a body of institutional knowledge to draw on. Just as important, though, were the ongoing interactions between Residents and the courtly elite that helped place these gifts in context. As Sanjay Subrahmanyam has pointed out, 'states and empires were very rarely ships that passed in the night of incommensurability'.[56] It was possible for Europeans and non-Europeans to arrive at a mutual understanding, even if it required some effort to construct. Indian rulers often made explicit precisely how they wished a gift to be interpreted, usually through an accompanying letter. In their return letters, British officials likewise alluded openly to the meanings underlying their receipt of gifts, signalling their awareness of the gift's symbolic value. Governor General the Earl of Minto specifically thanked the royal women of Delhi for their gifts of shawls, whose 'principal value', he wrote, 'consists in their having been worn by persons of your royal Highness's rank.' Such a present was, he recognized, 'a distinguished mark of favor and condescension'.[57]

Nor can we forget the Indian experts who considered it their job to educate Residents in the nuances of gift-giving. Residents could and often did refer to the munshis who acted as secretaries and political agents, or the ministers who so often mediated between the Residency and the monarch.[58] In cases where the Resident appeared blind to the

---

[54] Richard Jenkins, Resident at Nagpur, begged his mother for portraits of her and his sisters, urging her to spare no expense on 'what will be to me an inestimable treasure'. BL, APAC, Mss Eur E111, Richard Jenkins to his mother, 28 December 1813, p. 210.

[55] Cynthia Klekar, '"Prisoners in Silken Bonds": Obligation, Trade, and Diplomacy in English Voyages to Japan and China', *Journal for Early Modern Cultural Studies* 6, no. 1 (2006): 84–105; Maija Jansson, 'Measured Reciprocity: English Ambassadorial Gift Exchange in the 17th and 18th Centuries', *Journal of Early Modern History* 9, no. 3 (2005): 348–370.

[56] Subrahmanyam, *Courtly Encounters*, p. 29.

[57] NLS, Minto Papers, MS 11579, Earl of Minto to Kudsia Begam, 8 March 1809, p. 32.

[58] For example, BL, APAC, Mss Eur F228/11, J. A. Kirkpatrick to William Kirkpatrick, 28 October 1799, p. 277.

implications of a failure to follow the proper protocol, the minister or munshi could alert him to the meanings that might be read into such an act. For instance, the minister at Hyderabad intervened when Thomas Sydenham neglected to host Sikander Jah at his Residency. Sydenham recognized that such an occasion would require him to present the nizam with presents and would therefore put the Company to considerable expense, but the minister convinced Sydenham of the necessity of the measure by pointing out that it 'would be extremely gratifying to his Highness and might conduce to a familiar Intercourse between his Highness and myself [Sydenham]'.[59]

If the Residents accepted the social and symbolic functions that gifts could have, and were able to participate in these exchanges with some degree of cultural competence, what messages did they try to convey through the gifts that they presented and received? Christian Windler, commenting on political gift-giving in nineteenth-century Franco-Tunisian diplomacy, concluded that the giving of timepieces was 'only the most persistent instance of a cultural ascendancy communicated by the carefully designed composition of presents'.[60] In an Indian context, however, there is little to suggest that Residents chose presents intended to symbolize British technological advancement. The objective, at least according to surviving sources, was to conciliate the ruler in question by catering to Indian tastes as Residents understood them. Thomas Sydenham explicitly sought out 'such rare and curious Machines and Trinkets as I thought suited to the Nizams Fancy', including telescopes, air pumps, thermometers, hand organs, opera glasses, spectacles, and an electrical machine.[61] Mountstuart Elphinstone similarly tracked down timepieces at the desire of Raghuji Bhonsle, noting that 'the Raja is very curious in watches & is well provided in every thing but repeaters' (a clock that audibly chimes the hour, usually by pulling a cord).[62] Although war and ceremonial were considered crucial to the construction of an 'empire of opinion', political gifts seem to have been used primarily to accrue social, rather than symbolic, capital; their purpose was to amuse and entertain.[63]

Apart from giving and receiving gifts of their own, Residents also tried to monitor and control the exchange of gifts between courts as part of a

---

[59] BL, APAC, IOR/F/4/296/6833, Thomas Sydenham to Earl of Minto, 26 August 1808, pp. 29–30.

[60] Christian Windler, 'Tributes and Presents in Franco-Tunisian Diplomacy', *Journal of Early Modern History* 4, no. 2 (2000): 186.

[61] BL, APAC, IOR/F/4/296/6833, Thomas Sydenham to Earl of Minto, 26 August 1808, p. 31.

[62] BL, APAC, Mss Eur F109/88, Mountstuart Elphinstone to John Adam, 4 March 1804.

[63] On 'empire of opinion', see Sramek, *Gender, Morality, and Race*, p. 2.

broader strategy of subordinate isolation. Company administrators were particularly keen to preclude the exchange of gifts between Maratha courts, given the existential threat posed by an anti-British Maratha alliance. In 1803, the Company signed a treaty with the nominal head of the Marathas, the peshwa of Pune, that was designed to position the Company as chief mediator between the different Maratha courts. To cement this new political configuration, the Residents refused to allow the Marathas to exchange the usual gifts of coin and ceremonial robes. Despite his protestations, the Resident also denied Yashwant Rao Holkar the right to a robe of investiture, traditionally offered by the peshwa of Pune to royal heirs as a public recognition of their right to succeed. The Resident's justification for refusing these requests was that they implied a pre-eminence on the part of the peshwa contrary to the stipulations of the treaty, which was supposed to have placed the Marathas on an equal footing. Maratha aspirations to give and receive gifts were clearly taken seriously, since Resident Barry Close (then absent on military campaigns) informed his substitute at court that 'as the question is of a very delicate nature, I shall be happy if you will correspond with me minutely on every point that may occur relating to its future agitation or progress'.[64]

Company officials likewise tried to manipulate or evade these rituals to accentuate their own status. Successive governors general were keen to ensure that their participation was not interpreted as a form of submission. Resistance to these rituals increased over time. Governor General Richard Wellesley accepted gifts of ceremonial cloth from Indian rulers on his tour of the Northwest Provinces but insisted that these robes be presented to him on trays rather than ritually draped over his person. In this way, Wellesley attenuated the incorporative function of the ritual.[65] A few years later, when Akbar Shah II dispatched an emissary to present the Earl of Minto with an honorary dress, the governor general angrily refused to accede to what he considered to be 'a public acknowledgement of vassalage and submission on the part of the British Government to the throne of Delhi'.[66] Minto's successor, the Marquess of Hastings, similarly denied the emperor's request to bestow him with a khilat; Hastings bypassed Delhi altogether on his tour of the Upper Provinces, anxious to

---

[64] Barry Close to William Hamilton, 24 September 1809, in *PRC,* VII, p. 410. Holkar continued to make such applications during the Residency of Close's successor, Mountstuart Elphinstone; see *PRC,* XII, pp. 5, 17, and 20, for example.

[65] Valentia, *Voyages and Travels,* I, p. 99.

[66] BL, APAC, IOR/F/4/393/10009, Extract Political Letter to Bengal, 4 September 1811, pp. 2–3.

avoid 'a ceremonial which was to imply his Majesty's being the liege lord of the British possessions'.[67] Not wishing to offend Akbar Shah, Hastings did however send a deputation to Delhi headed by prominent members of his escort, who were instructed to present nazrs on their own account, and a 'gaudy state chariot' from Hastings himself. Hastings recorded in his diary that 'as an article of convenience and splendour, it was the most striking that I could send; and I wished to show the attention, as I had so much shorn the pretensions of his Majesty to supremacy'.[68] The fact that Hastings was still willing to furnish the Mughal emperor with such a lavish present suggests that the issue was not the monetary expense incurred by the exchange of gifts; the objection, clearly, was to the meanings that would be read into Hastings' acceptance of particular kinds of presents.

The Residents for their part did participate in rituals of subservience to Indian rulers. The exchange of gifts between Resident and ruler was considered by the Resident to be an important means of expressing and reaffirming their mutual importance to each other. For this reason, the Resident at Travancore issued a formal objection to the governor general when the Commercial Resident at Anchuthengu made a present to the raja at a marriage ceremony. Although the Resident referred to the presents as 'trifling', the issue was considered significant enough to prohibit further communication between the Commercial Resident and the court at Travancore on the basis that it undermined the Resident's personal influence and authority at court.[69]

Residents also turned the ritual to their advantage by distributing ceremonial robes of their own to courtiers and officials, thereby establishing themselves as dispensers of patronage in their own right.[70] For instance, following the construction of a water tank in Hyderabad Resident Henry Russell requested to be present at the ceremonial opening; once there, Russell handed out gifts of shawls and money to the minister's servants who had superintended the work, thereby stressing his instrumental role in ensuring the tank's completion.[71] As we shall see in Chapter 5,

---

[67] Bute, ed., *Private Journal*, p. 318.

[68] Ibid., p. 330.

[69] BL, APAC, IOR/F/4/244/5536, Colin Macaulay to Fort St. George, 27 August 1807, pp. 52–53.

[70] Mountstuart Elphinstone recommends this tactic in BL, APAC, Mss Eur F88/219, Report on the Deckan, p. 92. See BL, APAC, IOR/F/4/527/12633, p. 30 for description of shawls presented by Resident of Mysore to his munshi and other servants. See descriptions of similar offerings by a Resident to his munshi in BL, APAC, Mss Eur D514/1, Richard Strachey to J. W. Sherer, 14 March 1812, p. 85.

[71] BL, APAC, IOR/ F/4/403/10119, Henry Russell to N. B. Edmonstone, 10 August 1812, pp. 4–5.

Residents also regularly made public gifts of khilat to their munshis as a way of visibly co-opting the munshi's social and cultural capital and marking him out as a Residency agent. These rituals were a critical plank in the Resident's representational strategies.

Overall, gift-giving served an important function for Residents and their superiors. In addition to conciliating the ruling monarch and his ministers, participation in rituals of exchange served to some extent to naturalize the Company's place within the Indian political order. Viewed in this light, Anglo-Indian gift-exchange seems to exemplify Bourdieu's theory of the gift. For Bourdieu, the practice of gift exchange is only ever a counterfeit of the pure form of giving it is meant to represent, 'a fake circulation of fake coin'. Gift-giving functions (in principle, at least) as 'a kind of social alchemy' transforming 'overt domination into misrecognized, "socially recognized" domination, in other words, *legitimate authority*.'[72] Yet, upon closer examination the metaphor of the gift as a counterfeit coin does not quite hold, at least for this period in the Company's history. The exchange of gifts might well have been self-interested on the Company's side, but this does not mean that these exchanges, or the items thus exchanged, were considered worthless or empty of meaning. To the contrary, precisely because of their important political functions, gifts were carefully selected, deliberately and ceremonially presented, and dutifully recorded by Residents.

To the extent that gift-giving during this period was treated as if it could or should be nothing more than an exchange of commodities, it was usually by Company officials based outside of political capitals rather than the Residents themselves. Though recognizing the value of such activities, auditors and administrators in Calcutta, Madras, and Bombay were broadly uncomfortable with this facet of Indian political culture, and accordingly tried to limit and, in their view, rationalize these practices. The objective was to transform the exchange of gifts into something more commoditized and controlled, and, in so doing, to limit expenses and to confine relationships between the Company and the Indian elite within a narrowly contractual sphere. For instance, the Company administration urged Residents to treat the exchange of coins and ceremonial robes as a direct transaction congruent with the exchange of commodities for money, which entailed giving only gifts whose value they might expect to receive directly in return.[73] Where services were rendered, the Company preferred the Resident to pay for them in cash rather than reciprocating

---

[72] Pierre Bourdieu, *Outline of a Theory of Practice*, trans. Richard Nice (Cambridge, 1987), p. 192.
[73] BL, APAC, IOR/F/4/527/12633, p. 28.

with presents. The civil auditor of Madras chastised Arthur Henry Cole for presenting two shawl pieces to the raja of Coorg in recompense for repairs to an elephant saddle since the shawls were valued at a higher price than the saddle itself.[74]

Because of this assiduous account-keeping, the meaningful exchange of gifts sometimes appeared to be an empty exercise. In her travel journal, Lady Hood, a visitor to the court of Mysore, described such an exchange of jewels between the Resident and the raja: 'this reciprocation of presents', she wrote, 'was rather farcical, as they were on both sides to be lodged next day in the Company's treasury and put to the account of Debtor and Creditor.'[75] The British at court were not blind to the absurdity of such an arrangement, and were well aware that these measures were contrary to the spirit of the practice. By attempting to regulate gift-giving in this way, Company administrators were not betraying their ignorance, but rather, trying to force Indian political practices into a more narrowly defined framework of their choosing, thereby cutting down on costs and limiting relationships of obligation.

This kind of strict reciprocity was not easy to enforce, however. For one thing, it was impossible to anticipate how a gift would be reciprocated. Sometimes a generous gift would be purchased, according to the high status of the recipient, and a mere token given in return. The peshwa's brother, Amrit Rao, though he was greeted with a rich array of presents upon his arrival at Banaras, reciprocated with very paltry gifts, including a horse so old and broken down that the Resident had to prevail on an old *fakir* (religious ascetic) to take the animal off his hands.[76] Circumstances beyond the Resident's control also sometimes dictated the giving of gifts where there could be no assurance of reciprocity, for instance at birthdays or weddings. Finally, the Resident's pre-eminence at court sometimes precluded him from receiving gifts in turn. The Resident at Hyderabad James Achilles Kirkpatrick objected to the Company's emphasis on total reciprocity on the grounds that his position of high distinction prohibited this kind of equivalence. Out of respect for his position, visitors to Hyderabad were expected to pay Kirkpatrick the first visit. Kirkpatrick, for his part, rarely repaid that visit except as a mark of special respect and attention. This meant that Kirkpatrick could not

---

[74] BL, APAC, IOR/F/4/527/12633, George Moore, Civil Auditor, to Chief Secretary to Government, 24 November 1815, p. 6.

[75] NAS, Seaforth Papers, GD46/17/39, Lady Hood, 'Sketch of a Journey to Seringapatam & Mysoor', p. 117. See also Mundy, *Pen and Pencil Sketches*, I, pp. 19–20.

[76] UPSAA, Benares Residency Records, Letters Received by the Agent to the Governor General, January–July 1805, basta no. 11, book no. 46, T. Brooke to W. A. Brooke, 1 August 1808, pp. 160, 162.

expect to be reimbursed in kind for his munificence, since it was the host who was normally responsible for offering presents to his guests.[77] The lack of equivalence between the gifts given, and gifts received, signalled and at the same time cemented Kirkpatrick's pre-eminence.

As the example of Kirkpatrick suggests, the Residents themselves chafed at financial restraints imposed on them from on high. Through the lens of gift-giving, we see a split between Company auditors in government headquarters and the Resident on the ground. Gifts expressed social cachet as well as conciliating figures of political import at court. Consequently, many Residents found the administration's emphasis on money frustrating because the exchange of gifts clearly had social and political implications that could not be tallied in terms of rupees spent or received. As Bourdieu argued in his influential theory of the gift, gift-giving, though seemingly disinterested, is often motivated by the desire to translate one's wealth into influence and social prestige.[78] While the Resident's superiors sought to shore up the Company's stock of economic capital, from the Resident's perspective this money was practically meaningless. A capital of obligations and debts, by comparison, could help the Resident to do his job by ensuring the cooperation of important figures at court. From the Residents' point of view, money spent on gift-giving could hardly be considered lost, merely transformed into a more useful currency.

This clash between Residents and Company auditors was one important flashpoint in a broader field of combat, namely, the Resident's expense claims. In addition to a small monthly salary, the Resident was also permitted to claim certain expenses on a monthly basis because of the public duties incumbent on him as a government representative (except at Lucknow, where the Resident retained the prerogative of a larger salary until 1821).[79] Legitimate costs included office establishment, table attendance and camp equipage, daks, intelligence, charity, and articles purchased for presents. According to a Company policy of 1805, these expense claims could not exceed Rs 5193 per month, a sum that was meant to constitute a hard maximum rather than a fixed monthly allowance.[80] Once submitted, expense claims were closely scrutinized by the civil auditor, who evaluated whether or not the costs laid

---

[77] BL, APAC, Mss Eur F228/82, J. A. Kirkpatrick to John Lumsden, 17 June 1800, pp. 19–20.

[78] Bourdieu, *Outline of a Theory of Practice*, p. 192.

[79] House of Commons Papers, *Return of Civil Offices*, p. 2.

[80] BL, APAC, IOR/F/4/527/12633, Memorandum of rules observed in the adjustment and audit of the accounts of Residencies at foreign courts under the Bengal government, pp. 22–29.

out by the Resident were public and essential and therefore fit to be covered by the Company, or whether the charges represented private or non-essential expenses to be defrayed by the Resident. The civil auditor and the Resident frequently disagreed on the status of various expenses, thus requiring the intervention of the governor general or occasionally the Court of Directors to decide the issue. These disagreements were symptomatic of larger uncertainties concerning the vague boundary between the Resident's public and private life as well as the disputed nature of the Company's influence and how it should be expressed. These squabbles over money, though no doubt motivated to some degree by the personal interests of the people involved, are therefore more revealing than they might at first appear of the shifting and ill-defined nature of the Residency system in its early years.

4.3   The Spectre of the 'Sultanised Englishman'

After Colin Macaulay's home was looted during an 1809 insurrection, he drew up an inventory of items lost or damaged as a result, hoping to reclaim his estimated losses from the Travancore government. The inventory provides a fascinating glimpse into the material life of the Residency. The first impression is an abundance of textiles: of shirts, waistcoats, pantaloons, stockings, and handkerchiefs numbering into the hundreds. Other missing items include books; stationary; two telescopes; a magnifying glass; four pairs of spectacles; an opera glass; a collection of swords and pistols; a repeating watch. Some items are singled out for their associations: a seal engraved with a Persian title obtained from the Mughal emperor (likely Shah Alam) by John Duncan while Resident at Benares; a diamond ring received from the governor general (likely Richard Wellesley); two rings purchased at Srirangapatnam; a gold medal depicting Cornwallis's reception of Tipu Sultan's sons by following the Second Mysore War. Added to this is a mass of tableware: toasting forks; nutmeg graters, cheese knives; bread baskets; butter dishes; teaspoons; complete sets of fine English earthenware, china ware, table and dessert service. Finally, large quantities of madeira, claret, constantia, hock, beer, port wine, tea, rum, perry, cider, and cherry brandy.[81]

The inventory evokes the complex blend of public and private life occurring within the Residency precincts. On the one hand, the inventory includes some of Macaulay's most intimate possessions, from the rudimentary basics (his handkerchiefs, his slippers) to the sentimental and the commemorative. Equally, the inventory attests to Macaulay's

[81] BL, APAC, IOR/F/4/338/7682, 24 May 1809, pp. 12–17.

participation in eighteenth-century consumer culture, the world of silver buckles, porcelain dishes, and nankeen trousers described by historian Maxine Berg.[82] Finally, the inventory is a testament to Macaulay's representative functions, and the Residency's place as a centre of British hospitality: a generous table where visiting soldiers and officials could count on lavish dinners and a steady flow of spirits.

The dual role of the Residency, as private home and public, political space, complicated Residency finances. Compared to other branches of the civil service, Residents' salaries were relatively small, because their household expenses were meant to be covered by the Company. The arrangement ran counter to developing trends within the Company and across Britain at large, however, where distinctions were increasingly drawn between 'public' and 'private' life. Just as Pitt and other reformers within the British government sought to systematize the civil service through the payment of salaries in place of stipends, so too did the governor-general-in-council hope that closer scrutiny of the Residents' expenses would save money and preclude corruption.

The Residency, however, was a troubling reminder that the distinction between public and private remained far from clear in the early nineteenth century, particularly where diplomacy was concerned. The difficulty was how to distinguish between the Resident's personal needs and his public, representative role. The Resident was, after all, the Company's physical embodiment in far-flung Indian kingdoms; it made sense for him to be arrayed so as to reflect the Company's status. It was therefore difficult to determine a limit to be set to the Resident's spending, whether on gifts to be dispensed at court, or on carriages and personal attendants. If the sumptuousness of the Resident's establishment did not match or exceed that of his peers at court, it could, after all, reflect ill on the Company, producing, Thomas Sydenham argued, 'Impressions on all ranks of People, very unfavorable to the former notions of our Power and resources'.[83]

As the Company's influence expanded, the Residency's expenses, and arguments about them, increased accordingly. Throughout his tenure at Hyderabad, James Achilles Kirkpatrick was at pains to convey that his greater expenditure (relative to his predecessors) was an inevitable consequence of the changed relationship between the Company and the court. The establishment of a subsidiary force, as well as the larger number of visitors passing to and from the Residency, represented a significant drain

---

[82] Maxine Berg, *Luxury and Pleasure in Eighteenth-Century Britain* (Oxford, 2005).
[83] BL, APAC, IOR/F/4/311/7096, Thomas Sydenham to N. B. Edmonstone, 7 August 1806, pp. 14–15.

upon the Residency's table expenses. The Residents' expanded business, meanwhile, required an increased staff of scribes and accountants as well as household servants.[84] Overall, Residents were required to devote more money and attention to their public image. Elphinstone agreed; writing in 1812 to propose the construction of a new Residency building at Pune, Elphinstone pointed out that the current Residency had been built in 1786 'at a time when Pune was never visited by an English gentleman, except attached to the Residency, and it was made as small as possible to avoid exciting the [peshwa's] Jealousy'. Elphinstone complained that some of the bungalows in the military cantonment surpassed those of the Residency, concluding that '[t]he nature of his office, and the practice of the government, seem to establish that a Resident should possess a spacious and commodious dwelling and that the general appearance of his furniture and establishment should be superior to that ordinarily met with at the place where he resides.'[85]

Seizing on the distinctive nature of their work, Residents argued for increased personal allowances on the grounds that their position put them at a financial disadvantage relative to other Company servants. The contention was that their public responsibilities precluded the frugal habits they might otherwise have espoused. John Munro for instance contrasted his previous life as 'a private member of society' when he 'was at perfect liberty to live in whatever manner might be most suitable to my income or views', with his current situation where as 'the Organ of the authority of the British Government, and as ostensibly occupying the first place of the community, I must from considerations of public Duty support the establishments and incur the expences that are necessary for the maintenance of that weight and respect which the Natives attach to certain appearances of state'.[86] The governor general, when presenting Archibald Seton's claims before the Court of Directors, similarly noted that in Seton's previous role as provincial judge his 'personal habits' had 'admitted of his reserving a portion of his allowances, [...] larger than the amount which he is able to set aside from the Salary of the Resident at Delhi'.[87]

It was near impossible to determine the truth of such statements, however, since the government could only take the Resident at his word

---

[84] NAI, FSP, James Achilles Kirkpatrick to N. B. Edmonstone, 29 February 1804, pp. 11054–11055.

[85] BL, APAC, IOR/F/4/384/9790, Mountstuart Elphinstone to N. B. Edmonstone, 17 April 1812, pp. 7–10.

[86] BL, APAC, IOR/F/4/481/11553, John Munro to Chief Secretary to Government, 16 March 1814, pp. 16–17.

[87] BL, APAC, IOR/F/4/312/7119, Governor General's Minute, 4 August 1809, p. 36.

when it came to how he had previously disposed of his personal salary, or how he intended to employ his present allowances. In support of Archibald Seton's claim for an enlarged monthly allowance, the Earl of Minto assured the Court of Directors of Seton's 'high spirit of public zeal and honour', arguing that he would 'never be induced with views of personal emolument to retrench those personal establishments which are essentially necessary for the maintenance of the dignity and influence of the Government which he presents.'[88] In advancing this argument, however, Minto implicitly admitted the possibility that a Resident could mishandle Company funds in such a manner. Despite his position of public authority, the Resident was also a private person whose own desires might lead him to misrepresent the political necessity of his expenses. Given these conflicting interests, it was difficult to determine whether the Resident was driven by concern for the public good, or his personal fortunes.

Residents' geographical distance from administrative centres exacerbated the issue. Their isolation rendered them eminently suspect since their activities were difficult to monitor from Calcutta. At the same time, it was this very distance that allowed Residents to claim the local expertise necessary to decide on questions relating to the Residency's budget. For instance, Metcalfe defended his expenses from the Directors' accusations of exorbitance by emphasizing the large number of Europeans that he was expected to host at Delhi on a routine basis. Metcalfe then proceeded to question 'the equity of a condemnation passed on me by persons, who however high in authority, however respectable individually, however sacred collectively, cannot intuitively judge in London, what expenses may be necessary or superfluous at the Residency at Delhi.'[89] Residents could boast a kind of localized knowledge that Company administrators in far-away Presidency capitals, let alone London, could hardly pretend to.[90] The Resident was the man on the scene, and could plausibly claim to be a better judge of local conceptions of British prestige than his superiors.

Moreover, as the agent on the ground the Resident was also the one whose reputation and authority was most directly at stake. Parsimony might, after all, create an impression of weakness and insignificance in the opinion of the court. Thomas Sydenham complained that reductions in Residency expenses at Hyderabad had convinced the

---

[88] Ibid., p. 41.
[89] BL, APAC, IOR/F/4/552/13387, C. T. Metcalfe to John Adam, 23 July 1815, p. 50.
[90] This was acknowledged by the governor-general-in-council in a letter to the Court of Directors, BL, APAC, IOR/F/4/311/7096, 4 August 1809, p. 6.

nizam 'that my diplomatic Powers & rank were not equal to those of my Predecessors'.[91] Henry Russell, Sydenham's successor, stubbornly demanded a personal escort of cavalry, which he argued was one of the only marks of distinction that visibly identified him as a figure of public importance at Hyderabad. This visual sign of authority was important, according to Russell, since the local population 'can judge of power and authority by no other standard than the external marks of it, and if they saw a Resident with less state than his predecessors, nothing would convince them but that he had less power too.'[92] The Resident's professional credibility was thus perceived to hang in the balance; again, his appearance of grandeur constituted a kind of social capital which, for political purposes, was of more immediate use than money in the bank.

The Resident's private reputation within the European community was equally implicated in these disputes. The Resident's auditors used exceedingly moralizing language when contesting expense claims, accusing Metcalfe, for example, of 'a spirit of [...] profuse extravagance' and 'a lack of wholesome control'.[93] The Residents were very sensitive to these allegations, particularly since rumours of their supposed ostentation sometimes reached their family and friends in Britain. Archibald Seton was very frustrated by talk of his own prodigality, since it appears to have caused his friends and family in Scotland to believe that he had already accumulated a sufficient fortune, and to doubt the sincerity of his intention to return home. As Seton put it in a letter to a family friend, 'I cannot sufficiently regret the busy officiousness of ignorant people who, upon this as upon many other occasions, have misled you by fallacious accounts'. Reacting to gossip that he gave away large sums of money, and that his expenses were needlessly great, Seton countered that 'I do not give away money – and for this simple reason, that I have it not to give.' Of his expenses in general, he wrote, 'to call them large, wears almost an appearance of mockery'.[94] Charles Metcalfe likewise urged his sister to ignore 'idle tales' that he had a hundred horses in his stable. 'I detest wasteful and frivolous expenditure', he assured her, 'and whatever

[91] BL, APAC, IOR/F/4/311/7096, Thomas Sydenham to N. B. Edmonstone, 7 August 1806, p. 15.

[92] BL, APAC, IOR/F/4/372/9248, Henry Russell to N. B. Edmonstone, 31 August 1811, p. 45. A similar point is made in BL, APAC, IOR/F/4/311/7096, Thomas Sydenham to N. B. Edmonstone, 7 August 1806, pp. 14–15.

[93] BL, APAC, IOR/F/4/552/13387, Extract political letter to Bengal, 30 September 1814, p. 7; Metcalfe interpreted this as a serious attack on his character; see BL, APAC, IOR/F/4/552/13387, C. T. Metcalfe to John Adam, 23 July 1815, pp. 30–31.

[94] BL, APAC, IOR Neg 11664, Archibald Seton to Henry Steuart, 18 December 1808.

I do, in that way, is from respect to the situation which I hold'.[95] The disputes over monthly expense claims thus carried personal, as well as professional, connotations. Unsurprisingly, these disputes created serious rifts between the Residents and the men responsible for auditing them, resentments that always lurked close beneath the surface of their correspondence.

Yet, the question of how much money Residents could legitimately claim also had an important ideological dimension that has previously been overlooked. Arguments in favour of large monthly stipends were founded mostly on contemporary stereotypes of Indian political culture.[96] Conventional wisdom was that so-called Oriental polities vested great weight in appearances, and many Company employees expressed the belief that Indians straightforwardly equated conspicuous displays of affluence with power. Governor General the Marquess of Hastings defended the Residents' expenses on the grounds that 'the native Chiefs have seen Power and a certain degree of parade so invariably identified, that they cannot disconnect the notions'. Accordingly, a measure of magnificence was essential 'to prevent the Residents' appearing in a discreditable contrast before those who can only judge by the Eye'.[97] Some contemporaries certainly seem to have recognized the mythic dimensions of this stereotype. Henry Russell described with amusement his father's disappointment upon first sight of the nizam's palace, repeating Henry Russell Sr's complaint that the only establishment he had seen in India that he considered entitled to be called a palace was the Hyderabad Residency. For Russell, the moral of the story was that 'People in Europe are very apt to form their notions of Oriental splendour upon the Arabian Nights, and other Tales of the same kind, and are therefore sure to be disappointed.'[98] Still, even men with long experience of India were apt to cast Indian monarchs into this stereotypical mould. Russell, though he made light of his father's assumptions about Oriental grandeur, nevertheless made a point of attending carefully to appearances, noting to his brother that

---

[95] Lincoln, Lincolnshire Archives, Monson Papers, MON 28/B/23/16/19, C. T. Metcalfe to Emily Viscountess Ashbrook, 6 September 1829. Henry Russell was similarly frustrated by accusations of profligacy; see Bodl. Oxf., Russell Papers, MS. Eng. Misc. c. 327, Henry Russell, Notes and drafts of letters on Indian affairs, p. 236.

[96] BL, APAC, IOR/F/4/552/13387, C. T. Metcalfe to John Adam, 23 July 1815, p. 43; BL, APAC, IOR/F/4/552/13387, Archibald Seton to John Adam, 25 October 1816, p. 87.

[97] BL, APAC, IOR/F/4/552/13387, the Marquess of Hastings to the Court of Directors, 27 October 1816, pp. 74–75.

[98] Bodl. Oxf., Russell Papers, MS. Eng. lett. d. 164, Henry Russell to Charles Russell, February 1813, p. 15.

'the influence of state at Hyderabad is so powerful, that I mean on all Occasions to keep up as much of it as I can'.[99]

Once again, Britons in India were discursively distancing themselves from a feature of Indian society that was not so alien to their own. Royal legitimacy in India did depend to some extent on the ability to project one's power through visual spectacle. The ruler was meant to dazzle his subjects, reflecting his association with the divine.[100] Yet, Europeans, too, saw correlations between power, status, and visible grandeur. Historian Tim Blanning has famously traced the ways in which European monarchs expressed their authority and legitimacy visually in the eighteenth century, whether within the confines of the royal court or in view of the broader public.[101] At the highest levels, ceremonial costume helped distinguish and reinforce the rights and privileges of the monarch and the aristocracy. Among the general population, too, clothes signalled a person's rank and status.[102] The idea that Residents ought to be arrayed in grand fashion, in a manner that adequately represented the standing of the Company, thus accorded with British assumptions concerning the relationship between power and appearances.

At the same time, Britons also possessed a particularly charged notion of 'luxury' and its debilitating power that equally informed contemporary attitudes to the Residents' establishments. Although in the eighteenth century luxury was beginning to have positive connotations of comfort and convenience, it was still weighted with negative associations originating in the classical and Christian tradition.[103] In principle, luxury betrayed the kind of absorption in one's own material well-being which signalled, first, a disregard for the wellbeing of others, and second, a repudiation of God and his spiritual kingdom. Historically, luxury was associated with Roman imperial decline; according to the widely cited Roman moralist Sallust, luxury was imported to Rome from Asia Minor by the returning army, resulting in a civilizational collapse that was at once moral, social, and political. Given the extent to which Roman history served as a model and a frame of reference for the British empire in the late eighteenth century, it should come as no surprise that the

[99] Bodl. Oxf., Russell Papers, MSS. Eng. lett. d. 152, Henry Russell to Charles Russell, 1 April 1811, p. 153. See also BL, APAC, IOR/F/4/372/9248, Henry Russell to N. B. Edmonstone, 31 August 1811, p. 45.
[100] Brittlebank, *Tipu Sultan*, p. 131.
[101] T. C. W. Blanning, *The Culture of Power and the Power of Culture: Old Regime Europe 1660–1789* (Oxford, 2002), p. 5.
[102] Aileen Ribeiro, *Dress in Eighteenth-Century Europe 1715–1789* (London, 1984), pp. 115–131.
[103] John E. Crowley, 'The Sensibility of Comfort', *AHR* 104, no. 3 (1999): 762.

adoption of an Indian lifestyle was similarly feared to have a morally corrosive effect on Britons sojourning there.[104]

Visitors to the Residencies often commented on the Residents' seeming addiction to grandeur (or, perhaps equally telling, expressed surprise when Residents maintained a kind of dignified moderation).[105] As historian Kathleen Wilson has noted, in the eighteenth century character was considered to be contingent on shared language, laws, government, and social organization.[106] Because personalities and behaviours were believed to be intimately related to social and material context, people were not always trusted to act in a civilized manner, that is, in reasoning or virtuous ways, when uprooted from the British context.[107] In line with this conceptualization of mind and body, engaging in Indian forms of ceremonial and spectacle, and living in the manner of an Indian ruler, was feared to have pernicious effects on Britons in India. The Resident at Shinde's court from 1798 to 1804, nicknamed 'King Collins' (whose equipage 'might have served for the Great Mogul' according to John Blakiston), was perhaps the classic example of what James Mackintosh termed '*the Sultanised Englishman*'.[108] Far from being taken for granted, the 'civilisation' of Britons in India, that quality that supposedly differentiated them from Indians (generally defined as control over oneself through use of reason, judgement, and understanding rather than instinct), was considered exceedingly fragile.[109]

The question of how British prestige ought to be made visible in India was further complicated by the fact that the very nature of the Company's administration in India, and the source of its legitimacy, was itself contested during this period. In the mid-eighteenth century, as historian Robert Travers has demonstrated, the British justified their empire in India on the grounds that they were restoring the subcontinent to a pre-Mughal golden age. The Company's legitimacy derived from the claim

---

[104] Philip Ayres, *Classical Culture and the Idea of Rome in Eighteenth-Century England* (Cambridge, 1997), pp. 42–46.

[105] Maria Nugent described Charles Metcalfe as 'a plain, sensible young man, without any show or ostentation', in contrast to John Baillie's 'love of display'. Nugent, *Journal*, pp. 408 and 311, respectively.

[106] Kathleen Wilson, *The Island Race: Englishness, Empire and Gender in the Eighteenth Century* (London, 2003), p. 8.

[107] Ibid.

[108] For a description of John Collins (nicknamed King Collins), see John Blakiston, *Twelve Years Military Adventure in Three Quarters of the Globe* (London, 1829), p. 144. For James Mackintosh's description of the 'Sultanised Englishman' (and his opposite, 'the Braminised Englishman'), see Robert Mackintosh, ed., *Memoirs of the Life of the Right Honorable Sir James Mackintosh,* 2nd ed. (London, 1836), p. 212.

[109] Sheldon Rothblatt, *Tradition and Change in English Liberal Education: An Essay in History and Culture* (London, 1976), p. 17.

that it was introducing a form of government that was more rational and just than that of the Mughals, but which was at the same time consonant with Indian tradition.[110] Administration in such an Indian idiom seemed to require an element of conspicuous consumption and display. Pageantry served both to obscure the Company's commercial origins and to mark its role as successor to the Mughals. The most obvious example of such stately magnificence was Governor General Richard Wellesley's Palladian government house in Calcutta.[111] In his account of his travels to India, Viscount Valentia famously justified his uncle's building project on the grounds that 'India is a country of splendor, of extravagance, and of outward appearances', and that 'the Head of a mighty empire ought to conform himself to the prejudices of the country he rules over'.[112]

As ideas about the Company's role and responsibilities in India began to change, however, so too did beliefs about how its power ought to be made manifest. In the late eighteenth century, as evangelical and utilitarian ideologies began to gain ground in Britain, commentators both within and outside the Company increasingly began to justify the Company's rule in India in terms of the benefits that would accrue to the Indian population through the imposition of supposedly British institutions like private property, rule of law, and Christianity. As the Company's right to rule was increasingly seen to subsist in an inherent British superiority, the Company's administration was accordingly less and less interested in expressing its power in what was perceived to be an Indian idiom.[113] Historian E. M. Collingham has charted these ideological shifts, and the ways in which they were enacted in the bodily practices of the Company's colonial administrators. She notes the decline in pomp and pageantry, seeing it as part of a broader change, namely, the transformation of the nabob, 'the flamboyant, effeminate and wealthy East India Company servant, open to Indian influences and into whose self-identity India was incorporated', into the burra sahib, 'a sober, bureaucratic representative of the Crown'.[114]

What is missing from this account is the unevenness of this transition. Dividing her analysis between the nabob and the burra sahib, Collingham neglects the ways in which the awkward coexistence of two competing ideologies regarding the Company's rule in India posed practical ambiguities for those responsible for enacting the Company's

---

[110] Travers, *Ideology*, p. 7.

[111] E. M. Collingham, *Imperial Bodies: The Physical Experience of the Raj, c. 1800–1947* (Cambridge, 2001), pp. 20, 15

[112] Valentia, *Voyages and Travels*, I, p. 235.

[113] Collingham, *Imperial Bodies*, pp. 51–52.

[114] Ibid., p. 3.

power on the ground. The gap between these rival systems produced an ongoing tension that the Residents were required to negotiate.

This tension is evident in a letter issued by the governor-general-in-council to Thomas Sydenham in response to Sydenham's requests for money to cover the expenses of decorative trappings for elephants and camels. The council refused to cover Sydenham's bills, arguing that 'the dignity and respectability of the British Representatives should be made to rest as in fact it does on more solid foundations than the maintenance of state and splendour borrowed from the manners & habits of the natives [...],in a great degree inconsistent with our national character'.[115] At the same time, the council was careful to complicate this hard stance by assuring Sydenham that 'it is not intended to intimate, [...] that it is unnecessary to adapt our Arrangements, in matters of this nature, to the perceptions and prejudices of the Natives of India. A certain degree of pomp and retinue, must in all situations be the concomitant of Rank and Authority'.[116] What were Residents to make of such equivocation? There was no fixed model to which they could refer. Revealingly, when Mountstuart Elphinstone first took up his position at Nagpur, his letters are full of questions about the money to be spent on gifts and the degree of state to be maintained at the Residency.[117] His uncertainty, and the priority that he placed on his establishment (which he deemed 'so much a public concern'), illustrate the extent to which the matter of Residency finances was perceived to be a significant problem without a clear solution.

4.4 Conclusion

Over time, the emphasis on appearances at the Residencies does seem to have declined. In 1819, Henry Russell abolished the practice of gift-exchange at Hyderabad (though it persisted elsewhere). As Russell explained in his report, '[t]he footing in which we stand is now too high to require that we should exact presents either as an observance of courtesy or as a recognition of the rank of our public Officers and of the servants of the Nizam's Government'.[118] This decision anticipated broader changes in attitude. In 1829, the Court of Directors issued a letter to Governor General William Bentinck urging him to make retrenchments in the

---

[115] BL, APAC, IOR/F/4/311/7096, Extract Political Letter from Bengal, 4 August 1809, pp. 8–9.
[116] Ibid., pp. 27–28.
[117] BL, APAC, Mss Eur F109/88, Mountstuart Elphinstone to John Adam, 13 April 1804; Mountstuart Elphinstone to John Adam, 24 April 1804.
[118] BL, APAC, IOR/F/4/774/20920, Henry Russell to Charles Theophilus Metcalfe, 20 April 1819, pp. 16–17.

political line. The letter declared that the Residencies no longer needed to be maintained at the same expense as before given the changed relationship between the Company and its allies. 'When our power in India was less predominant than it is now become, your political residents were often engaged in conducting difficult negotiations, detecting dangerous intrigues, and defeating formidable combinations against our interests', the directors observed. '[T]heir characters as representatives of the British government, combined with their important avocations, required on public grounds establishments calculated for display, and a corresponding degree of magnificence in their style of living.'[119] Since their Residents now acted more as counsellors than diplomats, however, it was no longer so important that they maintain the same degree of splendour as before. The Court of Directors had always resisted high Residency budgets, but whereas in the past there had been a strong counterargument in favour of magnificence, now the strength of that argument was beginning to diminish in proportion to the perceived significance of Indian rulers. In the aftermath of 1857, ceremonial would be invested with renewed importance, but in a different way, with the emphasis instead on incorporating Indian rulers within a larger, global imperial order rather than establishing and expressing influence at court.[120]

This chapter has demonstrated, however, that during the early years of the Residency system, imperial administrators were hardly so confident when it came to questions of gift-giving and display.[121] Archibald Seton, Resident at Delhi, observing the apparently trivial points of ceremony upon which the Mughal emperor continued to insist in spite of his limited practical authority, wrote cautiously to the governor-general-in-council that 'under the cover of the formal homage, which a tenderness for his personal feelings alone prompts us to render him, he seeks to advance a silent and gradual claim to the Substantial attributes of Empire'.[122] The border between political theatre and 'substantial' power was porous; through consumption and exchange, rulers could assert their sovereign status. Residents, meanwhile, could not guarantee that their 'substantial' power would be accepted as such if it were not performed in a visible, recognizable fashion.

---

[119] Court of Directors to Bengal Government, 18 February 1829, in Philips, ed., *Correspondence of Lord William Cavendish Bentinck*, I, pp. 159–160.

[120] Dick Kooiman, 'Meeting at the Threshold, at the Edge of the Carpet or Somewhere in between? Questions of Ceremonial in Princely India', *IESHR* 40, no. 3 (2003): 315.

[121] Nicholas B. Dirks, *The Hollow Crown: Ethnohistory of an Indian Kingdom* (Cambridge, 1987), p. 354.

[122] BL, APAC, IOR/F/4/334/7656, Extract Political Letter to Bengal, 4 September 1811, p. 19.

This uncertain relationship between power and appearances meant that the upper echelons of the Company could never quite decide how much money Residents should be allowed to spend, particularly when it came to the purchase and exchange of gifts. It seems clear that the desire to regulate the Residents' expenditure was informed by pragmatic efforts at retrenchment and the desire to avoid future corruption scandals. We cannot know for sure how much Residents profited from illicit exchanges at court, but there is good reason to think that they did. Underlying these practical concerns, however, were deeper ideological ambiguities. Members of the political line were aware of the symbolism of gifts and their efficacy at securing relationships both vertically and horizontally. After all, gifts played a similar role in British society, and even were that not the case, the agency of Indian munshis and ministers meant that British officials could hardly be ignorant of their importance. British awareness of the gift's political implications is clearly manifest in their efforts to monitor and regulate gift-giving between courts. The attempt on the part of Company auditors to impose a rigid, contractual framework on gift-giving was therefore not a sign of their disregard, but, instead, a betrayal of their anxious desire to set limits to such relationships of obligation. The Residents, however, resented these restraints; a currency of debts and obligations was crucial to their work as mediators and information gatherers.

This rift between the Residents and their superiors on the issue of gift-giving was part of a broader conflict surrounding Residents' expense claims. Though partly explicable with reference to opposed interests and institutional structures, at their heart these dissensions were about British ambivalence concerning conspicuous consumption and display as well as differences of opinion regarding the basis of the Company's legitimacy in India. Attitudes within the Company were deeply divided when it came to the desirability of adopting Indian ways of life and styles of rule, particularly when it came to courtly pageantry. Residents argued for the political necessity of such tactics, but other Company officials remained unconvinced. By definition, indirect rule required accommodating to existing political culture, but there was widespread discomfort within the Company about what this kind of cultural immersion on the part of their political representatives might entail in practice, and whether it represented the best means of consolidating their influence at court.

Underlying these debates about expenses were concerns about the Resident's ability to act independently on the political stage, and the different relationships of obligation that might counteract that autonomy. Of these, one relationship loomed large: that between a Resident and his munshi. Previous chapters have alluded to the role that Indian secretaries played in composing and interpreting letters and advising on gift-exchange and ceremonial, but in the following chapter, the dynamics of these cross-cultural relationships take centre stage. This chapter will consider how Residents endeavoured to manage their ambivalent relationships with Residency munshis as well as the practical risks and rewards that these relationships carried for munshis themselves.

5   Weak Ties in a Tangled Web

In 1805, the Resident at Hyderabad wrote a letter to Acting Governor General George Hilario Barlow about a munshi. Munshi, a Hindi word meaning scribe or clerk, was a term that Britons commonly applied to their Indian or Persian language tutors, interpreters, and secretaries. The subject of this particular letter was Azizullah, the Hyderabad Residency's long-time head munshi, and the topic was Azizullah's proposed retirement. For more than twelve years, Azizullah had played a crucial role in the Residents' negotiations with the nizam of Hyderabad and his ministers, so much so that the former governor general Richard Wellesley had awarded the munshi a pay rise and a pension in recognition of his vital work. In 1805, Acting Resident Henry Russell wrote to inform the acting governor general of the munshi's imminent retirement, and to remind him of Wellesley's promise. Russell also took the opportunity to express his own 'high Estimation of the Character and Talents of Meer Uzeez Oollah'. Based on many years spent working alongside the mir, Russell confirmed that Azizullah had performed important services in the name of the Company, and had, in so doing, earned the respect and admiration of his British superior officers.[1]

Russell's earnest commemoration of Azizullah's services at the twilight of his career speaks to the distinction that Indians sometimes acquired within the political line. Like most Company employees, the Residents were heavily reliant on the work of Indian clerks and scribes to do their job. In recognition of this broad pattern, the role of cultural intermediaries in imperial administration and the construction of colonial knowledge has been a point of enduring interest in the historiography of British imperialism in South Asia. Recent interventions have highlighted the importance of Indian expertise as a basis for British understandings of

---

[1] BL, APAC, Mss Eur F228/51, Henry Russell to George Barlow, 20 November 1805, pp. 6–7.

Indian history, geography, tax collection, and jurisprudence.[2] Despite this proliferation of scholarship on other branches of the Company's service, however, munshis' essential contribution to Company diplomacy has continued to be overlooked since Michael Fisher first highlighted it as an object of consideration in his general survey of the Residencies, written almost thirty years ago.[3]

Yet, the relationship between Resident and munshi is worth investigating further since it differs in key respects from the cross-cultural working relationships usually described by historians of the Company state. Importantly, Residency munshis operated in predominantly Indian social environments regulated by courtly norms that privileged munshis' social and cultural capital over that of the Resident. More than a simple translator or informant, a munshi's expertise inhered just as much, if not more, in his internalization of courtly practices and ideals of behaviour, and his ability to perform on the stage of courtly politics. This kind of embodied knowledge was not easily or quickly learned, meaning that a munshi often acted in the Resident's stead, rather than simply furnishing him with the information requisite to do his duty. Munshis in the political line were thus able to acquire status and influence that was arguably unmatched by any other munshi in the Company's employ. At the same time, Residents were senior officials intended to represent the power and authority of the Company at Indian courts; as such, it was important for the Resident to establish and maintain an image of control and incorruptibility. The question of how much responsibility could or should be delegated to a munshi was thus particularly difficult to resolve conclusively in the Residency system, where the issue of public opinion was vested with so much importance (as preceding chapters have illustrated), and the political stakes were perceived to be exceedingly high.

The relationships between Residents and munshis differed according to the personalities, habits, and convictions of the individuals involved.

---

[2] Philip B. Wagoner, 'Precolonial Intellectuals and the Production of Colonial Knowledge', *Comparative Studies in Society and History* 45, no. 4 (2003): 783–814; Michael Dodson, *Orientalism, Empire, and National Culture* (Basingstoke, 2007), p. 1; Matthew Edney, *Mapping an Empire: The Geographical Construction of British India, 1765–1843* (Chicago, IL, 1990), p. 25; Kapil Raj, 'Mapping Knowledge: Go-Betweens in Calcutta, 1770–1820', in *The Brokered World: Go-Betweens and Global Intelligence, 1770–1820*, eds. Simon Schaffer et al. (Sagamore Beach, MA, 2009), p. 122; Hayden Bellenoit, 'Between Qanungos and Clerks: The Cultural and Service Worlds of Hindustan's Pensmen, c. 1750–1850', *MAS* 48, no. 4 (2014): 872–910; Kapil Raj, 'Refashioning Civilities, Engineering Trust: William Jones, Indian Intermediaries and the Production of Reliable Legal Knowledge in Late Eighteenth-Century Bengal', *Studies in History* 17, no. 2 (2001): 175–209.

[3] Fisher, *Indirect Rule*, p. 316.

Although there is not a clear, paradigmatic type of Resident–munshi relationship, there are nevertheless patterns that emerge when the major Residencies are considered side by side. This chapter identifies some of the common features of these relationships as they took shape across the subcontinent against the backdrop of the Company's political expansion. Section 1 provides basic context by describing who munshis were and how they were perceived by their British employers. Section 2 shows that despite the Residents' attempts to limit the influence of munshis, munshis remained crucial to the operation of the Residency, and their recognised importance gave them the leverage to secure interests of their own. Having outlined the dynamics that characterized the Resident–munshi relationship, Section 3 shows how this dyadic interaction was shaped by the larger political and corporate culture of which it was a part. There is sometimes a tendency within global history to romanticize the ingenuity of go-betweens, but the experiences of Residents and munshis, both cultural brokers in their own way, clearly demonstrates some of the perils of in-betweenness.[4]

5.1   Stereotypes and Suspicions

Residency munshis formed part of a broad corps of clerks and writers who made their living through 'mastery of the pen'.[5] Some sold their services in the bazaar, others worked for commercial firms or individual notables. The greatest prestige was attached to royal munshis, state secretaries operating at the highest level of politics.[6] Munshis came to their work largely by way of family precedents, deploying networks of friends and kin to learn the craft and find employment. Entry and advancement depended on skills and connections rather than formal qualifications.[7] A munshi's skillset generally included penmanship and accountancy, as well as an in-depth knowledge of social etiquette, political norms, and literary conventions.[8] The East India Company's Residents employed a number of munshis to perform a range of administrative tasks, but most important was the head munshi or mir munshi, the Resident's personal agent.

[4] Sanjay Subrahmanyam, 'Between a Rock and a Hard Place: Some Afterthoughts', in Schaffer et al., *The Brokered World*, p. 440.
[5] Bayly, *Empire and Information*, p. 74.
[6] Ibid.
[7] J. F. Richards, 'Norms of Comportment among Imperial Mughal Officers', in *Moral Conduct and Authority: The Place of* Adab *in South Asian Islam,* ed. Barbara Daly Metcalf (Berkeley, CA, 1984), p. 256.
[8] Rajeev Kinra, 'Master and Munshi: A Brahman Secretary's Guide to Mughal Governance', *IESHR* 47, no. 4 (2010): 530.

Mir munshis generally came from good families, and were for the most part, though not always, Muslim.[9] While some were of local provenance, their families already firmly established within the administrative world of the court, many mir munshis acquired the position because of their personal connection to the Resident in office or his network of friends and kin.[10] Practices varied from Resident to Resident, but in addition to overseeing the Residency's Indian staff, the head munshi usually met with ministers and other notables on the Resident's behalf.

The available sources describing these relationships are patchy. Included among the voluminous papers of the major Residencies are a number of reports, authored by munshis, detailing their meetings with rulers and ministers. The Residents' own everyday working relationship with their munshis, however, often went undocumented. The Resident and munshi met in person to discuss points of policy, and these conversations were only occasionally recorded in writing. When corresponding with the governor-general-in-council in Calcutta or their families in Britain, Residents conventionally passed over the mechanics of the Residency, including the activities of its Indian staff. When taken to task by his mother for failing to adequately describe his 'habits and life', Alexander Fraser, secretary to the Resident at Delhi, explained that such elisions were only to be expected in letters from Indian officials, 'since the history of his life is a mere routine of business, whose nature is nearly unknown in Europe; or whose variety & complication renders it difficult to describe'.[11] Kate Teltscher has characterized the familiar letter as a theatre for dramatizing the colonial self, 'a form of performance where the letter-writer stages the encounter between cultures, locations, and peoples', but it is for precisely this reason that many of the more complicated or banal elements of the Residents' day-to-day life were elided; they simply did not make for easy or compelling reading.[12] As a result of these kinds of epistolary conventions, even some of the more distinguished or notorious munshis make only sporadic appearances in the sources, occasionally disappearing from view entirely. In consequence, certain aspects of these relationships have proven elusive to the historian, particularly how they were viewed and experienced by munshis themselves.

[9] Fisher, *Indirect Rule*, p. 321.
[10] Ibid., p. 332.
[11] NRAS, Fraser of Reelig Papers, vol. 33, Alexander Fraser to his mother, 20 August 1810, p. 208.
[12] Kate Teltscher, 'Writing Home and Crossing Cultures: George Bogle in Bengal and Tibet, 1770–1775', in ed. Kathleen Wilson, *A New Imperial History: Culture, Identity, and Modernity in Britain and the Empire, 1660–1840* (Cambridge, 2004), p. 282.

When reflecting on why munshis might have attached themselves to British Residents, it seems logical to assume that their trajectory was at least partly shaped by their history. Most analyses of human agency, while recognizing the importance of emergent events, nevertheless stress the 'conditioning quality' of the past.[13] When confronting new situations, we generally draw, albeit creatively, on previous experiences and pre-existing repertoires. Munshis appear to have reacted in a similar fashion as the Company emerged as a major political player in the Indian subcontinent. At Indian royal capitals, there was a long historical precedent of service gentry seeking patronage from the local representatives of rival Indian powers.[14] C. A. Bayly has argued that Indians in the eighteenth century had a strong sense of attachment to particular homelands, customs, or political and religious institutions, which he terms 'old patriotism', but he made some exception for the munshis who depended for their livelihood on elite patrons.[15] Many munshis were itinerant, moving from the land of their birth to regional cultural capitals in pursuit of learning or employment opportunities.[16] Their identity was tied up in particular forms of expertise and family traditions of service to the state.[17] As historians of early modern India have observed, this scribal elite had long been flexible and diverse, bridging regional Brahmanical traditions and a wider Indo-Islamicate culture; they were accustomed to negotiating religious and cultural difference.[18] Accordingly, when munshis found employment with the Company, they were adjusting to changing circumstances, but there was some continuity in the nature of their employment.

There is even reason to think that munshis and Residents might have had broadly similar impressions of the reciprocal services to be expected from such a relationship. In India, relationships between elite patrons and their munshis could be powerful and long-lasting, almost resembling a family connection.[19] Similarly, Naomi Tadmor has illustrated

[13] Mustafa Emirbayer and Ann Mische, 'What Is Agency?', *American Journal of Sociology* 103 (1998): 975.
[14] Leonard, *Social History of an Indian Caste*, p. 22.
[15] C. A. Bayly, *Origins of Nationality in South Asia: Patriotism and Ethical Government in the Making of Modern India* (Oxford, 1998), p. 4.
[16] Maria Szuppe, 'Circulation des lettrés et cercles littéraires: Entre Asie Centrale, Iran et Inde du Nord (xve-xviiie siècle)', *Annales. Histoire, Sciences Sociales* 59 (2004): 997–1018.
[17] Kumkum Chatterjee, 'History as Self-Representation: The Recasting of a Political Tradition in Late Eighteenth-Century Eastern India', *MAS* 32, no. 4 (1998): 931.
[18] Kumkum Chatterjee, 'Scribal Elites in Sultanate and Mughal Bengal', *IESHR* 47, no. 4 (2010): 463; Muzaffar Alam and Sanjay Subrahmanyam, 'The Making of a Munshi', *Comparative Studies of South Asia, Africa, and the Middle East* 24, no. 2 (2003): 71.
[19] Alam and Subrahmanyam, 'Making of a Munshi', p. 65.

how in the British context membership of the 'household-family' was flexible and capacious, encompassing servants, apprentices, and other dependants.[20] The servant's recognized place within the patriarchal household meant that the household head had a responsibility towards him or her.[21] In line with these prescriptions, Residents acknowledged a certain accountability for their munshi's welfare, even after the working relationship had ended. Henry Russell, for instance, found a post for his former munshi (who he called 'Munshi Bankir') at Hyderabad upon that munshi's request. 'He has Claims upon me', Russell explained, 'from having been my first moonshy at Hyderabad; and I will cheerfully do for him every thing that I can with Propriety.'[22] Richard Jenkins likewise appealed to a Company official at Bareilly on behalf of a former munshi Ghulam Hussain, for, in his words, 'notwithstanding the unfortunate circumstances under which I parted with Gholaum Hoossein, I am still as solicitous as ever to serve him.'[23] This vertical relationship of mutual obligation approximated the connection that a munshi would have historically shared with Indian patrons.[24] Historians have been inclined to draw stark distinctions between the modern, bureaucratic Company and a more patrimonial Indian political culture, but in both British and Indian society, vertical relationships of service and obligation like this were an integral part of the texture of social and political life.[25]

Still, there were no doubt disjunctions, aspects of munshis' experiences in the Company's service that were shaped by the particular beliefs and assumptions of their British employers. Prominent among these was the distrust with which British officials tended to regard munshis as a group. Tellingly, although Resident John Munro strenuously denied the charges of corruption levelled at him by the inhabitants of Travancore, where he was stationed, he was far less enthusiastic in defending the good name of his munshi, Reddy Rao. While Munro's investigation into Reddy Rao's conduct produced no evidence of wrongdoing, Munro concluded that 'however high my opinion of Reddy Rows integrity may be, yet, it is impossible that I can positively affirm that his conduct, or that

---

[20] Tadmor, *Family and Friends*, p. 19.

[21] Cissie Fairchilds, *Domestic Enemies: Servants & Their Masters in Old Regime France* (Baltimore, MD, 1984), p. 139.

[22] Bodl. Oxf, Russell Papers, MSS Eng. lett. d. 151, Henry Russell to Charles Russell, 4 June 1810, p. 101.

[23] BL, APAC, Mss Eur E11, Richard Jenkins to J. Brooke, 21 July 1811, p. 149.

[24] Alam and Subrahmanyam, 'Making of a Munshi', p. 65.

[25] For the first point, see for example Dirks, *Hollow Crown*, p. 354; for patronage in Indian and British society, respectively, see Leonard, *Social History of an Indian Caste*, p. 22; Perkin, *Origins of Modern English Society*, p. 44.

of any other native servant has invariably been pure and honorable.'[26] From John Munro's perspective, Reddy Rao's status as a native servant meant that his probity could not be vouchsafed. Though Residents sometimes ascribed positive traits to specific munshis in this way, they almost always described munshis in general using negative, highly stereotyped language.[27]

The underlying foundations of this prejudice are difficult to disentangle. In part this indeterminacy is a product of the sources; Residents often repeated these stereotypes, but rarely reflected on them at length. The influence of nascent biological conceptions of 'race' is not readily apparent, though it is possible that Residents were simply unwilling to enter into explicit discussions of racial ideologies or racist practices in their letters to professional colleagues, and rarely discussed these relationships at all when writing to family.

Of more obvious significance were contemporary attitudes towards Indian political culture; to some extent, the Residents' attitudes towards munshis seem to have been informed by a more generalised set of British preconceptions. The gist of these stereotypes is evident in a passage from John Blakiston's published memoirs of his military service in India, where Blakiston writes that a unique feature of Indian society was 'their policy to withhold every fact they possess, even though it cost them nothing to give it; and to deceive you by every means in their power, even when they can themselves derive no apparent benefit from so doing.'[28] Alena K. Alamgir has identified a long-term continuity in the language of mistrust with which Britons described their relationships with Indians; in the personal papers of the Residents, Indian courtly politics were certainly characterized in terms that resonated with this convention.[29] The long-time Resident at Pune Sir Charles Warre Malet (Resident 1793–1798) compared the position of the Company in India to 'that of an honest Man thrown by Circumstances into the society of Swindlers [...] & Highwaymen.'[30] In line with this general view of Indian politics, Residents often described their munshis' activities as crafty or conniving. Henry Russell claimed to have been obliged to expel his munshi from the Residency at

---

[26] BL, APAC, IOR/F/4/445/10674, John Munro, 'Observations on a Petition Delivered to the Government Dated 16 September 1813', p. 97.

[27] This is characteristic of representations of out-groups. See Mark Knights, 'Historical Stereotypes and Histories of Stereotypes', in *Psychology and History: Interdisciplinary Explorations,* eds. Christian Tileagă and Jovan Byford (Cambridge, 2014), p. 246.

[28] Blakiston, *Twelve Years Military Adventure,* p. 107.

[29] Alena K. Alamgir, '"The Learned Brahmen, Who Assists Me": Changing Colonial Relationships in 18th and 19th Century India', *Journal of Historical Sociology* 19, no. 4 (2006): 426.

[30] BL, APAC, Mss Eur F149/56, C. W. Malet to G. F. Cherry, p. 167.

Pune for 'intriguing', as he put it, commenting that 'there is something in the air of Poona which is not only villainous itself, but is also the Cause of Villainy in others.'[31]

To what extent was socioeconomic difference a factor explaining the Residents' distrust of munshis? Ann Stoler has theorized that racial and class language were not only parallels of one another but were in fact overlapping and interchangeable ways of constructing and explaining what contemporaries considered to be similar kinds of human differences, to do with variant attitudes and behaviours.[32] It is crucial to point out here that munshis formed a hereditary class of respected and highly trained service gentry; Susan Bayly has shown how these specialists emerged as a prominent and prestigious class of people in the eighteenth century as the proliferating Mughal successor states competed for administrative expertise and royal legitimacy.[33] Residents also chose, as much as possible, munshis of good family and reputation, believing that this would increase the munshi's credit in the eyes of the courtly elite, as well as acting as a form of insurance for his good behaviour.[34] Still, in his pamphlet directed at members of the political line diplomatist John Malcolm highlighted a munshi's class as an object of consideration when he warned his readers from investing them with too much power or favour, contending that Indian employees 'cannot be supposed to have even the same motives with those of native rulers for good conduct, much less the same title to regard.'[35] Despite their education and gentility, munshis were still viewed as subordinate figures who were not always trusted to act honourably. Tellingly, when writing to the secretary to government about his Residency expenses, Henry Russell refused to reduce the wages of his head munshi on the grounds that 'it is vain to expect honesty from any Native Servant, who is not placed beyond the reach of ordinary Temptation.'[36]

Accusations of immoral behaviour levelled at munshis by their British employers mirrored language used to describe the lower social orders in

[31] Bodl. Oxf., Russell Papers, MSS. Eng. lett. d. 152, Henry Russell to Charles Russell, 18 December 1810, p. 63.
[32] Ann Laura Stoler, *Race and the Education of Desire: Foucault's History of Sexuality and the Colonial Order of Things* (Durham, NC, 1995), p. 127.
[33] Susan Bayly, *Caste, Society, and Politics in India from the Eighteenth Century to the Modern Age* (Cambridge, 1999), p. 66; see also Richards, 'Formulation of Imperial Authority', p. 311.
[34] Fisher, *Indirect Rule*, p. 321
[35] John Malcolm, 'Notes of Instruction', in Briggs, *Letters*, p. 203.
[36] BL, APAC, Mss Eur F88/60, Henry Russell to John Adam, 5 September 1816, p. 149.

Europe.[37] In the words of Thomas Williamson, munshis, 'having only to attend their employers at stated hours, and the residue of their time being wholly unoccupied, it is not to be wondered, that, with their liberal salaries, they should rather court, than shun, pleasure.' Williamson elaborated that 'what with venery, drinking, smoking, &c. nine in ten of them exhale the most intolerable effluvia!'[38] This complaint features prominently in the correspondence of Resident Mountstuart Elphinstone while at Nagpur, who grumbled to his friend and cousin John Adam that he was 'very ill off for natives', having 'a Moonshee who is drunk half the day & an intelligencer who is drunk the whole day.' To give substance to his grievances, Elphinstone recounted how when he sent his munshi to wait on Raghuji, 'he [the munshi] was so drunk that he could not stand, was taken sick during the interview & fell off his horse on the way home.'[39] These allegations, though they echo the rhetoric surrounding the lower social orders more broadly, also resemble the discourse of a supposed 'servant problem' in England. Elphinstone's complaints call to mind the prevalence within British court records and family papers of dysfunctional relationships between masters and servants in which servants are ceaselessly charged with vice, cheating, idleness, and drunkenness.[40]

Like servants, munshis also worked in close quarters with their employers. In both cases, intimacy could be viewed as potentially threatening.[41] Elphinstone, at least, made it quite clear that he viewed munshis as dangerous interlopers when he assured Lady Hood, in a personal letter, 'that no native of Asia can be admitted to table without his interrupting the comfort of the Company on which he is a spy & that above all no Persian servant of any rank can be allowed such a distinction without its tempting him to encroach.'[42] The remark was made with reference to a munshi who joined the Hyderabad Resident at his table; for Elphinstone, the munshi's background and the nature of his employment together marked him out as an outsider to be kept at a distance. John Briggs, in a letter of advice to a young man just entering the civil line of the Company, similarly reminded his correspondents to be wary when setting up a household, '[s]ervants in all countries have it greatly

---

[37] R. C. Richardson, *Household Servants in Early Modern England* (Manchester, 2010), p. 175.
[38] Williamson, *East India Vade-Mecum*, I, p. 194.
[39] BL, APAC, Mss Eur F109/88, Mountstuart Elphinstone to John Adam, 3 May 1804.
[40] Richardson, *Household Servants*, p. 176.
[41] Fairchilds, *Domestic Enemies*, pp. 154–155.
[42] NRS, Seaforth Papers, GD46/17/42, Mountstuart Elphinstone to Lady Hood, 26 May 1813.

in their power to contribute to our comforts as well as to impose on us, and even sometimes to inflict on us positive distress,' but that 'this must be particularly the case in a strange land like this.'[43] John Malcolm warned his readers that an Indian employee's 'real or supposed influence will, under any circumstances that they are allowed frequent approach to an European officer in the exercise of authority, give them opportunities of abusing his confidence if they desire it', contending that 'there is no science at which the more artful among the natives are greater adepts, than that of turning to account the real or supposed confidence of their superiors.'[44] It seems possible that the munshi's status as a non-European, as well as his access to the details of the Resident's professional life, might have combined to make him doubly threatening from the Resident's perspective.

The munshi's close association with the Resident, and his access to the Residency papers, did mean that he had it in his power to throw relations between the Company and the court into disarray. To some extent, the munshi's personal connection to the Resident allowed him to partake of the Resident's public authority, muddying hierarchies of power that the Resident would have preferred to keep clear-cut. There are a few examples of munshis extorting money from courtly figures with promises of bringing their influence to bear on the Resident, but none perhaps is more extraordinary than the case of Muhammad Sadiq Khan, or illustrates so well the extreme possibility that munshis could infiltrate the Residency and use its authority for their own purposes.[45] In the year 1809, the Governor General the Earl of Minto received a mysterious letter from Shahamat Khan, second brother to Nawab Vizier Saadat Ali Khan, alluding vaguely to promises made to him by the recently deceased John Collins (Resident at Lucknow between 1804 and 1807). Further investigation by the newly appointed Resident John Baillie unearthed a plot orchestrated by a deputy munshi in Collins's office. The munshi, it transpired, had forged letters purporting to be from John Collins and the governor general, in which he promised to oust the current nawab vizier and to place Shahamat Khan on the throne in his place. The use of the Resident's official seal, combined with the munshi's status as representative of the Resident, appear to have convinced Shahamat Khan of the legitimacy of the plan, allowing the munshi to use the proposed coup d'état as a pretext for extorting

---

[43] Briggs, *Letters*, p. 11.

[44] Malcolm, 'Notes of Instruction', in Briggs, *Letters*, pp. 203, 206–207.

[45] See BL, APAC, IOR/F/4/311/7620, Extract Political Letter from Bengal, 9 May 1810, pp. 2–4 for example of Sayyid Reza Khan, dismissed for corrupt practises; for similar accusations of Elphinstone's agent at Poona see also BL, APAC, Mss Eur F88/60, 5 January 1817 and 8 February 1817.

large sums of money. The Resident's exposure of the plot, and Shahamat Khan's subsequent exile to Company-ruled Patna, marked the end of the conspiracy.[46] At the same time, this exceptional occurrence forcefully illustrates the subversive potential of the munshi, no doubt explaining why some Residents regarded their munshis with wariness. The very possibility of such a misappropriation of Company authority was a source of anxiety, however baseless such anxieties might have been in practice given that these acts of corruption seem to have been rare, or at least were rarely exposed.

This brings us to perhaps the clearest source of British anxieties about the munshi, namely, his role as middleman and translator. Munshis were regularly responsible for reading out, translating, and explaining communications of Company policy to the ruler and his ministers, thereby giving them a vital role in negotiations between Indian courts and the Company.[47] Given this position of influence, Residents and their superiors were unsurprisingly fearful of being misled or misrepresented by munshis. This anxiety was not unique to Residents. Throughout India, the Company was dependent on the mediation of clerks, moneychangers, bankers, and commercial middlemen.[48] Accordingly, the problem of translation and interpretation, and the danger of misrepresentation, was at the forefront of every Company employee's consciousness. In his *Vade Mecum,* a popular guide for young men about to enter the service, Thomas Williamson urged his readers to familiarize themselves with Indian languages, for until they were able to dispense with an interpreter, 'no person can be deemed independent; far less, capable of acting in any civil, military, or commercial capacity with effect.'[49] Munshis, then, were the subject of many of the same anxieties that have historically coalesced around the figure of the translator.[50] It was a fear that sprang from munshis' relative power, as well as their perceived 'otherness'. What made

---

[46] See BL, APAC, IOR/F/4/248/5584, Extract Political Letter from Bengal, 2 February 1808, pp. 1–22 for a description of this series of events.

[47] For descriptions of munshi's role as interpreter, see NAI, HRR, box no. 2, vol. 38, Thomas Sydenham to Earl Minto, 30 August 1809, p. 12, or Richard Jenkins to the Marquess of Hastings, 17 July 1814, in *NRR,* III, p. 487.

[48] Lakshmi Subramanian, 'Banias and the British: The Role of Indigenous Credit in the Process of Imperial Expansion in Western India in the Second Half of the Eighteenth Century', *MAS* 21, no. 3 (1987): 473–510.

[49] Williamson, *East India Vade-Mecum,* I, p. 172.

[50] For North American context see James H. Merrell, *Into the American Woods: Negotiators on the Pennsylvania Frontier* (New York, NY, 1999), p. 32. For African context, see Benjamin N. Lawrance, Emily Lynn Osborn, and Richard L. Roberts, eds., *Intermediaries, Interpreters, and Clerks: African Employees in the Making of Colonial Africa* (Madison, WI, 2006), p. 11.

the relationship particularly fraught was the disruption of clear lines of authority within the Residency; it was always possible that the munshi might act in the Resident's stead to pursue his own interests or inclinations, perhaps without the Resident even realizing it.

At the heart of these various overlapping stereotypes about munshis, then, were the Residents' anxieties about their own incapacity, and the fear that the munshi might take advantage of it. The question, from the Company's perspective, was how the Resident could ensure that the munshi did not use this power to frustrate or impede the Residency's operations. As Kapil Raj has illustrated, this problem of intercultural trust was a primary concern for Company administrators reliant on the skill and expertise of Indian agents.[51] Under pressure from the governor general, Residents accordingly devised strategies to manage the perceived risks represented by munshis. As Henry Russell advised his brother, 'without searching for perfect Instruments, which are not to be found, we must be content to make the best use we can of those which Circumstances have placed within our reach.'[52]

Yet, the question of what constituted 'the best use' for Residency munshis remained a conundrum. At Pune, Charles Warre Malet and William Palmer had both relied heavily on Mir Fakhir al-Din; at Hyderabad, meanwhile, William Kirkpatrick and his brother James Achilles had placed their full trust in Azizullah. By contrast, Colonel Close, who succeeded Palmer at Pune, and Thomas Sydenham, who succeed James Achilles Kirkpatrick at Hyderabad, were both determined to conduct their business without the aid of a munshi. Close argued that this observance would 'prevent misconceptions and give precision to the delivery of our sentiments', while Sydenham averred that 'at present it is often very uncertain whether the representations made to the Minister by the British Resident be faithfully conveyed to the peshwa, and that uncertainty would be increased by the mediation of another agent between His Highness and the Resident.'[53] With time, however, their resolve weakened. Henry Russell, who worked under both Thomas Sydenham and Barry Close as Assistant Resident and Acting Resident, respectively, remarked that neither man successfully enacted their ambitions. According to Russell, 'they both of them began their Administrations with a decided Resolution to conduct their Business without the Agency of

---

[51] Raj, 'Refashioning Civilities, Engineering Trust', pp. 175–209.
[52] Bodl. Oxf., Russell Papers, MSS Eng. lett. d. 151, Henry Russell to Charles Russell, 10 June 1810, p. 119.
[53] Barry Close to Marquess Wellesley, 21 December 1801, in *PRC*, VII, p. 6; Thomas Sydenham to Arthur Wellesley, 29 January 1805, in *PRC*, VII, p. 188.

a moonshy: and yet, perhaps, there never was a Time at which more was done by natives, or more entrusted to them, than there was then at Hyderabad under Captain Sydenham, and at Pune under Colonel Close.' This led Russell to conclude, when it came time for him to take up the mantle of Resident at Hyderabad in 1811, that 'a native servant must be employed [...] call him what you will, but such a man must be had, must very frequently be employed and trusted.'[54] The following section explores the strategies that Residents like Barry Close and Thomas Sydenham used to try to sidestep the influence of Residency munshis, and demonstrates why these grand aspirations so often foundered in practice.

5.2   The Dialectic of Control

The clearest means of mitigating the munshi's power was by learning Indian languages. Even William Jones, perhaps the most famous Orientalist of the eighteenth century, was motivated to learn Sanskrit primarily in order to more closely monitor the Indian officials who assisted him in his work at the Supreme Court in Calcutta.[55] The Company's administration similarly sought to preclude a dependence on Indian interpreters by placing a deliberate emphasis on language skills. This prioritization of languages applied particularly to aspiring members of the political line, but to some extent British officials of all kinds were expected to be conversant in the Indian languages relevant to their posts. During the late eighteenth century Persian and Hindustani language instruction was gradually institutionalized in the form of grammars and dictionaries, treatises, translations, and class books directed to native English speakers. In the early nineteenth century, the Company founded colleges at Fort William (in 1800) and Haileybury (in 1806) where students were also instructed in Arabic and Bengali.[56] By 1828, John Briggs proclaimed proudly and in print that 'hardly an instance now exists of any European holding a civil situation of responsibility removed from the presidencies, who is ignorant of the language of the district in which he resides.'[57]

In fact, the situation varied from court to court. Most Residents had a thorough grounding in Persian and Hindustani; these were languages

---

[54] Bodl. Oxf., Russell Papers, MSS Eng. lett. d. 151, Henry Russell to Charles Russell, 14 June 1810, pp. 119–120.
[55] Rosane Rocher, 'Weaving Knowledge: Sir William Jones and Indian Pundits', in *Objects of Enquiry: The Life Contributions and Influences of Sir William Jones (1746–1794)*, eds. Garland Cannon and Kevin R. Brine (New York, NY, 1995), p. 54.
[56] Cohn, *Colonialism and Its Forms of Knowledge*, p. 21.
[57] Briggs, *Letters*, p. 6.

that were heavily weighted within the curriculums at Haileybury and Fort William and used throughout India. By contrast, most Residents stationed at Maratha courts during this period seem to have had little grasp of Marathi; Josiah Webbe was conversant in it, and Elphinstone claimed to understand it (though not to speak it), but otherwise there is little evidence to suggest that the Residents had any knowledge of Marathi at all.[58] At Pune, the problem was mitigated by the fact that Baji Rao was fluent in Hindustani and often (though not always) willing to converse directly with the Resident in this language. At Nagpur, however, the language barrier posed more of an obstacle, since Raghuji was understandably hesitant to talk politics in anything other than his native tongue; here, the practice seems to have been for the Resident to communicate with the munshi in Persian, and for the munshi to translate from Persian into Marathi.[59] In general, then, Residents stationed at these courts had no option but to speak through an interpreter of some kind. In not speaking Marathi, the Resident found himself placed at an obvious remove from the courtly culture of which he was nominally a part.

Even at royal centres where the dominant languages were Persian and Hindustani, Residents were still discouraged from acting independently of their munshis in their dealings with the court. Even John Baillie, previously a professor of Persian at Fort William, was scolded by Governor General the Marquess of Hastings for assuming that he could dispense with a munshi in his meetings with the nawab vizier and his ministers. As Hastings put it, 'the reliance of Major John Baillie on his correct possession of a polished idiom was likely to betray him beyond the exact line of established usage.'[60] However fluent the Residents were by European standards, their linguistic abilities were not expected to rival the eloquence and refinement of experienced munshis. In a context where an individual's grasp of Persian was a point of personal prestige, minute idiomatic details mattered; to quote historian Muzaffar Alam, 'deficiency in elegant self-expression meant cultural failure'.[61]

Nevertheless, Residents were still proficient enough to intervene, to some extent, when they felt they were being misrepresented by their translators, even, it appears, at Maratha courts. While H. T. Colebrooke

---

[58] On Elphinstone, see Briggs, *Letters,* 47; MSA, PRCOP, vol. 44 (1817), pp. 62–63. On Close, see MSA, PRCOP, vol. 39 (1801/2), p. 422; MSA, PRCOP, vol. 40 (1802/1803), p. 262.

[59] H. T. Colebrooke to Marquess Wellesley, 26 March 1799, in *NRR,* I, p. 108.

[60] BL, APAC, IOR/F/4/510/12267, p. 17.

[61] Muzaffar Alam, 'The Culture and Politics of Persian in Precolonial Hindustan', in *Literary Cultures in History: Reconstructions from South Asia,* ed. Sheldon Pollock (Berkeley, CA, 2003), p. 167.

was in the process of negotiating a treaty of defensive alliance with the raja of Nagpur through the mediation of his munshi, he noticed that the munshi had omitted the word 'quadruple' in his description of the proposed alliance, presenting it to the raja as an alliance between the two states exclusively rather than a joint alliance with the Company, the peshwa of Pune, and the nizam of Hyderabad; Colebrooke subsequently corrected the mistake.[62] Similarly, John Collins carefully attended to the munshi Kaval Nain's translation of the Treaty of Bassein to Daulat Rao Shinde. In his papers, Collins noted that 'when the moonshee came to the 12th Article [...] he by no means gave that force to the words thereof which he ought to have done, I was, therefore, under the necessity of assisting him, & embraced the occasion of giving the clearest explanation of that important stipulation.'[63] Residents sought, as much as possible, to monitor and control the way in which Company policy was represented to Indian rulers and ministers via the channel of the munshi, even taking over entirely when the munshi was considered to have misspoken.

The problem, from the Residents' perspective, was that in order to achieve their political ends it was not enough to be linguistically competent. Indian courtly politics were governed by a larger Indo-Persian system of meanings, a dense web of moral, ethical, and administrative ideals. The munshi was extensively trained in these Indo-Persian principles, and therefore better able to frame and present the Resident's demands or queries. These scribal elite were widely read from a young age in poetry, politics, ethics, history, and epistolography.[64] Contemporaries outside of the diplomatic line sometimes belittled this kind of expertise. Captain Thomas Williamson, a soldier, scoffed that 'a few volumes of tales, the lives of those great men who have either invaded, or ruled, the empire, some moral tracts, and the Koran [...] constitute the acquirements of this haughty class of servants.'[65] Those in the political departments, however, clearly recognized the munshi's worth.

Munshis' mastery of letter-writing and courtly etiquette was particularly important. The Persian *insha* tradition of *belles lettres* comprised a complex blend of formula and invention, producing documents with a poetic bent 'heavily imbued with rhymed prose, verse, figurative language,

---

[62] BL, Add MS 13589, H. T. Colebrooke to Marquess Wellesley, 19 April 1799, p. 1.
[63] BL, APAC, Mss Eur F228/77, John Collins to Marquess Wellesley, 29 May 1803, p. 8.
[64] Alam and Subrahmanyam, 'Making of a Munshi', p. 63; see also Chatterjee, 'Scribal Elites', p. 462.
[65] Williamson, *East India Vade Mecum*, pp. 192–193.

and rhetorical embellishment', to quote historian Colin Mitchell.[66] The Resident's working knowledge of Persian hardly sufficed for the composition of the highly stylized prose requisite for corresponding officially with the Indian elite.[67] As Dick Kooiman demonstrated in his study of late nineteenth-century Residencies, ceremonial and questions of precedence were also taken very seriously as reflections of the status and prestige of those concerned.[68] A munshi could be an invaluable resource in this regard, as even the most grudging Residents were forced to acknowledge.[69] The munshi was of vital assistance in determining questions of protocol when arranging meetings between the Resident and other figures of political importance, avoiding offence or indignity on either side.[70] All in all, the munshi had the cultural capital so crucial to the success of the Resident's diplomatic endeavours. It was a particular kind of know-how which, having been painstakingly acquired over the course of the munshi's lifetime, was not easily transmitted to British officials.[71]

Because of this savoir-faire, munshis were often better equipped than the Resident to negotiate sensitive diplomatic situations. Indian rulers and their ministers were sometimes willing to extend a degree of trust to the munshi that they withheld from the Resident, and this trust could be taken advantage of by the Resident if he was willing to use a munshi as his agent. When Richard Strachey (then Resident at Lucknow) was having trouble reaching an agreement with Ghazi ud-Din Haidar Khan in 1816, he dispatched his munshi to initiate a second round of negotiations. The nawab vizier expressed his willingness to draft a written engagement and asked the munshi to assist in formulating that treaty. The munshi reported this conversation to Strachey, at which point Strachey himself drafted a treaty, which 'was submitted to the Vizier by the moonshee as if from himself'.[72] In this case, Strachey clearly felt that, by presenting the draft as the munshi's own work, Ghazi ud-Din would be more likely to accept the treaty as a reflection of his own best interests. The most effective munshis were often individuals who were able to elicit the Indian

---

[66] Mitchell, 'Safavid Imperial *Tarassul* and the Persian *Insha* Tradition', p. 182; for the importance of poetry in the *insha* tradition, see pp. 200–201.

[67] Fisher, *Indirect Rule,* p. 319.

[68] Dick Kooiman, 'Meeting at the Threshold', pp. 311–333.

[69] BL, APAC, Mss Eur F109/88, Mountstuart Elphinstone to John Adam, 3 May 1804.

[70] For example, see description of a munshi arranging the first meeting between the new Resident at Nagpur and the raja in Mountstuart Elphinstone to Marquess Wellesley, 1 January 1804, in *NRR*, I, p. 17.

[71] Pierre Bourdieu, 'The Forms of Capital', in *Readings in Economic Sociology*, ed. Nicole Woolsey (Malden, MA, 2002), p. 283.

[72] BL, APAC, Mss Eur D514/3, Richard Strachey to John Adam, 29 April 1816, p. 116.

ruler's trust in this way, creating the sense that they were serving both parties at the same time. Azizullah, for instance, was said (according to a letter penned by the first minister of the nizam of Hyderabad) to have shown 'sincere attachment to the Interests of both States', and to have acted always 'with due regard and consideration towards the ministers of his Highness'.[73] Rulers often seem to have preferred working through munshis, finding it easier to broach sensitive topics than with the Resident himself. In addition to the munshi's cultural capital, the munshi's lower status (relative to the Resident) and more tenuous links to the Company meant that conversations could proceed on a more informal, and less threatening, basis.[74]

Although Residents could profit by employing munshis in this fashion, this intermediary role also clearly invested the munshi with precisely the kind of influence that the Resident sought to monopolize for himself. Accordingly, some Residents vacillated when it came to relying on the munshi in this way. Early on in his career at Pune, Mountstuart Elphinstone found that the intercession of a munshi could help smooth over disputes; as Elphinstone put it, 'when transacting business with me on such occasions, they [the ruler and his ministers] are so intent on resisting my proposals and on guarding against committing themselves, that a great deal of the effect of all arguments and explanations is lost.' Rather than attending on the minister himself, then, Elphinstone preferred to send his munshi.[75] Later, however, Elphinstone appears to have second-guessed his inclination to confide in the munshi so readily. In a letter of 1814, Elphinstone reported that though Cursetji Sait had proved very useful in past negotiations with the peshwa, he (Elphinstone) no longer thought it expedient to use Cursetji Sait as a channel for communication with the court. As Elphinstone put it, the peshwa's favour as well as Cursetji Sait's position as agent of the British Residency had 'given the natives an exaggerated idea of his consequence'. This led Elphinstone to 'discontinue employing him to the extent which had been usual'. Once again, the spectre of undue influence made the Resident unwilling to place too much trust in an individual whom he nevertheless continued to recognize as 'zealous and useful'.[76]

---

[73] NAI, For. Sec., file no. 66–68, Mir Alam to Thomas Sydenham, 8 January 1806, p. 6.

[74] For example, at a time when the Company was attempting to interfere in the nomination of a minister, the nizam preferred to discuss the issue with the Residency munshi; when the Resident James Achilles Kirkpatrick protested, the nizam explained that he was not yet prepared to receive the Resident. NAI, FSC, 9 August 1804, no. 55, James Achilles Kirkpatrick to Marquis Wellesley, 27 June 1804, p. 2.

[75] Mountstuart Elphinstone to Lord Minto, 7 July 1812, in *PRC*, XII, p. 183.

[76] Mountstuart Elphinstone to John Adam, 7 May 1814, in *PRC*, XII, p. 323.

Cursetji figures prominently in Pune Residency records, and his story suggests the ways in which courtly mediators could profit from their in-between status. Cursetji was a Parsi from Gujerat who came to Pune with the Resident Sir Charles Warre Malet in 1786. Cursetji was initially employed as an accountant at the Residency, and continued to be described in these terms in Residency records, but increasingly began to act as a political agent with the peshwa. In the difficult period preceding the Treaty of Bassein, Cursetji provided a channel of communication between the durbar and the Residency and continued to be employed in this capacity by Barry Close after the treaty was signed.[77] Cursetji acquired the reputation of being in favour both at the Residency and at the durbar, and used this reputation to fashion himself as an invaluable aid to both the peshwa and the Resident. Cursetji worked in close alliance with the peshwa's favoured ministers, first Shedasheo Mankesir, and then Trimbakji, to influence the peshwa's policy.

Yet, Cursetji would become a problem for the Resident. He was believed by Elphinstone's Assistant Secretary James Grant Duff to have turned the peshwa against Elphinstone out of resentment at Elphinstone's attempt to displace him from the position of chief mediator between court and Company.[78] This was also the opinion of Gangadhar Shastri, emissary of the Gaekwad of Baroda. In 1814, Elphinstone was in the process of mediating between the Gaekwad and the peshwa regarding an expired lease. In May of that year, with no end to the negotiations in sight, the Shastri approached Elphinstone with a suggestion, namely, that the Residency's head servant Cursetji should be more closely involved in the mediation process. According to Elphinstone's account of the conversation, the Shastri 'said he observed that the Sait was not in my confidence, that a disaffected servant was worse than an enemy.' When asked to elaborate further, the Shastri replied 'that the Sait possessed great influence with the peshwa, and would be tempted to employ it in thwarting our views.'[79] Though ultimately the Shastri's suggestions do not seem to have shaken Elphinstone's determination to sideline the Sait, they nevertheless imply the potential dangers of bypassing a munshi. Not only was the Resident perhaps needlessly prolonging negotiations, he might even have been actively though unintentionally sabotaging his own plans by sowing resentments.

Despite the language of malfeasance and mistrust with which so many Residents spoke about them, munshis were nevertheless integral to the workings of the Residency. Even in cases where Residents discovered evidence of misconduct, they were sometimes forced to keep the munshi

[77] Ibid., pp. 323–324.
[78] Grant Duff, *History of the Mahrattas*, p. 347.
[79] Ibid., p. 322.

in question in their employ, at least temporarily. When Richard Jenkins
set out to make additions to the Residency compound, building a dining
bungalow and a set of offices and out-houses, the Residency munshi
was entrusted with superintending the construction. Upon discovering
a discrepancy between the anticipated budget and the actual charges, to
the sum of 10,000 Rs, Jenkins instigated an investigation into the munshi's accounts, discovering that he had been overcharged for the price of
materials. Although the munshi was immediately divested of all involvement in the Residency's finances, Jenkins was forced to retain the munshi in his service to conduct the Residency's Marathi correspondence.[80]

Residents were apt to do anything in their power to keep a skilled munshi
in their employ. Munshi Azizullah, for one, had to petition several times
for a pension enabling him to retire; his first effort earned him only an
increased salary, with, as Resident James Achilles Kirkpatrick noted sar-
castically, 'the pleasing prospect of being a drudge in office for nearly the
remainder of his days, for it is not reasonable to suppose that Government
will dispense with the services of so useful a man, as long as they think they
can have any service out of him.'[81] Though Residents sometimes spoke
of munshis as a group with suspicion, in many cases these partnerships
lasted decades, often surviving the Resident's professional peregrinations
throughout the subcontinent. Charles Metcalfe met Hafiz ud-Din during
his student days at Fort William College; he attributed his conversancy in
Persian to Hafiz ud-Din's instruction and brought the munshi with him
to Delhi when he was appointed Resident there.[82] Peri Lal served under
Archibald Seton for 24 years in Bengal, Bihar, Bareilly, and, finally, at
the Residency at Delhi; Seton described Peri Lal as 'able and zealous',
declaring that 'he has served me with credit to himself & with the utmost
fidelity.'[83] It is worth observing that in this case Seton was writing a character reference in support of Peri Lal's application for a pension; these
kinds of reference letters constitute the main instances in which Residents
openly expressed their gratitude to their munshis, and they typically did
so in very generic terms.[84] Still, the fact of the Resident's support for his

[80] BL, APAC, IOR/P/118/29, Richard Jenkins to N. B. Edmonstone, 3 October 1808,
pp. 248–249.
[81] BL, APAC, Mss Eur F228/12, J. A. Kirkpatrick to William Kirkpatrick, 14 November
1800, p. 259
[82] Thompson, *Life of Charles, Lord Metcalfe*, p. 57.
[83] BL, APAC, IOR/F/4/371/9244. Other examples of long-serving munshis include Ali
Naqi Khan, John Baillie's munshi for thirty years (see VL, APAC, IOR/F/4/372/9249),
Cursetji Sait who served at Poona for thirty years, and Ghulam Muhammad who served
Richard Jenkins for eight years (BL, APAC, IOR/F/4/1473/5782).
[84] Letters of recommendation were a recognized and highly coded genre. See Tavor
Bannet, *Empire of Letters*, pp. 61–62.

munshi, added to the longevity of the relationship, substantiates these affirmations of admiration and attachment.

The degree of respect conferred on the munshi was made manifest in the customary practice of endowing them with ceremonial robes. The khilat was granted to the munshi as, in the words of Resident Richard Strachey, 'a public acknowledgement of his services'.[85] This ceremony was a self-conscious appropriation of Mughal court ritual. Khilats were given as a means of establishing and proclaiming an almost organic bond between an authority figure and a subordinate, symbolically incorporating the recipient into the body of the giver.[86] Residents like Strachey sought purposefully to take on the role of Indian patrons, and to behave to their subordinates in what they perceived to be a manner that would be intelligible to munshis and their peers.[87] This was a form of 'position-taking'.[88] Through this public performance, the Resident actively affirmed and advertised his vertical relationship with the munshi, thereby visibly establishing his own authority while at the same time clearly co-opting the munshi's social capital.

These vertical relationships could yield practical benefits. The experiences of munshi Muhammad Hanif exemplify the favours a munshi could secure through the intercession of his British patrons over the course of his life. To begin with, Colonel Barry Close, formerly Resident at Pune, wrote to Henry Russell, the newly appointed Resident, recommending Muhammad Hanif for the position of head munshi; Muhammad Hanif, the Colonel claimed, 'writes Mahratta as well as the Persian Language and is well acquainted with characters and affairs in the Deccan.'[89] Later, when Muhammad Hanif was ready to retire, Close interposed to secure him a land grant and the command of a body of horse at Hyderabad, ensuring him an income that would see him through his remaining years. When financial reforms in Hyderabad put Muhammad Hanif's tax collection rights in peril, Resident Mountstuart Elphinstone, who had known the munshi at Pune, intervened to get Muhammad Hanif a substitute land grant in Company territory in the Deccan.[90] Throughout

---

[85] BL, APAC, Mss Eur D514/1, Richard Strachey to J. W. Sherer, 14 March 1812, p. 85.

[86] Cohn, 'Representing Authority in Victorian India', pp. 168–169.

[87] For examples of Residents dispensing khilats to munshis see memorandum enclosed in BL, APAC, IOR/F/4/527/12633, G. Moore, Civil Auditor, to Arthur Henry Cole, 24 November 1815, pp. 8–9; BL, APAC, IOR/F/4/1473/5782, Richard Jenkins to John Adam, 12 February 1816, p. 4.

[88] Ira J. Cohen, *Structuration Theory: Anthony Giddens and the Constitution of Social Life* (Houndmills, Basingstoke, 1989), p. 210.

[89] BL, APAC, Mss Eur D1053, Barry Close to Henry Russell, 24 June 1810.

[90] BL, APAC, IOR/F/4/762/20696, Extract Political Letter from Bombay, 2 March 1822, pp. 1–3.

his life, Muhammad Hanif appears to have been able to call on the aid of Company officials to pursue his own ends, demonstrating how munshis could put their personal connections with their British employers to practical use.

The interaction between Resident and munshi, in short, illustrates what Anthony Giddens termed 'the dialectic of control'. In Giddens's view, even when relationships are deeply asymmetrical, they nevertheless retain a degree of complementarity; the superior figure might have greater resources at his command, but he depends on his subordinate to undertake certain tasks. The dialectic of control, to quote sociologist Ira J. Cohen, 'refers to this universal presence of imbalanced degrees of autonomy and dependence that constitute power relations in systems and reproduction circuits of all kinds.'[91] Even though Residents sought to limit the munshi's field of autonomy, munshis were nevertheless able to secure certain advantages through the provision of services that were indispensable to the Residency, belying the disparaging stereotypes that were so prevalent within the political line. At the same time, although this relationship with the Resident created opportunities for the munshi, it also produced frictions. A munshi's relationship with the Resident seems to have been complicated by the fact that the Resident, too, was an intermediary; the Resident's place within the Company, as well as his pre-eminent position at court, meant that the munshi was doubly exposed to the caprices of Company and courtly politics. To properly evaluate the munshi's position, his relationship with the Resident needs to be situated within this wider fabric of social relations of which it was a part. In so doing, it becomes clearer how disparate lines of personal and professional affiliation could come into conflict, often to the munshi's disadvantage.

5.3 Broadening the Scope of Analysis

The Resident was a representative figure who derived his authority from his position in the Company; it was this corporate connection that made him valuable as a patron. For one thing, the Company could bring significant economic resources to bear because of its access to British credit. It has been convincingly argued that the Company's army provided more reliable salaries, pensions, and other kinds of benefits for its soldiers, which in turn allowed the Company to monopolize the Indian military market; the same might be said, to some extent, of its Residencies.[92] Although the provision of pensions was only properly institutionalized in

---

[91] Cohen, *Structuration Theory*, p. 151.
[92] Cooper, *Anglo-Maratha Campaigns*, p. 311.

the 1830s, from an early period many Residency munshis were provided with life-long salaries or grants of land to reward them for their services, and after their deaths it was not unusual for the Company to continue to support their wives and families.[93] Some munshis were certainly left in dire financial straits, but their petitions to the Company suggest that they had had reasonable expectations of provision for their old age on the basis of these kinds of precedents.[94] Bhagwant Rao, munshi at the court of Daulat Rao Shinde, reproached the governor general that 'having long served the British Government with fidelity and zeal I am now reduced to great want and ready to expire.' Bhagwant Rao pointed bitterly to the example of his predecessor in office munshi Kaval Nain, who had been awarded a jagir just a few years previously, arguing that 'I who have been a faithful servant of the British Government for a period of 30 years am better entitled then him to the favour of the honorable Company.'[95] Bhagwant Rao had been betrayed by the system, but his allusions to the favours to which he felt entitled suggest the financial motivations he might have had for associating himself with the Company in the first place. Enam Allah, a former munshi of the Resident John Collins who also found himself in a dismal financial situation, similarly appealed to 'the established practice of the British Government which abandons none of its servants or dependants to wander abroad in search of bread', thereby securing for himself a pension of Rs 200 per month.[96]

Perhaps just as enticing was access to the patronage of other Company officials, indeed, to a whole institutional network that the munshi could draw upon for support and assistance. Residents regularly manipulated the munshi's ties to serve their own ends, using the munshi's acquaintance with literati at other courts as a channel for political information.[97] Munshis, however, also cashed in on the Residents' social capital. Given the geographical spread of the Company as an institution, it made sense for munshis to cultivate good relationships with British

[93] Fisher, *Indirect Rule*, p. 332. For examples of these arrangements, see BL, APAC, IOR/F/4/1473/57822, John Adam to Richard Jenkins, 17 August 1816, p. 13; BL, APAC, IOR/F/4/762/20696, Extract Political Letter from Bombay, 2 March 1822, pp. 1–3.

[94] NLS, Minto Papers, MS 11583, Mir Ibn Alli to N. B. Edmonstone, 7 October 1810, pp. 174–175.

[95] NLS, Minto Papers, MS 11583, Bhugwunt Rao to Earl of Minto, 13 July 1810, pp. 24–25.

[96] BL, APAC, IOR/F/4/297/6840, Enam Allah to Minto, received 28 August 1808, p. 6.

[97] Fisher, *Indirect Rule*, p. 326. For example William Palmer to Marquess Wellesley, 8 April 1799, in *PRC*, VI, pp. 388–390; before war with Tipu, William Palmer's munshi passed on information he'd received from a friend in the service of a rival power that the peshwa and Shinde were conspiring to attack the nizam and form an alliance with Tipu Sultan.

officials who could help forge connections with patrons in other parts of India. Munshis fully exploited this perk of the job; the correspondence of the Residents is rife with examples of letters written to colleagues on behalf of Indian secretaries. Often it was in pursuit of legal aid, usually respecting the munshi's landholdings or investments in distant parts of the subcontinent. The Resident at Nagpur Richard Jenkins, for instance, appealed to John Baillie, Resident at Lucknow, seeking legal aid for his former munshi, Mir Ghulam, who complained that a person named Sadiq Ali was building on a piece of his property in Faizabad. Jenkins asked Baillie, on behalf of Mir Ghulam, to ensure that the affair would be properly adjudicated.[98] Through access to the Resident's personal and professional network the munshi was also able to enjoy a range of employment opportunities. To take just one example, Mir Kazim Hussain, initially employed by Mountstuart Elphinstone as second in the Persian Department on Elphinstone's mission to Afghanistan, was able, once the mission was over, to acquire a position under Elphinstone's close friend Richard Strachey at Shinde's camp.[99] A connection with the Company therefore opened up lines of communication and aid to the munshi that might otherwise have been closed to him. The Resident's position in the Company bureaucracy put him at the centre of a network of relationships, and this administrative machinery could be set in motion to the munshi's advantage.

At the same time, the nature of the Company as a bureaucratic institution, and the Resident's place as a subordinate within that wider hierarchy, posed problems for the munshi. In particular, there was no guarantee of how long a Resident would remain at court. It could be dangerous for a munshi to rely too heavily on an individual who might well be stationed elsewhere and in any case would likely return permanently to Britain at some point. To some extent, the munshi could expect to benefit from the networks of the Resident or those of the Company more generally to furnish him with employment or other kinds of financial support upon the Resident's departure from court. As previously mentioned, Enam Allah Kahn, who declared himself 'dependent on Colonel Collins' and who on Collins death was 'exposed [...] to alarm and distress', was subsequently able to secure a Company pension.[100] Still, depending upon the circumstances of the Resident's withdrawal, the munshi might be left with nothing. Ibn Ali, for instance, seems to have had a good thing

---

[98] BL, APAC, Mss Eur E111, Richard Jenkins to John Baillie, 21 July 1811, pp. 148–149.
[99] BL, APAC, Mss Eur D514/3, Richard Strachey to C. A. Molony, 4 January 1817, p. 225.
[100] BL, APAC, IOR/F/4/297/6840, Enam Allah Khan to Minto, received 28 August 1808, p. 5.

going as Thomas Sydenham's head munshi at Hyderabad. According to Henry Russell, Sydenham's assistant, 'Ibn i Ally has exercised more Authority than ever Uzeez Oolah [his predecessor] did in the very zenith of his Power.' This power had made Ibn Ali an important patron in his own right; Russell referred bitterly to 'the Swarm of Locusts that he has invited from the Countries of the north.' In 1810, however, Thomas Sydenham was disgraced because of his association with an army uprising. After Sydenham's departure from the Residency, Ibn Ali was left without protection, and Henry Russell's first act on taking up the Residency was to send him away.[101] Ibn Ali's reversal of fortunes highlights the insecurity of the munshi's position given that the Resident was often his single, unstable link to the Company and its resources. It also suggests the dangers of acquiring too much power within the Residency; the appearance of influence could alienate the munshi from other employees of the Company who might, ultimately, replace the Resident upon whose complicity the munshi, to some degree, depended.

Allegations of impropriety, and the appearance of undue influence on the part of a munshi, were also interpreted as a reflection on the morals and character of the Resident in question. To return to the previous example, though Henry Russell determined to replace Ibn Ali as head munshi at Hyderabad, he also decided, as he put it, to let the munshi go 'quietly, and without any digging into his past Conduct.' In so doing, Russell was explicitly motivated by 'Delicacy towards Sydenham', who would be implicated in any misdeeds that Russell might unearth.[102] By contrast, when Resident at Delhi Edward Colebrooke was accused of corruption, he defended himself by lashing out at his predecessors in office, suggesting that the fortunes made by former Residency munshis evidenced a long tradition of corruption at Delhi that made his own alleged malfeasance seem innocuous by comparison. According to Colebrooke, it was widely known within the city that Charles Metcalfe's munshi Hafiz ud-Din had retired with a fortune of four lakhs, while Seton's munshi, Peri Lal, was supposed to be worth upwards of six lakhs; the wealth of Ochterlony's late munshi, Barkat Ali Khan, was described as 'unbounded'.[103] Bhavani Raman has argued that, in the context of the local revenue office, Company officers often portrayed their Indian subordinates as

---

[101] Bodl. Oxf., Russell Papers, MSS Eng. lett. d. 151, Henry to Charles Russell, 31 May 1810, p. 93.

[102] Ibid.

[103] James Edward Colebrooke, *Papers Relative to the Case at Issue between Sir Edward Colebrooke, Bt., and the Bengal Government* (London, 1833), p. 15.

corrupt as a way of deflecting these allegations from themselves.[104] In the political line, however, it seems that it was less easy for Residents to dissociate themselves from their munshis. This intimate connection was the subject of scrutiny and suspicion, given broader reformist trends within the Company and Britain at large, whereby accountability and transparency in the civil service were increasingly emphasized.[105] The problem was that in practice the close working relationship between Residents and munshis made questions of responsibility difficult to resolve conclusively; it was hard to determine who to blame when things went wrong, particularly given the Residency's geographical isolation from the Company's administrative centres.

The example of John Baillie and munshi Ali Naqi Khan illustrates this entanglement. Baillie and Ali Naqi Khan had traversed the subcontinent together filling various Company posts over the course of several years before finally settling at the Lucknow Residency. When the munshi faced the potential loss of some landholdings, primarily because of a disputed will, Baillie tried to use his influence with the nawab vizier to restore Ali Naqi Khan's property. When his exhortations to the Nawab Vizier Saadat Ali Khan proved unsuccessful, Baillie brought the munshi's petition before the government, arguing that the munshi's long service to the Company entitled him to the governor general's support. At that time, the then-Governor-General the Earl of Minto interpreted the munshi's difficulties, and the nawab vizier's unwillingness to intercede in his favour, as part and parcel of the nawab vizier's opposition to the Company. Accordingly, Minto pressured the nawab vizier to restore Ali Naqi Khan's property.[106] A few years later, however, when the Marquess of Hastings took office as governor general, he saw the entire affair in a different light. Hastings viewed the supposed restoration of Ali Naqi Khan's property, a transaction that had taken place without any due investigation into competing claims, as clear proof that Baillie was using the Company's power, and his status as Company representative, to pursue his own ends. Hastings's belief was that political instability in India was at least partly a consequence of the Residents' tyrannical treatment of Indian rulers, and Baillie's actions in favour of Ali Naqi Khan appeared to substantiate this view. In Hastings's mind, the problem was that Baillie had developed extensive patronage networks that were beginning to spiral out of control, impeding Baillie's

---

[104] Raman, *Document Raj*, p. 26.
[105] Philip Harling, *The Waning of 'Old Corruption': The Politics of Economical Reform in Britain, 1779–1846* (Oxford, 1996), p. 22.
[106] BL, APAC, IOR/F/4/372/9249, Extract Political Letter from Bengal, 24 July 1811, p. 2.

ability to fulfil his responsibilities. As Hastings put it, because Baillie's Indian agents were 'essentially recognised depositories of his Power', Baillie 'could not sacrifice those dependents to His Excellency's indignation without giving up all hope of keeping together a Party', and was therefore 'constrained to uphold them in confessed opposition to their Sovereign.'[107] In line with this interpretation of the relationship between Resident and munshi, the property that had been reclaimed by Ali Naqi Khan was restored to his rivals, and a commission was created to investigate the dispute; John Baillie was removed from Lucknow shortly thereafter.[108] In this case, the personal fortunes of Ali Naqi Khan and John Baillie were subject to shifts in Company personnel and policy, in light of which their relationship came to seem suspicious; in the end, their interests were determined to be dangerously linked.[109]

Figures at court and the surrounding area were equally apt to bracket Residents and munshis together, albeit often to the munshi's disadvantage. To revert to the previous example, when asked to explain the reasons for his conflict with Resident John Baillie, Saadat Ali Khan's successor, Ghazi ud-Din Haidar Khan, blamed the tensions between them on a misunderstanding generated by Baillie's munshi Ali Naqi Khan, claiming 'that Col. Baillie was a good man but that he had been misled by the moonshee.'[110] Similarly, when a petition was presented to the government of Fort St George on behalf of some inhabitants of Travancore, accusing the Resident John Munro of tyranny and corruption, most of the accusations actually centred on the activities of Munro's munshi. Reddy Rao was accused of accepting bribes, and of conferring titles upon the as a pretext for taking gifts from her. Reddy Rao was even blamed for causing a three-month-long famine by ordering merchants not to sell their stores of rice. John Munro was implicated in these crimes only because, as the petition stipulated, 'Colonel Munro reposing all his confidence on his said Dewan Reddee Royer behaves himself pursuant to the said Reddee Royers evil persuasions. So that they seem to have one Soul in two bodies and consequently their conduct is arbitrary and tyrannical.'[111] Conditions in Travancore were thus attributed to Reddy Rao's evil influence rather than to the Resident himself, who was

---

[107] BL, APAC, IOR/F/4/510/12267, p. 114.

[108] BL, APAC, IOR/F/4/510/12266, John Adam to John Baillie, 1 July 1815, p. 40.

[109] Baillie also alienated the nawab vizier by intervening on behalf of an agent of the Residency treasury; see BL, APAC, IOR/P/118/30, John Baillie to Secretary to Government, 10 October 1808, no. 23.

[110] BL, APAC, Mss Eur D514/3, Richard Strachey to John Adam, 8 December 1815, pp. 18, 19.

[111] BL, APAC, IOR/F/4/445/10674, 'Petition of Soobba Royer and Sanagara Lingum Pillary', Extract Fort St. George Political Consultations, 14 October 1813, p. 15.

portrayed rather as Reddy Rao's willing puppet. Passages like these are difficult to interpret. It is entirely possible that these munshis did exert a potent influence over the Residents, just as they were accused of doing, but it is also possible that these accusations were made strategically, based on the assumption that the munshi was a more amenable target for criticism than the Resident himself. In general, the influence of munshis is difficult to ascertain, since Residents were unlikely to describe themselves as being under the thumb of their secretaries, though onlookers might describe the relationship in precisely these terms.

Whatever the basis for these accusations might have been, there is no doubt that the munshi's relationship with the Resident placed him in a position of visibility at court that made him susceptible to these kinds of allegations. Indeed, the munshi's association with the Resident seems to have made him an object of antagonism in his own right. This, at least, is what is suggested to us by a petition written by Raja Kaval Nain, the appointed mediator between the Resident and Daulat Rao Shinde. Kaval Nain presented himself as an adherent of both parties; as he put it, 'the attachment and loyalty which I have from first to last evinced in my conduct towards the two states is well known and has been often proved.' Shinde's first minister, however, apparently used Kaval Nain's affiliation with the Company against him in an attempt to reduce the munshi's influence with Shinde by arguing that Kaval Nain's first loyalty was to the British. Indeed, according to Kaval Nain, the minister 'treated me in a bad and improper manner, in order that no one for the future might exert himself to support the friendship between the states.'[112] Though Kaval Nain claimed never to have lost Shinde's ear, and to be continually advising him to ally with the English (thereby trying, no doubt, to emphasize his own continuing utility to the Company), the first minister nevertheless succeeded in confiscating Kaval Nain's property and expropriating a large sum of the munshi's money, the reacquisition of which was the motive for Kaval Nain's petition to the governor general. Kaval Nain certainly had practical reasons for framing events in this way; by presenting his loyalty to the Company as the chief source of his problems at court, he thereby had some justification for holding the Company accountable for his loss. Still, incidents at other courts would appear to support the idea that a munshi's association with the Company could be a liability. Gopal Rao, the peshwa's agent at the Pune Residency, was also accused of being 'an adherent of the Company', and consequently was 'much alarmed for

---

[112] BL, APAC, IOR/H/625, Kavel Nyne to John Malcolm, 23 June 1805, p. 155.

his own safety', according to Resident William Palmer.[113] In the words of Thomas Sydenham, who briefly substituted for Palmer at Pune, 'every person who is at all supported by us, becomes an object of persecution to the Minister.'[114] Not only was the munshi vulnerable to the vagaries of Company policy, but his association with it also made him a target for the jealousies and resentments of the courtly elite.

The Resident would occasionally intercede in the munshi's favour, but only when personal obligations and public responsibilities were in alignment. For instance, Richard Strachey, newly appointed to the position of Political Resident at Lucknow, refused to dismiss munshi Ali Naqi Khan when the nawab vizier demanded it; Strachey declared that he 'could not admit the propriety of his [Ghazi ud-Din's] interference [...] regarding the members of my household.'[115] Significantly, Richard Strachey described Ali Naqi Khan as a member of his household, a concept widely current in eighteenth-century Britain and defined in terms of spheres of authority and domestic management.[116] By intervening in the Resident's household, the nawab vizier was thus infringing on the Resident's domestic authority. The Company's authority was implicated as well on such an occasion; to surrender one of its employees would be tantamount to suggesting that the Company was incapable of looking out for its own. In instances such as these, the Company's reputation for good faith was perceived to be at stake, and, in the words of John Malcolm in his 'Notes of Instruction', 'whenever that is concerned, the tone of our feeling should be very high.'[117] When the Resident at Pune intervened to protect munshi Byaji Naik against the peshwa's first minister, the Resident explicitly justified his intervention on the grounds that it would act as 'a wholesome check upon the Minister', showing him that the Company were prepared to use their influence over the peshwa when necessary.[118] An association with the Company could, it seems, occasionally counteract the disfavour of notable figures at court; it could not, however, be trusted implicitly in a context where personal and professional affiliations were not infrequently in conflict.

From the Resident's perspective, the joint demands of fulfilling his official duties and conciliating the local monarch generally took

---

[113] BL, APAC, IOR/H/576, William Palmer to Marquess Wellesley, 16 May 1800, p. 126. Also BL, APAC, IOR/H/576, William Palmer to Marquess Wellesley, 20 March 1801, pp. 631–632.

[114] Thomas Sydenham to Barry Close, 17 June 1805, in *PRR*, X, p. 259.

[115] BL, APAC, Mss Eur D514/3, Richard Strachey to John Adam, 5 December 1815, p. 19.

[116] Tadmor, *Family and Friends*, pp. 20, 24.

[117] Malcolm, 'Notes of Instruction', in Briggs, *Letters*, p. 218

[118] Thomas Sydenham to Richard Wellesley, 1 February 1805, in *PRC*, X, p. 193.

precedence over his accountability to his Indian staff. The strict lines of authority within the Company sometimes competed with, and in these instances tended to outweigh, links of personal loyalty and dependence. In consequence, the Resident was often prepared to abandon his munshi by the wayside if circumstances seemed to demand it. In 1801 Resident William Palmer learned that his munshi Mir Fakhir al-Din was rumoured to be involved in a conspiracy to depose the current ruler of Pune. One of the conspirators had been arrested, and charges were now being brought against the munshi. The munshi solemnly denied any participation in the scheme. Indeed, Palmer himself recalled Fakhir al-Din mentioning certain ambiguous advances that had been made to him by some of the conspirators, though neither Palmer nor the munshi had then realized the full extent of the plot. Palmer was thus forced to conclude that 'if a mere knowledge of the Intrigue to this extent only is criminal towards the Peshwah, I am as culpable as Meer Fukir ul Dien.' Palmer explained away his own silence by claiming that it was not his responsibility to inform the Pune government of any plots against it, but felt that circumstances required that he dismiss Fakhir al-Din from his service, whether he was guilty of conspiracy or not. As Palmer put it,

though I know that I not only have a right, but it is my Duty as a public Minister to protect my Servants, until their conduct is proved to be unjustifiable, I will wave these Considerations rather than expose the public Business to interruption or afford the Peshwah a pretext for asserting that I countenance intrigue against his Person and Government.[119]

At a time when Palmer was under intense pressure to conclude a subsidiary alliance at Pune, he could not, he felt, risk alienating Baji Rao by standing up for Fakhir al-Din. Palmer thus sacrificed his munshi to the interests of the Company, concealing his knowledge of events that might have exculpated the man.

   William Palmer himself did not escape from this predicament entirely unscathed; his reputation does seem to have been somewhat tarnished by Fakhir al-Din's reputed activities. Henry Russell, for one, blamed Palmer for the munshi's alleged misconduct; Russell observed that 'under the Ascendancy of Sir Charles's [Malet] Talents and Dignity, he [Mir Fakhir al-Din] was honest and useful; but the weakness and good nature of Colonel Palmer encouraged and permitted him to be a

---

[119] BL, APAC, Mss Eur F228/13, William Palmer to J. A. Kirkpatrick, 18 July 1801, pp. 106–109; see also MSA, PRCOP, vol. 38 (1798–1801), William Palmer to Political Secretary, 18 July 1801, p. 1181; William Palmer to Political Secretary, 20 July 1801, p. 1195.

Rogue.'[120] Still, the fact of the matter was that Palmer kept his job and Fakhir al-Din lost his; Palmer, given his association with the Company and his status as Resident, was too prestigious to become collateral damage to courtly intrigues.

The munshi was therefore often forced to respond to circumstances not of his making, without even being able to place entire reliance on his patron. His position at the intersection of court and Company, though it opened up certain opportunities, also required him to be highly adaptive. The multiple contingencies to which the munshi was subject made the future difficult to judge, requiring him to be acutely attuned to changing circumstances in the present.[121] Though the munshi played a crucial part in the operations of the Residency, he could never quite enjoy the luxury of resting on his laurels and looking with confidence into the future. Like so many cultural brokers in similar situations around the world, maintaining his precarious position required the munshi to be constantly on the alert as he navigated the turbulent waters at the confluence of the local and the global.

The story of Mir Fakhir al-Din did not end with his dismissal, however. After leaving the Residency, Fakhir al-Din joined his brother at Hyderabad, where he lobbied on behalf of the peshwa's brother, Amrit Rao, and acted as a channel of communication between Amrit Rao and the nizam.[122] Gopal Rao, one of the peshwa's ministers, seemed to imply, in a conversation with Close, that Mir Fakhir al-Din's activities were a product of 'the chagrin that he must naturally sustain in consequence [of his removal from office and] the asperity of his feelings towards those to whom he attributes the loss of his station'.[123] Among the courtly elite at Pune, however, it was generally believed that Mir Fakhir al-Din had been acting in this capacity for some time, even prior to his dismissal from the Residency.[124] Mir Fakhir al-Din's political activities offer a tantalizing glimpse of cross-cutting loyalties, reminding us that a munshi's work for the Resident constituted only one dimension of his political life. A munshi's services were essential to the Residency, but they could never be entirely controlled, much to the Residents' discomfiture.

---

[120] Bodl. Oxf., Russell Papers, MSS Eng. lett. d. 151, Henry to Charles Russell, 14 June 1810, p. 120.

[121] Emirbayer and Mische, 'What Is Agency?', p. 994.

[122] MSA, PRCOP, vol. 39 (1801–1802), Barry Close to John Malcolm, 1 December 1802, p. 357.

[123] MSA, PRCOP, vol. 39 (1801–1802), Barry Close to Secretary to Government, 5 February 1802, p. 142.

[124] MSA, PRCOP, vol. 40 (1802–1803), Barry Close to James Achilles Kirkpatrick, 1 December 1802, pp. 363–365.

5.4   Conclusion

In conclusion, the relationship between Residents and munshis, though of great practical importance to both parties, was also a source of considerable risk. Though some Residents and munshis did develop lasting relationships, in many cases the written evidence suggests that the Residents' attitudes towards Residency munshis were inflected by negative stereotypes of Indian political culture, as well as their fear of being misled or misrepresented in a context where their grasp of the dominant language and political norms was weak. From the point of view of Residency munshis, an association with the Resident had definite practical benefits; the Resident was not only an attractive source of patronage in his own right but could provide access to a larger patronage network that spanned the subcontinent. Still, the Resident could be unreliable; while in some instances the Resident was able to protect the munshi from the disfavour of the monarch, his willingness to do so was entirely dependent on circumstances largely outside the munshi's control. Ultimately the Resident prioritized his own interests and those of the Company above the interests of his staff, privileging professional over personal responsibilities. Indeed, because of his intermediary status, and his prominent place within the Company and at court, an association with the Resident effectively doubled the potential problems from the munshi's point of view by exposing the munshi to scrutiny and suspicion from both British and Indian onlookers.

In the end, many Residents expressed uncertainty about how far they could, or should, trust the Residency munshi. Residents who relied too heavily on their munshis were liable to exploitation or suspicions of malversation; from an outsider's perspective, their agency could become indistinguishable from that of the munshi, over whom the Resident feared they could never enjoy complete control. Yet, Residents who dispensed with a munshi's services risked committing damaging social and political faux pas. To most Residents it seemed clear that there was a balance to be struck somewhere between the two, but where that middle ground was to be found remained a problem. Henry Russell was certain that a munshi's services were requisite at the Residency, but nevertheless remarked that the particular nature of that employment depended upon 'circumstances casual and fluctuating'. It was up to the Resident to determine, in his words, 'what Business is to be transacted verbally, and what in writing; upon which occasion the Resident is to appear himself, where he is to employ his Assistants, and where he is to confide in a native servant.'[125] This lack of definition sometimes created the opportunity for

---

[125] Henry Russell to Charles Russell, 14 June 1810, Russell Papers, MSS Eng. lett. d. 151, Bodl. Oxf., p. 119.

a munshi to acquire a position of recognized authority within the Residency, but it was equally likely to make him a target of resentment and distrust. This problem was both pervasive and intractable, and it lay at the very heart of the Residents' operations, suggesting how complicated even the most basic aspects of the Resident's job could be.

Though the resources available to them were very different, the members of the royal family were faced with a very similar problem to the munshis in the Residents' employ. As the Company's reach extended further across the subcontinent, Indian royalty had to decide for themselves how to secure their own best interests in an environment of instability and change. The solutions to this quandary differed dramatically from person to person; in some instances, royal family members were the Company's greatest allies, while in other cases they represented their greatest foes. Either way, royal family members found that they had to engage to some extent with the Resident if they were to continue to be players in the contested field of courtly politics. The Residents, meanwhile, recognized that royal family members had the power to promote or prevent their agendas from taking shape, and acknowledged that they could ill afford to ignore the kinds of patrimonial conflicts that they might have preferred to dismiss as family squabbles.

6   Kinship, Gender, and Dynastic Dramas

When the Marquess of Hastings decided to tour the Northwest Provinces shortly after his arrival in India in 1814, he charged the Resident at Delhi with a somewhat intractable problem. Archibald Seton was asked to manage the ceremonial encounter between the newly appointed governor general and the king of Delhi, as he was then designated by the Company, in a way that would reflect the Company's paramountcy, without offending the man widely venerated in India as the king of kings. Seton wracked his brain for ways of exempting Hastings from making the usual signs of deference, particularly the imperative to remain standing in the royal presence. Ultimately, Seton could recommend only one solution. 'I have [...] been endeavouring to discover a principle or precedent calculated to meet both the feelings of the King and the wishes of your Lordship', he wrote, 'and this I can only do by a reference to your Lordship's descent and illustrious pedigree', alluding to Hastings's distant connection to the British royal family. Princely descent was, in Seton's mind, 'unquestionably the plea most likely to be understood and admitted by the feelings of the king'.[1] Regardless of the power that the governor general wielded as the dominant political authority in the subcontinent and commander-in-chief of one of the largest standing armies in the world, it was his tenuous relation to the king of England that would permit him to break with precedent and approach the king of Delhi on a footing of near equality. In the end, Hastings preferred not to meet Akbar Shah at all.[2]

Whether Company officials liked it or not, in a hereditary monarchy family mattered; it entitled a person to privileges and respect. In consequence, the ruler's family exercised a kind of authority that even the most senior Company men had to take seriously. Yet, historians of the Company have focused on its engagement with Indian rulers at the expense of the wider royal family. Despite the existence of a few

---

[1] BL, APAC, Cleveland Public Library Papers, IOR Neg 4227, wq091.92 Ea77p9, Archibald Seton to Marquess of Hastings, 6 June 1814, pp. 118–120
[2] Bute, ed., *Private Journal*, p. 318.

significant studies on the early modern Mughal household, and on royal women in the late nineteenth and early twentieth century, the period of Company rule has been neglected.[3] A study of royal families might seem dangerously close to being an outdated history of great men and women, but to ignore the dynastic side of Indian politics, and the intrigue and revolt with which it was rife, is to ignore one of the biggest quandaries confronting the Residents at Indian courts. Power and charisma were conceived loosely in this context, belonging in some degree to the patriliny as a whole. Royal family members could muster significant social, cultural, and economic capital in support of their personal and political projects. As a result, royal family members, women as well as men, could be vital allies, dangerous foes, or a combination of the two. If the Resident was to succeed in this world, he could not ignore the extensive royal family, with its shifting internal rivalries, enmities, and affective bonds. As André Wink famously argued, *fitna* (roughly, intrigue and sedition) formed a crucial element of political practice in India, central to the establishment and maintenance of sovereignty.[4] *Fitna* entailed forging alliances and marshalling support, and in this context, as Sumit Guha has shown, 'the exploitation of both family loyalties and their dark face-familial hatreds – was an important resource'.[5]

This chapter shines a spotlight on the privileged place that royal men and women occupied at the centre of the sweeping maelstrom of early nineteenth-century Indian courtly politics. The first two sections focus on male relatives, and the obstacles and opportunities they represented from the Resident's perspective. Section 1 examines how Residents attempted to manage incipient succession crises by curtailing the ambitions of younger brothers, a process that tended to foment, rather than preclude, acts of princely resistance. Section 2 provides a broader perspective, illuminating the long-term significance of male relatives beyond moments of succession. The second half of the chapter is devoted to female relatives, who raised different issues from the Resident's perspective and are therefore analysed separately. Section 3 demonstrates how the Residents' engagement with Indian royal women was mediated by British preconceptions, as well as frustration at the influence that royal women were capable of exercising.

---

[3] Ruby Lal, *Domesticity and Power in the Early Mughal World* (Cambridge, 2005); Ellison Banks Findly, *Nur Jahan: Empress of Mughal India* (New York, 1993); Angma Dey Jhala, *Courtly Indian Women in Late Imperial India* (London, 2008).

[4] André Wink, *Land and Sovereignty*, p. 26.

[5] Sumit Guha, 'The Family Feud as a Political Resource in Eighteenth-Century India', in *Unfamiliar Relations: Family and History in South Asia*, ed. Indrani Chatterjee (Delhi, 2004), p. 76.

Section 4 argues that despite these barriers, Residents and Indian royal
women forged important working relationships, in which the Residents
often found themselves working for the benefit of royal women rather
than the other way around. This chapter therefore introduces a vital
but previously neglected dimension to the Resident's work, namely, the
delicate job of managing the royal family. Because of the importance of
royal family members within courtly politics, Residents regularly found
themselves drawn into family dramas that they could not always understand or control, and which often had the effect of complicating their
work at court.

6.1   Sex, Succession, and Princely Resistance

The period of transition from one ruler to another was a potentially
critical juncture from the Company's perspective; a capable but compli-
ant ruler could greatly facilitate the Company's political and military
projects, while a resistant successor could spell instability or even war.
Even before the Company had begun to station Residents at Indian
courts, therefore, they had already meddled in succession disputes, most
famously in the Carnatic in the mid-eighteenth century.[6] These early
conflicts were proxy wars designed to secure British influence at Indian
courts at the expense of the French Compagnie des Indes. A hundred
years later, it was through the notorious 'doctrine of lapse' that the Company pursued its expansionist policies, by annexing states that lacked an
officially recognized heir.[7] Succession disputes were therefore an important element of the Company's history from first to last. The aggressive
interventionism of the later nineteenth century, however, was preceded
by a period in which the Company's main concern was stability and
control. Usually, Residents pre-empted the threat of succession crises by
deciding the heir apparent well in advance and supporting his succession
by keeping a military force close at hand.[8] This policy, however, did not
go unopposed.

   At the courts examined in this study, succession was open ended,
meaning that there were usually a handful of claimants rather than a single heir. To some degree, questions of inheritance and legitimacy were
complicated by polygyny, the practice of taking many wives. Not only

---

[6] Fisher, *Indirect Rule*, p. 141.
[7] Ibid., pp. 257–258.
[8] See for example events following death of nawab vizier in UPSAA, Benares Residency
Records, Letters Received by the Agent to the Governor General, basta no. 12, book no.
55, John Baillie to John Adam, 17 July 1814, pp. 287–288.

were the inhabitants of the zenana many, sometimes numbering into the hundreds, but they were differentiated according to multiple, graded forms of marriage and cohabitation; in theory, contractual marriages were distinguished from partnerships of pleasure, which in turn were distinct from women given as gifts, or concubines purchased or taken by force. Each form could imply different rights and expectations, but these hierarchies were not rigidly maintained, and concubines could acquire influence through the ruler's favour.[9] Perhaps most confusingly, from a British perspective, slavery and kinship could exist on a spectrum; sometimes the two were virtually indistinguishable, as Indrani Chatterjee has pointed out.[10] Since wives, lovers, and slaves mixed and intermingled, the line between legitimate and illegitimate children within royal families was negotiable. What mattered was less the legal status of the marriage, than the importance accorded it by the ruler in question; the favoured son of the ruler was usually the offspring of a favourite wife, whatever her family origins. Adoption allowed the ruler to remould kinship at will, and childless kings regularly adopted the sons of brothers, sisters, or even the children of menial servants to succeed them.[11]

To smooth the path to succession for a favoured son, the ruler placed the young man in administrative or military positions, thereby expressing his trust in his son's abilities and his intention to pass the reins of government to him. In the process, the youth acquired political experience and established himself at court. The ruler's preference was not incontrovertible, however, and court factions could and did intervene in succession disputes. The claim of the heir apparent was frequently contested by uncles or brothers, legitimate and illegitimate, biological or adopted.[12] Though the Nawab Vizier of Awadh Asaf ud-Daula went to great lengths to identify Vizier Ali as his heir, investing him with numerous offices and titles in addition to financing his lavish wedding to the daughter of a Lucknow courtier, powerful figures at court nevertheless united with the Company to depose him.[13] Vizier Ali's uncles were perceived to have just as much, if not more, of a claim to the throne. Qualities

[9] Michael H. Fisher, 'Women and the Feminine in the Court and High Culture of Awadh, 1722–1856', in *Women in the Medieval Islamic World: Power, Patronage, and Piety,* ed. Gavin R. Hambly (Houndmills, Basingstoke, 1998), pp. 491–493.

[10] Indrani Chatterjee, *Gender, Slavery and Law in Colonial India* (New Delhi, 1999), pp. 26–27.

[11] BL, APAC, IOR/L/PS/20/H17, Book of Nomenclature, p. 23.

[12] Fisher, *Indirect Rule,* p. 140.

[13] BL, APAC, Cleveland Public Library Papers, IOR Neg 4227, wq091.92 Ea77p9, John Monckton, 'Translation of the Narrative of Vizier Ali', 2 June 1814, pp. 333–334; John Monckton, 'Memorandum Respecting the State of Vizier Ali's Family as far as It Is Known', p. 239.

and connections sometimes trumped blood or seniority. Heredity was only one facet of royal legitimacy; personal charisma and the ability to maintain order were also key.[14]

In opposition to this more flexible pattern of royal inheritance, the Company began to deploy a narrow conception of legitimacy to undermine competing claims in succession crises. The deposition of Vizier Ali in 1798 is a well-documented instance of this. At first, individuals high up in the Company's administration doubted their ability to penetrate the harem of Vizier Ali's putative father, Asaf ud-Daula, and discover its secrets. In response to rumours circulating about the spurious birth of the recently crowned nawab vizier, Governor General John Shore reaffirmed his support for Vizier Ali's claim on the grounds that the truth or falsity of the rumours could not be conveniently proven. In Shore's mind, the crux of the problem inhered in the nature of Indian elite family life: 'the secrets of a Haram are seldom penetrable, and if it were otherwise, the attempt to unveil them would be an insult, and no Prince in a situation to resist enquiry would admit of it'.[15] In any case, Shore averred that 'to institute a public investigation into the secrets of the seraglio, would affect our reputation in a degree which no professions of our regard for Justice would ever efface'.[16] Despite his professed repugnance at attempting to unravel the mysteries of the zenana, however, Shore subsequently plunged into precisely such an investigation, minutely probing into the most private aspects of the former nawab vizier's sexual activities to ascertain the legitimacy of his successor. Reliant primarily on the testimony of the former nawab vizier's trusted eunuch and leading figure at court, Almas Ali Khan, the governor general reported that Asaf-ud-Daula was not only sexually impotent, but known to have procured pregnant menial servants to compensate for his childlessness; Vizier Ali was apparently the product of such a transaction.[17] While Shore argued that to support the succession of a known bastard would disgrace the Company in the eyes of the Indian elite, one wonders whether Vizier Ali's chief crime was his refusal to sanction the influence of the Company's agents at court.[18] After all, when the Company decided to intervene to support the succession of Sikander Jah at Hyderabad, Wellesley justified

---

[14] Stewart Gordon, 'Legitimacy and Loyalty in Some Successor States of the Eighteenth Century', in *Kingship and Authority in South Asia,* ed. J. F. Richards (Delhi, 1998), p. 341.

[15] BL, APAC, Cleveland Public Library Papers, IOR Neg 4215, wq091.92 Ea77m5, Minute of the Governor General, 20 October 1797, p. 246

[16] Ibid., p. 254

[17] BL, APAC, Cleveland Public Library Papers, IOR Neg 4215, wq091.92 Ea77m5, Minute of the Governor General, 13 January 1798, pp. 362, 357.

[18] Ibid.

his claim not simply in terms of the right of primogeniture but because 'his connections are among those persons best affected towards our interest; he is the only son of the Nizam who has ever maintained any authorised intercourse with us, or who has ever manifested any desire to cultivate our friendship.'[19] Still, the example of Vizier Ali illustrates how sexuality and heredity could become political, how the salacious gossip of the bazaar could become the stuff of official reports.

The Company were deeply interested in marriage and reproduction, because in India, as in Britain, royal marriages were strategic, used to cement alliances and accrue resources and status.[20] Births and marriages within royal families were rigorously recorded to amass useful political intelligence and trace emerging configurations of power. When the Qutlugh Begum (widow of Prince Jahander Shah, eldest son of the deceased Mughal emperor Shah Alam) attempted to marry her granddaughters to the princes of Delhi in 1808, for instance, she was reprimanded by the governor-general-in-council for not communicating her intent through official channels. The Resident at Benares (where the begum was living) was instructed to remind her of her duty to the governor general, and to 'request her royal highness to specify the princes to whom her granddaughters have been betrothed and report their names for the information of the government'.[21] In this instance, Minto was probably concerned that this marriage might augment the status of one of the Mughal emperor's younger sons, thereby undermining the claim of the Company's candidate for the throne. By keeping track of royal marriages, Residents and other Company officials sought to pre-empt the formation of courtly factions and the possibility of succession crises that would have to be stifled or resolved if the Resident were to maintain control.

Despite the Residents' best efforts, disputes could and did erupt at court, and, because of the Company's intervention, resistance during this period often centred on British officials. Perhaps the most famous instance of dynastic struggle of this kind was when the exiled former nawab Vizier Ali, assisted by a few close retainers, murdered the senior judge at Benares and his four guests on 15 January 1799, shortly after breakfast. Evading British forces, Vizier Ali fled the city to unite with

---

[19] Mornington to J. A. Kirkpatrick, 6 November 1799, in *Wellesley Despatches*, II, p. 136.
[20] Stephen P. Blake, 'Returning the Household to the Patrimonial-Bureaucratic Empire: Gender, Succession, and Ritual in the Mughal, Safavid and Ottoman Empires', in *Tributary Empires in Global History*, eds. Peter Fibier Bang and C. A. Bayly (Houndmills, Basingstoke, 2011), pp. 18–19.
[21] UPSAA, Benares Residency Records, Letters Received by the Agent to the Governor General at Benares (1807–1808), basta no. 11, book no. 48, N. B. Edmonstone to W. A. Brooke, 18 January 1808, p. 92.

his supporters and mount a full-scale rebellion to reclaim the throne of Awadh. Over the course of the following months, Vizier Ali joined with bands of marauders to plague British troops, before finally surrendering to capture and living out his days in exile, imprisoned in the British fortress at Vellore.[22] Though the account of Judge George Cherry's tragic death made Vizier Ali a villain of the highest order in British public opinion, the events leading up to that armed confrontation over the breakfast table were not so very unusual. Bypassed or disempowered male relatives were apt to resent the outsiders who were seen to have robbed them of their birthright, and this resentment could easily translate into violence.

This was particularly true of younger sons. To avoid political instability, Residents threw their weight behind older siblings on point of principle. Understandably, this policy generated significant tensions at court. Suddenly, age hierarchies and ideas of legitimacy that had previously been negotiable were rendered rigid and unbending. This policy created a conflict of interests between the Resident and royal brothers, some of whom aligned themselves against the Company, occasionally to the point of outright rebellion. One notorious incident occurred at Delhi when Prince Mirza Jahangir, the third and favoured son of Akbar Shah II, briefly took control of the Red Fort in 1809. Irritated at the Resident Archibald Seton's attempt to control his drinking by prohibiting wine vendors from selling their wares in the palace precincts, the young prince barred the gates of the fort against the Resident. Shots were fired, but the revolt proved short lived; Mirza Jahangir ultimately surrendered to the Resident and was confined in the fortress at Agra.[23] One of the Resident's secretaries attributed Mirza Jahangir's attempted insurrection to his association with European gentlemen, through which he 'had imbibed notions of liberty very inimical to the policy of our Government respecting native princes'.[24] Also clearly at issue, however, was the Resident's persistent opposition to Mirza Jahangir's status as favoured son and heir apparent, much to the dismay of the Mughal emperor and his favourite wife, Mumtaz Mahal.[25]

A similar incident occurred at Hyderabad a few years later, where Mubariz ud-Daula, one of Nizam Sikander Jah's younger sons, described as 'headstrong, obstinate and rapacious', was particularly known to have

---

[22] UPSAA, Benares Residency Records, Letters Issued by the Agent to the Governor General at Benares, basta no. 1, register no. 3, John Neave to George Barlow, 15 January 1799, p. 220.

[23] BL, APAC, IOR/F/4/334/7657, Extract of Letter from Bengal, 19 October 1809, pp. 2–4.

[24] NRAS, Fraser of Reelig Papers, vol. 33, Alexander Fraser to his mother, 23 December 1810, p. 219.

[25] Panikkar, *British Diplomacy in North India*, pp. 20–42.

'always hated the English'. According to the Resident Henry Russell, 'when the Nizam insisted on posting a guard from Captain Hare's brigade at Moobariz ood Dowlah's house, the latter declared "that he would lose his Life rather than suffer a Guard to be posted over him from any Corps commanded by a European".'[26] After a long period of escalating tensions, the crisis came to a point in 1815 when the twenty-year-old Mubariz ud-Daula and his brother Shams ud-Daula seized Henry Russell's tailor, purportedly to extort money from him. The infantry posted near the city attempted, but failed, to take Mubariz ud-Daula's house. Afraid of a general insurrection, Russell ordered them to wait for reinforcements. Eventually the ferment in the city subsided of itself and the princes surrendered to the nizam, who acceded to the Resident's request to imprison them in the nearby fortress of Golconda.[27]

Just over fifteen years later, however, Mubariz ud-Daula once again became associated with unrest in the city, this time during the reign of his brother Nasir ud-Daula. With the backing of disaffected Arab and Afghan mercenaries who had been displaced by the Company's subsidiary forces, Mubariz fortified his house and began to press claims against his brother.[28] Once again, British forces marched into the city and induced the prince to surrender. Mubariz then withdrew to the fortress of Golconda, the previous site of his imprisonment, but turned the tables on his brother by refusing access to the treasury there. Once again British and Hyderabadi forces were assembled, with many days spent negotiating before the nizam and his brother were finally reconciled through the mediation of their mother, the Chandni Begum, who Nasir ud-Daula sent as his representative. In 1839, Mubariz ud-Daula found himself confined at Golconda for the third and final time, in this instance because of his ties to Muslim reformist networks and his involvement in the purported 'Wahhabi conspiracy' to overturn British rule in India. Mubariz lived out the remainder of his days in Golconda as a state prisoner.[29] The prince was described, even within the unsympathetic pages of the Residency records, as 'personally brave and determined'; he was a proficient rider, and skilled in the use of the sword, spear, and bow. This 'manly and soldier like' prince, seemingly destined for great things, had good reason to chafe at the restraints imposed on him by the Resident.[30]

[26] BL, APAC, Mss Eur F88/60, Notes and intelligence of Mountstuart Elphinstone regarding the Peshwa and Trimbuckjee, p. 35.

[27] Prinsep, *History*, pp. 263–265.

[28] Chandra Mallampalli, *A Muslim Conspiracy in British India? Politics and Paranoia in the Early Nineteenth-Century Deccan* (Cambridge, 2017), pp. 76–77.

[29] Mallampalli, *Muslim Conspiracy*, pp. 66–105.

[30] BL, APAC, Mss Eur F88/60, p. 35.

The consequences of Company interference in royal successions are difficult to assess; elder sons were not necessarily any more receptive to the Company's influence than their younger siblings, and many were outright inimical to it. Company interference might, however, have caused potentially more suitable candidates to be bypassed, forced to give way to older siblings who might not have possessed their interest or ability. While princely infighting was seen as a weak point of Indian polities in the nineteenth century (and is sometimes still described in these terms even today), the Company might well have been stifling a process that would have reinvigorated reigning dynasties by encouraging competing princes to reinforce vertical ties of patronage and obligation among the broader population, as Munis Faruqui has argued for the seventeenth-century Mughal dynasty.[31] Although the Company might have been contributing to the weakness or stagnation of Indian monarchies, however, this strategy had its price. Historians have interpreted the Company's management of succession disputes as a sign of their growing power over Indian kingdoms, but the Company's influence in this regard did not go unchallenged.[32] Although the Company sought to preclude succession crises by intervening in support of elder sons, in practice this policy fomented the ambitions of younger brothers who knew they had historical precedent on their side. These insurrections were easily stamped out, but they were nevertheless recurring. Aggrieved royals could always find supporters to rally to their cause, suggesting that many people refused to accept the legitimacy of the rules imposed by the Company.

6.2   Bad Blood: Arbitrating Fraternal Conflict

Violent uprisings exemplify opposition in its most extreme form, but even in the absence of such acts of rebellion, the fluidity of the rules governing royal succession soured relations between brothers whose shared heredity made them rival claimants. Siblings Baji Rao, Chimnaji Appa, and Amrit Rao were apparently very close as children living together in political exile, but their friendship was almost irredeemably dispelled when the musnud unexpectedly came into play after their cousin Madhav Rao II fell from a balcony in 1795.[33] As a child Baji Rao was said to have been particularly fond of Amrit Rao, but henceforward his relationship

---

[31] Munis Faruqui, *The Princes of the Mughal Empire 1504–1719* (Cambridge, 2012), p. 12.
[32] Fisher, *Indirect Rule*, p. 144; Ramusack, *Indian Princes*, p. 138.
[33] UPSAA, Benares Residency Records, Letters Received by the Agent to the Governor General at Benares (1810), basta no. 11, book no. 51, Henry Russell to John Monckton, 23 September 1810, enclosed in John Monckton to W. A. Brooke, 10 November 1810, p. 245.

with his erstwhile favourite brother would always be tense. Amrit Rao would become the focus of oppositional politics at court, culminating in an attempt to place his son Benaik Rao on the throne during the Second Maratha War. Even after Amrit Rao had voluntarily withdrawn to the Company's dominions after the war, Baji Rao continued to hold his adherents, as well as their family and servants, in confinement.[34] Male relatives of the ruler were usually subject to suspicion and surveillance, and not infrequently to imprisonment or exile.[35] Even Baji Rao's loyal younger brother Chimnaji Appa eventually became a subject of his 'jealousy and hatred'.[36] As Baji Rao's biological brother (Amrit Rao was adopted), numerous schemes at Pune had revolved around placing Chimnaji on the musnud; yet, Chimnaji had always resisted the role laid out for him by Baji Rao's enemies, consistently exposing their conspiracies to his brother and even joining Baji Rao in exile during the Second Maratha War.[37] For years, Chimnaji was Baji Rao's closest confidant and a constant presence at his side; yet, in 1808, Baji Rao protested that Chimnaji had become reserved and unaccommodating, and by 1810, the two were thoroughly estranged. Chimnaji complained that he was not granted the honours and attentions due to his rank; he resented having to report his movements outside the city, and to present receipts for his stipend. In Chimnaji's view, these restrictions were a poor reward for his loyalty to his brother.[38] In contrast to his strained relationships with his brothers, the peshwa's closest associates were individuals of lowly origins. In a context where the ruler's kin posed a threat through their claims to the musnud, vulnerable rulers were understandably prone to attach themselves to people who presented no such challenge.[39]

The rulers' preference for slaves and servants above members of their own family was a tendency that Residents found perplexing and disagreeable; unsurprising, perhaps, given the centrality of kinship

---

[34] BL, APAC, Mss Eur E216, Arthur Wellesley to Barry Close, 14 December 1804, p. 52.

[35] Henry Russell notes that the nizam's brothers 'live in an easy kind of restraint, and never appear in public'. BL, APAC, Mss Eur F88/60, p. 37.

[36] BL, APAC, Cleveland Public Library Papers, IOR Neg 4226, wq091.92 Ea77p5, Mountstuart Elphinstone to Marquess of Hastings, 20 November 1815, p. 251.

[37] MSA, PRCOP, vol. 38 (1798–1801), William Palmer to Richard Wellesley, 18 September 1801, p. 1210; vol. 39 (1801–1802), Barry Close to Richard Wellesley, 3 July 1802, p. 401.

[38] For intimacy between Chimnaji and Baji Rao, see MSA, PRCOP, vol. 39 (1801–1802), Barry Close to Richard Wellesley, 13 February 1802, p. 170; 19 July 1802, p. 421; 1 November 1802, p. 180; vol. 40 (1802–1803), Barry Close to Richard Wellesley, 14 May 1803, p. 541. For growing tensions between the two, see BL, APAC, IOR/F/4/311/7097, p. 13; UPSAA, BRR, LRA, basta no. 11, book no. 51, Henry Russell to John Monckton, 23 September 1810.

[39] Chatterjee, Gender, Slavery and Law, p. 43.

networks to the pursuit of the economic and political aspirations of the gentry in Britain and its empire.[40] Indian rulers were frequently condemned for their neglect or ill-treatment of close relatives, behaviour that seemed to many Residents to require direct British intervention. The Residents at Pune consistently mediated between the peshwa and Amrit Rao, even though their negotiations on Amrit Rao's behalf were recognized to undermine their position in the peshwa's favour. The inconvenience was mitigated by the confidence they felt in occupying the moral high ground, as they saw it.[41] Similarly, the governor-general-in-council belittled Nawab Vizier Saadat Ali Khan's mistrust of his second brother, Mirza Jangli, and regretted that 'His Excellency should condescend to distinguish by his public favour men notorious for the depravity of their lives and the infamy of their characters', who were 'calumniators of the most respectable subjects of his Government' (meaning his relatives).[42] David Ochterlony, while briefly Resident at Delhi, entered into a particularly bitter dispute with Shah Alam, who, he believed, was allowing his favourites to 'wallow [...] in affluence' at the expense of his children, contrary to the dictates of 'parental affection'. Ochterlony could not help interfering, even though, as Shah Alam pointed out, it was his right to spend his monthly allowance as he pleased, 'in Alms to the poor, in reward to his servants, or in short in any way that he thinks proper'.[43] In cases like these, Residents seem to have found it difficult to resist trying to impose their own models of appropriate family behaviour.

The Residents' frustration, however, belies the fact that these recurring tensions often worked to the Company's benefit. As a counterpoint to the ill will of the ruler, male relatives were sometimes inclined to seek a rapprochement with the Resident, exchanging vital political intelligence in return for the Company's protection and support.[44] These transactions were a recurring feature of life at the court of Nagpur.[45] Vyankoji

[40] Will Coster, *Family and Kinship in England 1450–1800* (Harlow, 2001), p. 44; Julia Adams, *The Familial State: Ruling Families and Merchant Capitalism in Early Modern Europe* (Ithaca, NY, 2005), pp. 32–33; Margot Finn, 'Anglo-Indian Lives in the Later Eighteenth and Early Nineteenth Centuries', *Journal for Eighteenth-Century Studies* 33, no. 1 (2010): 49.

[41] BL, APAC, Cleveland Public Library Papers, IOR Neg 4226, wq091.92 Ea77p5, Mountstuart Elphinstone to Marquess of Hastings, 20 November 1815, pp. 248–249.

[42] BL, APAC, IOR/F/4/311/7097, Extract Political Letter to Bengal, 14 September 1808, pp. 2, 5. See also BL, APAC, IOR/F/4/216/4755, Extract Secret Letter from Bengal, 20 August 1806, p. 5.

[43] NAI, FSC 31 January 1804, David Ochterlony to General Lake, 18 November 1803, p. 24.

[44] BL, APAC, Mss Eur F88/60, p. 37.

[45] BL, APAC, IOR/H/626, Mountstuart Elphinstone to Marquess Wellesley, 20 December 1804, p. 566.

Bhonsle, Raghuji's brother, looked to the Company as a crucial safeguard at a time when he was detained at the capital and beginning to fear for his life. As the Resident interpreted it, 'if the influence of the British Government were established at this Court he naturally judged that it would be restraint on Raja Raghojee Bhonsle sufficient to prevent any gross injustice or act of violence', and therefore 'showed himself zealous to promote the measure'.[46] This zeal was manifest in Vyankoji's willingness to transmit important information regarding the activities of his brother, including Raghuji's endeavours to unite the Marathas against the British in the prelude to the Second Maratha War.[47] Similarly, in 1817 Gujaba Dada, Raghuji's nephew, took refuge at the Residency for fear of assassination at the hands of his jealous cousin, Appa Sahib, who had recently succeeded to the musnud; Gujaba Dada even went so far as to seek asylum in Company territory for a few years.[48] Richard Jenkins, Resident at Nagpur, had anticipated this rapprochement, recognising the use that alienated relatives like Gujaba could have. In 1816, prior to Raghuji's death, Jenkins had reported to the governor general that 'in the discontents [...] of his Nephew, and of the old adherents of that branch of the family, means of no inconsiderable force to shake the foundations of the state of Nagpore, might be found.'[49] Gujaba Dada subsequently repaid his debt to the Company in the days leading up to the final Maratha War, when he and his family provided invaluable support. 'To them', Jenkins claimed, 'I owe much of the intelligence which has enabled me to defeat the Rajah's treacherous designs'.[50]

Relying on royal family members in this way was not without hazard, however. Male relatives had their own agendas, as well as being the target of others' schemes. Despite his professed loyalty, Amrit Rao repeatedly disappointed the Resident at Pune by failing to exert any influence in the Company's favour as they tried to conclude a subsidiary alliance with the peshwa at the turn of the nineteenth century. As William Palmer

---

[46] H. T. Colebrooke to Marquess Wellesley, 21 March 1801, in *NRR*, I, p. 146. Also, BL, APAC, Mackenzie General Collection, Mss Eur Mack Gen XLIII, A collection of original memoirs illustrative of the revenues, resources, statistics and governments of the modern states of the Dekan, p. 308.

[47] H. T. Colebrooke to Marquess Wellesley, 22 May 1801, in *NRR*, I, p. 3; H. T. Colebrooke to Marquess Wellesley, 14 May 1801, in *NRR*, I, p. 149.

[48] BL, APAC, IOR/H/506a, Papers on Hindustan, Nagpur, and Maratha Affairs, p. 190; BL, APAC, IOR/F/4/718/19537, Extract Political Letter from Bengal, 15 January 1820, pp. 1–3.

[49] BL, APAC, Cleveland Public Library Papers, IOR Neg 4226, wq091.92 Ea77p5, Richard Jenkins to Marquess of Hastings, 5 September 1816, p. 434.

[50] BL, APAC, Mss Eur F311/10, Richard Jenkins to Marquess of Hastings, 7 December 1817, p. 34.

observed with frustration in the prelude to the Second Maratha War, 'Emrut Rhow with an undoubted attachment to & predilection for our nation & government will sacrifice these sentiments & expose the safety of his Brother & the state to the silly Ambition of occupying a station for which he is totally unqualified', referring to his ambition to become his brother's minister.[51] By becoming too closely implicated with royal family members, Residents risked becoming party to their ambitions.

By becoming too intimate with the ruler's family, the Resident also risked exciting the resentment of the ruler himself, who was, after all, the person most able to advance, or to thwart, the Company's designs at court. A common feature of subsidiary alliances during this period was a clause that barred the Company from interfering in the household affairs of Indian rulers. Rulers insisted on this point precisely to prevent these strategic relationships from forming. If the Resident wanted to cultivate both sides at once, he had to do so discreetly, without making too many promises. To revert to a previous example, when Vyankoji Bhonsle desired to meet with the Resident's munshi to establish communications shortly after the Residency was first founded in 1801, the two arranged to rendezvous 'as if by accident at a place of worship'.[52] Later, when Vyankoji dispatched confidential agents to the Residency with secret information, Resident H. T. Colebrooke was careful to ensure that he 'neither flattered his hopes, nor excited his expectations', and in fact displayed a decided 'aversion from intrigue'. Colebrooke's objective in so doing was to guarantee plausible deniability if these exchanges ever came to light; not only was the information unsolicited, but Colebrooke could say that he had discouraged Vyankoji's secretive conduct (nominally, at least).[53]

Sometimes, to keep relations with the ruler on a solid footing, Residents rejected the assistance of male relatives outright. The risk was that, by accepting their help, Residents might empower the relative concerned at the expense of the ruler in power. For instance, while the Company enthusiastically accepted a sizeable loan from Ghazi ud-Din Haidar to fund their war with the Gurkhas, they deemed it 'inexpeditious' to accept such a loan from his brother Shams ud-Daula, the second son who had been favoured by the deceased Nawab Saadat Ali Khan with offices and titles and was therefore perceived as a rival

---

[51] MSA, PRCOP, vol. 38 (1798–1801), William Palmer to Governor-General-in-Council, 18 August 1798, p. 168; William Palmer to Governor-General-in-Council, 13 October 1798, p. 260.

[52] H. T. Colebrooke to Marquess Wellesley, 14 May 1801, in *NRR*, I, p. 149.

[53] Ibid., 22 May 1801, p. 3. Colebrooke refused to meet with one of the raja's nephews out of a desire to avoid secret meetings; see H. T. Colebrooke to Marquess Wellesley, 24 August 1800, in *NRR*, I, p. 127.

by the reigning nawab vizier.[54] By accepting this loan, the Company would have conferred a degree of prestige on Shams ud-Daula that would have attracted the jealousy of the ruling nawab vizier, since it would, by implication, have placed them on an equal footing in terms of their respective relations with the Company.

When the Company failed to maintain good relations between male relatives, they usually took it upon themselves to arrange for exile in Company territory. Shams ud-Daula, for instance, was given permission to retire to Benares, where he lived on a considerable stipend paid out to him from the Company's treasury.[55] The conditions of exile depended upon the extent of the individual's misconduct; rebellious relatives were usually confined in military fortresses far from the land of their birth and kept separate from their wives and children, while relatives who were perceived as more of an existential threat to the ruler in power were generally allowed to live independently in establishments of their own in places of their choosing.[56] Banishment of political rivals or vanquished rebels had a long tradition in Europe as in India; the underlying rationale was that once out of sight, the individual in question could no longer act as a rallying point for resistance. His absence would allow him to be conveniently forgotten, whereas his execution might have rendered him a martyr.[57] Exile was a particularly attractive option given powerful taboos against flogging or executing Brahmins; banishment was a way of punishing high-status individuals without social stigma.[58] Male relatives sometimes even chose exile of their own volition, preferring to escape the jealous gaze of their royal siblings, and to retire to the relative calm of the country, or to religious and cultural centres like Benares. Amrit Rao voluntarily retreated from Pune in 1804; he claimed to have 'laid aside all worldly concerns', and to have 'nothing to do with the contentions of Princes'.[59] Even in cases like these, however, royal exiles were

[54] UPSAA, Benares Residency Records, Letters Received by the Agent to the Governor General in Benares (1815), basta no. 13, book no. 56, J. Monckton to W. A. Brooke, 26 July 1815, p. 299.
[55] BL, APAC, IOR/F/4/508/12261, p. 1.
[56] Contrast Amrit Rao, who brought his family and a large establishment to join him in Benares, with the fate of Vizier Ali, who was imprisoned in a fortress and separated forever from his wives and children; see BL, APAC, Cleveland Public Library Papers, IOR Neg 4227, wq091.92 Ea77p9, J. Monckton to Marquess Wellesley, 2 June 1814, p. 263.
[57] Robert Aldrich, 'Out of Ceylon: The Exile of the Last King of Kandy', in Exile in Colonial Asia: Kings, Convicts, Commemoration, ed. Ronit Ricci (Honolulu, HI, 2016), p. 49.
[58] Clare Anderson, 'A Global History of Exile in Asia, c. 1700–1900', in Exile in Colonial Asia, ed. Ricci, p. 22.
[59] BL, APAC, IOR/H/626, Mountstuart Elphinstone to Marquess Wellesley, 20 December 1804, p. 556.

encouraged to settle within easy reach of a military cantonment, where they could be monitored by a Company commissioner.[60]

Exile to British territories was viewed as a useful means of developing ties with Indian royals. These men made attractive claimants when succession crises broke out, given their perceived attachment to the Company. Saadat Ali Khan, after many years of living in exile in Company territory following an unsuccessful plot against his brother, Asaf ud-Daula, in 1775, was said to have acquired 'a fondness for every thing European'. He was excessively devoted to hunting and horse-racing in the English style and was even known to dress in English riding kit.[61] When in 1798 the Company decided to dethrone his nephew, Vizier Ali, Saadat was the obvious choice to replace him as nawab vizier of Awadh. Similarly, when Vyankoji Bhonsle and his family sought refuge in Company territory, the family's resulting attachment to the British was viewed as an asset that could be deployed to the Company's advantage. When Vyankoji's son Appa Sahib made his bid for power at Nagpur in 1816, acting as regent for his young cousin Parsoji, the Resident supported his claim because his personal history was believed to have made him sympathetic to the Company. In Jenkins's view, Appa Sahib's time in Benares, 'combined with the lessons of his father, who looked up to us for support against the Rajah', rendered him 'superior to the vulgar prejudices of the dangers of a connection with us', leading him 'to trust implicitly to our honor and good faith'.[62] In both cases, however, British officials overestimated the exiles' attachment to the Company; Appa Sahib, for one, openly revolted in 1817. The benefits of accommodating a royal family member in British territory were not always what British officials hoped they might be.

Male relatives were also an onerous burden for the British officials responsible for managing their interests and concerns.[63] The Company was charged with paying out stipends and often took on the additional task of overseeing budgets as a means of precluding financial embarrassments; officials seem to have feared that royal relatives would incur debts

---

[60] UPSAA, Benares Residency Records, Letters Received by the Agent to the Governor General in Benares, basta no. 12, book no. 55, G. Dowdeswell to the Board of Commissions, 18 June 1814, enclosed in N. B. Edmonstone to W. A. Brooke, 23 June 1814, p. 268.

[61] Charles Madan, *Two Private Letters to a Gentleman in England, from His Son Who Accompanied Earl Cornwallis, on His Expedition to Lucknow in the Year 1787* (Peterborough, 1788), p. 33. For Saadat Ali Khan's plot against his brother, see Fisher, *Indirect Rule*, p. 63.

[62] BL, APAC, IOR/H/506a, Papers on Hindustan, Nagpur, and Maratha Affairs, p. 189.

[63] UPSAA, BRR, LIA (January 1798–February 1799), basta no. 1, register no. 3, pp. 25, 26, 44, 147, 66, for description of work that agent at Benares did (including repairing houses and dispensing stipends) to help Vizier Ali settle down in the city.

and find themselves in the shameful position of being put on public trial.[64] After all, the behaviour and lifestyle of brothers could have implications for family honour, meaning that male relatives had it within their power to besmirch the prestige of the ruler concerned if they did not adhere to certain standards of respectability. Tellingly, Akbar Jah threatened his brother Nizam Sikander Jah that if he did not receive land revenues said to have been granted to him by their late father, he would 'retire to a holy Hill in the neighbourhood of the city [...] assuming the Dress and Habits of a Fakeer', or religious mendicant.[65] When Baji Rao urged his brother Chimnaji to take a wife, Chimnaji refused until his demands for reinstatement into Baji Rao's inner circle were met.[66] Royal brothers could use public perceptions of family honour as leverage, knowing that their siblings cared how they comported themselves. Even Saadat Ali Khan was keen to ensure that Vizier Ali, the exiled nephew whom he had deposed, continued to be attended by a chobdar, or stick bearer, to signal his noble status.[67] By failing to calibrate their own conduct or the conduct of their charges according to fine gradations of status, Company officials risked undermining the whole system of hereditary power upon which their influence rested. Officials were therefore keen to pay the recognition due to these royal family members, carefully regulating ritual practices including the exchange of nazr and khilat and the frequency of visits, for example. Attending to all these concerns, however, was almost a full-time job in and of itself.[68]

The presence of royal exiles could also create disruptions within the communities where they settled. Magistrates regularly complained that the followers and attendants of royal exiles clashed with local inhabitants and perpetrated acts of 'outrage'.[69] This was particularly true of Muslim royals who sought asylum in Benares and offended the locals with allegedly immoderate celebrations of Muslim religious holidays.[70] Given their rank and stores of treasure, however, royal exiles could justify large numbers of soldiers and attendants 'for the Purposes of Parade and the

[64] UPSAA, BRR, LIA, basta no. 1, register no. 3, G. F. Cherry to George Barlow, 26 February 1798, p. 25; G. F. Cherry to Alured Clarke, 5 January 1799, p. 215.

[65] NAI, HRR, box no. 2, vol. 38, Charles Russell to Minto, 2 March 1811, p. 123.

[66] BL, APAC, IOR/F/4/311/7097, Barry Close to Minto, 24 June 1809, pp. 38–41.

[67] UPSAA, BRR, LIA, basta no. 1, register no. 3, G. F. Cherry to J. Lumsden, 19 April 1798, p. 66.

[68] For example, see discussion of regulation of ceremonial intercourse with exiled prince Mirza Jahangir in UPSAA, BRR, LRA, basta no. 12, book no. 53, Richard Strachey to W. A. Brooke, June 1812, pp. 149–151.

[69] UPSAA, BRR, LIA, basta no. 3, book no. 14, W. A. Brooke to John Adam, 7 September 1818, p. 66; UPSAA, BRR, LIA (January 1798–February 1799), basta no. 1, register no. 3, W. A. Brooke to Barlow, 26 February 1798, p. 25.

[70] UPSAA, BRR, LRA, basta no. 10, book no. 42, Samuel Davis to G. F. Cherry, 21 June 1798, p. 235.

protection of [...] property', as the Resident at Benares affirmed, even though the followers of Amrit Rao, at least, were described as having the appearance 'more of a colony than an army'.[71]

Finally, even when living comfortably abroad, some male relatives found it difficult to put their political careers behind them. Though Amrit Rao purported to be perfectly content to live a life of peaceful reflection at Benares, his son, Benaik Rao, who had been briefly installed as peshwa under his father's tutelage during the Second Maratha War, proved more restless. Having become 'impatient of the inactive state in which he is compelled to remain at this place', as the magistrate of Benares described it, Benaik Rao 'fell into the hands of associates equally restless, and ill disposed with himself'. Together with his friends, Benaik Rao planned to flee the city and seek his fortune, before his intentions were discovered and aborted by his father in early 1814. For a young man like Benaik Rao, being forced to live a quiet life far from the stage of war and politics on which he might otherwise have distinguished himself was punishment indeed. Having had a brief taste of power, his exile was even more galling. The Company had to be careful of men like these; Benaik Rao could assemble military men to his cause, and could give the Company significant embarrassment and trouble, as the magistrate at Benares recognized.[72]

All in all, male relatives were considered as a necessary evil to be managed with care. Fraternal conflicts, though distasteful to the Resident, could be exploited for valuable political intelligence. Suitably Anglicized royal family members also made attractive claimants to the throne when succession crises did break out. An alliance with a royal family member could equally, however, expose the Resident to distrust from the ruler in question. Nor could the attachment of royal brothers and cousins necessarily be relied upon. To the contrary, male relatives regularly proved unruly and irrepressible, even when tucked away safely in Company territory. The Residents' greatest censure, however, was usually reserved for women of the royal household.

6.3   Petticoat Influence from behind the Purdah

'A nasty Dame & Bitch': this is how a Company soldier stationed in Delhi described the favourite wife of Mughal Emperor Akbar Shah II.[73] The language is crude, but the sentiment was not unusual; British commentators commonly described royal wives, mothers,

---

[71] UPSAA, BRR, LRA (1804–1805), basta no. 10, book no. 45, E. A. Broughton to N. B. Edmonstone, p. 121.
[72] For information contained in this paragraph see BL, APAC, IOR/F/4/470/11324, Extract of Political Letter from Bengal, 31 March 1814, pp. 1–11.
[73] NRAS, Fraser of Reelig Papers, B436, Robert Macpherson to William Fraser, 21 June, p. 16.

grandmothers, and concubines as harridans exercising undue influence over emasculated Indian rulers. The stereotype had deep roots; in published accounts of the first British embassy to the court of the Mughal Emperor Shah Jahan almost two hundred years before, Thomas Roe depicted Shah Jahan's romance with his favourite wife in similar terms. 'His motion is inward among women', Roe observed, 'of which sort, though he keepe a thousand, yet one governs him, and wynds him up at her pleasure'.[74]

Despite the prevalence of these defamatory portraits of ambitious women in British accounts of Indian courtly life, female agency has been pushed to the margins in recent scholarship on the Residency system. To the extent that historians have discussed the women in the Residents' lives, the focus has been on their Indian wives and concubines.[75] This tendency is part of a broader trend wherein the history of conjugal relations between European men and non-European women is used to demonstrate the entanglement of the personal and the political, of private lives and larger patterns of imperial rule.[76] In this view, intimate relationships were a key theatre for the construction and consolidation of racial and gender hierarchies, as well as the development of colonial knowledge.[77] Though compelling, this line of inquiry has distracted from the Residents' relationships with the women of the royal zenana, relationships that were, if not intimate, then nevertheless politically significant, emotionally fraught, and comparatively well documented. In her study of imperial families, Durba Ghosh had to sift through baptismal records to bring her 'nameless' subjects to light; Indian royal women are, by contrast, almost inescapable from the historian's perspective, their names scattered liberally through the records

---

[74] William Foster (ed.), *The Embassy of Sir Thomas Roe to India 1616–1919* (London, 1926), pp. 170–171.

[75] Ghosh, *Sex and the Family*, pp. 69–106, for William Palmer and James Achilles Kirkpatrick. A recent exception is Rochisha Narayan, 'A Mughal Matriarch and the Politics of Motherhood in Early Colonial India', *Journal of Women's History* 32, no. 2 (2020): 12–36, which examines the relationship between the Company and the Qutlugh Begum, a Mughal noblewoman resident at Benares.

[76] Elisa Camiscioli, 'Women, Gender, Intimacy, and Empire', *Journal of Women's History* 25, no. 4 (2013): 138–148; Tony Ballantyne and Antoinette Burton, 'Introduction: The Politics of Intimacy in an Age of Empire', in *Moving Subjects: Gender, Mobility, and Intimacy in an Age of Global Empire*, eds. Tony Ballantyne and Antoinette Burton (Urbana, IL, 2009), pp. 5–7.

[77] Ann Laura Stoler is the predominant influence in this field; see especially *Carnal Knowledge and Imperial Power*, p. 9. For knowledge production, see Lynn Zastoupil, 'Intimacy and Colonial Knowledge', *Journal of Colonialism and Colonial History* 3, no. 2 (2002).

and correspondence of the Residents.[78] These were women who made themselves heard, sometimes to the exasperation of the Company officials responsible for managing their concerns.

British attitudes towards these women were powerfully shaped by contemporary preconceptions about the harem, or women's quarters. Harems were usually associated in British thought with Muslim courts and portrayed in European art and literature as spaces of chaos and disorder, of material and sexual excess. The basis for this cloud of fear and fantasy encircling the zenana (to give it its Persian name) was its relative inaccessibility to European men due to the observation of rules of seclusion or *pardanishin*. Because of these restrictions, the zenana accrued a reputation in colonial circles as a site of gossip and speculation, of imagined theft, slavery, infanticide, and murder.[79] As one nineteenth-century historian imagined it, 'there were things done within the precincts of that vast privileged asylum, and duly reported to the Resident, in violation of all laws human and divine'.[80] The zenana as an institution existed at Muslim, Hindu, Sikh, and Buddhist courts, but Residents seem to have reserved their greatest calumny for the zenanas of Muslim dynasties in the subcontinent. In this, Residents reflect an older tradition that particularly associated Muslim women with the harem and with the sexual excess assumed to take place there.[81] Historians have noted that the figure of 'the degraded "Hindoo" woman' was a recurring trope in nineteenth-century colonial discourse, with British commentators invoking child marriage, sati, and polygamy as justifications for British interventions in the domestic realm.[82] Within Residency records, letters, and contemporary travelogues, however, this stereotype is notable for its absence. Maratha women were often contrasted favourably with Muslim women who, it was said, 'do nothing but adorn their persons, study deception, and smoke their *hookahs*'.[83]

Despite this dismissive language, in practice Residents had no choice but to take royal women seriously. Most obviously, women's dynastic,

[78] Durba Ghosh, 'Decoding the Nameless: Gender, Subjectivity, and Historical Methodologies in Reading the Archives of Colonial India', in *A New Imperial History: Culture, Identity, and Modernity, 1600–1840*, ed. Kathleen Wilson (Cambridge, 2004), pp. 297–316.
[79] Janaki Nair, 'Uncovering the Zenana: Visions of Indian Womanhood in Englishwomen's Writings, 1813–1940', *Journal of Women's History* 2, no. 1 (1990): 11.
[80] Kaye, ed., *Life and Correspondence of Charles, Lord Metcalfe*, p. 249.
[81] Kate Teltscher, *India Inscribed*, p. 38.
[82] Catherine Hall, 'Of Gender and Empire: Reflections on the Nineteenth Century', in *Gender and Empire*, ed. Philippa Levine (Oxford, 2004), p. 54.
[83] Deane, *Tour*, p. 94. See also Joan DelPlato, *Multiple Wives, Multiple Pleasures: Representing the Harem, 1800–1875* (Cranbury, NJ, 2002), pp. 162, 164.

reproductive functions sometimes placed them at the centre of factional intrigue. When Mahdav Rao fell from a balcony, for example, his wife, Yasodha Bai, was viewed by competing forces at Pune as an instrument for legitimating rival claimants to the musnud. First, scheming ministers forced her to adopt Baji Rao's brother Chimnaji Appa, an adoption that was subsequently disqualified by Brahmin experts after Baji Rao seized control. Later, rumours circulated at Pune that Amrit Rao planned to elevate his son Benaik Rao by 'causing him to be adopted' by Yasodha Bai, too.[84] Consequently, Baji Rao monitored Yasodha Bai's movements and tried to compel her to leave the city, though Resident Barry Close reported that 'she firmly resists all his entreaties repeating her determined resolution to part with her life rather than change her place of residence'.[85] When Pune itself was threatened by Yashwant Rao Holkar's approaching troops, Baji Rao renewed his efforts to get Yasodha Bai to leave, unwilling to depart himself without first securing her from his enemies. Yasodha Bai continued to defy him, however, 'protesting that she should not be removed from her present habitation alive'.[86] The peshwa had no choice but to remain in the capital a few more weeks until he was finally able to send her to a nearby fortress in the company of his brother, Chimnaji Appa.[87] A month later, observing that the garrisons in the region appeared to have abandoned Baji Rao's cause, Close speculated that the widow would be seized by Amrit Rao's adherents and made to adopt his son.[88] As troops approached her place of confinement, she was withdrawn by the peshwa and brought with him to Bassein, where his treaty with the Company was negotiated.[89] After Baji Rao's return to Pune, Yasodha Bai seems to disappear from the Residency records until her death in 1820. Not long afterwards, however, amidst disturbances in the Gwalior region in 1826, a woman claiming to be Yasodha Bai 'collected around her a considerable rabble'. The threat was considered sufficient for the Resident at Gwalior to offer her asylum within the Company's dominions, though he emphasized that the Company would provide her with no financial support and were prepared to publicly dispute her identity if she crossed them.[90] Throughout her life,

---

[84] MSA, PRCOP, vol. 39 (1801–1802), Barry Close to Richard Wellesley, 27 June 1802, p. 387.

[85] MSA, PRCOP, vol. 39 (1801–1802), Barry Close to Wellesley, 27 June 1802, p. 387–388. See also Close to Wellesley, 3 June 1803, pp. 392–393.

[86] MSA, PRCOP, vol. 40 (1802–1803), Barry Close to Wellesley, 28 September 1802, pp. 39–40.

[87] MSA, PRCOP, vol. 40 (1802–1803) Barry Close to Wellesley, 10 October 1802, p. 114.

[88] Ibid., Barry Close to Wellesley, 9 November 1802, pp. 204–205.

[89] Ibid., Barry Close to Jonathan Duncan, 23 November 1802, p. 307.

[90] BL, APAC, IOR/F/4/26168, pp. 112–113.

Yasodha Bai resisted the attempts of men to instrumentalize her in their quests for political advantage, and even after her death, her name and symbolic power were still being appropriated by those keen to profit by them.

If Yasodha Bai sometimes seems more like a pawn in the schemes of men than a director of her own fate, other examples exist to show that women could and did harness their symbolic power for their own purposes. Perhaps the most dramatic instance of this is the campaign spearheaded by the women of Mahadji Shinde's household in the early years of Daulat Rao's reign. When Mahadji passed away in 1795, he left his three widows (referred to by contemporaries as 'the bais') in the care of his nephew, adopted son, and successor, Daulat Rao. Daulat Rao had promised to provide for them but failed to settle his adopted father's household in their own permanent establishment. Rising tensions came to a head when the elder widows charged Daulat Rao with engaging in a 'criminal intercourse' with the young widow Bhagirathi Bai, 'at which they openly expressed their abhorrence, and declared they could no longer consider as a son the incestuous defiler of his father's bed.'[91] They tried to use this language of disgrace to secure an independent livelihood separate from Daulat Rao's household, arguing that his cohabiting with Mahadji's young widow 'is dishonourable to the Family and is an indelible stain on his own Character'.[92] As it transpired, the allegations only provoked Daulat Rao; the women were seized and flogged. Their treatment, however, drew some of Daulat Rao's chief Brahmin officers to their cause. Assisted by powerful Maratha *sirdars* (nobles or officers of rank), the ladies escaped Daulat Rao's clutches and assembled a large body of troops, refusing to negotiate until Daulat Rao had met their demands for their future security and subsistence.[93] At first, Resident William Palmer was inclined to believe that the plot had been orchestrated by Baji Rao, long under Daulat Rao's thumb and therefore interested in undermining him. Eventually, however, Palmer was forced to concede that there was no evidence to suggest that the peshwa had concerted the measure, though he was obviously delighted to take advantage of the situation; rumour had it he intended to support a rival candidate to the raj as selected by Mahadji Shinde's senior widow.[94]

---

[91] Grant Duff, *History of the Mahrattas*, III, p. 162.
[92] MSA, PRCOP, vol. 38 (1798–1801), William Palmer to the Governor-General in-Council, 1 June 1798, p. 61.
[93] Ibid., William Palmer to the Governor-General-in-Council, 25 May 1798, p. 61.
[94] Ibid., William Palmer to the Governor-General-in-Council, 1 June 1798, p. 70; William Palmer to Governor-General-in-Council, 8 June 1798, pp. 77–78.

Though the women's forces were initially small, they benefited from the support of Shinde's army, many of whom expressed resentment at his treatment of the ladies and even deserted to their cause.[95] As their numbers grew, Shinde was faced with an insoluble quandary. He was humiliated by his inability to control dissensions within his family, but at the same time could not countenance the use of force, particularly since he seems to have doubted whether his troops would have backed him up in the event of a violent confrontation.[96] After nearly a year's stalemate in which the conflict 'entirely engrosse[d] the public attention', Shinde finally acceded to the ladies' demands, restoring their favoured minister to power, granting them the city of Burhanpur and its dependencies, and a fort at Assir for their future security.[97] The women no doubt benefited from the fact that Shinde was struggling to pay his soldiers, whose loyalty to him was consequently tenuous. Still, women clearly had negotiating power because of their affiliation with the royal dynasty; individual honour was closely bound up with lineage, and the honour of families was reflected in the conduct and treatment of its women.[98] Although caricatures of the royal household portrayed women as spoiled and indolent, as members of the ruling dynasty women were endowed with recognized charisma. In addition to securing an establishment of their own, the women, considering 'their Safety & Interests as inseparable from those of Tantia' (one of Shinde's chief ministers), were able to bring to bear a military force of five or six thousand men in their efforts to coerce Shinde to release the minister from confinement and return him to his privileged position within the council.[99]

The women of Shinde's family were able to muster material resources as well as family associations in support of their cause. Contrary to the Resident's depictions of the women of the harem as frivolous and indolent, historians have clearly demonstrated the range of activities engaged in by female elites in South Asia. Women collected tax, invested in inland and overseas trade, and profited from the sale of textiles, minerals, and agricultural goods, as well as the duties collected from merchants travelling through their dominions.[100]

The history of Faizabad presents a clear example of the kind of establishment that royal women were capable of sustaining. When

---

[95] Ibid., William Palmer to the Governor-General-in-Council, 24 May 1798, p. 61; William Palmer to the Governor-General-in-Council, 28 May 1798, p. 62.

[96] Ibid., William Palmer to the Governor-General-in-Council, 8 June 1798, p. 76.

[97] Ibid., William Palmer to Governor-General-in-Council, 5 June 1798, p. 83. William Palmer to the Governor-General-in-Council, 16 July 1799, in *PRC*, VI, p. 462.

[98] William Palmer to the Governor-General-in-Council, 16 July 1799, in *PRC*, VI, p. 462.

[99] BL, APAC, IOR/H/576, William Palmer to Marquess Wellesley, 28 April 1800, p. 72.

[100] Findly, *Nur Jahan*, p. 110.

Asaf ud-Daula succeeded his father in 1775, he shifted the capital of Awadh from Faizabad to Lucknow; his mother, known as Bahu Begum, and his grandmother, known as Nawab Begum, remained behind. One of the munshis in their employ later wrote a poignant portrait of their life in the city. The elder begum's household included: a guard of four hundred sepoys; an establishment of eunuchs employed as clerks, bankers, assayers; and staff to oversee her carriage-houses and stables of elephants. Her home in Moti Bagh was also, he remembered, a centre for learned men, physicians, and nobles, as well as descendants of the best Delhi families. In all, Muhammad Faiz Bakhsh estimated 'about one thousand souls [...] dependent upon her bounty', not including the men who managed her parganas at Bihar, Aligang, Bahuta, Begumganj, and Raeganj. The younger begum's lands were even more extensive. She possessed her own stables filled with horses and elephants, and employed an army of eunuchs, house servants, messengers, slaves, mace bearers, accountants, and artisans. Writing after her death, the munshi mourned 'this august of ladies', who, when at the 'zenith of her glory', boasted 'ten thousand troops, horse and foot, scores of elephants, and countless horses. The people who earned their bread directly or indirectly through her bounty must have been more than a hundred thousand.' Bahu Begum's memory lingers in the city even today, in the form of the mausoleum and mosque built to commemorate her death, on the site of the garden where she used to sit.[101]

Bahu Begum operated out of her own power base at Faizabad, but others exercised their influence in the heart of the capital. Tinat un-Nissa Begum, one of the dominant women within the Hyderabad zenana, is a good example of an important female power broker. Born around 1740 to 'a Person in a very low station of Life', according to Henry Russell's investigations, at twenty Tinat un-Nissa Begum was purchased and employed as a servant by the Bakshi Begum, favourite wife of Nizam Ali Khan. Tinat un-Nissa Begum subsequently gave birth to two of the nizam's sons, including his successor, Sikander Jah. Russell condemned the begum as 'weak, ignorant, selfish, meddling, and covetous', but this invective simply reflects his frustration at her interference 'in every Arrangement of the Government from the most important to the most trivial.'[102] She actively intervened on behalf of her favourites, for example, by negotiating the marriage of Sikander Jah's eldest daughter with the son of the exiled courtier Mumtaz

---

[101] Muhammad Faiz Bakhsh, *Memoirs of Delhi and Faizabad*, trans. William Hoey (Allahabad, 1889), pp. 60–61, 294–295.
[102] BL, APAC, Mss Eur F88/60, Notes and Intelligence of Mountstuart Elphinstone, p. 36.

ul-Umara in order to effect his recall.[103] She was a noted supporter of minister Munir ul-Mulk, who had 'contrived to obtain the support and Assistance of most of the Females of his Highness's family but particularly that of the Tunent oo Nissa Begum'.[104] The records of the *daftar-i-diwani* note that it was because of 'the recommendation of a consort' that Munir ul-Mulk was once again welcomed at court levees after three months of exile.[105] Chandu Lal, Munir ul-Mulk's rival in office, was well aware of this strategy and attempted to replicate it; when the begum asked for permission to visit a garden belonging to him, Chandu Lal 'paid her great Attention, gave her valuable Presents, represented his condition to her, expressed the most cordial Attachment to her Interests, and those of her Family, and sent her Home very much gratified with her reception.'[106]

For the Residents, Tinat un-Nissa Begum was a troubling reminder of how women of lowly descent could access the springs of power. Residents often invoked the humble origins of zenana women while denigrating their role at court. '[R]aised to the Honor of the late Nizam's [Ali Khan's] Bed from a servile situation in the service of the Bukshy Begum', women like her were, in the view of the Residents, 'strongly marked with those characteristicks which frequently attend a great and sudden elevation', being 'haughty, tyrannical, rapacious and officious'.[107] The issue, however, was clearly her political activity at court, and not her background. Even women with respectable lineages, like Jahan Parwar Begum, daughter of the former minister Azim ul-Umara and niece to Munir ul-Mulk, were, if they resisted the Resident in any way, liable to be described as women 'debased by the lowest propensities', and 'addicted to all the disgusting vices which prevail among many of the women of Indian seraglios'.[108] By contrast, women like Chandni Begum, apparently the illegitimate daughter of a slave girl, could be considered 'mild, unassuming' and 'very respectable', so long as they 'seldom interfered in publick affairs'.[109] The Residents' rhetorical attacks on Indian women increased in proportion to their political activity.

---

[103] NAI, HRR, box no. 2, vol. 33, N. B. Edmonstone to Thomas Sydenham, 4 August 1807, pp. 395–396.

[104] NAI, HRR, box no. 2, vol. 38, Charles Russell to Minto, 4 August 1810, pp. 79–80.

[105] Central Records Office, *Chronology of Modern Hyderabad,* pp. 110–111.

[106] NAI, HRR, box no. 2, vol. 38, Charles Russell to Minto, 25 September 1810, pp. 97–98.

[107] Ibid., Charles Russell to Earl of Minto, 4 August 1810, pp. 79–82.

[108] BL, APAC, Mss Eur F88/60, Notes and Intelligence of Mountstuart Elphinstone, p. 35.

[109] Bodl. Oxf., Russell Papers, MS. Eng. Misc. c. 324, Henry Russell, The Conditions and Resources of the Nizam's Government, p. 50.

Though Residents might have used viciously moralizing language to depreciate the zenana, they simultaneously recognized its importance as a political space, and the political advantages enjoyed by the women who resided there. For example, despite their disparagement of her, the Residents nevertheless recognized Tinat un-Nissa's usefulness, and bemoaned her antagonism to them; 'it is unfortunate that the Tuhnent oo Nissa Begum is so much under the influence of Mooneer ool Moolk', Charles Russell complained, 'as the Nizam seldom adopts any measure without her Advice and Concurrence.'[110] Power in these political systems flowed out from the ruler; accordingly, proximity to the ruler was a source of influence. As occupants of the palace's private quarters, royal women were also placed at a key nexus of the Indian information order, as C. A. Bayly has pointed out. In the ruler's private quarters, newsletters were read out and agents examined in the women's presence.[111] Royal women themselves corresponded widely and maintained links with geographically distant kin; consequently, they were sometimes the first to hear of events at rival courts. All this made them attractive informants. Jahan Parwar Begum was apparently especially 'useful in communicating Intelligence to [Munir ul-Mulk] and conveying his private notes and messages to the Nizam', while Chandu Lal appealed to the female attendants of Tinat un-Nissa Begum to confirm reports about the intentions of the rebel Mahipat Ram.[112]

The Residents' relative exclusion from these spaces of leisure and conversation was a recognized obstacle to the transaction of Residency business. To be sure, Residents were far from being entirely disconnected from the world of the zenana, whose boundaries, historians have argued, were always more porous than we might suppose.[113] In addition to corresponding with Residents, royal women also sometimes conversed with them in person, separated only by a fabric screen or curtain; at Maratha courts, these conversations took place face to face. European women, meanwhile, could, and did, enter the precincts of the zenana to socialize with royal women; these visits figure prominently in contemporary travel literature.[114] Still, these interactions were not so frequent and open as some Residents would have preferred. All the major European diplomatic

---

[110] NAI, HRR, box no. 2, vol. 38, Charles Russell to Minto, 4 August 1810, pp. 79–80.

[111] Bayly, *Empire and Information*, p. 18.

[112] Bodl. Oxf., Russell Papers, MS. Eng. misc. c. 324, Henry Russell, 'The Condition and Resources of the Nizam's Government', p. 50; NAI, For. Sec., no. 1, Thomas Sydenham to Minto, 17 April 1808, p. 38.

[113] Ruby Lal, *Domesticity and Power in the Early Mughal World* (Cambridge, 2005), p. 4; Angma Dey Jhala, *Courtly Indian Women in Late Imperial India* (London, 2008), pp. 44–45.

[114] Nugent, *Journal*, pp. 420–425; Deane, *Tour*, p. 105; Bute, *Private Journal*, I, p. 83.

manuals emphasized the importance of sociability in an informal context, observing that 'when people begin to be a little warmed with wine, they often discover secrets of importance', yet the Residents were rarely invited into the spaces of leisure and conversation where the ruler and his friends and family congregated.[115] Henry Russell openly begrudged the manner in which the Hyderabadi habit of retiring to the zenana in the evenings precluded homosocial activities, noting that 'they never meet together, but upon occasions of ceremony or business, and every man passes his hours of relaxation and retirement in the secluded privacy of his female apartments'.[116] William Palmer bemoaned his infrequent communications with the peshwa and 'the Forms and reserve with which his Intercourse is clogged', while Mountstuart Elphinstone similarly opined that the peshwa was 'very difficult of access', preferring to enjoy the company of 'his favorites in large assemblies of women, where he enjoys the coarsest ribaldry and buffoonery'.[117] Elphinstone's complaint is typical; Indian rulers were commonly denounced for spending too much time with the women of their household or for taking their counsel too seriously.

The language used to describe Indian rulers reflected the charges of 'effeminacy' that permeated eighteenth-century British political discourse and everyday parlance. To be 'effeminate' was to be unmanly or self-indulgent, to associate too much with women or to have sex with men; these were private vices that threatened to seep into public life, impeding a man's ability to act rationally and independently on the public stage.[118] T. D. Broughton, a member of the Resident's military escort at Shinde's camp, was convinced that the temptations of the zenana had clouded Daulat Rao Shinde's judgement; in Broughton's words, 'women and low company have been his bane; and appear to have quite corrupted a heart and mind originally meant for better things'.[119] Similarly, when a contemporary book authored by a British soldier in India

---

[115] de Callières, *Art of Diplomacy*, p. 116. John Malcolm also advised that it was in 'an unceremonious interchange of visits with the most respectable' that a member of the political line could best effect his objectives, in his 'Notes of Instruction', in Briggs, *Letters*, p. 202.

[116] Bodl. Oxf., Russell Papers, MS. Eng. misc. c. 324, Henry Russell, 'The Condition and Resources of the Nizam's government', p. 7. See also BL, APAC, IOR/F/4/394/10019, Extract letters to Bengal, 1 March 1812, p. 1.

[117] BL, APAC, IOR/H/576, William Palmer to Marquess Wellesley, 16 June 1800, p. 177; BL, APAC, Cleveland Public Library Papers, IOR Neg 4226, wq091.92 Ea77p5, Mountstuart Elphinstone to Marquess of Hastings, 20 November 1815, pp. 251, 250. See also BL, APAC, Mss Eur F88/219, Report on the Deckan, p. 91.

[118] John Tosh, *Manliness and Masculinities in Nineteenth-Century Britain: Essays on Gender, Family, and Empire* (Harlow, 2005), pp. 70–73; Anna Clark, *Scandal: The Sexual Politics of the British Constitution* (Princeton, NJ, 2006), p. 10.

[119] Broughton, *Letters Written in a Mahratta Camp*, p. 124.

described Nizam Sikander Jah's unfitness for office, a key justification was that 'he lives almost entirely with women; his business is chiefly transacted by verbal messages communicated by female attendants, and he never goes from one chamber to another, without being followed by four or five women slaves.'[120] The Residents shared these views; when the begums of Hyderabad communicated a rumour to the nizam that the Company intended to depose him in favour of his brother, the Resident Thomas Sydenham condescendingly, in his words, 'expressed my compassion only that his Highness should seriously entertain such unmanly and absurd suspicions upon the base assertions of ignorant Women'.[121] The Resident's belittling remarks bely the serious frustration he felt at his inability to repress or control the influence that women could exercise in the privacy of the zenana. At Travancore, the Resident Colin Macaulay (there from 1800 to 1810) even resorted to the extreme measure of banishing the raja's favourite wife Arumenah Mah as a means of insulating the ruler from faction and intrigue.[122] Their access to and perceived influence over the ruler meant that royal women were taken seriously as a potential threat, sometimes requiring Residents to take direct action to mitigate their activities.

Examining the Residency records from this period, what becomes clear is that much of the disparagement to which women were subject was directly proportionate to their political importance. Apart from their dynastic functions, many women had ambitions of their own, and could muster their symbolic power, to say nothing of their military, symbolic, and social resources, in pursuit of these agendas. The zenana was thus an important space both because of its association with the ruler and his family, and because it was a nexus for political brokerage and the exchange of information. To the extent that Residents complained about the zenana, then, it was largely because they resented this fact of life. They might have had more access to the zenana than we might at first assume, but it was still less permeable to them than they would have liked. Still, their complaints should not be allowed to conceal what was in fact a more complex

---

[120] An Officer, *Origin of the Pindaries*, p. 134. Sikander Jah's father, Nizam Ali Khan, was likewise described as 'Much addicted [...] to the pleasures of the Haram.' See BL, APAC, Mackenzie General Collection, Mss Eur Mack Gen XLIII, A collection of original memoirs illustrative of the revenues, resources, statistics and governments of the modern states of the Dekan, p. 301.

[121] BL, APAC, IOR/F/4/296/6833, Thomas Sydenham to Earl of Minto, 26 August 1808, p. 36.

[122] BL, APAC, IOR/F/4/445/10674, John Munro, 'Observations on a Petition Delivered to the Government', 16 September 1813, p. 114. See also a letter from the vakils of the Rajah of Travancore to Minto, NLS, Minto Papers, MS 11582, 21 December 1809, p. 102.

reality, in which Residents and royal women sometimes worked in sync. While gender norms in Britain are often assumed to have predisposed the Residents to disregard the workings of the zenana, precisely the opposite is true, as the following section will show.

6.4   Bridging the Gender Frontier

When Residents ascribed women's political interventions to base avarice and accused them of sexual promiscuity, they echoed condemnations levelled at aristocratic women deemed to have taken an inappropriately active role in British public life. As Anna Clark has shown, allegations of sexual misconduct and prostitution were prominent motifs in eighteenth- and nineteenth-century British politics. Famously, when Georgiana, Duchess of Devonshire, canvassed for Charles James Fox in the Westminster elections of 1784, contemporaries speculated that she was trying to pay off her gambling debts, and accused her of being sexually involved with the candidate; caricatures depicted her kissing butchers for votes.[123] Similarly, Tinat un-Nissa Begum was said by Henry Russell to be 'not particularly attached to any Party, but takes bribes from all and for the time espouses that side which pays the highest', with chastity 'by no means unimpeached'.[124] This kind of dismissive attitude would seem to foreclose the possibility that the Resident and the women of the zenana could fruitfully act in concert.

Yet, Residents readily acknowledged that women could be useful political allies. Although in theory British politics was conceived as belonging to the masculine domain, in practice politics in Britain, as in India, was familial and social. As such, women could and did participate, as hostesses, patronesses, sociopolitical 'fixers' and confidantes, as Elaine Chalus has illustrated.[125] According to historian Amanda Vickery, at a time where so much of a propertied gentleman's engagement with public life took place within the context of the home, the oppositions that historians have drawn between the public spheres occupied by men, and the private spheres occupied by women, do not make much sense.[126] A recent study of the typical 'political day' of an English Lord or MP shows how much of their working life was spent in domestic spaces.[127] In European diplomatic culture, as well, the same rules and opportunities

---

[123] Clark, *Scandal*, pp. 73–74.

[124] Bodl. Oxf., Russell Papers, MS. Eng. misc. c. 324, Henry Russell, 'The condition and resources of the Nizam's government', p. 51.

[125] Elaine Chalus, *Elite Women in English Political Life, c. 1754–1790* (Oxford, 2005), pp. 4, 12–13.

[126] Vickery, *Gentleman's Daughter*, p. 9.

[127] Hannah Greig and Amanda Vickery, 'The Political Day in London, c. 1697–1834' *P&P*. Accessed 24 June 2021, https://doi.org/10.1093/pastj/gtaa016.

applied; de Callières advised diplomats to go to great lengths to endear themselves with the ladies of the court, arguing that 'the power of their charms has often an influence over the most important resolutions, on which the greatest events depend'.[128] Indrani Chatterjee has described the political configurations of Indian political courts as 'an inversion of dominant Western notions of the politically significant as 'outer' or public and male and the politically marginal as 'inner' or private and domestic'.[129] Yet, even in Britain itself these distinctions were not clear cut.

Residents were not necessarily averse to women exercising political agency, particularly within the bounds of what they considered to be more conventional feminine activities. Ideally, Residents wanted royal women to exercise a moralizing influence, paralleling an emergent model of female domestic influence that Anna Clark attributes to the rising tide of British evangelicalism and the philosophy of sensibility.[130] Royal women were valued as effective mediators, able to salve the resentments of fathers, brothers, and sons. Raja Raghuji Bhonsle's mother, Chuma Bai, was particularly adept at managing the often-fractious relations between her two sons. Raja Raghuji himself observed that had it not been for his mother 'the differences between him & Nana Sahib must ere this have led to a civil war', and held that it was out of respect for her that he did not punish his brother for his armed depredations along their shared territorial borders.[131] After her death, the Resident anticipated ruptures between the brothers and worried about the extortionate activities that the brothers might engage in without her moderating influence. As Richard Jenkins noted, 'there must be many who having formerly owed their safety from the Rajah's exactions, to the Bai's influence, now tremble for their persons and property'.[132]

Royal women like Chuma Bai were valued, even venerated, for the softening influence they were perceived to exercise over their male relatives. Residents were keen to harness this influence for their own purposes. Thomas Sydenham was explicitly instructed to cultivate a connection with the Bakshi Begum at Hyderabad and to use her as an instrument to conciliate Sikander Jah and stop him from corresponding with the rebellious former minister Mahipat Ram.[133] According to the Resident

[128] de Callières, *Art of Diplomacy*, p. 78.
[129] Chatterjee, *Gender, Slavery and Law*, p. 37.
[130] Clark, *Scandal*, pp. 11–12.
[131] BL, APAC, IOR/H/626, Mountstuart Elphinstone to Marquess Wellesley, 20 December 1804, p. 566.
[132] Richard Jenkins to Barry Close, 23 December 1809, in *NRR*, II, p. 21.
[133] NAI, HRR, box 2, vol. 33, N. B. Edmonstone to Thomas Sydenham, 3 November 1806, p. 436. Sydenham's successor, Henry Russell, relied on the Nizam's favourite wife Chandni Begum to moderate the behaviour of her sons when they returned to Hyderabad from their exile in Golconda. See BL, APAC, IOR/F/4/796/21427, Henry Russell to Marquess of Hastings, 10 November 1820, p. 28.

Henry Russell (who succeeded Sydenham), when Bakshi Begum chose to intervene in the administration of her adopted son Sikander Jah, 'it was with so much dignity and good sense [...] that I always lamented she did not possess or would not exercise that Influence, to which her age, her Rank, the soundness of her understanding and the rectitude of her Intentions justly entitled her.'[134] Her death was deemed to be 'a great public loss'.[135]

Not all the Company's female allies fit this mould; their relationship with Bahu Begum, the widow of Nawab Vizier Shuja ud-Daula, was much more complicated. Bahu Begum had been the nawab vizier's chief consort and had provided critical support to him at key points in his reign; to show his gratitude, Shuja entrusted her with much of his wealth.[136] As described earlier, she oversaw a significant establishment at Faizabad. After Shuja's death this vast property gave her great clout in the politics of Awadh, but it also made her a target. Despite her important role in securing his succession in 1775, her son Asaf ud-Daula made increasingly aggressive attempts to appropriate her wealth. The Company offered her their protection, but their guarantee was less than sincere since they clearly viewed her treasure as a possible resource that Asaf could draw on to pay off his debts. When the raja of Benares revolted against the Company in 1781, Bahu Begum supported him with money and men, disillusioned by the promises that the Company had made to her and fearful for the future of Awadh.[137] As punishment, Asaf and Governor General Warren Hastings helped themselves to her treasure, an act that would figure prominently in Hastings's impeachment trial.[138] Despite expressing deference for her age and status, the Company's overriding interest was in her wealth.

Regime changes in the late eighteenth century entailed dramatic shifts in the begum's relationship with the Company. Although Asaf and his mother were alienated for much of his reign, they reconciled on the eve of his death, and she provided crucial support to his young son, Vizier Ali. Her presentation of the khilat of investiture 'will perhaps by the native princes of Hindostan, be deemed the most satisfactory refutation of the Reports which have been propagated to the prejudice of

---

[134] BL, APAC, IOR/P/120/9, consultation no. 49, Henry Russell to Marquess of Hastings, 23 December 1813.
[135] BL, APAC, IOR/L/PS/6/27, Political Letters Received from Bengal, 31 March 1814, p. 425.
[136] Barnett, *North India*, p. 76.
[137] Ibid., pp. 193, 200.
[138] Clark, *Scandal*, p. 84.

his birth', according to Governor General John Shore's assessment.[139] General opinion, so far as the Resident at Lucknow could learn, was that the young nawab attracted many followers thanks to the begum's influence.[140] When Vizier Ali was deposed, it was Bahu Begum who the Company most feared would upset the new political order; they called on her to use her influence to quell unrest in Lucknow, and to bestow the khilat on the new nawab vizier, Saadat Ali Khan, with her own hand.[141] Despite her role in settling the succession, however, Saadat and the begum soon found themselves at odds; she turned to the Company to enlist their support as a guarantor of the promises made to her by the nawab vizier that he would respect her position and property.

Subsequently, Bahu Begum claimed to regard herself as being entirely under the protection of the Company.[142] She maintained a regular correspondence with the governor general, sometimes passing on critical political intelligence.[143] During her lifetime, the Bahu Begum promised to make the Company her legatee, and used this promise as leverage to secure their assistance in defending her financial interests from Saadat Ali's encroachments, for instance by incentivizing the governor general to take her side in disputes over the inheritance of the wealthy *amil* (or revenue official) Almas Ali Khan.[144] After her death, the Company was indeed made the trustee of her considerable treasury, along with that of her daughter-in-law and the widow of Asaf ud-Daula, Shams un-Nissa Begum, who similarly relied on the Company to defend her interests at court. This trusteeship enabled the Company to acquire a position of authority relative to the begums' significant body of dependents, which included politically powerful eunuchs and other courtly adherents, as well as relatives.[145]

By investing the Company with this trust, the begums were not necessarily seeking to empower the Company relative to the ruling nawab vizier of Awadh, who deeply resented the Company's encroachment into

---

[139] BL, APAC, Cleveland Public Library Papers, IOR Neg 4215, wq091.92 Ea77m5, Minute of the Governor General, 20 October 1797, p. 252. See also Barnett, *North India*, p. 100.
[140] BL, APAC, Cleveland Public Library Papers, IOR Neg 4215, wq091.92 Ea77m5, Minute of the Governor General, 13 January 1798, p. 317.
[141] NAI, FSC no. 6, John Shore to Peter Speke, 22 January 1798, pp. 130–131.
[142] BL, APAC, IOR/F/4/304/7000, Extract of political letter from Bengal, 13 January 1809, p. 8.
[143] For instance, when Bahu Begum received unauthorized correspondence from the Mughal emperor, she transmitted it to the Resident at Lucknow. BL, APAC, IOR/F/4/331/7624, Extract of political letter from Bengal, 9 May 1810, p. 5.
[144] BL, APAC, IOR/F/4/304/7000, Bahu Begum to Governor General, 3 October 1808, p. 48.
[145] For the begum's wealth and influence in eighteenth-century Lucknow, see Barnett, *North India*, p. 102.

this family affair. Rather, they were trying to provide for their households and supporters, to ensure that they would be looked after and sheltered from the ruler's disfavour. Shams un-Nissa Begum placed her servants, adherents, and relatives under the care of the governor general so that, in her words, 'they may be protected from all molestation and oppression', passing on her lands, vessels of gold and silver, and the revenues of the bazaar attached to her palace, to be distributed among her dependents through the agency of the Company.[146] While the actions of these women might have consolidated the Company's influence in Awadh by amassing wealth and patronage in the Resident's hands, the begums' primary intent was to secure the futures of those dear to them. As Durba Ghosh observed of women's engagements with the Company more generally, although women sometimes exploited the possibilities made available to them in an imperial context, 'this should not lead us to the facile conclusion that colonialism [...] benefited native women.' Rather, 'the activities of the Company opened up limited social, material, and legal opportunities for native women, allowing them some mobility within positions of relative powerlessness.'[147] Royal women, while enjoying all the privileges of wealth and even sometimes political influence, nevertheless had to contend with the fact that the conditions of their lives were still subject, at least to some extent, to the dictates of powerful men, be they blood relatives or strangers from across the sea.

At the same time as Residents endeavoured to enlist royal women in their cause, royal women therefore sought to mobilize Residents in their interests. Women might, for example, ask for Company troops to quell disturbances in their dominions to facilitate the collection of tax.[148] And, as the Company began to expand its political and commercial activities across the subcontinent, royal women were not averse to deploying these networks in support of their personal enterprises, particularly by soliciting exemption from customs duties.[149] Aside from their business concerns, royal women were also prime builders, particularly noted for the construction of mosques, tombs, and caravanserais

---

[146] NLS, Minto Papers, MS 11574, Shams un-Nissa Begum to Minto, 13 January 1808, pp. 24–25.

[147] Ghosh, *Sex and the Family*, pp. 16–17.

[148] John Baillie was described as 'sedulously employed in effecting an arrangement for the commutation on fair and just principles of your Highness's [Shumsoo Nissa Begum's] jaggeer and Khassa for a regular payment of money', NLS, Minto Papers, MS 11594, Minto to Shumsoo Nissa Begum, 2 July 1813, p. 120.

[149] See for example UPSAA, BRR, LRA, basta no. 12, book no. 53, N. B. Edmonstone to W. A. Brooke, 28 August 1812, p. 220; Richard Strachey to W. A. Brooke, 17 October 1812, p. 257; N. B. Edmonstone to W. A. Brooke, 12 December 1812, p. 290.

that publicly expressed their piety and prestige, and contributed to the honour and good reputation of their family.[150] Bala Bai, daughter of Mahadji Shinde, adoptive sister of Daulat Rao and a prominent lady in his zenana, used the channel of the Resident to acquire the aid of the Commissioners for the Ceded and Conquered Provinces in Farrukhabad for planting an avenue of trees, constructing a road, and digging several wells between Mathura (a sacred Hindu city) and Bindrabin (the site of a popular temple) for the convenience of pilgrims and travellers. Bala Bai forwarded a plan of the proposed work to the Resident and asked the commissioners to provide her agents with letters of reference that would assist them in the collection of labourers and materials.[151] In so doing, she marshalled the local expertise of the Company's agents to help her in a project that would materially manifest her piety and benevolence. Women who enjoyed such status and connections were endowed with the leverage necessary to use the Company to facilitate projects designed to augment their financial and cultural capital.

One powerful way in which women could enlist the Company in their cause was to use the idiom of protection. Although women were often characterized as the main instigators and abettors of family conflict, they were also considered to be its chief victims, leading the Residents to position themselves as protectors even in relation to women whom they otherwise condemned for their scheming.[152] At Delhi, Archibald Seton was convinced that 'the Mother of the Heir Apparent was at the bottom of all the Disturbances in the Palace'.[153] Though Mumtaz Mahal was reproached for her ongoing campaign to secure Company recognition for her son Mirza Jahangir as heir apparent, the Resident was still shocked to witness how Mirza Jahangir repaid his mother's indulgence with insult, and 'carried his excesses to such a height, as frequently to strike his Mother; which unnatural conduct, through the misplaced affection of His Majesty, was always suffered to go unpunished'.[154] The Residents' stance relative to royal women was thus powerfully shaped

[150] Gregory C. Kozlowski, 'Private Lives and Public Piety: Women and the Practice of Islam in Mughal India', in *Women in the Medieval Islamic World: Power, Patronage, and Piety*, ed. Gavin R. Hambly (Houndmills, Basingstoke, 1998), pp. 475–477.
[151] BL, APAC, Mss Eur D514/1, Richard Strachey to J. E. Colebrooke and John Deane, 31 July 1812, pp. 110–111.
[152] For instance, though Henry Russell condemned Jahan Parwar Begam as 'ignorant, selfish deceitful and intriguing', he observed that 'the nizam treats her with little or no consideration.' Bodl. Oxf., Russell Papers, MS. Eng. misc. c. 324, Henry Russell, 'The conditions and resources of the Nizam's government', p. 50.
[153] NAI, For. Sec., series no. 7, file no. 54, Archibald Seton to N. B. Edmonstone, 13 January 1806, pp. 8–9.
[154] BL, APAC, IOR/F/4/334/7657, Extract of Political Letter from Bengal, 19 October 1809, pp. 1–2.

by British assumptions of civilizational superiority which postulated that British men had a responsibility to protect Indian women from Indian men.[155] In consequence, royal women figure prominently in the Residents' letters and papers in diametrically opposed roles, as victims to be protected as well as villains to be censured.

If so inclined, women could play the victim to counterbalance the influence of male relatives, exploiting the Residents' desire to position themselves as the protectors of Indian womanhood.[156] In part, this pattern reflected the zenana's nature as an intergenerational space. When a ruler died, his successor was expected to provide for the women of his predecessor's zenana. While rulers often venerated their own mothers and grandmothers, they were apt to resent the favourite wives of the men who had preceded them; these women sometimes paid a bitter price for the difficult relationships between male relatives. In such cases, particularly where a ruler was hostile to the English, it was not unusual for his female relatives to seek closer ties with the Company in pursuit of honours and benefits perhaps denied them by the ruler in question. For instance, Shams un-Nissa Begum, widow of Nawab Asaf ud-Daula, vowed that 'the Almighty is my witness that I have no kind friend nor protector but the faithful English Gentlemen'.[157] She called on the government to help her resolve disputes in her *zamindaris* (revenue-yielding lands) and her bazaar, and to rectify the ill treatment of Nawab Vizier Saadat Ali.[158] Eventually, Shams un-Nissa retired to Company territories. Though unwilling to assume the burden of looking after her or risk the nawab's resentment, 'the Begums sufferings under the Viziers most discreditable persecution and enmity and under the pressure of a severe malady however were considered to be sufficient to over balance those motives'.[159] By claiming the identity of 'the weaker vessel', women had a claim to Company support that Residents and other officials found extremely difficult to gainsay.

The compulsion to intervene on behalf of women who demanded their protection sometimes put Company officials in a difficult position;

---

[155] Gayatri Chakravorty Spivak, 'Can the Subaltern Speak?' in *Colonial Discourse and Post-colonial Theory: A Reader,* eds. Patrick Williams and Laura Chrisman (London, 1993), p. 93.

[156] Thomas Metcalf, *Ideologies of the Raj* (Cambridge, 1995), p. 94.

[157] NLS, Minto Papers, MS 11574, Shams un-Nissa Begum to Minto, 13 January 1808, pp. 24–25.

[158] NLS, Minto Papers, MS 11587, Shams un-Nissa Begum to Minto, 11 October 1811, pp. 112–113.

[159] BL, APAC, IOR/F/4/394/10025, Extract Political Letter from Bengal, 1 March 1812, pp. 3, 5. BL, APAC, IOR/F/4/308/7057, Extract Political Letter from Bengal, 1 May 1809, p. 1.

to revert to the previous example, they did not really want to provide asylum to Shams un-Nissa but felt compelled to do so because of her appeal to their protection. Similarly, after the rebellion of Vizier Ali, British officials sought, without success, to convince his wives to return to their family homes at Lucknow. The head wife Banu Begum expressed her unwillingness to leave Benares because of the apparent coldness shown her by her father, a Lucknow courtier.[160] After the Resident's repeated attempts to ensure her return, the begum responded in dramatic terms. 'As I regard the English Gentlemen as my father & guardians, and they have resolved to abandon me, surely death is to be preferred to life', she is reported to have said. 'All I want is a single loaf of Bread and to live under the shadow of the Protection of the English.' When further pressed, she responded, 'why do you talk to a person who is completely in your power, do whatever you please, I will not go to Lucknow to be disgraced [...] The English Gentlemen gave me honor, they ought to be the guardians of it.'[161] By emphasizing her own powerlessness, Banu Begum placed responsibility for her fate in the Company's hands.

Ultimately, Banu Begum returned to Lucknow to visit her mother, who was ill; otherwise, nothing the Company did, including cutting off her stipend, succeeded in convincing her.[162] While deeply unwilling to use force against a woman of status, the Resident at Benares was beginning to consider violent methods, worried that her present condition of penury, 'tho it is induced by her own disobedience of orders, may possibly, however erroneously, be ascribed to motives the very reverse of those which would govern your Lordship upon such occasions as the present.'[163] By holding her ground, Banu Begum forced the Company to resort to unflattering methods, subverting their claims to civilizational superiority. Undoubtedly, the Company would have prevailed against her, if pressed, but it is telling that for many months the begum was able to successfully fend off the attempts of the British to displace her, all the while claiming the moral high ground. In this context, basic similarities across the 'gender frontier' gave Indian women the tools to mobilize the British political elite in their interests.[164]

---

[160] UPSAA, BRR, LIA, basta no. 1, book no. 4, D. Vanderheyden to George Barlow, 18 May 1799, p. 56.

[161] Translation of the report of Ganesh Peshaud, munshi to the agent of the Governor General at Benares, enclosure to Ibid., pp. 88–89.

[162] UPSAA, BRR, LIA, basta no. 1, book no. 4, D. Vanderheyden to William Kirkpatrick, 1 May 1800, p. 178.

[163] Ibid., D. Vanderheyden to Marquess Wellesley, 20 September 1799, p. 119.

[164] For this concept, see Kathleen M. Brown, 'The Anglo-Algonquian Gender Frontier', in *Negotiators of Change: Historical Perspectives on Native American Women*, ed. Nancy Shoemaker (New York, NY, 1995), p. 27.

6.5   Conclusion

The endeavour to consolidate control at Indian courts required Residents to confront the complex and changeable form of Indian royal families and the highly adaptable rules governing succession. The Company was able, with time, to impose strict principles of primogeniture at Indian courts, but they did so at the hazard of inciting younger brothers to revolt. Even royal brothers who submitted to Company protection were sometimes more trouble than they were worth. Fraternal squabbles could serve the Company's interests, since it motivated royal family members to supply the Company with information. Exile to Company territories could also conciliate male relatives to British habits, helping to cultivate future heirs who might be more amenable to the Company's policies. In practice, however, forming alliances with royal brothers required delicate manoeuvring. In cultivating these relationships, Residents risked alienating the ruler in power. Royal exiles, meanwhile, also represented a considerable drain on time and resources, and rarely proved as loyal as anticipated. Residents' desire to impose their own models of family behaviour often led them to act as mediators between brothers, but the risks of this strategy were just as apparent as the rewards.

The Residents' relationships with royal women were, if anything, even more politically significant and emotionally fraught. Though Residents might have described royal women in derogatory terms, these women, particularly royal mothers, were nevertheless recognized power brokers at court. Residents might have resented this influence in some cases, but this did not mean they were blind to it or unwilling to mobilize it where and when they could. Royal women, for their part, used their status to call on the support of the Resident in fulfilment of personal projects, often strengthening their claim through the idiom of kinship and protection. Because of this moralising discourse, Residents sometimes found themselves implicated in family dramas against their will because of their desire to appear in the guise of protectors of Indian womanhood. As with so much else in the Resident's line of work, relationships with the royal family were apt to get messy, exposing the Resident to entanglements that he would have preferred to avoid. To the Residents' frustration, the dynamics of Indian royal families persistently refused to be constrained by the models of appropriate family relationships that the Company hoped to impose, as younger brothers continued to aspire to the throne, and royal women continued to involve themselves in matters of state. Working through existing dynasties, rather than simplifying matters, in fact posed unique problems of its own.

Conclusion

This book has described the strategies used to consolidate British political influence at Indian royal courts during a transformative period in the history of the British empire in India. From its inception in the seventeenth century, the East India Company was required to engage with Indian politics, but in so doing, their primary concern was to secure a stable commercial environment. As the Company became increasingly militarized over the course of the eighteenth century, first in response to French rivalry and then in the interests of defending its territories in Bengal, the nature of these relationships shifted; Indian allies began to be seen as a source of income to support the Company's growing political and military establishments. Until the close of the eighteenth century, however, the Company's relationships with Indian kingdoms were still, by and large, bilateral. The Company's main interest was to ensure that neighbouring states paid their subsidies where requisite and did not disrupt British trade or imperial governance. The Company was not, at this stage, averse to Indian rulers fighting one another; in fact, these divisions were seen as useful distractions that weakened potential rivals and prevented the formation of anti-British coalitions.; Under Wellesley, however, a new vision for Company rule in the subcontinent was articulated. Wellesley's administration introduced a moralizing dimension to the Company's policy, emphasizing its duty to impose 'tranquillity' across the Indian landscape by mediating between Indian kingdoms. Wellesley's ideas became the cornerstone for a system of paramountcy, whereby the Company assumed the mantle of political arbiter over the kingdoms of central India.

This expanded role had implications for the day-to-day work of the Residents, dramatically amplifying their sphere of action. Prior to Wellesley's arrival, Residents had transmitted intelligence, negotiated loans, subsidies, and war reparations, and carefully overseen royal successions, but their intervention in Indian administrations was generally limited; at Maratha courts, Residents exercised very little control at all, and maintained only uneasy diplomatic relations interspersed with periods of war. From the 1790s, not only were Residents charged with excluding European powers and military expertise from Indian courts, but they were also responsible for eliminating communications between different Indian centres. Added to this was an increasing tendency on the part of the Company to espouse a tutelary role towards their Indian allies; Residents were supposed to exercise a positive influence by managing disputes between states as well as by urging Indian rulers to adhere to European models of good government within their own dominions and even, in some cases, within their own families. The degree to which Residents intervened in the affairs of their respective courts differed across space and time; in Awadh, the terms of the 1801 treaty laid the ground for the Company to take a more aggressive tone for the good government of the country, even if they avoided taking direct action, whereas at Nagpur the lack of a subsidiary alliance meant that Residents were less prone to offer council, and did not enjoin reforms in the same way. Still, across the different courts there was a shared assumption that the Company had a right as well as a responsibility to exert its influence, and that Residents were the medium whereby that influence would be exercised.

Amid these transformations, Residents developed strategies for wielding influence at court, as well as building their credit within the Company. They were concerned as much with their own personal fortunes as with those of their employers. These interests, though clearly connected, were not inextricable. Not only did Residents endeavour to control the public image of the Company at royal capitals by closely monitoring the flow of letters and rumours, but they also used their position as the exclusive channel of communication with the governor general to cast their activities in a flattering light and to consolidate their credibility in Calcutta at the expense of the rulers to whom they were attached. Recognizing the efficacy of coercive measures, Residents asserted their rights to employ force or the threat of force and justified these measures in their letters to Calcutta by building on pre-existing conceptions of Indian kingdoms as lawless zones of perpetual warfare. Residents surrounded themselves with material finery that reinforced their status at court, as well as exchanging lavish presents that implanted relations of obligation with the ruler and his ministers at the same time as they concealed the growing asymmetry of the subsidiary alliance system with a veneer of reciprocity. Finally, and perhaps most importantly, Residents sought with varying degrees of success to harness the influence and expertise of munshis and royal family members to their cause. Throughout, Residents were concerned to construct themselves as in-between. At court, they emphasized their connections to the power and resources of the Company. In their correspondence with the Company, they fashioned themselves as invaluable by emphasizing their local expertise within the world of the court.

Despite these tactics, the consolidation of the Resident's influence at court was far from straightforward. To the contrary, the changing nature of the Residency system was a major source of conflict, even within the Company itself. Lacking clear precedents, Residents and their superiors in London and Calcutta debated how the Company's influence over Indian courts should be exercised, and what it should look like. To what extent should Residents embrace the use of exemplary violence, supposedly such a vital aspect of Indian sovereignty? Should Residents engage in the same acts of pageantry and benevolence as the rulers whose authority they were increasingly seeking to supplant? The controversies surrounding these questions reveal conflicting visions about the basis and legitimacy of Company power in the subcontinent, namely, whether the Company should present themselves as successors to the Mughals, or whether it was in fact their civilizational superiority, as Britons, that undergirded their right to rule. Historians like Robert Travers and Thomas Metcalfe have elaborated these changes in ruling ideologies, but this book has shown how these models competed for prominence in the routine business of empire.[1] Uncertainty about the Company's role in India was more than an abstract concern; it permeated every aspect of the Resident's day-to-day life, including the clothes they wore, the house they lived in, whether they flogged criminals or shot them from a cannon.

Even where Company policy was clear, translating these policies into practice could prove challenging. For instance, although Residents were instructed to exchange political gifts according to a strict principle of reciprocity, in practice this principle was difficult to enforce since Residents could neither anticipate nor control the presents they received in return. Similarly, although members of the political line were chosen for their fluency in Indian languages, to most Residents it became apparent that fluency by European standards was hardly sufficient to enable them to act independently on the political stage. This gap between ideals and reality produced persistent tensions between the governor-general-in-council, who issued the instructions, and the Resident, who was responsible for enacting them.

One of the overarching aims of this book, therefore, has been to counter widespread assumptions that the subsidiary alliance system was obvious, expedient, and uncontested. To the contrary, within the political line many of the issues connected with the Company's rapidly expanding

---

[1] Travers, *Ideology*, pp. 6–7; Metcalf, *Ideologies*, p. 24.

empire became exceptionally acute. As the Company's sphere of control encompassed ever greater expanses of territory, officials in Calcutta and London were faced with the problem of how to ensure the good conduct of the men who acted in their name at distant imperial outposts. Given their geographical distance from administrative centres, and their relative isolation from officials of equal standing to themselves, Residents were particular objects of uncertainty in this regard. The Company's inability to closely supervise its own agents produced anxieties about what these young men might be getting up to, an uneasiness that the ever-increasing stream of official reports from Indian capitals could never quite allay; after all, administrators in Company centres were keenly aware of the Residents' ability to whitewash their misdeeds in carefully worded letters, as Chapter 2 has shown. Suspicions centred around the question of where the Resident's loyalties lay: were his British virtues intact, or had he become 'Indianized', his dispositions and attachments shaped by his long sojourn at court? The very feature that has made the Residents so attractive in the eyes of modern historians was thus precisely the aspect of their work that most concerned their superiors in office.

More troubling even than the issue of 'Indianization' was the question of whether Residents were motivated by public benefits, or personal gains. Although there was a developing discourse of transparency and merit in Britain in the early nineteenth century, public and private interests had long been intertwined and in practise proved difficult to disentangle. The concerns about governance and public accountability that preoccupied domestic British society in the nineteenth century acquired greater urgency in a context of indirect rule. For one thing, the representative function of the Residents made the boundaries between public and private especially difficult to demarcate. The Resident was the embodiment of the Company's authority at Indian royal courts. In consequence, how he dressed, the style in which he lived, the carriage that transported him through the streets, could all be said to form a part of his official duties and representative functions, since they were believed to imbue him with status and significance in the eyes of the courtly elite. The Residents' personal relationships were also seen to have public implications; the forging of interpersonal ties constituted an important aspect of his work, partly because Indian politics were conceived as especially personalistic, but also because diplomacy itself was viewed as a line of work that relied on the cultivation of personal connections. Still, the Residents' superiors were unsettled to find the Residents forming an intricate web of interpersonal ties, the nature and extent of which administrators in London and Calcutta could not always discern. These concerns relating to the dissolving boundaries between public and private, Briton and

Indian, both came particularly to the fore in contemporary anxieties surrounding munshis, the subject of Chapter 5.

Because of these entanglements, Residents proved particularly impervious to the professionalizing impulses that swept with varying degrees of resistance through other branches of the Company. The Residents' experiences at Indian courts convinced them of the efficacy of personalistic forms of rule according to Indian idioms, meaning that the men who cut their teeth within the political line would become leading opponents of Anglicization. The Residencies were the seedbed within which the 'Romantic' ideological currents identified by Stokes and Metcalfe began to germinate.[2]

Still, even though some members of the political line became important advocates of conservativism within the Company, there was nevertheless a widespread recognition among them of the practical limits curtailing this policy. When Elphinstone oversaw the annexation of the peshwa's dominions in the aftermath of the Third Maratha War, his objective was to preserve existing institutions as far as possible; however, he conceded that the simple fact of the administration being assumed by Europeans meant that distortions were inevitable. Even within their more limited spheres of action, Residents recognized that their mere presence, to say nothing of the presence of the subsidiary forces, introduced a disruptive element into Indian courtly politics. To pursue a truly non-interventionist path, Residents began to recognize, they would have to withdraw from court entirely, but doing so seemed unethical if not impossible because of the moralizing tendency that had begun to infuse Company policy. If the Company, through the Residents, was the only power capable of arbitrating between Indian states, then surely it had a responsibility to do so; the fate of individual dynasties paled, in their eyes, when compared to their vision of 'tranquillity' in the subcontinent. The turn of the century thus represented a moment in which prominent members of the Company began to grapple with the implications of their policies in India, all the while believing in the impossibility of retracing their steps.

Although Residents' place within Indian courtly politics meant that they espoused a more personalistic approach to their careers in India, this should not, therefore, be interpreted to mean that they rejected the Company's political agenda. Another overarching argument of this book has been that it is important not to romanticize the Residencies as cosmopolitan spaces, ignoring the political functions that they were primarily designed to serve. Some Residents certainly criticized the Company for its treatment of its nominal allies; James Achilles Kirkpatrick is the most notorious example of this, as William Dalrymple famously showed. In general,

---

[2] Stokes, *English Utilitarians*, p. 14; Metcalf, *Ideologies*, p. 24.

however, the Residents' assimilation into Indian political culture should be interpreted as part of a larger strategy that included the use of force as well as the sharing of meals and the offering of gifts. Similarly, while Residents did develop close relationships with Indian elites, particularly with their munshis, these relationships did not take shape within a political vacuum. Friendly though they might have been, these relationships were moulded by the imperial context within which they emerged. From the Residents' perspective, they were implements for consolidating control.

Indians too, however, instrumentalized these relationships for their own purposes; because of their connections and cultural competence, Indian political actors had the leverage necessary to make the Residency system work for them, to some extent. Company networks were used to make claims to property, secure jobs, expedite building projects, and serve a variety of other ends conducive to the social, cultural, and economic capital of the individuals concerned. The Resident could be a valuable counterpoint to rival factions at court, protecting administrators from the disfavour of the ruler; he could also shield brothers and cousins from the resentment of the monarch, and side with royal women against the interventions of male relatives. Previous studies of the Residencies during this period have focused either on emotional attachments (friendships, marriages), or else have devoted their attention to ritual encounters circumscribed in space and time. This book has sought instead to illuminate the stream of letters, petitions, gifts, and services that made up Anglo-Indian exchange and formed the bedrock of the Company's developing system of imperial influence.

These interactions were facilitated by broad similarities between British and Indian political and family culture. This point cannot be pushed too far; there were prominent differences undergirding the Company's claims to paramountcy during this period. A conflict in military cultures spawned accusations of tyranny and inhumanity, for example, while the fraternal strife characteristic of Indian royal families was sharply censured given British assumptions about the importance of family solidarity to social, political, and economic advancement. Still, social and political life in India and Britain were structured in comparable, albeit distinct, ways, and these parallels provided a common ground on which British and Indian political actors could cooperate. Both British Residents and their munshis, for instance, would have had roughly similar expectations of the obligations entailed by their patron–client relationships, given that these vertical relationships of dependency were the basic fabric of which both societies were composed. Similarly, while British and Indian family structures differed in many respects, common assumptions about kinship and gender gave Indian royal women the tools to form alliances and mobilize the Residents in their interests through the imposition of compelling moral imperatives of protection and guardianship. By examining the Resident's day-to-day work, other commonalities also emerge, suggesting why Residents could cement their position at Indian courts so effectively. Many features of Indian courtly life would have resonated with Residents, who came from a society that similarly emphasized the intermingling of the social and the material in the form of gift-giving and grandeur, and that also had a sophisticated epistolary culture where readers and writers attended carefully to language and format.

While the Residencies were thus prominent sites of cooperation between British officials and Indian administrators and elites, they were also targets of opposition. British letters were forged, stolen, or waylaid; misinformation was industriously spread. Princes and ministers organized violent uprisings, while rebels and marauders plundered Company domains. These acts of overt resistance might seem starkly opposed to the practical support provided by the Resident's Indian allies, who we might be tempted to label as collaborators; this book, however, has tried to upset these binaries. Life at Indian courts was complicated and occasionally cut-throat; to the extent that munshis, ministers, or royal women assisted the Resident, it was usually in pursuit of their own objectives, and sometimes even for fear of their life. The Resident was only one player in a diverse field of interests and factions, and it was these configurations of power that usually determined the activities of the Indian political actors described in this book, from ministers and queen mothers to informants and intelligencers of lowly origins. To draw too sharp a line between the Company's allies and adversaries is also reductive because many people acted in both capacities, most famously Bahu Begum, who went from being the Company's most committed enemy to their most devoted supporter, as discussed in Chapter 6. Loyalties were rarely set in stone, and individuals who had previously shown an unwillingness to work with the Resident were apt to change tactics if the stakes were high enough, while those who had previously supported the Company could and did revolt if the opportunity presented itself. In sum, the Resident was reliant on people whose commitments, and consequently the assistance that they provided, were often partial and contingent.

The Residents' activities were mostly restricted to the royal court, but the development of the subsidiary alliance system had ramifications beyond the city limits. Outside the capitals, the story was less one of negotiation and political intrigue than it was of flight and famine in the wake of pillaging and warfare.[3] For the general population, the traditional

---

[3] BL, APAC, Mss Eur D1086, John Macdonald Kinneir to J. A. Graham, 18 February 1806; Bodl. Oxf., Russell Papers, MS. Eng. lett. c. 151, Henry Russell to Henry Russell Sr., 4 March 1811, p. 9; Henry Russell to Henry Russell Sr., 3 April 1811, p. 20.

strategies for combatting this kind of deprivation were migration and marauding. These activities had repercussions for the ill-defined and shifting borders between princely states and British-administered country, producing recurring disputes over law, order, and extraterritoriality which in turn expose changing ideas about sovereignty and interstate relations. The movement of people required Company officials and their Indian counterparts to clarify their relationship to one another and their obligations to their subjects; indeed, it required them to theorize about how the idea of subjecthood itself should be defined. Future work on the princely states might therefore fruitfully focus on the borders. This approach would foreground the agency of the broader population, showing how practices in the peripheries informed diplomatic activities at the capital, where courtiers and colonial officials found themselves debating the legal status of peasants, mercenaries, and merchants.

As this suggests, the subsidiary alliance system never ceased to inspire debate. Over the following decades, the Company experimented with different degrees of intervention. The disillusionment of the Third Maratha War set in train a pattern of more aggressive interference, particularly at Nagpur and Hyderabad where Company officials assumed administrative responsibilities. Yet the perceived failures of the 1820s (including severe economic depression in Hyderabad and a series of corruption scandals across major Residencies) subsequently brought the desirability of this model into question.[4] In response, succeeding administrations explicitly advocated a policy of non-intervention (even if they failed to implement it in practice). The regime of James Andrew Broun Ramsay, first Marquess of Dalhousie appeared to mark another change of direction; his policy was imbued with cynicism about the viability of working through Indian regimes. Dalhousie's approach, in turn, would be undermined by the events of 1857.

The Uprising is usually treated as a turning point wherein relationships between the British government and the Indian princely states were fundamentally transformed. According to conventional narratives, 1857 was interpreted as a cautionary tale of the dangers of Dalhousie's policy of annexation.[5] While dispossessed rulers numbered among the Company's most virulent enemies, their surviving allies had emerged as their staunchest supporters. Trying to make sense of the conflict in

---

[4] For Hyderabad, see Sunil Chander, 'From a Pre-colonial Order to a Princely State: Hyderabad in Transition, c. 1748–1865' (PhD diss., University of Cambridge, 1987), p. 129. On corruption scandals, see Margot Finn, 'Material Turns in British History: II. Corruption: Imperial Power, Princely Politics and Gifts Gone Rogue', *Transactions of the Royal Historical Society* 29 (2019): 1–25; Karen Leonard, 'Palmer and Company: An Indian Banking Firm in Hyderabad State', *MAS* 47, no. 4 (2014): 1157–1184.

[5] Metcalf, *Aftermath of Revolt*, p. 220.

its immediate aftermath, one thing seemed clear; maintaining and protecting the sovereign status of Indian allies was the safest expedient for
ensuring social and political stability in India. Financially, too, retaining
the existing system of subsidiary alliances made the most sense considering the Company's indebtedness. Accordingly, the government of India
set about strengthening its relationships with Indian states by confirming
their rights and privileges. Historians have therefore tended to interpret
post-1857 policy as inherently conservative, in contrast to the liberal,
reformist model of empire which, they argue, preceded it. In Mahmood
Mamdani's words, 'the colonial mission was redefined – from civilization to conservation and from progress to order.'[6] The ruptures of 1857,
according to this view, had dashed optimistic visions of reform, convincing contemporaries of the essential difference of their imperial subjects;
whereas previously imperial rule had been justified through the rhetoric
of a civilizing mission, now it was the fundamental difference of Indians
which, instead, required protection and preservation by the paramount
power. To quote Karuna Mantena, 'the ethical dilemma at the heart
of late empire was not about what right (and for what ethical purpose)
Britain ruled India, but a diminished moral duty to stay, as the lesser evil
compared to leaving India to collapse on her own.'[7]

These views, however, were being aired from very early on in the history of the subsidiary alliance system; Henry Russell had expressed his
interpretation of the Company's role in the subcontinent in very similar
terms. The rule of difference, and the concept of 'protection', were built
into the subsidiary alliance's very foundations. On closer examination,
1857 seems like less of a watershed than is usually assumed. A contemporary observer, the future historian of the Uprising, John William Kaye,
argued as much in the pages of *Blackwood's Edinburgh Magazine*. Himself a former soldier in the Company's army and recently employed in its
London establishment, Kaye was keen to emphasize that this new empire
in India was built on the foundations of the old. In his view, the pledge
that the Queen made to the Indian princes was from 'first to last [...]
little more than the traditional policy of the East India Company.'[8]
Kaye pointed out that the awkward coexistence of, first, the repudiation of territorial expansion, and, second, the commitment to prosperity, peace, and good government within allied territories, were precisely
the two imperatives that had informed the Company's relationship with

---

[6] Mamdani, *Define and Rule*, p. 8.
[7] Mantena, *Alibis*, p. 149.
[8] John William Kaye, 'The Royal Proclamation to India', *Blackwood's Edinburgh Magazine*
85, no. 519 (1859): 114.

Indian states in the first half of the nineteenth century. What is more, Kaye highlighted that the nature and limits of the 'rights' guaranteed by the proclamation were suspiciously undefined. 'We pledge ourselves to respect the rights of the native princes of India. But what are those rights? Is "The divine right of kings to govern wrong" henceforth to be one of them?'[9] Far from being a clear blueprint for the future relationship between the British government and Indian princely states, the proclamation was a reiteration of those very principles that had created problems for the East India Company in the past.

Kaye's purpose in writing was to vindicate the Company and pay tribute to 'that magnificent Past'; in so doing, however, he usefully brings into question the stark distinctions usually drawn between the Company and the Raj in the history of the princely states.[10] Despite British promises to protect and preserve Indian sovereignty, the post-1857 period was far from being a golden age for Indian rulers. Disorder and misgovernment continued to be invoked as the basis for circumscribing ruler's powers, as the government of India continued to maintain ministers in office against the sovereign's will, to interfere in succession disputes, and even to depose rulers (as in Baroda in 1875).[11] As alluded to in Chapter 1, theorists like Charles Lewis Tupper also continued to invoke the precedents set during the period 1798–1818 to justify Indian rulers' subordinate status in international law.[12]

The twentieth century witnessed crucial changes in the relationship between Britain and the princely states, but amidst these transformations, the traces of much older ideas are still visible. In the same way that the events of 1857 had proven the worth of the princely states, so too did the threat of nationalism and global warfare render them important and highly valued pillars of support. In 1909, in recognition of the aid that the princes had provided in the face of nationalist agitation, the government of India introduced a policy of laissez-faire, refuting the high-handed measures that had prevailed under Viceroy George Nathaniel Curzon, Marquess Curzon, at the turn of the century.[13] In the aftermath of World War I, a Chamber of Princes was created with the intention of establishing a channel for consultation between the government and its allies.[14] Yet, as always, British promises proved disappointing in practice; laissez-faire was implemented unevenly on the ground, and the Chamber of

---

[9] Ibid., p. 117.
[10] Ibid., p. 114.
[11] Keen, *Princely India*, p. 18.
[12] Tupper, *Our Indian Protectorate*, p. 62.
[13] Copland, *Princes of India*, pp. 29–31.
[14] Ibid., p. 41.

Princes was a less effective mechanism for political participation than the princes had hoped, particularly since prominent Indian rulers, including the nizam of Hyderabad, refused to participate. Finally, the British government continued to adhere to the model of paramountcy established by 'usage', even in the face of repeated princely attempts to insist on the rights guaranteed to them by treaty.[15]

The greatest let-down, of course, was Britain's failure to support or even deal plainly with Indian rulers in the lead-up to independence in 1947, at which point the states, with varying degrees of resistance, were submerged within a newly independent India.[16] Only Hyderabad, awkwardly positioned as a Muslim state in the heart of peninsular India, made a bid for independence. Following its appeal to the United Nations, however, Hyderabad was violently annexed in the so-called Police Action, forcing the last nizam to cede his dream of resuming independent control over the kingdom.[17] Though members of some these formerly royal dynasties would become important players in post-colonial politics, in 1948 kingship in India was abruptly brought to an end, and with it, the network of Indian Residencies.

Elsewhere, however, the Residency system persisted. The Gulf Residency, formed in 1822 out of an amalgamation of the East India Company Residencies at Basra and Bushehr, survived until 1971. In his study of this institution, James Onley has emphasized the influence of Indian precedents, observing that nearly every British political officer in the Gulf had previous experience of Residency work in India.[18] The Gulf Residency is just one example of how the Residency as an institution was exported internationally, with remarkably lasting consequences. Over the course of the nineteenth century, Residencies were also established across Asia and Africa, from the Nigerian emirates to the Malaysian archipelago.

Yet, the difficulties of the early Residency system may also have acted as a counterexample, a cautionary tale of the dangers of political intervention. When Stamford Raffles (1781–1826, colonial governor and founder of Singapore) proposed extending British influence across Southeast Asia through the appointment of a network of Residents at key ports, the plan met with disapproval in London. In 1815, the Secret Committee of the Court of Directors condemned 'the extension in any degree to the Eastern Islands of that system of subsidiary alliance which

---

[15] Ibid., p. 70.
[16] Ibid., p. 276.
[17] Sunil Purushotham, 'Internal Violence: The "Police Action" in Hyderabad', *Comparative Studies in Society and History* 57, no. 2 (2015): 435–466.
[18] James Onley, *The Arabian Frontier of the British Raj: Merchants, Rulers, and the British in the Nineteenth-Century Gulf* (Oxford, 2007), p. 28.

has prevailed perhaps too widely in India.'[19] For decades, the East India Company and its successors loudly declared their determination to avoid political entanglements in Southeast Asia; a Residency system was not established in the Malay states until 1874.[20] Even in the Gulf, Guillemette Crouzet has argued, strategies devised in the Indian subcontinent were implemented 'only belatedly, and almost haphazardly, after a range of other options had been tested and exhausted.'[21] The Indian Residency system is often assumed to have provided a clear model for subsequent iterations of indirect rule around the world, but these examples suggests a more uneven trajectory. By adopting a comparative perspective, future research might trace this circuitous history, helping us understand how ideas and practices of indirect rule changed over time and between places. As this book has argued, indirect rule presented British colonial administrations and their agents with a host of practical and ideological problems. By elucidating some of these issues, I hope to have shown that indirect rule has a distinctive cultural history of its own, with many questions remaining to be answered.

---

[19] Quoted in Nicholas Tarling, 'The Establishment of Colonial Régimes', in *The Cambridge History of Southeast Asia*, 2 vols (Cambridge, 1993), II, p. 16.

[20] Rupert Emerson, *Malaysia: A Study in Direct and Indirect Rule* (Kuala Lumpur, 1964), pp. 112–135.

[21] Guillemette Crouzet, *Inventing the Middle East: Britain and the Persian Gulf in the Age of Global Imperialism* (Montreal, 2022), p. 68.

Glossary

akhbar	court newsletter
amil	revenue official
begum	lady of rank
bai	lady; often appended to a woman's name as a respectful form of address
chobdar	staff-bearer; attendant of the nobility
dak	a relay system for the transmission of post
dak dauriya	postal runner
diwan	chief minister of state, particularly concerned with finance
durbar	the court or levee of a prince; an audience chamber
firman	a mandate, command, order, or royal patent
hircarrah	a messenger, a courier; an emissary or spy
jagir	assignment of land revenues
khilat	honorific dress
lakh	unit of 100,000
mansabdar	holder of a Mughal office commanding specified number of men
musnud	a large cushion, equivalent to a throne
mohur	Mughal gold coins
munshi	a writer, author, secretary, tutor, or language-master
nabob	term used to designate returning Company servants; usually derogatory
nautch	dance performed by women; a public stage entertainment
nawab	Muslim noble or ruler; viceroy of the Mughal emperor
naubat	a very large kettle-drum, struck at stated hours; a musical band playing at stated times before the palace of a king or prince
nazr	ceremonial present or offering from an inferior to a superior
omrah	Anglo-Indian term for Muslim nobleman or court official – from the Arabic *umara*
paan	preparation of betel leaf and areca nut, chewed for its stimulant effects
peshkash	offering, tribute, or present
purdah	seclusion of women; from *parda,* a curtain screening women from the sight of men
sanad	an order, a written authority for holding either land or office

sepoys	in Anglo-Indian use, an Indian soldier disciplined and dressed in European style
sirdar	a nobleman or officer of rank
toshakhana	repository of articles received as presents or intended to be given as presents
vakil	an ambassador, agent, or other authorized representative
vizier	a counsellor of state, minister, viceregent, or lieutenant of a king
zamindar	landholder responsible for collecting revenues
zenana	women's apartments; also used to refer to the women themselves

Bibliography

Manuscripts

Government Records

British Library, London
Bengal Proceedings (IOR/P/118–120)
Board's Collections (IOR/F/4)
Court of Directors Correspondence with India (IOR/E/4)
Home Miscellaneous (IOR/H)
Political and Secret Department Records (IOR/L/PS)

National Archives of India, New Delhi
Foreign Department Secret Branch Consultations
Foreign Department Secret Branch Proceedings
Foreign Secret Department
Hyderabad Residency Records

Maharashtra State Archives, Mumbai
Poona Residency Correspondence

Uttar Pradesh State Archives, Allahabad
Benares Residency Records

Private Papers

Bodleian Library, Oxford
Russell Papers

British Library, London
Arthur Wellesley Papers (Mss Eur E216)
Charles Theophilus Metcalfe Papers (Mss Eur B233)
Cleveland Public Library Papers (IOR Neg 4211–32)
Diaries and Papers of Sir Charles Malet (Mss Eur F149)
Elphinstone Collection (Mss Eur F88)

Gilbert Elliot-Murray-Kynynmound Papers (Mss Eur D1086)
Grant-Duff Papers (Mss Eur F311)
John Adam Papers (Mss Eur D585)
Letter Books of Sir Richard Jenkins (Mss Eur E111)
Mackenzie General Collection (Mss Eur Mack Gen 1–75)
Maria Sykes Papers (Mss Eur C799)
Metcalfe Family Papers (Mss Eur F656)
Official and Private Correspondence and Papers of Warren Hastings (Add MS
    28973–29236)
Papers of 1st Earl Amherst (Mss Eur F140)
Papers of Hugh Smith, alias Seton (IOR Neg 11664)
Papers of John Adam (Mss Eur F109)
Papers of Maj-Gen William Kirkpatrick (Mss Eur F228)
Papers of Sir George Barlow (Mss Eur F176)
Richard Strachey Papers (Mss Eur D514)
Richard Wellesley Papers (Add MS 12564–13915)
Sir Barry Close Papers (Mss Eur D1053)
Sutton Court Collection (Mss Eur F128)

Lincolnshire County Archives, Lincoln
Monson Papers

National Library of Scotland, Edinburgh
Minto Papers
Seton of Touch Papers

National Records of Scotland, Edinburgh
Seaforth Papers

National Register of Archives, Scotland
Fraser of Reelig Papers

Newspapers and Periodicals

Asiatic Journal and Monthly Register
Blackwood's Edinburgh Magazine
The Annual Register
The Gentleman's Magazine
The Parliamentary Register
The Times

Parliamentary Papers

Hansard Parliamentary Debates. 1st series (1803–1820).
House of Commons. *Papers Relating to Oude*. London, 1856.

House of Commons. *Report from the Select Committee on the Affairs of the East India Company.* London, 1832.

House of Commons. *Report of the Indian States Committee, 1928–1929*, 1929, Cmd. 3302.

House of Commons. *Return of Civil Offices and Establishments under Presidencies of Bengal, Madras, and Bombay, 1817 and 1827.* London, 1830.

House of Commons. *Treaty between East India Company and Maha-Rajah Ragojee Bhonsla, 1826; Reports on Failure of Heirs of late Rajah of Berar, and Annexation of Berar Territory; Despatches and Correspondence with Lord Dalhousie.* London, 1854.

Printed Primary Sources

Aitchison, C. U. *A Collection of Treaties, Engagements and Sunnuds.* Calcutta, 1864.

An Officer in the Service of the East India Company. *Origin of the Pindaries; Preceded by Historical Notices on the Rise of the Different Mahratta States.* London, 1818.

Anonymous. *Considerations Relative to the Military Establishments in India Belonging to the British, and Those of the Native Princes.* London, 1803.

Anonymous. *Notes Relative to the Peace Concluded between the British Government and the Marhatta Chieftains, and to the Various Questions Arising Out of the Terms of the Pacification.* London, 1805.

Baird, J. G. A. *Private Letters of the Marquess of Dalhousie.* Edinburgh, 1910.

Bakhsh, Muhammad Faiz. *Memoirs of Delhi and Faizabad.* Translated by William Hoey. Allahabad, 1889.

Blakiston, John. *Twelve Years Military Adventure in Three Quarters of the Globe.* London, 1829.

Briggs, John. *Letters Addressed to a Young Person in India.* London, 1828.

Broughton, Thomas Duer. *Letters Written in a Mahratta Camp during the Year 1809.* London, 1813.

Bute, Marchioness, ed. *The Private Journal of the Marquess of Hastings*, 2 vols. London, 1858.

Callières, Francois de. *The Art of Diplomacy.* Edited by Maurice Keens-Soper and Karl W. Schweizer. New York, NY, 1983.

Clunes, John. *An Historical Sketch of the Princes of India, Stipendiary, Subsidiary, Protected, Tributary, and Feudatory; with a Sketch of the Origin and Progress of British Power in India.* Edinburgh, 1833.

Colebrooke, James Edward. *Papers Relative to the Case at Issue between Sir Edward Colebrooke, Bt., and the Bengal Government.* London, 1833.

Colebrooke, T. E. *Life of the Honourable Mountstuart Elphinstone.* London, 1884.

Deane, Anne. *A Tour through the Upper Provinces of Hindostan.* London, 1823.

Duff, James Grant. *A History of the Mahrattas.* London, 1826.

Elliot-Murray-Kynynmound, Emma Eleanor Elizabeth, Countess of Minto, ed. *Lord Minto in India: Life and Letters of Gilbert Elliot, First Earl of Minto.* London, 1880.

Forbes, James. *Oriental Memoirs: A Narrative of Seventeen Years Residence in India*, 2nd edn, 2 vols. London, 1834.

Foster, William, ed. *The Embassy of Sir Thomas Roe to India 1616–1919.* London, 1926.

Furber, Holden, ed. *Private Record of a Governor-Generalship: The Correspondence of Sir John Shore, Governor-General with Henry Dundas, President of the Board of Control, 1793–1798*. Cambridge, MA, 1933.

Gleig, G. R. Memoirs of the Life of the Right Hon. *Warren Hastings*, 3 vols. London, 1841.

Grotius, Hugo. The Rights of War and Peace. Edited by Richard Tuck. Indianapolis, IN, 2005.

Hastings, Francis Rawdon, Marquess. *The Marquis of Hastings' Summary of the Operations in India, with Their Results*. London, 1824.

Hyderabad, Central Records Office. *The Chronology of Modern Hyderabad 1720–1890*. Hyderabad, 1954.

Ingram, Edward, ed. *Two Views of British India: The Private Correspondence of Mr Dundas and Lord Wellesley, 1798–1801*. Bath, 1970.

Jenkins, Richard. *Report on the Territories of the Rajah of Nagpore*. Calcutta, 1827.

Kaye, John William, ed. *The Life and Correspondence of Charles, Lord Metcalfe*. London, 1858.

Kaye, John William, ed. *Selections from the Papers of Lord Metcalfe*. London, 1855.

Law, Algernon, ed. *India under Lord Ellenborough, March 1842–June 1844*. London, 1922.

Madan, Charles. *Two Private Letters to a Gentleman in England, from His Son Who Accompanied Earl Cornwallis, on His Expedition to Lucknow in the Year 1787*. Peterborough, 1788.

Malcolm, John. *The Political History of India, from 1784–1823*. 2 vols. London, 1826.

Martens, Karl von. *Le guide diplomatique*. Leipzig, 1832.

Martin, Robert Montgomery, ed. The Despatches, Minutes, and Correspondence of the Marquess Wellesley, K. G., during his Administration in India. 5 vols. London, 1836; repr. Cambridge, 2012.

Mundy, Godfrey Charles. *Pen and Pencil Sketches, Being the Journal of a Tour in India*. London, 1832.

Nugent, Maria. *A Journal from the Year 1811 to the Year 1815, Including a Voyage to and Residence in India*. London, 1839.

Philips, C. H., ed. *Correspondence of Lord William Cavendish Bentinck*. 2 vols. Oxford, 1977.

Prinsep, Henry T. *History of the Political and Military Transactions in India during the Administration of the Marquess of Hastings 1813–1823*. London, 1825.

Pufendorf, Samuel. *De jure naturae et gentium libri octo*, 1688 edn, 2 vols. trans. C. H. Oldfather and W. A. Oldfather. Oxford, 1934.

Robert, Mackintosh, ed., *Memoirs of the Life of the Right Honorable Sir James Mackintosh*, 2nd edn, London, 1836.

Roebuck, Thomas, ed. *The Annals of the College of Fort William*. Calcutta, 1819.

Ross, Charles, ed. Correspondence of Charles, First Marquis Cornwallis, 3 vols. Cambridge, 2011.

Sardesai, G. S., ed. *English Records of Maratha History Poona Residency Correspondence*. 15 vols. Bombay, 1936–1951.

Sinha, H. N., ed. *Selections from the Nagpur Residency Records*. 5 vols. Nagpur, 1950–1957.

Srinivasachari, C. S., ed. *Fort William – India House Correspondence*, 21 vols. Delhi, 1962.

Sutherland, James. *Sketches of the Relations Subsisting between the British Government in India, and the Different Native States.* Calcutta, 1833.

Thorn, William. *Memoir of the War in India.* London, 1818.

Tupper, Charles Lewis. *Our Indian Protectorate.* London, 1898.

Vattel, Emer de. *The Law of Nations, or, the Principles of the Law of Nature, Applied to the Conduct and Affairs of Nations and Sovereigns.* Edited by Béla Kapossy and Richard Whatmore. Indianapolis, IN, 2008.

Viscount Valentia, George. *Voyages and Travels in India, Ceylon, the Red Sea, Abyssinia, and Egypt.* 2 vols. London, 1809.

Welsh, James. *Military Reminiscences, Extracted from a Journal of Nearly Forty Years' Active Service in the East Indies.* 2 vols. London, 1830.

White, Adam. *Considerations on the State of British India.* Edinburgh, 1822.

Wicquefort, Abraham de. *The Embassador and his Functions.* London, 1716.

Williamson, Thomas. *The East India Vade-Mecum, or Complete Guide to Gentlemen Intended for the Civil, Military, or Naval Services of the Hon. East India Company.* 2 vols. London, 1810.

Wilson, W. J. *History of the Madras Army.* 3 vols. Madras, 1883.

Wolff, Christian. *Jus gentium method scientifica pertractatum,* 3 vols. trans. Joseph H. Drake, Oxford, 1934.

Unpublished Dissertations

Chander, Sunil. '*From a Pre-colonial Order to a Princely State: Hyderabad in Transition, c. 1758–1865*'. PhD diss., University of Cambridge, 1987.

Ehrlich, Joshua. '*The East India Company and the Politics of Knowledge*'. PhD diss., Harvard University, 2018.

Secondary Sources

Adams, Julia. *The Familial State: Ruling Families and Merchant Capitalism in Early Modern Europe.* Ithaca, NY, 2005.

Alam, Muzaffar. *The Crisis of Empire in Mughal North India.* Delhi, 1986.

Alam, Muzaffar. 'The Culture and Politics of Persian in Precolonial Hindustan'. In *Literary Cultures in History: Reconstructions from South Asia,* edited by Sheldon Pollock. Berkeley, CA, 2003.

Alam, Muzaffar and Sanjay Subrahmanyam. 'The Making of a Munshi'. *Comparative Studies of South Asia, Africa, and the Middle East* 24, no. 2 (2003).

Alamgir, Alena K. '"The Learned Brahmen, Who Assists Me": Changing Colonial Relationships in 18th and 19th Century India'. *Journal of Historical Sociology* 19, Eno. 4 (2006).

Alavi, Seema, ed. *The Eighteenth Century in India.* Oxford, 2002.

Alavi, Seema, *Sepoys and the Company: Tradition and Transition in Northern India, 1770–1830.* Oxford, 1995.

Alexandrowicz, C. H. *An Introduction to the History of the Law of Nations in the East Indies (Sixteenth, Seventeenth, and Eighteenth Centuries).* Oxford, 1967.

Allport, Gordon W. and Leo Postman. *The Psychology of Rumor.* New York, 1947.

Amussen, Susan Dwyer. 'Punishment, Discipline, and Power: The Social Meanings of Violence in Early Modern England'. *Journal of British Studies* 34, no. 1 (1995): 1–34.

Anderson, Clare. *Subaltern Lives: Biographies of Colonialism in the Indian Ocean World, 1790–1920*. Cambridge, 2012.

Anghie, Antony. *Imperialism, Sovereignty, and the Making of International Law*. Cambridge, 2004.

Armitage, David. *The Ideological Origins of the British Empire*. Cambridge, 2004.

Ayres, Philip. *Classical Culture and the Idea of Rome in Eighteenth-Century England*. Cambridge, 1997.

Ballantyne, Tony. 'Archive, Discipline, State: Power and Knowledge in South Asian Historiography'. *New Zealand Journal of Asian Studies* 3, no. 1 (2001): 87–105.

Ballantyne, Tony and Antoinette Burton, eds. *Moving Subjects: Gender, Mobility, and Intimacy in an Age of Global Empire*. Urbana, IL, 2009.

Bannet, Eve Tavor. *Empire of Letters: Letter Manuals and Transatlantic Correspondence, 1688–1820*. Cambridge, 2005.

Barnett, Richard B. *North India between Empires: Awadh, the Mughals, and the British 1720–1801*. Berkeley, CA, 1980.

Bayly, C. A. *Empire and Information: Intelligence Gathering and Social Communication in India, 1780–1870*. Cambridge, 1996.

Bayly, C. A. 'The First Age of Global Imperialism, c. 1760–1830'. *The Journal of Imperial and Commonwealth History* 26, no. 2 (1998): 28–47.

Bayly, C. A. *Imperial Meridian: The British Empire and the World 1780–1830*. London, 1989.

Bayly, C. A. *Indian Society and the Making of the British Empire*. Cambridge, 1988.

Bayly, C. A. 'Knowing the Country: Empire and Information in India'. *Modern Asian Studies* 27, no. 1 (1993): 3–43.

Bayly, C. A. *Origins of Nationality in South Asia: Patriotism and Ethical Government in the Making of Modern India*. Oxford, 1998.

Bayly, C. A. 'The Origins of Swadeshi (Home Industry): Cloth and Indian Society, 1700–1930'. In *The Social Life of Things: Commodities in Cultural Perspective*, edited by Arjun Appadurai. Cambridge, 1986.

Bayly, C. A. *Rulers, Townsmen and Bazaars: North Indian Society in the Age of British Expansion, 1770–1870*. Delhi, 1993.

Bayly, C. A. 'The Second British Empire'. In *The Oxford History of the British Empire*, ed. Robin Winks, 5 vols. Oxford, 1999, V.

Bayly, Susan. *Caste, Society and Politics in India from the Eighteenth Century to the Modern Age*. Cambridge, 1999.

Bayly, Susan. 'Hindu Kingship and the Origin of Community: Religion, State and Society in Kerala, 1750–1850'. *Modern Asian Studies* 18, no. 2 (1984): 177–213.

Bell, David A. *The Cult of the Nation in France: Inventing Nationalism, 1680–1800*. Cambridge, MA, 2001.

Bell, Duncan. 'Dissolving Distance: Technology, Space, and Empire in British Political Thought, 1770–1900'. *Journal of Modern History* 77, no. 3 (2005): 523–562.

Bell, Duncan. 'From Ancient to Modern in Victorian Imperial Thought'. *The Historical Journal* 49, no. 3 (2006): 735–759.

Bellenoit, Hayden. 'Between Qanungos and Clerks: The Cultural and Service Worlds of Hindustan's Pensmen, c. 1750–1850'. *Modern Asian Studies* 48, no. 4 (2014): 872–910.

Bellenoit, Hayden. *The Formation of the Colonial State in India: Scribes, Paper, and Taxes, 1760–1860.* London, 2017.

Ben-Amos, Ilana Krausman. *The Culture of Giving: Informal Support and Gift-Exchange in Early Modern England.* Cambridge, 2008.

Benton, Lauren. *A Search for Sovereignty: Law and Geography in European Empires, 1400–1900.* Cambridge, 2009.

Benton, Lauren and Lisa Ford. *Rage for Order: The British Empire and the Origins of International Law 1800–1850.* Cambridge, MA, 2016.

Berg, Maxine. *Luxury and Pleasure in Eighteenth-Century Britain.* Oxford, 2005.

Berry, Sara. 'Hegemony on a Shoestring: Indirect Rule and Access to Agricultural Land'. *Africa* 62, no. 3 (1992): 327–355.

Beverley, Eric Lewis. *Hyderabad, British India, and the World: Muslim Networks and Minor Sovereignty, c. 1850–1950.* Cambridge, 2015.

Bhagavan, Manu. *Sovereign Spheres: Princes, Education and Empire in Colonial India.* Oxford, 2003.

Biedermann, Zoltán, Anne Gerritsen and Giorgio Riello, eds. *Global Gifts: The Material Culture of Diplomacy in Early Modern Eurasia.* Cambridge, 2017.

Blake, Stephen P. 'Returning the Household to the Patrimonial-Bureaucratic Empire: Gender, Succession, and Ritual in the Mughal, Safavid and Ottoman Empires'. In *Tributary Empires in Global History*, edited by Peter Fibier Bang and C. A. Bayly. Houndmills, Basingstoke, 2011.

Blanning, T. C. W. *The Culture of Power and the Power of Culture: Old Regime Europe 1660–1789.* Oxford, 2002.

Bourdieu, Pierre. 'The Forms of Capital'. In *Readings in Economic Sociology*, edited by Nicole Woolsey. Malden, MA, 2002.

Bourdieu, Pierre. *Outline of a Theory of Practice.* Translated by Richard Nice. Cambridge, 1987.

Bowen, H. V. *The Business of Empire: The East India Company and Imperial Britain, 1756–1833.* Cambridge, 2006.

Brant, Clare. *Eighteenth-Century Letters and British Culture.* Houndmills, Basingstoke, 2006.

Brittlebank, Kate. *Tipu Sultan's Search for Legitimacy: Islam and Kingship in a Hindu Domain.* Delhi, 1997.

Brown, Kathleen M. 'The Anglo-Algonquian Gender Frontier'. In *Negotiators of Change: Historical Perspectives on Native American Women*, edited by Nancy Shoemaker. New York, NY, 1995.

Brown, Matthew, ed. *Informal Empire in Latin America: Culture, Commerce, and Capital.* Oxford, 2008.

Burke, Peter. *A Social History of Knowledge from Gutenberg to Diderot.* Cambridge, 2000.

Burns, Arthur and Joanna Innes, eds. *Rethinking the Age of Reform: Britain 1780–1850.* Cambridge, 2007.

Camiscioli, Elisa. 'Women, Gender, Intimacy, and Empire'. *Journal of Women's History* 25, no. 4 (2013): 138–148.

Chalus, Elaine. *Elite Women in English Political Life, c. 1754–1790.* Oxford, 2005.

Chartrand, Alix. 'Comparing Comparisons: The Role of Religion in British-Produced Histories of Ireland and India, c. 1650–1800'. *Journal of Colonialism and Colonial History* 18, no. 3 (2017).

Chatterjee, Indrani. *Gender, Slavery and Law in Colonial India*. New Delhi, 1999.

Chatterjee, Kumkum. 'History as Self-Representation: The Recasting of a Political Tradition in Late Eighteenth-Century Eastern India'. *Modern Asian Studies* 32, no. 4 (1998): 913–948.

Chatterjee, Kumkum. 'Scribal Elites in Sultanate and Mughal Bengal'. *Indian Economic and Social History Review* 47, no. 4 (2010): 445–472.

Chatterjee, Partha. *The Black Hole of Empire: History of a Global Practice of Power*. Princeton, NJ, 2012.

Clark, Anna. *Scandal: The Sexual Politics of the British Constitution*. Princeton, NJ, 2006.

Cohen, Benjamin B. *Kingship and Colonialism in India's Deccan: 1850–1948*. Basingstoke, 2007.

Cohen, Ira J. *Structuration Theory: Anthony Giddens and the Constitution of Social Life*. Houndmills, Basingstoke, 1989.

Cohn, Bernard S. *Colonialism and Its Forms of Knowledge: The British in India*. Princeton, NJ, 1998.

Cohn, Bernard S. 'Representing Authority in Victorian India'. In *The Invention of Tradition*, edited by Eric Hobsbawm and Terence Ranger. Cambridge, 1983.

Cohn, Bernard S. 'The Role of the Gosains in the Economy of Eighteenth and Nineteenth Century Upper India'. *IESHR* 1, no. 4 (1964): 175–182.

Collin Davies, Cuthbert. *Warren Hastings and Oudh*. Oxford, 1939.

Collingham, E. M. *Imperial Bodies: The Physical Experience of the Raj, c. 1800–1947*. Cambridge, 2001.

Condos, Mark. *The Insecurity State: Punjab and the Making of Colonial Power in British India*. Cambridge, 2017.

Condos, Mark. 'Licence to Kill: The Murderous Outrages Act and the Rule of Law in Colonial India, 1867–1925'. *Modern Asian Studies* 50, no. 2 (2016): 479–517.

Cooper, Frederick. *Colonialism in Question: Theory, Knowledge, History*. Berkeley, CA, 2005.

Cooper, Randolf G. S. *The Anglo-Maratha Campaigns and the Contest for India: The Struggle for Control of the South Asian Military Economy*. Cambridge, 2003.

Copland, Ian. *The Princes of India in the Endgame of Empire, 1917–1947*. Cambridge, 1997.

Coster, Will. *Family and Kinship in England 1450–1800*. Harlow, 2001.

Cotton, H. E. A. 'The Story of James Paull'. *Bengal Past & Present* 28, no. 55–56 (1924): 69–109.

Crouzet, Guillemette. *Inventing the Middle East: Britain and the Persian Gulf in the Age of Global Imperialism*. Montreal, 2022.

Crowley, John E. 'The Sensibility of Comfort'. *American Historical Review* 104, no. 3 (1999): 749–782.

Dalrymple, William. *White Mughals: Love and Betrayal in Eighteenth-Century India*. London, 2004.

De, Rohit and Robert Travers. 'Petitioning and Political Cultures in South Asia'. *Modern Asian Studies* 53, no. 1 (2019): 1–20.

De Costa, Ravi. 'Identity, Authority, and the Moral Worlds of Indigenous Petitions'. *Comparative Studies in Society and History* 48, no. 3 (2006): 669–698.

DelPlato, Joan. *Multiple Wives, Multiple Pleasures: Representing the Harem, 1800–1875*. Cranbury, NJ, 2002.

Dirks, Nicholas B. *The Hollow Crown: Ethnohistory of an Indian Kingdom*. Cambridge, 1987.

Dodson, Michael. *Orientalism, Empire, and National Culture*. Houndmills, Basingstoke, 2007.

Donnan, Hastings and Thomas M. Wilson. *Borders: Frontiers of Identity, Nation and State*. Oxford, 1999.

Duncan, Alison. 'The Sword and the Pen: The Role of Correspondence in the Advancement Tactics of Eighteenth-Century Military Officers'. *Journal of Scottish Historical Studies* 29, no. 2 (2009): 106–122.

Dwyer, Philip G. 'Violence and the Revolutionary and Napoleonic Wars: Massacre, Conquest and the Imperial Enterprise'. *Journal of Genocide Research* 15, no. 2 (2013): 117–131.

Earle, Rebecca, ed. *Epistolary Selves: Letters and Letter-Writers, 1600–1945*. Aldershot, 1999.

Eaton, Natasha. 'Between Mimesis and Alterity: Art, Gift, and Diplomacy in Colonial India, 1770–1800'. *Comparative Studies in Society and History* 46, no. 4 (2004): 816–844.

Edelstein, Dan. *The Terror of Natural Right: Republicanism, the Cult of Nature, and the French Revolution*. Chicago, IL, 2010.

Edney, Matthew. *Mapping an Empire: The Geographical Construction of British India, 1765–1843*. Chicago, IL, 1990.

Emerson, Rupert. *Malaysia: A Study in Direct and Indirect Rule*. Kuala Lumpur, 1964.

Emirbayer, Mustafa and Ann Mische. 'What Is Agency?', *American Journal of Sociology*, 103 (1998).

Epstein, James. *Scandal of Colonial Rule: Power and Subversion in the British Atlantic during the Age of Revolution*. Cambridge, 2012.

Fairchilds, Cissie. *Domestic Enemies: Servants & Their Masters in Old Regime France*. Baltimore, MD, 1984.

Farge, Arlette and Jacques Revel. *The Vanishing Children of Paris: Rumor and Politics before the French Revolution*. Translated by Claudia Miéville. Cambridge, MA, 1991.

Faruqui, Munis. *The Princes of the Mughal Empire 1504–1719*. Cambridge, 2012.

Findly, Ellison Banks. *Nur Jahan: Empress of Mughal India*. New York, 1993.

Finn, Margot. 'Anglo-Indian Lives in the Later Eighteenth and Early Nineteenth Centuries'. *Journal for Eighteenth-Century Studies* 33, no. 1 (2010): 49–65.

Finn, Margot. *The Character of Credit: Personal Debt in English Culture, 1740–1914*. Cambridge, 2003.

Finn, Margot. 'Colonial Gifts: Family Politics and the Exchange of Goods in British India, c. 1780–1820'. *Modern Asian Studies* 40, no. 1 (2006): 203–231.

Finn, Margot. 'Material Turns in British History: II. Corruption: Imperial Power, Princely Politics and Gifts Gone Rogue'. *Transactions of the Royal Historical Society* 29 (2019): 1–25.

Finn, Margot. 'Men's Things: Masculine Possession in the Consumer Revolution'. *Social History* 25, no. 2 (2000): 133–155.

Finn, Margot and Kate Smith, eds. *The East India Company at Home 1757–1857*. London, 2018.

Fisch, Jörg. *Cheap Lives and Dear Limbs: The British Transformation of the Bengal Criminal Law 1769–1817*. Wiesbaden, 1983.

Fisher, Michael H. *A Clash of Cultures: Awadh, the British, and the Mughals*. New Delhi, 1987.

Fisher, Michael H. 'The East India Company's Suppression of the Native Dak'. *Indian Economic and Social History Review* 31, no. 3 (1994): 311–348.

Fisher, Michael H. *Indirect Rule in India: Residents and the Residency System 1764–1858*. Delhi, 1991.

Fisher, Michael H. 'The Office of Akhbar Nawis: The Transition from Mughal to British Forms'. *Modern Asian Studies* 27, no. 1 (1993): 45–82.

Fisher, Michael H. 'Women and the Feminine in the Court and High Culture of Awadh, 1722–1856'. In *Women in the Medieval Islamic World: Power, Patronage, and Piety*, edited by Gavin R. Hambly. Houndmills, Basingstoke, 1998.

Gallagher, John, and Ronald Robinson. 'The Imperialism of Free Trade'. *Economic History Review* 6, no. 1 (1953): 1–15.

Gatrell, V. A. *The Hanging Tree: Execution and the English People 1770–1868*. Oxford, 1994.

Gerber, David A. *Authors of Their Lives: The Personal Correspondence of British Immigrants to North America in the Nineteenth Century*. New York, NY, 2006.

Ghosh, Durba. 'Decoding the Nameless: Gender, Subjectivity, and Historical Methodologies in Reading the Archives of Colonial India', in *A New Imperial History: Culture, Identity, and Modernity, 1600–1840*, edited by Kathleen Wilson. Cambridge, 2004.

Ghosh, Durba. Sex and the Family in Colonial India: The Making of Empire.

Gill, Ellen. '"Children of the Service": Paternalism, Patronage and Friendship in the Georgian Navy'. *Journal for Maritime Research* 15, no. 2 (2013): 149–165.

Gordon, Stewart. 'Legitimacy and Loyalty in Some Successor States of the Eighteenth Century'. In *Kingship and Authority in South Asia*, edited by J. F. Richards. Delhi, 1998.

Gordon, Stewart. *The Marathas 1600–1818*. Cambridge, 1993.

Gordon, Stewart. *Marathas, Marauders, and State Formation in Eighteenth-Century India*. Delhi, 1994.

Gordon, Stewart. 'Robes of Honour: A "Transactional" Kingly Ceremony'. *Indian Economic and Social History Review* 33, no. 3 (1996): 225–242.

Gould, Eliga. 'Zones of Law, Zones of Violence: The Legal Geography of the British Atlantic, circa 1772'. *The William & Mary Quarterly* 60, no. 3 (2003): 471–510.

Guha, Ranajit. *Elementary Aspects of Peasant Insurgency in Colonial India*. Delhi, 1983.

Guha, Ranajit. *A Rule of Property for Bengal: An Essay on the Idea of Permanent Settlement*. Paris, 1963.

Guha, Sumit. *Environment and Ethnicity in India, 1200–1991*. Cambridge, 1999.

Guha, Sumit. 'The Family Feud as a Political Resource in Eighteenth-Century India'. In *Unfamiliar Relations: Family and History in South Asia*, edited by Indrani Chatterjee. Delhi, 2004.

Hagerman, C. A. *Britain's Imperial Muse: The Classics, Imperialism, and the Indian Empire, 1784–1914*. Houndmills, Basingstoke, 2013.

Harling, Philip. 'Rethinking "Old Corruption"'. *Past & Present* 147 (1995): 127–158.

Harling, Philip. *The Waning of 'Old Corruption': The Politics of Economical Reform in Britain, 1779–1846*. Oxford, 1996.

Harlow, Vincent T. *The Founding of the Second British Empire 1763–1793*. 2 vols. London, 1952–64.

Heath, Deana. *Colonial Terror: Torture and State Violence in Colonial India*. Oxford, 2021.

Heathcote, T. A. *The Military in British India: The Development of British Land Forces in South Asia, 1600–1947*. Manchester, 1995; repr. Barnsley, 2013.

Hunt, Lynn. *Inventing Human Rights: A History*. New York, 2007.

Ignatieff, Michael. *A Just Measure of Pain: The Penitentiary in the Industrial Revolution, 1750–1850*. London, 1978.

Jansson, Maija. 'Measured Reciprocity: English Ambassadorial Gift Exchange in the 17th and 18th Centuries'. *Journal of Early Modern History* 9, no. 3 (2005): 348–370.

Jasanoff, Maya. *Edge of Empire: Lives, Culture, and Conquest in the East, 1750–1850*. New York, 2006.

Jeffrey, Robin. 'The Politics of "Indirect Rule": Types of Relationship among Rulers, Ministers and Residents in a "Native State"'. *Journal of Commonwealth & Comparative Politics* 13, no. 3 (1975): 261–281.

Jhala, Angma Dey. *Courtly Indian Women in Late Imperial India*. London, 2008.

Joshi, Chitra. 'Dak Roads, Dak Runners, and the Reordering of the Communication Networks'. *International Review of Social History* 57, no. 2 (2012): 169–189.

Jupp, Peter. 'The Landed Elite and Political Authority in Britain, ca. 1760–1850'. *Journal of British Studies* 29, no. 1 (1990): 53–79.

Kapila, Shruti. 'Race Matters: Orientalism and Religion, India and Beyond c. 1770–1880'. *Modern Asian Studies* 41, no. 3 (2007): 471–513.

Keen, Caroline. *Princely India and the British: Political Development and the Operation of Empire*. London, 2012.

Kidd, Colin. *British Identities before Nationalism: Ethnicity and Nationhood in the Atlantic World, 1600–1800*. Cambridge, 2006.

Kinra, Rajeev. 'Master and Munshi: A Brahman Secretary's Guide to Mughal Governance'. *Indian Economic and Social History Review* 47, no. 4 (2010): 527–561.

Klekar, Cynthia. '"Prisoners in Silken Bonds": Obligation, Trade, and Diplomacy in English Voyages to Japan and China'. *Journal for Early Modern Cultural Studies* 6, no. 1 (2006): 84–105.

Knights, Mark. 'Historical Stereotypes and Histories of Stereotypes'. In *Psychology and History: Interdisciplinary Explorations*, edited by Christian Christian Tileagă and Jovan Byford. Cambridge, 2014.

Kolsky, Elizabeth. 'The Colonial Rule of Law and the Legal Regime of Exception: Frontier "Fanaticism" and State Violence in British India'. *American Historical Review* 120, no. 4 (2015): 1218–1246.

Kooiman, Dick. 'Meeting at the Threshold, at the Edge of the Carpet or Somewhere in Between? Questions of Ceremonial in Princely India'. *Indian Economic and Social History Review* 40, no. 3 (2003): 311–333.

Kozlowski, Gregory C. 'Private Lives and Public Piety: Women and the Practice of Islam in Mughal India'. In *Women in the Medieval Islamic World: Power, Patronage, and Piety*, edited by Gavin R. Hambly. Houndmills, Basingstoke, 1998.

Kunju, A. P. Ibrahim. *Rise of Travancore: A Study in the Life and Times of Martanda Varma*. Trivandrum, 1976.

Lal, Ruby. *Domesticity and Power in the Early Mughal World*. Cambridge, 2005.

Lally, Jagjeet. 'Empires and Equines: The Horse in Art and Exchange in South Asia, ca. 1600-ca. 1850'. *Comparative Studies of South Asia, Africa, and the Middle East* 25, no. 1 (2015): 96–116.

Lawrance, Benjamin N., Emily Lynn Osborn, and Richard L. Roberts, eds. *Intermediaries, Interpreters, and Clerks: African Employees in the Making of Colonial Africa*. Madison, WI, 2006.

Lefebvre, Georges. *The Great Fear of 1789: Rural Panic in Revolutionary France*. Translated by Joan White. Princeton, NJ, 1983.

Lemieux, Cyril. 'A quoi sert l'analyse des controverses'. *Mil neuf cent* 25 (2007): 191–212.

Leonard, Karen. 'The Deccani Synthesis in Old Hyderabad: An Historiographical Essay'. *Journal of the Pakistan Historical Society* 21, no. 4 (1973): 1157–1184.

Leonard, Karen. 'The Hyderabad Political System and Its Participants'. *The Journal of Asian Studies* 30, no. 3 (1971): 569–582.

Leonard, Karen. 'Palmer and Company: An Indian Banking Firm in Hyderabad State'. *Modern Asian Studies* 47, no. 4 (2013): 1157–1184.

Leonard, Karen. *Social History of an Indian Caste: The Kayasths of Hyderabad*. Berkeley, CA, 1978.

Lewellyn-Jones, Rosie. *Engaging Scoundrels: True Tales of Old Lucknow*. Delhi, 2000.

Lewellyn-Jones, Rosie. *A Fatal Friendship: The Nawabs, the British, and the City of Lucknow*. Delhi, 1985.

Louis, William Roger, ed. *Imperialism: The Robinson and Gallagher Controversy*. New York, 1976.

Maier, Charles. *Among Empires: American Ascendancy and Its Predecessors*. Cambridge, MA, 2007.

Mallampalli, Chandra. *A Muslim Conspiracy in British India? Politics and Paranoia in the Early Nineteenth-Century Deccan*. Cambridge, 2017.

Mamdani, Mahmood. *Define and Rule: Native as Political Identity*. Cambridge, MA, 2012.

Mandler, Peter. *The English National Character: The History of an Idea from Edmund Burke to Tony Blair*. London, 2006.

Mantena, Karuna. *Alibis of Empire: Henry Maine and the Ends of Liberal Imperialism*. Princeton, NJ, 2010.

Marshall, P. J. *Bengal: The British Bridgehead – Eastern India 1740–1828*. Cambridge, 1988.

Marshall, P. J. *The Impeachment of Warren Hastings*. Oxford, 1965.

Mason, Philip. *The Men Who Ruled India*. London, 1985.

McClure, Alastair. 'Archaic Sovereignty and Colonial Law: The Reintroduction of Corporal Punishment in Colonial India, 1864–1909'. *Modern Asian Studies* 54, no. 5 (2020): 1712–1747.

McGowen, Randall. 'The Body and Punishment in Eighteenth-Century England'. *Journal of Modern History* 59, no. 4 (1987): 652–679.

McLane, John R. *Land and Local Kingship in Eighteenth-Century Bengal*. Cambridge, 1993.

Mehta, Uday Singh. *Liberalism and Empire: A Study in Nineteenth-Century British Liberal Thought*. Chicago, 1999.

Melo, Joao. 'Seeking Prestige and Survival: Gift-Exchange Practices between the Portuguese Estado da India and Asian Rulers'. *Journal of the Economic and Social History of the Orient* 56, no. 4/5 (2013): 672–695.

Merrell, James H. *Into the American Woods: Negotiators on the Pennsylvania Frontier*. New York, 1999.

Metcalf, Thomas R. *Aftermath of Revolt: India 1857–1970*. Princeton, NJ, repr. 2015.

Metcalf, Thomas R. *Ideologies of the Raj*. Cambridge, 1995.

Mitchell, Colin. 'Safavid Imperial Tarassul and the Persian Insha Tradition'. *Studia Iranica* 26, no. 2 (1997).

Mitchell, Linda C. 'Letter-Writing Instruction Manuals in Seventeenth- and Eighteenth-Century England'. In *Letter-Writing Manuals and Instruction from Antiquity to the Present: Historical and Bibliographic Studies*, eds. Carol Poster and Linda C. Mitchell. Columbia, SC, 2007.

Mohiuddin, Momin. *The Chancellery and Persian Epistolography under the Mughals*. Calcutta, 1971.

Morieux, Renaud. 'Patriotisme humanitaire et prisonniers de guerre en France et en Angleterre pendant la Révolution francaise et l'Empire'. In *La politique par les armes, Conflits internationaux et politization, XVe-XIXe siècles*, edited by Laurent Bourquin et. al. Rennes, 2014.

Nair, Janaki. 'Uncovering the Zenana: Visions of Indian Womanhood in Englishwomen's Writings, 1813–1940'. *Journal of Women's History* 2, no. 1 (1990).

Nakhimovsky, Isaac. 'Carl Schmitt, Vattel and the Law of Nations: Between Enlightenment and Revolution', *Grotiana* 31, no. 1 (2010): 141–164.

Narayan, Roschisha. 'A Mughal Matriarch and the Politics of Motherhood in Early Colonial India'. *Journal of Women's History* 32, no. 2 (2020): 12–36.

Naseemullah, Adnan and Paul Staniland. 'Indirect Rule and Varieties of Governance'. *Governance: An International Journal of Policy, Administration, and Institutions* 29, no. 1 (2016): 13–30.

O'Hanlon, Rosalind. 'Entrepreneurs in Diplomacy: Maratha Expansion in the Age of the Vakil'. *Indian Economic and Social History Review* 57, no. 4 (2020): 503–534.

Onley, James. *The Arabian Frontier of the British Raj: Merchants, Rulers, and the British in the Nineteenth-Century Gulf*. Oxford, 2007.

Panikkar, K. N. *British Diplomacy in North India: A Study of the Delhi Residency, 1803–1857*. New Delhi, 1968.

Parry, Jonathan and Maurice Bloch, eds. *Money and the Morality of Exchange.* Cambridge, 1989.

Pavarala, Vinod. 'Cultures of Corruption and the Corruption of Culture: The East India Company and the Hastings Impeachment'. In *Corrupt Histories,* edited by Emmanuel Kreike and William Chester Jordan. Rochester, NY, 2004.

Pearsall, Sarah. *Atlantic Families Lives and Letters in the Later Eighteenth Century.* Oxford, 2008.

Peers, Douglas M. *Between Mars and Mammon: Colonial Armies and the Garrison State in Early Nineteenth_Century India.* London, 1995.

Perice, Glen A. 'Rumors and Politics in Haiti'. *Anthropological Quarterly* 70, no. 1 (1997): 1–10.

Perkin, Harold. *The Origins of Modern English Society 1780–1880.* London, 1969.

Peterson, Indira Viswanathan. 'The Cabinet of King Serfoji of Tanjore: A European Collection in Early Nineteenth Century India'. *The Journal of the History of Collections* 1, no. 1 (1999): 71–93.

Philips, C. H. *The East India Company 1784–1834.* Manchester, 1961.

Pitts, Jennifer. *Boundaries of the International: Law and Empire.* Cambridge, MA, 2018.

Pitts, Jennifer. 'Empire and Legal Universalisms in the Eighteenth Century'. *American Historical Review* 117, no. 1 (2012): 92–121.

Prasad, Dharmendra. *Social and Cultural Geography of Hyderabad City: A Historical Perspective.* New Delhi, 1986.

Pratt, Mary Louise. *Imperial Eyes: Travel Writing and Transculturation.* London, 2008.

Purushotham, Sunil. 'Internal Violence: The "Police Action" in Hyderabad'. *Comparative Studies in Society and History* 57, no. 2 (2015): 435–466.

Raj, Kapil. 'Mapping Knowledge: Go-Betweens in Calcutta, 1770–1820'. In *The Brokered World: Go-Betweens and Global Intelligence, 1770–1820,* edited by Simon Schaffer et al. Sagamore Beach, MA, 2009.

Raj, Kapil. 'Refashioning Civilities, Engineering Trust: William Jones, Indian Intermediaries and the Production of Reliable Legal Knowledge in Late Eighteenth-Century Bengal'. *Studies in History* 17, no. 2 (2001): 175–209.

Raman, Bhavani. *Document Raj: Writings and Scribes in Early Colonial South India.* Chicago, 2012.

Ramusack, Barbara. *The Indian Princes and Their States.* Cambridge, 2004.

Rao, Anupama and Steven Pierce. 'Discipline and the Other Body: Humanitarianism, Violence, and the Colonial Exception'. In *Discipline and the Other Body: Correction, Corporeality, Colonialism.* Durham, NC, 2006.

Recchia, Stefano and Jennifer M. Welsh, eds. *Just and Unjust Military Intervention: European Thinkers from Vitoria to Mill.* Cambridge, 2013.

Redford, Bruce. *The Converse of the Pen: Acts of Intimacy in the Eighteenth-Century Familiar Letter.* Chicago, IL, 1986.

Regani, Sarojini. *Nizam-British Relations 1724–1857.* New Delhi, 1963; repr. 1988.

Ribeiro, Aileen. *Dress in Eighteenth-Century Europe 1715–1789.* London, 1984.

Ricci, Ronit, ed. *Exile in Colonial Asia: Kings, Convicts, Commemoration.* Honolulu, HI, 2016.

Richards, J. F. 'The Formulation of Imperial Authority under Akbar and Jahangir'. In *Kingship and Authority in South Asia*, edited by J. F. Richards. Madison, WI, 1978.

Richards, J. F. 'Norms of Comportment among Imperial Mughal Officers'. In *Moral Conduct and Authority: The Place of Adab in South Asian Islam*, edited by Barbara Daly Metcalf. Berkeley, CA, 1984.

Richards, Thomas. *The Imperial Archive: Knowledge and the Fantasy of Empire*. London, 1993.

Richardson, R. C. *Household Servants in Early Modern England*. Manchester, 2010.

Rocher, Rosane. 'Weaving Knowledge: Sir William Jones and Indian Pundits'. In *Objects of Enquiry: The Life Contributions and Influences of Sir William Jones (1746–1794)*, edited by Garland Cannon and Kevin R. Brine. New York, 1995.

Rosenthal, Joel T. 'The King's "Wicked Advisers" and Medieval Baronial Rebellions'. *Political Science Quarterly* 82, no. 4 (1967): 595–618.

Rosnow, Ralph L. and Gary Alan Fine. *Rumor and Gossip: The Social Psychology of Hearsay*. New York, 1976.

Rothblatt, Sheldon. *Tradition and Change in English Liberal Education: An Essay in History and Culture*. London, 1976.

Rothman, E. Natalie. *Brokering Empire: Trans-Imperial Subjects between Venice and Istanbul*. Ithaca, NY, 2012.

Roy, Kaushik. *The Oxford Companion to Modern Warfare in India: From the Eighteenth Century to Present Times*. Oxford, 2009.

Roy, Kaushik. *War, Culture and Society in Early Modern South Asia, 1740–1849*. Florence, KY, 2011.

Roy, Tirthankar. 'Economic Conditions in Early Modern Bengal: A Contribution to the Divergence Debate'. *The Journal of Economic History* 70, no. 1 (2010): 179–194.

Rudolph, Lloyd I. and Susanne Hoeber Rudolph. 'The Subcontinental Empire and the Regional Kingdom in Indian State Formation'. In *Region and Nation in India*, edited by Paul Wallace. New Delhi, 1985.

Schaffer, Simon, Lissa Roberts, Kapil Raj, and James Delbourgo, eds. *The Brokered World: Go-Betweens and Global Intelligence, 1770–1820*. Sagamore Beach, MA, 2009.

Schechter, Ronald. *A Genealogy of Terror in Eighteenth-Century France*. Chicago, IL, 2018.

Schwartz, Joan M. and Terry Cook. 'Archives, Records, and Power: The Making of Modern Memory'. *Archival Science* 2, no. 1–2 (2002): 1–19.

Scott, James C. *Weapons of the Weak: Everyday Forms of Peasant Resistance*. New Haven, CT, 1985.

Sen, S. P. *The French in India 1763–1816*. New Delhi, 1971.

Sen, Sailendra Nath. *Anglo-Maratha Relations during the Administration of Warren Hastings, 1772–1785*. London, 1995.

Sen, Sudipta. *Distant Sovereignty: National Imperialism and the Origins of British India*. New York, 2002.

Sharpe, J. A. *Judicial Punishment in England*. London, 1990.

Sherman, Taylor. *State Violence and Punishment in India*. Abingdon, 2010.

Shibutani, Tamotsu. *Improvised News: A Sociological Study of Rumor*. Indianapolis, IN, 1966.

Shorto, Sylvia. *British Houses in Late Mughal Delhi*. Woodbridge, 2018.

Siebenhuner, Kim. 'Approaching Diplomatic and Courtly Gift-Giving in Europe and Mughal India: Shared Practices and Cultural Diversity'. *The Medieval History Journal* 16, no. 2 (2013): 525–546.

Singha, Radhika. *A Despotism of Law: Crime and Justice in Early Colonial India*. Delhi, 1998.

Sivaramakrishnan,K. *Modern Forests: Statemaking and Environmental Change in Colonial Eastern India*. Stanford, CA, 1999.

Sivasundaram, Sujit. 'Trading Knowledge: The East India Company's Elephants in India and Britain'. *The Historical Journal* 48, no. 1 (2005): 27–63.

Smith, Kate. 'Amidst Things: New Histories of Commodities, Capital, and Consumption'. *The Historical Journal* 61, no. 3 (2018): 841–861.

Smolenski, John and Thomas J. Humphrey, eds. *New World Orders: Violence, Sanction, and Authority in the Colonial Americas*. Philadelphia, PA, 2005.

Spadafora, David. *The Idea of Progress in Eighteenth-Century Britain*. New Haven, CT, 1990.

Spear, T. G. P. *The Nabobs: A Study of the Social Life of the English in Eighteenth Century India*. Oxford, 1932.

Spivak, Gayatri Chakravorty. 'Can the Subaltern Speak?' In *Colonial Discourse and Post-Colonial Theory: A Reader*, edited by Patrick Williams and Laura Chrisman. London, 1993.

Sramek, Joseph. *Gender, Morality, and Race in Company India, 1765–1858*. New York, 2011.

Stephens, Julia. 'A Bureaucracy of Rejection: Petitioning and the Impoverished Paternalism of the British-Indian Raj'. *Modern Asian Studies* 53, no. 1 (2019): 177–202.

Sternberg, Giora. 'Epistolary Ceremonial: Corresponding Status at the Time of Louis XIV'. *Past & Present* 204 (2009).

Stokes, Eric. *The English Utilitarians and India*. Delhi, 1959.

Stoler, Ann Laura. *Carnal Knowledge and Imperial Power: Race and the Intimate in Colonial Rule*. Berkeley, CA, 2002.

Stoler, Ann Laura. 'In Cold Blood: Hierarchies of Credibility and the Politics of Colonial Narratives'. *Representations* 37 (1992): 151–189.

Stoler, Ann Laura. 'On Degrees of Imperial Sovereignty'. *Public Culture* 18, no. 1 (2006): 125–146.

Stoler, Ann Laura. *Race and the Education of Desire: Foucault's History of Sexuality and the Colonial Order of Things*. Durham, NC, 1995.

Subrahmanyam, Sanjay. *Courtly Encounters: Translating Courtliness and Violence in Early Modern Eurasia*. Cambridge, MA, 2012.

Subramanian, Lakshmi. 'Banias and the British: The Role of Indigenous Credit in the Process of Imperial Expansion in Western India in the Second Half of the Eighteenth Century'. *Modern Asian Studies* 21, no. 3 (1987): 473–510.

Szuppe, Maria. 'Circulation des lettrés et cercles littéraires: Entre Asie Centrale, Iran et Inde du Nord (xve-xviiie siècle)'. *Annales. Histoire, sciences sociales* 59 (2004): 997–1018.

Tadmor, Naomi. *Family and Friends in Eighteenth-Century England: Household, Kinship, and Patronage*. Cambridge, 2001.

Tarling, Nicholas. 'The Establishment of Colonial Régimes'. In *The Cambridge History of Southeast Asia*, edited by Nicholas Tarling. Cambridge, 1993.

Taussig, Michael. *Shamanism, Colonialism, and the Wild Man: A Study in Terror and Healing*. Chicago, IL, 1986.

Taylor, Miles. *Empress: Queen Victoria and India*. New Haven, CT, 2018.

Teltscher, Kate. '"The Fearful Name of the Black Hole": Fashioning an Imperial Myth'. In *Writing India 1757–1990: The Literature of British India*, edited by Bart Moore-Gilbert. Manchester, 1996.

Teltscher, Kate. *India Inscribed: European and British Writing on India 1600–1800*. Delhi, 1995.

Teltscher, Kate. 'Writing Home and Crossing Cultures: George Bogle in Bengal and Tibet, 1770–1775'. In *A New Imperial History: Culture, Identity, and Modernity in Britain and the Empire, 1660–1840*, edited by Kathleen Wilson. Cambridge, 2004.

Thompson, Edward. *The Life of Charles, Lord Metcalfe*. London, 1937.

Tosh, John. *Manliness and Masculinities in Nineteenth-Century Britain: Essays on Gender, Family, and Empire*. Harlow, 2005.

Travers, Robert. *Ideology and Empire in Eighteenth-Century India: The British in Bengal*. Cambridge, 2007.

Trim, David. 'Intervention in European History, c. 1520–1850'. In *Just and Unjust Military Intervention: European Thinkers from Vitoria to Mill*, edited by Stefano Recchia and Jennifer M. Welsh. Cambridge, 2013.

Tuck, Richard. *The Rights of War and Peace: Political Thought and the International Order from Grotius to Kant*. Oxford, 1999.

Urbach, Karina. 'Diplomatic History since the Cultural Turn'. *The Historical Journal* 46, no. 4 (2003).

Van Meersbergen, Guido. 'The Diplomatic Repertoires of the East India Companies in Mughal South Asia, 1608–1717'. *The Historical Journal* 62, no. 4 (2019): 875–898.

Van Meersbergen, Guido. *Ethnography and Encounter: The Dutch and English in Seventeenth-Century South Asia*. Leiden, 2021.

Van Meersbergen, Guido. '"Intirely the Kings Vassalls": East India Company Gifting Practices and Anglo-Mughal Political Exchange (c.1670–1720)'. *Diplomatica* 2, no. 2 (2020).

Van Voss, Lex Heerma. *Petitions in Social History*. Cambridge, 2001.

Vaughn, James M. *The Politics of Empire at the Accession of George III*. New Haven, CT, 2019.

Vickery, Amanda. *The Gentleman's Daughter: Women's Lives in Georgian England*. New Haven, CT, 1998.

Wagner, Kim. '"Calculated to Strike Terror": The Amritsar Massacre and the Spectacle of Colonial Violence'. *Past & Present* 233, no. 1 (2016): 185–225.

Wagoner, Philip B. 'Precolonial Intellectuals and the Production of Colonial Knowledge'. *Comparative Studies in Society and History* 45, no. 4 (2003): 783–814.

Watt, Carey A. 'The Relevance and Complexity of Civilizing Missions c. 1800–2010'. In *Civilizing Missions in Colonial and Postcolonial South Asia: From Improvement to Development*, edited by Carey A. Watt and Michael Mann. Cambridge, 2012.

Watts, John. 'The Problem of the Personal: Tackling Corruption in Later Medieval England, 1250–1550'. In *Anti-Corruption in History: From Antiquity to the Modern Era*, edited by Ronald Kroeze, André Vitória, and Guy Geltner. Oxford, 2017.

Weintraub, Jeff. 'The Theory and Politics of the Public/Private Distinction'. In *Public and Private in Thought and Practice: Perspectives on a Grand Dichotomy*, edited by Jeff Weintraub and Krishan Kumar. Chicago, IL, 1997.

Whatmore, Richard. '"Neither Masters nor Slaves": Small States and Empire in the Long Eighteenth Century'. In *Lineages of Empire: The Historical Roots of British Imperial Thought*, edited by Duncan Kelly. Oxford, 2009.

Whatmore, Richard. 'Vattel, Britain and Peace in Europe'. *Grotiana* 31, no. 1 (2010): 85–107.

Wheeler, Roxann. *The Complexion of Race: Categories of Difference in Eighteenth-Century British Culture*. Philadelphia, PA, 2000.

White, Luise. *Speaking with Vampires: Rumor and History in Colonial Africa*. Berkeley, CA, 2000.

White, Richard. *The Middle Ground: Indians, Empires, and Republics in the Great Lakes Region, 1650–1815*. Cambridge, 1991.

Whitman, James Q. *The Verdict of Battle*. Cambridge, MA, 2012.

Wilkinson, Callie. 'The East India College Debate and the Fashioning of Imperial Officials, 1806–1858'. *The Historical Journal* 60, no. 4 (2017): 943–969.

Wilson, Jon E. *The Domination of Strangers: Modern Governance in Eastern India, 1780–1835*. Houndmills, Basingstoke, 2008.

Wilson, Kathleen. *The Island Race: Englishness, Empire and Gender in the Eighteenth Century*. London, 2003.

Windler, Christian. 'Tributes and Presents in Franco-Tunisian Diplomacy'. *Journal of Early Modern History* 4, no. 2 (2000): 168–199.

Wink, André. *Land and Sovereignty in India: Agrarian Society and Politics under the Eighteenth-Century Maratha Svarajya*. Cambridge, 1986.

Yang, Anand A. 'A Conversation of Rumors: The Language of Popular "Mentalités" in Late Nineteenth-Century Colonial India'. *Journal of Social History* 20, no. 3 (1987): 485–505.

Yazdani, Kaveh. 'Haidar 'Ali and Tipu Sultan: Mysore's Eighteenth-Century Rulers in Transition'. *Itinerario* 38, no. 2 (2014): 103–104.

Yazdani, Zubaida. *Hyderabad during the Residency of Henry Russell, 1811–1820: A Case Study of the Subsidiary Alliance System*. Oxford, 1976.

Zastoupil, Lynn. 'Intimacy and Colonial Knowledge'. *Journal of Colonialism and Colonial History* 3, no. 2 (2002).

Zutshi, Chitralekha. 'Re-visioning Princely States in South Asian Historiography: A Review', *Indian Economic and Social History Review* 46, no. 3 (2009): 303–313.

Index

Printed in the USA
CPSIA information can be obtained
at www.ICGtesting.com
CBHW062241310824
13927CB00006B/428